TOTEMICA

TOTEMICA

A SUPPLEMENT TO
TOTEMISM AND EXOGAMY

BY

SIR JAMES GEORGE FRAZER
O.M., F.R.S., F.B.A.

FELLOW OF TRINITY COLLEGE, CAMBRIDGE
ASSOCIATE MEMBER OF THE "INSTITUT DE FRANCE"

GN
491
F84

1968
DAWSONS OF PALL MALL
London

First published by Messrs Macmillan & Co. Ltd., 1937.
© This edition Trinity College, Cambridge, 1937.
Reprinted 1968
Dawsons of Pall Mall
16 Pall Mall, London, S.W.1
SBN: 7129 0277 5

Printed in Great Britain
by Photolithography
Unwin Brothers Limited
Woking and London

TO

SIR ROBERT MOND

THE GENEROUS FRIEND OF LEARNING
AND WORTHY SCION OF HIS NOBLE RACE
I DEDICATE THIS BOOK.
IN GRATITUDE AND HIGH ESTEEM

JAMES GEORGE FRAZER

MAY 1937

PREFACE

SINCE the publication of my book *Totemism and Exogamy* in 1910, much fresh information on the subject has been collected in various parts of the world by many enquirers well fitted by their training and abilities to do justice to the theme. In this volume I have endeavoured to present to the reader a clear view of the principal results of their researches, arranged in a roughly geographical order. Beginning with Australia, the classical land of Totemism, I shall ask the reader to follow me through Melanesia to New Guinea, thence on to India and Africa. Finally we shall end in America, from which our first knowledge of the name and institution of *Totemism* was derived. The stream of new information has flowed chiefly from Australia, hence I have been led to treat Australian evidence at much greater length than any other part of my subject, but not at greater length, I hope, than the importance of the new matter deserves ; for it is to Australia, with its varied and very primitive forms of Totemism, that we must ultimately look, if we are ever to find a clue to the problem of the origin and meaning of the institution.

J. G. FRAZER

CAMBRIDGE
11th April 1937

CONTENTS

BOOK I

TOTEMISM IN AUSTRALIA

BOOK II

TOTEMISM IN MELANESIA

BOOK III

TOTEMISM IN NEW GUINEA

BOOK IV

TOTEMISM IN INDIA

BOOK V

TOTEMISM IN AFRICA

BOOK VI

TOTEMISM IN NORTH AMERICA

BOOK I

TOTEMISM IN AUSTRALIA

CHAPTER I

ANY enquiry into the geographical distribution of totemism in the world should begin with an examination of totemism among the aborigines of Australia, which may be called the great motherland of totemism, for not only is the institution characteristic of the whole aboriginal race of that continent, but some of its forms seem to shed a strong light on the vexed question of the origin and meaning of totemism in general. On this point I will quote the opinion of Professor A. P. Elkin of Sydney University, who by his personal researches in many of the tribes and his careful sifting of the evidence in all has earned him the right to speak with high authority on every question of Australian totemism.

" Australia has long been considered the ideal ' laboratory ' for the study of totemism, and it still is so, not only because totemism is found everywhere on the continent, but also because almost every conceivable variety—both as regards distribution and function—seems to be found in it. And what is more, in several tribes we can see several varieties existing and functioning together. Thus in the tribes of north-eastern South Australia, matrilineal social totemism, patrilineal cult totemism, matrilineal cult totemism, dream totemism, and sex totemism function together in a most interesting manner, and serve to form the social and religious unity of the tribe." [1]

And with regard to the importance of the study of Australian totemism for the whole outlook of the aboriginals

---

[1] A. P. Elkin, " Totemism in North-Western Australia (The Kim- berley Division)," in *Oceania*, vol. iii. No. 3 (Melbourne, March 1933), p. 258.

on the world of man and Nature, Professor Elkin observes :
" Totemism then is our key to the understanding of the
aboriginal philosophy and the universe—a philosophy which
regards man and Nature as one corporate whole for social,
ceremonial, and religious purposes, a philosophy which from
one aspect is pre-animistic but from another is animistic, a
philosophy which is historical, being formed on the heroic
acts of the past which provide the sanctions for the present,
a philosophy which, indeed, passes into the realm of religion
and provides that faith, hope, and courage in the face of his
daily needs which man must have if he is to persevere and
persist, both as an individual and as a social being." [1]

In what follows I shall attempt to give some account of
the more important discoveries in Australian totemism which
have been made since the publication of my book, *Totemism
and Exogamy*, in 1910, arranging the materials in a roughly
geographical order. I shall begin with Melville and Bathurst
Islands, lying off the north-west coast of the continent, and
then follow the coastline through West Australia to South
Australia, and then northward along the eastern coast to
Queensland. Finally I shall take some notice of the tribes
of the centre, the subjects of the comprehensive and now
classical researches of Sir Baldwin Spencer and F. J. Gillen,
to which subsequent enquiry seems to have added little of
importance.

A clear and comprehensive summary of our knowledge of
Australian totemism down to 1930, based partly on personal
researches in various parts of the continent, has been given
by Prof. A. R. Radcliffe-Brown.[2] The convenient terminology which he proposes for the exogamous divisions of the
Australian tribes (hordes, moieties, sections, and sub-sections)
is now generally accepted, and will be followed by me in this
work in preference to the terms phratries, classes, and sub-
classes which I had used in my previous work.

To explain much that follows with regard to the social
organisation of the Australian tribes I will here add that they

---

[1] A. P. Elkin, " Studies in Australian Totemism," in *Oceania*, vol. iv.
No. 2 (Dec. 1933), p. 131.
   [2] A. R. Radcliffe-Brown, *The*

*Social Organization of the Australian
Tribe*, Oceania Monograph, No. 1
(Melbourne and London, 1931).

are normally distributed into two, four, or eight exogamous subdivisions, that is, subdivisions in which men may not marry women within their own subdivision. It is highly significant that the subdivisions are invariably two or multiples of two in number, and seem to have been produced by successive bisections of the tribe, at first into two, then into four, and finally into eight subdivisions, for in many parts of Australia, especially in the centre and in the north-west, these subdivisions are actually spreading at the present day. It is also highly significant with regard to the meaning of these successive subdivisions that the effect of dividing a tribe into two exogamous subdivisions is to prevent the marriage of brothers and sisters ; that the division of the tribe into four subdivisions excludes the marriage of parents with children ; and that the final division into eight subdivisions excludes the marriage of own first or cross-cousins, which before the final subdivision had already been prohibited in many tribes. It seems difficult or impossible to believe that these successive exogamous divisions were not made for the express purpose which they now serve, namely to prevent the marriage of near kin, the successive subdivisions indicating a growing scruple as to the marriage of such persons. These successive subdivisions are normally totemic, that is, are associated with totems ; but elsewhere I have shown reason for thinking that totemism existed in Australia before the introduction of the exogamous divisions, in other words, that in Australia totemism as a social institution is older then exogamy.[1]

It is interesting to observe that on the question whether close inbreeding is injurious or not to the stock that practises it, a question on which modern science is still divided, the very primitive aborigines of Australia have adopted so decided an opinion of the extremely prejudicial tendency of close inbreeding that they have actually, to all appearances, unanimously and from time immemorial, instituted an elaborate and very effective form of social organisation for the express purpose of preventing it. For any serious breach of the social order thus established, the usual penalty was death. When we consider the extremely backward state in which

---

[1] J. G. Frazer, *Totemism and Exogamy* (London, 1910 and 1935), iv. 9 *sqq.*

CHAPTER II

TOTEMISM OF THE TIWI OF MELVILLE AND BATHURST ISLANDS, IN THE NORTHERN TERRITORY

LYING off the coast of the Northern Territory, in north-west Australia, are the two large islands of Melville and Bathurst. Of these Melville is the largest island in the possession of the Australian Commonwealth with the exception of Tasmania and Papua. It is about 70 miles long by 40 miles wide. Though the islands were distant only some 50 miles from the mainland, which is visible in clear weather, the aboriginal inhabitants seem to have had no intercourse whatever with Australia, which they regarded as the abode of departed souls, the home of the dead. They seem to have called themselves *Tiwi*, but to have made little use of the name, having no reason to distinguish themselves from other people, of whose existence they were totally ignorant, believing apparently that they were the only people existing in the world.[1] These isolated islanders were first visited and described by Sir Baldwin Spencer, who paid them a visit of six weeks in 1912, and later in the year revisited them. His general account of the natives runs as follows :

" There was first of all the main separation of the natives into Melville Islanders and Bathurst Islanders. They speak the same language, perform the same ceremonies, use the same objects and make implements all quite distinct from those of the mainland, and yet, though separated only by the narrow Apsley Strait, are, in certain respects, apart from one another in feelings. The men of Melville Island periodi-

---

[1] C. W. M. Hart, " The Tiwi of Melville and Bathurst Islands," in *Oceania*, vol. i. No. 2 (Melbourne, July 1930), pp. 165-170.

cally raid the Bathurst territory—even carry off their women
—and vice versa. Each island, again, is divided up into
local areas, much like, for example, the counties of England,
the boundaries of which are well known and in each of which
there is a main camping ground, like a primitive county
capital, but in this case the buildings are only log and bark
huts. The Tjikalauulla and Malauulla are two of these
groups of Bathurst Island, and, after long enquiry, we were
able to find out the names of others. There seemed to be
more on Melville than on Bathurst Island, but, for some
reason, it was hard to find out the exact number. Probably
this is to be explained by the extraordinary reticence of a
native, that is, of one who is more or less in his natural state
and uncontaminated by contact with white men, to speak of
anything that concerns groups of people other than his own.
Officially, he is not supposed to know about such things : he
resents anyone prying into his own private matters, or those
that he regards as such, partly perhaps because, in many
cases, he thinks that strangers with too much knowledge
might be thereby helped in working him some harm. The
result is that it is often difficult to gain what seems to you to
be very simple and harmless knowledge from some special
man, while another will part with it to you freely. When
once the native is semi-civilised, this difficulty of gaining
information largely disappears, but then there arises another
one—how far is the information reliable, or how far is it due
to a desire to provide the white man with knowledge that the
native shrewdly sees he wants to have ? I think the list for
Melville Island, which I got later, with the help of Cooper,
is fairly complete, but, though we were now on Bathurst
Island, it was impossible to get the names of more than four
local groups. . . .

" So far as I could find out, no one married within his
own local group ; he had to obtain his wife from another,
and she also had to belong to a totem different from his own."[1]

Elsewhere, speaking of the social organisation of the
Australian tribes in general, Spencer observes : " There are
very wide differences between various tribes in regard to

[1] Baldwin Spencer, *Wanderings in Wild Australia*, ii. (London, 1928)
p. 911 *sq.*

organisation, and it is interesting to notice that what are presumably the most modified tribes, are met with on the far northern coastal districts and on Melville and Bathurst Islands. At the other extremity of Australia, in its extreme south-eastern corner, we meet with equally modified tribes, or did so until some years ago. In both parts—the north and the south—the most striking feature is that there is no trace left of classes,[1] or at most a very doubtful one, and that the organisation is essentially a local one, with, in the north, an attendant, well-marked totemic system.

" The tribes we are now dealing with may be divided into two main groups : (*A*) those without class organisation, and (*B*) those with class organisation.

Tribes without Class Organisation

Bathurst and Melville Islands

" These two islands are inhabited by a tribe of wild and, physically, remarkably well-developed natives, who are easily distinguishable from all others by the way in which they ornament their bodies with a series of V-shaped cicatrices, which they call *Miunga*, and are supposed to represent the barbs on their heavy spears. So far as my experience goes, the marks on these islanders are the only ones which serve to identify the particular tribe to which any special individual belongs. From the region of Lake Eyre in the south, across the continent to Darwin and away east to the Gulf of Carpentaria, though all natives are more or less marked with cicatrices, there is nothing in them which is in any way distinctive of totem, class, or particular tribe. The nearest approach to anything of this kind are the cuts made on the backs of adult men in the Urabunna, Dieri, Wonkgongaru, and other tribes, who have passed through the Wilyaru, or its equivalent, final initiation ceremony. These marks, however, are characteristic of the whole of the Dieri nation and not of any class, or special tribe. The Melville and Bathurst Islanders can, however, always be distinguished,

---

[1] By classes Spencer means the exogamous subdivisions of Australian tribes, which are now known as moieties, sections, and subsections.

and the fact that they can serves to emphasise still more strongly the absence of any such possibility in the case of all the mainland tribes in Central and Northern Australia.

"Despite repeated enquiries, I have not been able to find out any true tribal name for the islanders. There are definite and well-known names applied to local groups, but, though doubtless it exists, I tried in vain to find out a name equivalent to that of Larakia or Kakadu.[1] My informants, also, knew of the existence of these and other tribal names on the mainland. It is astonishing how difficult it often is to get reliable information in regard to a subject such as this, where there is, apparently, no question of the matter being of a sacred or secret nature. As a matter of fact, in all tribes the tribal name is not often used and, very often, there is one name applied by the members to themselves and quite a different one by outsiders. The Larakia natives at Darwin speak of Bathurst and Melville as Wongok ; the natives on the latter call both the mainland and the natives there Jeruula. The natives at Cape Donn, near Essington, call Melville Island, which they can see across the water, Wamuk.

"The natives, on both Bathurst and Melville Islands, are divided into a series of local groups, each of which is supposed to occupy and own a special well-defined district. . . . Though their language, customs, and beliefs are identical, there is only a certain amount of intercourse between the natives of the two islands, who are, at least, mutually distrustful of one another. Every now and then the men from a camp on one side of Apsley Strait will raid a camp on the other."

Spencer then gives a list of twelve groups on Melville and three on Bathurst.

"The separation of the local groups from one another is very clearly marked indeed if they come together for the performance of special ceremonies, such as those connected with mourning. When I was last on Bathurst Island, watching these ceremonies, there were representatives of two local groups present called respectively Malauulla and Tjikalauulla. They camped some distance away from one another,

---

[1] Two tribes of the mainland investigated by Spencer. See below. pp. 21 *sqq.*

and though they foregathered during the actual dancing, yet, immediately this was over, they separated.

"I was unable to ascertain anything definite in regard to the marriage system beyond the fact, as described in connection with the account of totemic systems, that it is closely associated with and regulated by the totemic groups. In some cases it is certainly concerned with the local group, a man of one group taking as a wife a woman of another, who then comes into his own group to which his children also belong, but, whether this is always the case, I cannot say positively, though I believe it to be so."[1]

"Amongst the Melville Islanders the totemic system is somewhat different from that of any tribes on the mainland. The word for totem is Pukui. If you say to a man, *Inta ananunga pukui*, he will reply, *Ingaga*, which means white cockatoo, *Irrungabi*, crocodile, or whatever may be the name of his totem. On the other hand, there is a special name applied to the members of the various totemic groups which is quite distinct from that of the totemic animal or plant. These curious double names are as follows :—

(1) Crocodile .	.	.	.	.	Irrungabi
Crocodile man	.	.	.	.	Urdungui
(1) Mullet .	.	.	.	.	Takaringa
Mullet man	.	.	.	.	Arriwidiwi
(2) Turtle .	.	.	.	:	Kurkulani
Turtle man	:	.	.	.	Andjului
(2) Rain .	.	.	.	.	Pakateringa
Rain man	.	.	.	.	Andjului
(3) Wild dog .	.	.	.	.	Teiaminni
Wild dog man	.	.	.	.	Namungarau
(3) Wood .	.	.	.	.	Timareringa
Wood man	.	.	.	.	Ukaringui
White cockatoo .	.	.	.	.	Ingaga
White cockatoo man	.	.	.	.	Jabijabui
Sea bird .	.	.	.	.	Witjerevi
Sea bird man	.	.	.	.	Mitjiwinilla
Pandanus .	.	.	.	.	Mierti
Pandanus man	.	.	.	.	Yirikiwi
Blood wood tree .	.	.	.	.	Umalaka
Blood wood tree man	.	.	.	.	Wanningetti

"Amongst these totemic groups there are three pairs,

[1] Baldwin Spencer, *The Native Tribes of the Northern Territory of Australia* (London, 1914), pp. 42-46.

indicated by the numbers (1), (2), and (3). These are regarded respectively as being what is called *amandinni*, that
is, mates. Crocodile and mullet are mates ; turtle and rain ;
wild dog and wood. The members of groups that are
amandinni are supposed to belong to the same ' skin,' or
pukui, and may not intermarry. Any man can marry any
woman, provided she does not belong to his *pukui*.

" Alligator and mullet marry cockatoo, blood wood, sea
bird, turtle, wild dog, wood, Pandanus, rain.

" Wild dog and wood marry crocodile, cockatoo, blood
wood, sea bird, turtle, mullet, Pandanus, rain.

" Turtle and rain marry crocodile, cockatoo, blood wood,
sea bird, wild dog, wood, mullet, Pandanus.

" Cockatoo, blood wood, sea bird, and Pandanus have no
amandinni and so may marry anyone save a member of
their own totemic group.

" The descent of the totem is strictly in the mother's line.

" There is something very abnormal about the Iwaidja
tribe at Port Essington,[1] which is evidently closely allied, in
some respects, to the Melville Islanders. As in the latter
there are local groups. My information was gained, with
the assistance of Mr. R. J. Cooper, from Port Essington
natives who knew their own and the Melville Island systems.
There are three divisions in the tribe, with totemic groups
attached to each. These three divisions again refer to local
groups, as do those on Melville Island and also those amongst
the Kakadu tribe,[2] to which, in other points, the Iwaidja
natives are closely allied. Their names and the totemic
groups associated with them are as follows :—

GROUP I : MUNBULKITJ

Barramunda	.	.	.	Mangauuli
Barramunda men	.	.	.	Munbulkitj
Goanna (lizard)	.	.	.	Wallwarra
Goanna man	.	.	.	Maiyak
Crocodile	.	.	.	Meirdneiai
Crocodile man	.	.	.	Munbulkitj
Mullet	.	.	.	Ngurilliak
Mullet man	.	.	.	Maiyak

[1] Port Essington is a town on the
coast of the Northern Territory nearly
opposite to Melville Island.

[2] As to Kakadu tribe, see below,
pp. 21 *sqq.*

GROUP 2 : MANJEROJELLI

Wild dog	Lang
Wild dog man	Allaquallurut
Wood	Allmara
Wood man	Manjerojelli

GROUP 3 : MANJEROWULI

Jungle fowl	Urgurgi
Jungle fowl man . . .	Manjerowuli
Turtle	Manbirri
Turtle man	Manjerowuli
Rain	Wailmat
Rain man	Manjerowuli
Blood wood tree . . .	Wubuin
Blood wood tree man . .	Imma-wubuin
Shark	Wanba
Shark man	Manjerowuli
Sea bird	Odjurn
Sea bird man	Allakwulwurjuring
Cockatoo	Allallak
Cockatoo man	Manjerimaringait

" It will be seen that, as in the Melville Island system, the totemic animal or plant has one name, the member of the group another. The Iwaidja word for totem is *Wailar*.

" Members of the Munbulkitj and Manjerojelli groups marry those of Manjerowuli, and *vice versa*. It will be noticed that in each case individuals belonging to certain totemic groups carry as their totemic name, if it can be called so, that of one of the local tribal divisions, Munbulkitj, Manjerojelli, or Manjerowuli. For example, Barramunda men are called Munbulkitj, wood men are called Manjerojelli, and turtle men are called Manjerowuli. The natives were quite clear on this point.

" The descent of the totem is in the female line. One of our informants was a cockatoo man, his mother was cockatoo and his father crocodile. His mother's brother was also cockatoo, and is married to a crocodile woman. They have a daughter who is crocodile and has been promised as wife, by her father, to the first-named cockatoo man. In this case the mother of the man and her brother have the same father but not the same mother. Another of our informants was a cockatoo man, his mother was cockatoo and his father a wood man." [1]

Subsequently to Sir Baldwin Spencer's investigations the social and totemic organisation of the Melville and Bathurst Islanders was examined by Mr. C. W. M. Hart, as a Science Research Scholar of the University of Sydney, with the aid of a grant from the Australian National Research Council. It confirms, supplements, and on one point at least claims to correct Spencer's account. For the sake of comparison I subjoin it in full.

" The Tiwi have a system of matrilineal totemic clans. Each clan has a special relation to one or sometimes to two and in two instances to three species of natural objects. The members of the clan have a solidarity of their own, helping each other in tribal fights, speaking of each other as ' brother ' despite the variation in their actual blood relationship, and not marrying women of their own totem. There are, however, few of the distinctive features of Australian totemism as known from other parts of the continent. They eat their totem without any restriction ; they have no ceremonies for the increase of the totem species.

" Since the totem of a child is that of its mother it follows that the members of one totemic clan are found in different hordes, and inversely each horde contains persons of several totemic clans. Nevertheless each totem is associated in the minds of the native with a particular locality or district. This association appears in the myths, there being a number of stories which connect particular natural species with particular localities. Thus each clan may be said to have its ancestral home or centre, but there is little or nothing of any feeling of reverence or ritual attachment to the home of one's totem. Taking it all in all Tiwi totemism does not amount to very much compared with the elaborate forms of totemism found in other parts of Australia.

" The word for totem and totemic clan is *pukui*. But the same word means also ' sun ' and in addition ' breath.' The connection between these three concepts denoted by one word is not at all apparent.

---

[1] B. Spencer, *Native Tribes of the Northern Territory of Australia*, pp. 200-203.

" The totems are grouped into three phratries.   The term phratry is here used in the sense of an exogamous group containing a number of clans and not being a moiety.   The phratries are unnamed.   Should a man want to mention a phratry he will call it by the name of one of the totemic clans composing it.   He will generally use the name of his own totem clan if his own phratry is in question, or that of the clan that is powerful in the phratry.   Thus the phratry that I am calling Phratry 1, will more often be called *Tjilarui* than anything else, because at the present time the *Tjilarui* clan is very numerous and many of them are the kind of people who are usually much in the public eye.   For a similar reason Phratry 2 is more often called *Timiririnui* than anything else, and Phratry 3 is usually *Tokwombui*.   There is a much stronger feeling of solidarity with one's clan than with one's phratry, which will perhaps explain that while the clan name is very important there seems no need, or much less need, for any specific name for the phratry."

A complete list of the clans and their totems is given below.

CLAN NAME	TOTEMS
Phratry 1	
(*a*) *Tjilati* (pl. *Tjilarui*) . .	Jaberoo
(*b*) *Ariri*	Mullet
(*c*) *Mundubaui* . . .	Fly
(*d*) *Uduna*	Crocodile
(*e*) *Milubruinila* . . .	Cockatoo
(*f*) *Mierdi*	Pandanus
(*g*) *Tanikini* . . .	Flying fox
(*h*) *Mutuninila* . . .	A fish
(*i*) *Timilani*	Sand-fly
Phratry 2	
(*a*) *Timiririnini* (pl. *Timiririnui*) .	Woolly-butt tree
(*b*) *Yarinabila* . . .	Red paint, sugar bag (wild honey)
(*c*) *Orandjani* . . .	Stingray
(*d*) *Paroliuŋinila* . . .	Mud
(*e*) *Iliti* . . .	(A wild fruit)
(*f*) *Andjulini* . . .	Rain, turtle

CLAN NAME			TOTEMS
Phratry 3			
(a) *Tokwombini* (pl. *Tokwombui*) .			A bird
(b) *Ariŋguinila*	.	.	. Stones
(c) *Pinaluwinila*	.	.	. Wood
(d) *Walikuinila*	.	.	. Stars
(e) *Wirnigiti* .	.	.	. Blood wood
(f) *Taparini* .	.	.	. Moon
(g) *Djabijabini*	.	.	. March fly

" In reference to the list it must be pointed out that among the Tiwi there are two languages ; one is used in common everyday conversation, and the other is a sacred language used on ceremonial occasions, in ritual songs, and formulae. Most of the clan-names of the above list are words belonging not to the ordinary language but to the esoteric language. Such words would never be used in ordinary conversation *except as totemic names*. . . . Of the twenty-two clans, nine are normally called by a word in use in the ordinary language ; the other thirteen have names taken from the sacred language.

" Sir Baldwin Spencer apparently failed to distinguish between the sacred and the ordinary language, with the result that his list of Tiwi clans and their totems is confused and inaccurate

" The Tiwi do not seem to associate very closely the totemic clan and the object that is the totem of the clan. For instance a man of the *Udunui* considers himself as *Udunini*, not as a crocodile, which he normally thinks of as *irungrabai*. The bond of solidarity is between one member of the clan and another rather than between a member of the clan and his totem.

" So much is this the case that it is occasionally difficult to ascertain what is the natural object which gives the clan its name, *i.e.* what is the totem of the clan. . . .

" With regard to the origin of the totemic clans and their names the natives say that the system of *pukui* was instituted by the old men a very long time ago. One old man said at some time in the distant past. . . . ' Udunui is my totem at Primandua,' and so every one knew his totem was *udunui*. Knowing their legends every one knew the connection between

Udunui and *Primandua* since it is at this place, a district in Bathurst Island, that *Munutuni*, the father of all crocodiles, still has his home.   Another old man decided upon *mandubaui* as his *pukui* because his favourite camping ground was at *Pripanyimili*, which has a mythological association with *mandubuka* (the sand-fly), such association being founded no doubt on the fact that sand-flies breed in great numbers in the mangrove swamps of that region.

" The *Ariŋgwila* (the stone totem) are closely associated with a famous rock in *Miŋgu* called *Wurukwompi* which, due no doubt to a hollow interior, gives forth a roll like thunder when beaten with a stick and hence is a sacred object to the natives.   The former home of the *Ariŋgwila* is in the vicinity of this rock, so the legend runs, and they are often called the *Wurukwompila*.

" The *Timiririŋui* are said to have come originally from a small island off the coast of *Wraŋgu* where the *timiririŋa* (woolly-butt tree) is especially prolific due to the fact that it was here that *Prondupu*, the original mythological woolly-butt, settled after the battle at *Taŋio* between the animal-men.

" So the story goes on throughout the list of totems.   It is not a myth properly so called since mythological figures are in it only incidentally.   As told by the Tiwi it is a rationalised explanation on a basis of local geography and the desires of old men generations ago.

" The clans vary greatly in size.   The largest clan, *Mierdui*, numbers 132 persons, whereas the *Paroliuŋibila* has only six and the *Taparui* only two." [1]

With regard to personal names amongst the Tiwi, we are told by Mr. Hart :   " Every member of the Tiwi has not one name but many, each of which belongs to him or her alone and each having an equal validity as a term of address or of description, though naturally some are used more frequently than others.   That is to say, although a man with five different names may be addressed or referred to by any one of those five names, nevertheless the normal thing is for one name to be much more generally used than any of the others,

[1] C. W. M. Hart, " The Tiwi of   *Oceania*, vol. i. No. 2 (July 1930), pp.
Melville   and   Bathurst   Islands,"   170-180.

it being for a native, as for us, much easier to think of a person by a single name than by several.

" The multiplicity of names is accounted for by the fact that quite a number of the relatives have the right to bestow names upon a new-born child and a certain proportion of them will always exercise that right. The father may always bestow names upon his own children, and the father's brothers, who are of course the classificatory fathers of the child, have the same power. The mother's brothers may also bestow names upon a child, should they so desire, and less frequently children will be found bearing names given to them by the older men of their own totem clan, that is not only the mother's brothers but also other relatives of the mother, such as the mother's mother's brother. The Tiwi have matrilineal totemic clans.

" Names are seldom bestowed upon an individual by women ; the only female relative having that power is the actual mother's mother. A mother is never in any circumstances allowed to name her own child. The reason for this is fairly obvious. The naming of children is a ritual affair, and as such is more or less forbidden to the women, for although their exclusion is not nearly so strict as in some other parts of Australia, they do not, among the Tiwi, take very much part in ritual affairs. The mother's mother, however, stands in a rather privileged position to her daughter's child. She is of the same totem and is normally a very old woman, and to a certain extent appears to become a symbol of the clan for her daughter's son. A boy, for example, will strongly resent and often endeavour to revenge any insult to his mother's mother, even if it means taking up arms against his own father. For example, during my stay a boy of twelve abused his father and quitted his father's camp for over a month because in a fight between hordes his father had injured the boy's mother's mother's brother. There was no particular respect or regard for the latter individual on the part of the boy, but the injury was a grave insult to his mother's mother.

" It must also be understood that it is impossible for any two people to have the same name. Should a father inadvertently bestow upon his child a name already in use he is guilty of a gross breach of etiquette, and to prevent such a possibility a man will refrain for a long time from coining a name until he is fairly certain that the one he decides upon is neither already in use nor was held by any person recently dead. Although the Tiwi number nearly eleven hundred people at the present time, and each one of these has on an average three names, a careful study of these three thousand three hundred names fails to reveal any two as being identical.

" By the time that a child reaches puberty he is the possessor of several names, since by then some at least of the people entitled to bestow names upon him will have exercised that privilege. In exceptional cases he may have six or seven names though sometimes only one. All of these will have been known at some time or other to the tribe at large, though it is usually possible to get a full list of a person's names only from that individual himself or his father or mother.

" It is not at all unusual in primitive societies for the death of a man to render his name tabu. This is the case among the Tiwi. All the names of a dead man become strictly *pukimani* (=tabu) immediately upon his death. Any one in the tribe who uses a name of a dead person at any time for years after his death, but especially in the period— usually about five to six months—that always elapses between the death and the funeral corroboree, violates one of the strictest social sanctions the tribe possesses. And this prohibition extends to all words in the ordinary language— though curiously enough not in the sacred language—which bear any resemblance in sound to any of the names of the dead man. It applies equally to English names in use by the tribe with resemblances to native or English words and to native words which resemble either English or native words. Thus a boy named *Tipuki* having died ' tobacco,' ' baccy,' *Tiparkitimiri* all equally became *pukimani*. Simi- larly when *Mulankina*, one of the Mandeimbula horde, died, *mulikina*, one of the commonest words in the language, meaning ' plenty,' ' full,' ' enough,' was dropped completely from the language.

" Nor does the *pukimani* stop there. Not only is the use of any of the names of the dead man prohibited, but there is an equally strong rule against the use of any of the personal names he has bestowed upon other people, be they his own children or children of others. A young child may only have one name, that given him by his father, but should his father die he must become nameless until he gets a new name from somewhere. This aspect of the *pukimani* does not extend to similar words in either the ordinary or the sacred language.

.   .   .   .

" The fact that death renders sacred all the concepts closely associated with the dead man does no doubt play a large part in causing the tabu on names he has bestowed upon other people. There is, I think, another factor which is even more important in the causation of this particular tabu. When a man marries a widow he becomes to the tribe not the foster father of her children but the actual father. It cannot be pointed out too often that the Australian blackfellow does not distinguish physiological and social fatherhood. The new husband is married to the widow, he therefore must be the father of her children. Her children change their position in the tribe, and the function of the changing of their names is to show this change and the new social relationships that have been imposed upon them by it. It will be remembered in this connection that the husband changes the names of *all* the woman's children whether of her last husband or not, and also that words in either the sacred or the ordinary language which are similar in sound to the former names of the children do not become tabu. That is, it is a social not a sacred change of name." [1]

[1] C. W. M. Hart, " Personal Names among the Tiwi," in *Oceania*, vol. i. No. 3 (Oct.-Dec. 1930). pp. 280-289.

CHAPTER III

TOTEMISM OF THE KAKADU AND OTHER TRIBES OF THE NORTHERN TERRITORY

THE totemic systems of the Kakadu and other tribes of the Northern Territory, together with the native legends of their mythical foundation, have been described by Sir Baldwin Spencer, from his personal researches and observations. He was resident in the Territory from December 1911 to December 1912, in the official capacity of Special Commissioner for the Aboriginals and Chief Protector in charge of the Department that the Government had instituted to safeguard the interests of the aboriginal population. His account runs as follows :—

" Being so accustomed to tribes like the Arunta in which there is a very definite class organisation,[1] it was very perplexing to find that apparently the Kakadu had no such system. Every individual belonged to a local group and had his or her totem name, but there was no such thing as any sections in the tribe corresponding to the Panunga, Purula, etc., of the Arunta. Whilst talking about old ancestors we met with a tradition relating to the far-past times during which a very celebrated ancestor lived, and this gave us a clue to the matter. The tradition, which seems to be common to the Kakadu and all the tribes now occupying the Coburg Peninsula and the country drained by the Alligator Rivers, is a very lengthy and detailed one, but it shows very clearly the ideas of the natives in regard to the

---

[1] By class organisation Spencer means the division of a tribe into exogamous moieties, sections, and sub-

sections. The change of nomenclatures has already been indicated. See above, p. 5.

origin of the members and different sections of the tribe and reveals a belief in reincarnation which is spread far and wide over Australia. I give an outline of what we found out during these days, because it shows how carefully the natives think these things out for themselves.

"A man named Wuraka came away from the west, walking through the sea. His feet were on the bottom, but he was so tall that his head was well over the water. He landed at a place called Allukuladi, between two hills now known as Mts. Bidwell and Roe, both of which he made, and so on to Aruwurkwain. A woman named Imberombera came from the north, landed at what is now called Malay Bay and travelled south, till she met Wuraka at Aruwurkwain and asked him, ' Where are you going ? ' He replied, ' I am going straight through the bush to the rising sun.' At that time they both spoke the Iwaidja language and there were no blackfellows. Imberombera wanted Wuraka to come with her, but he was very tired, so he sat down where he was, and a great rock, called by the natives *Wuraka* and by the whites Tor Rock, arose to mark the spot. Imberombera went on alone. She was of huge size and carried many children in her body, and wore a bamboo ring on her head from which numbers of dilly-bags hung down, full of yams. At two places, called Marpur and Muruni, she left boy and girl spirit children, telling them to speak Iwaidja. She also planted many yams and said, ' *Mungatidda jam*,' these are good to eat. Then she went on to Mamul, on what is now Cooper's Creek, to the north of the East Alligator River, leaving children here and telling them to speak the Umoriu language. The only food supply she left them were Cyperus bulbs. After this she stopped at different places, opening her dilly-bags, throwing out yams broadcast and sent spirit children to ten different parts, telling them, as she did so, to speak different languages, in each case instructing them as follows :—

    (1) Gnaruk ngeinyimma tjikâru, gnoro Koranger.
    (2) Watta ngeinyimma tjikaru, gnoro Kumboyo.
    (3) Kakadu ngeinyimma tjikaru, gnoro Munganillida.
    (4) Witji ngeinyimma tjikaru, gnoro Miortu.
    (5) Puneitja ngeinyimma tjikaru, gnoro Jaijipali.

(6) Koarnbut ngeinyimma tjikaru, gnoro Kapalgo.
(7) Ngorbur ngeinyimma tjikaru, gnoro Illari.
(8) Umbugwalur ngeinyimma tjikaru, gnoro Owe.
(9) Djowei ngeinyimma tjikaru, gnoro Nauillanja.
(10) Geimbo ngeinyimma tjikaru, gnoro Waimbi.

" The first word of each of these is the language the children were to speak ; *ngeinyimma* means you or yours, *tjikaru* is talk or language, *gnoro* is go, and the last word is the name of the place to which she sent them. It is difficult to feel quite sure whether these are the names of the tribes or of local groups, but each place is now the central ground of the group or tribe named.

" She came at last to Jaijipali, in Kakadu country, searched around for a good camping-place and, at first, sat down in a water-pool, but the leeches came in numbers and fastened on her, so she decided to camp on dry land, saying that she would go into the bush. Accordingly she did so and camped at Ibinjairi, where she became the great progenitor of the Kakadu people. While walking over the country she made creeks, hills, animals and plants, in fact she was responsible originally for everything. She had already, as described above, sent out large numbers of spirit children to various places and, later on, all of them entered women who, in their turn, were sent to the same places later on.

" I am using the term spirit-children as the equivalent of the Kakadu word *Iwaiyu* and the Arunta *Kuruna*. Each is what we should call the soul or simply the spirit of the individual, but the native regards it as something perhaps a little more concrete and definite than what we figure to ourselves as a soul. The essential feature of the *Iwaiyu* or spirit-child belief of the Kakadu, and the *Kuruna* of the Arunta, is that it is, definitely, something concrete ; every individual possesses one ; it may, at times, leave the body either temporarily or, as at death, permanently ; when it leaves the body at death it can, at will, enter a woman and so give rise to a new individual who is the reincarnation of the ancestor because it contains his unchanging *Iwaiyu* or *Kuruna*.

" From Ibinjaira, Imberombera sent out five pairs of men and women. The tradition, so far as I could find out, says nothing about these, either as to their relationship to one another or to their totems. Imberombera herself had no totem, but she is regarded as having instituted them all and given a totemic name to each of the spirit children that she deposited in different places. She is essentially the equivalent of the great Numbakulla amongst the Arunta, except that she is a woman. Starting from Imberombera, the succession of events, so far as the production of offspring is concerned, may be represented as follows :—

(1) Imberombera carrying large numbers of spirit children.

(2) Spirit children deposited by her before she got into the Kakadu country to give rise to

(*a*) Iwaidja people ;
(*b*) Umoriu people.

(3) Spirit children sent out by her during her wanderings before she came into Kakadu country, to give rise, later on, to ten different tribes or groups, as named in the table already given.

(4) Spirit children sent out by her from her camp at Ibinjaira to different parts of the Kakadu country.

(5) Five pairs of individuals, men and women, also carrying spirit children, sent out by her from Ibinjaira, her camping place in Kakadu country, to various places in the latter.

(6) Five pairs of individuals, men and women, sent out again by each of the pairs in No. 5 to various places in Kakadu country, giving twenty-five places in all.

" All the spirit children (included in Nos. (4) and (5)) originally sent out by Imberombera to various places entered into women of these twenty-five pairs and gave rise to the men and women who now form the different local groups into which the tribe is divided.

" It will be seen that Imberombera was responsible for everything, just as in the Arunta legend Numbakulla was ; she gave every spirit individual his or her totemic name, furnished all food supplies, gave to the five pairs (No. (5)) whom she sent out from Ibinjaira everything that they needed and full instructions as to where they were to go, telling them all about the *Jereipunga*, or totems, and ordered them to give these to the different spirit children. A peculiar feature of all the original lots of spirit children sent out is that they contained individuals of different totems, so that there is no special gathering together of men and women of the same name, such as emus and kangaroos, in any one locality in the way characteristic of the Arunta.

" The only thing that I could find out, that governed marriage at the present day, was that a man of one group had to marry a woman from another group, but it did not matter what his totem was, nor was there any descent of the totem from either father or mother to son or daughter." [1]

" There is considerable variation amongst the different tribes inhabiting the Northern Territory in regard to their totemic systems. In some tribes, such as the Waduman and Mudburra, the totemic name is transmitted in the maternal line ; in others, such as the Worgait and Djauan, in the paternal line.

" In some, the totemic groups are divided between the moieties, in others, such as the Djauan and Mungarai, they are divided between the classes or sub-classes,[2] so that the child cannot possibly inherit either its father's or its mother's totem.

" In some, such as the Waduman and Mudburra, there is no division of the totem groups between the moieties or classes, the same group occurring on both sides of the tribe, but the totemic groups are exogamous, and the totem descends in the female line. In others, moieties and classes do not exist, and in these there is no descent of the totem from parent to child, the latter receiving his totemic name in consequence of an intimation conveyed by a spirit individual to the parent.

" In all tribes, however, there is a very definite totemic system, which may or may not regulate marriage.

" In most tribes the totemic groups are exogamous, but in some, such as the Kakadu, they are not, though it is very rare to find a man married to a woman of the same totemic group as himself. Such a marriage, however, in the Kakadu and allied tribes would be quite allowable.

" Amongst these more northern tribes we may distinguish five main groups so far as totemic matters are concerned :—

[1] Baldwin Spencer, *Wanderings in Wild Australia*, ii. 752-756.

[2] By these terms Spencer designates what are now generally known as the four sections and eight subsections of an Australian tribe. See above, p. 5.

" (1) A group represented by the Larakia, Worgait, and Wulwullam, in which the totem groups are divided between the two moieties ; they are strictly exogamic and descent is counted in the male line.

" (2) A well-marked group of tribes including the Djauan, Mungarai, Warrai, Yungman, Mara, and Nullakan, in which the totem groups are divided between the classes or sub-classes so that a child passes into a totemic group belonging to the same side of the tribe to which his father belongs, but of necessity different in name from his father's, because different totemic groups are attached to different classes or sub-classes.

" (3) A well-marked group of tribes, including the Waduman, Mudburra, Ngainman, and Billianera, in which the same totemic groups are found on both sides of the tribe, and in which the descent of the totem is in the female line. The totemic groups are strictly exogamous.

" (4) Abnormal and modified coastal and island tribes, such as those on Melville Island and the Iwaidji, in which there are no moieties or classes, but in which there are local groups and in which certain restrictions with regard to marriage exist in connection with the totemic groups. The descent of the totem is in the female line.

" (5) Abnormal and evidently modified coastal tribes, such as the Kakadu and allied tribes, in which no moieties or classes are present, and in which the totem descends in neither the female nor the male line.

" In at all events many of the tribes, such as the Kakadu, Waduman and Mudburra, the men perform ceremonies that are the equivalent of the Intichiuma in the Arunta, and have for their object the increase of the totemic animal or plant.

" The Kakadu group of tribes is evidently much modified in many ways, and in none more so than in regard to their totemic system. The question of totems is closely bound up with their beliefs in regard to the origin of children. As described in connection with this subject, when an individual dies his spirit part remains with his bones in the form of what is called a Yalmuru. This, again, gives rise to a double of itself, called an Iwaiyu, which the Yalmuru places in some food, such as a sugar-bag or fish, that the father of the future child then secures ; aided by the Yalmuru in doing so. This food will be the totem of the future child. The Iwaiyu jumps out of the food before the man secures the latter, and rejoins the Yalmuru. Finally, in the form of a small frog, called Purnumanemo, it goes into its mother. The Yalmuru, at night time, comes to the father while he is asleep in his camp and tells him the name of the child and its totem. Originally, in the far past times, each individual had his totem, or *jereipunga*, given to him by the great ancestor of the tribe named Imberombera, or by men and women sent out by and acting under her instructions. At each re-incarnation the Yalmuru decides upon the Jereipunga, which may or may not be the same as that to which it belonged during a previous reincarnation. It has no reference of necessity to that of either the father or mother, nor is it concerned in any way with the marriage system. In the Kakadu tribe, indeed, there is no idea of heredity of the totemic name in either the male or female line. A few examples of actual families living in the Kakadu camp, while I was staying at Oenpelli, their central camping ground, will serve to illustrate this matter.

" (1) A man named Ungara whose totem is Kimberikara (Barramunda, a fish) ; his wife, Obaiya, is Mormo, sugar-bag. They have two children, Monmuna a boy, who is Kunbaritja, a small fish, and Murawillawill, whose totem is Erbinjori, crocodile. The totem of Ungara's father was Kunbaritja, and that of his mother Mormo.

" (2) A man named Mukalakki whose totem is Mormo. That of one wife, named Mitjunga, is Kunaitja, mullet ; that of another, named Numerialmak, is Kulekuli. His father, named Monmuna, was Kimberikara, his mother, named Kumbainba, was Eribinjori, a crocodile ; his brother was Murno, opossum ; the mother of Monmuna was Kintjilbara, a snake, his wife's mother was Kulekuli, cat-fish.

" (3) A man named Miniamaka, whose totem is Jameru, a small fish ; his wife named Murrapurnminni, is Kulekuli, cat-fish ; a son, called Naminjeya, is Kimberikara. His father and mother were both Kimberikara.

" (4) A man named Mitjeralak whose totem is Kalerungeni, flying-fox; his father, named Mitiunga, is Jameru, a small fish; his father's father was Eribinjori, crocodile.

"(5) A man named Kopereik whose totem is Kunaitja, mullet; his father is Kimberikara.

"(6) A man named Oogutjali whose totem is Kunbaritja, a fish; his wife, named Belgramma, is Narenma, a snake; a son, called Tjurabego, is Eribinjori, crocodile; a daughter, called Mikgeirne, is Kulekuli, cat-fish; a daughter, named Mirowargo, is Kalerungeni, flying-fox; a daughter, named Minagi, is also Kalerungeni, and another, called Mukarula, is Mormo, sugar-bag.

" It will be seen from these examples that there is a complete and most perplexing mixing up of the totems, so far as anything like descent of the totemic name is concerned. They have nothing whatever to do with regulating marriage, nor are they hereditary in either the paternal or maternal line. Further still, there is no attempt made for each individual to retain the totem of the old ancestor of whom he is supposed to be the reincarnation. In the case of the above-named individuals there is actually only one—the woman Mitiunga—in which the living person has the same totem as the old ancestor of whom he, or she, is supposed to be the reincarnation. In regard to their totemic system, the group of tribes that have the Imberombera legend, or its equivalent, appear to stand by themselves. In some respects, as, for example, in regard to the idea of definite local centres, people by spirit individuals, they call to mind the Arunta, but, on the other hand, they differ from them and from all others in the remarkable way in which each centre is the home of a definite group of individuals, the actual names of all of whom are known and handed down from generation to generation.

" The following is a list of the totemic groups in the Kakadu tribe. It is quite possible that there may be more than these, but they will, at all events, serve to indicate their nature in this tribe which may be taken as representative of the northern coastal tribes generally. The latter inhabit the well-watered country, where food is abundant, that lies between the Ranges and the sea. It will be noticed that, in every case, the totemic animal or plant is edible :—

Alberjiji, Whistling Duck
Banjil, a Fish
Baralil, a Fish
Biaka, a Wallaby
Boinmun, a Rat
Brutpenniweir, Jabiru
Eribinjori, Crocodile
Erlaungerla, Echidna
Eyenbumbo, Fish-Hawk
Gunumaramila, a Yam
Jailba, Sugar-bag
Jeluabi, a non-venomous Snake
Jeruober, Old-man Kangaroo
Jimeribunna, Native Companion
Jimmidauappa, a small Fish
Kaleiyu, White Cockatoo
Kalerungeni, Flying-Fox
Karakera, Spur-winged Plover
Kimberikara, Barramunda (a Fish)
Kintjilbara, a Carpet Snake
Kopereipi, Emu
Korunokadju, Wild Dog
Kudbauu, a Fish
Kudjalinga, Turtle
Kulabaga, Pied Egret
Kulawura, Jungle Fowl
Kulekuli, Cat-Fish
Kulijidbo, a Yam
Kuljoanjo, a non-venomous Snake
Kulori, a Yam
Kunaitja, Mullet
Kunbaritja, a small Fish
Kunjeama, a ' Plum '
Kupulapuli, White Crane
Kurnembo, Goose
Mangortji, wedge-tailed Eagle
Marabornji, brush-tailed Wallaby
Mimiorko, Bandicoot
Mimweluda-uda, Blue Mt. Parakeet
Minjiweya, a Yam
Miriwidjonga, Quail

Mitjiborla, a Wallaby
Moain, a small Fish
Mormo, Sugar-bag
Mornum, a Yam
Mudburraburra, native Cat
Mudebenbo, native Turkey
Mungalama, Lily Seed
Munmarwer, a Snake
Murarowa, a Cypress Bulb
Murkailpu, Sugar-bag
Murlappa, a Yam
Murmorlpa, a Rat
Murno, Opossum, M.
Murora, a small Wallaby
Nabapungeni, Black Kangaroo
Narenma, a Snake
Ngabadaua, a Snake
Ngulauer, a Fish
Nguloa, a Fish
Numberanerji, a Snake
Nuppadaitba, a Fish
Padauitja, a Sugar-bag
Parijiliji, Lily root
Pitjordu, Lizard
Puneri, a Lizard
Putamunga, Water Lizard
Tiradjuno, a Water Snake
Tjailba, Sugar-bag
Tjameru, a small Fish
Tjikali, Wood Grub
Tjilaka, Jew Fish
Tjimidaba, a long-nosed Fish
Tjinangu, a Sugar-bag
Tjunara, a Yam
Tjungoan, a Snake
Ulloa, a Fish
Unari, a Lizard
Worki, a Lily Root
Wuridjonga, Lily Seed and Roots
Yidaburabara, a Snake
Yinganga, small Crocodile

" Whilst investigating the initiation ceremonies in this tribe with Mr. Cahill, I came across a very interesting part of the final initiation ceremony that is called Muraian. This consisted in showing the older men certain very sacred sticks and stones intimately associated with the totems. They are as intensely *kumali* as are the churinga of the Arunta, and the natives when showing them to us and performing the ceremony took most elaborate precautions to prevent any women from having the slightest chance to see what was being done. Each stone or stick was wrapped up in sheet after sheet of paper bark.

" The first that we saw, and we came upon it by mere accident, was a small stone called Iwaija Kopereipi, or Emu egg. It measured about four inches in length by two and a half in diameter. It was sufficiently like an egg in shape as to suggest its name. . . . Its history was as follows : Long ago, for the egg has now passed through the hands of nine old men, one after the other, an old ancestor named Nauundel, was out in the bush, searching for sugar-bag, when he heard a curious hissing noise. He looked round and, in the distance, saw an egg and a snake coiled round it. It was the hissing of the snake that Nauundel heard. The snake was one now called Kintjilbara. Nauundel came close up, got a stick and began to poke the snake, which, by and by, went away. He did not attempt to injure it. The egg stood up on end and Nauundel lifted it from the ground and tied it up in paper bark. Then he cut some grass, laid it in his bag and put the egg, wrapped in paper bark, upon it, saying, *Geimbi kala muraian* ; *ngainma kala, kulapunna maleiappa*, which means, ' This is a Muraian stone all right ; it is mine all right, I put it in my bag.' All night he heard the egg saying *Prr, Prr,* as it moved about restlessly inside the paper bark. It moved about so much that it tossed all the grass out of the bag and, as it would not keep still, and Nauundel was afraid of losing it, he placed the mouth of the bag near the fire and stupefied the egg with the heat and smoke.

" Only Murabulba, that is, very old men, are allowed to see the egg. When its present possessor, a man named Narlinda, wishes to show it during the progress of the Muraian ceremonies, he says to the younger men . . . ' Food, go, all of you '—in other words, all of you go out into the bush and collect food. The young men know what he means, or, rather, that there is something that they must not see, and away they go. He says nothing to the other

men, but, as Narlinda told us, they know what he means
and nudge one another.   When the young men are far away,
Narlinda sits down by himself, a little distance away from
the old men, unwraps the paper bark, and calls the others up.
They come with their heads bent down.   Narlinda tells them
to come near and not be frightened because it will not
' growl,' that is, it will not be angry with them or do them
any harm.

" When they are going to hold these special ceremonies
there may be only one or two, or several, of these sacred
objects brought on to the ceremonial ground, which is most
carefully placed and, if necessary, as in the one we saw,
closed in with bushes.   At one of these ceremonies, after
the men have brought in their sacred sticks and stones, each
one being in the charge of some special individual, they are
placed on the ground to one side of the enclosed space.   If
there are any men present who have not seen them before,
but are judged to be old enough to do so, an old man, such
as Narlinda, says, ' Look, these are Muraian, do not quarrel
or, by and by, all your fingers will swell up.'   The performance itself is a very curious one and the men become
very excited. . . . When we saw it enacted, two of the men
stood to one side, one clanging sticks, the other clapping
his hands.   First of all a stick representing a fish, called
Jimidauappa, was brought in by a man to whom it belonged.
Followed by the other men, he came from behind some
bushes, creeping along with the sticks in his hands.   On the
ground he stood in the middle, all the other men circling
round and round him, while he pointed the stick at each of
them.   At first they sang the words—

> *Ka kai ka ka le*
> *Ka lulla le,*

and, after dancing for some time, they all extended their
arms towards the stick, time after time, drawing them back
rapidly and yelling, *Brau, brau,* which means, ' Give, give.'
They were supposed to be demanding a plentiful supply of
the fish Jimidauappa.

" Finally, the man fixed the stick upright in the ground
and they all danced round and round, pretending to rub

their hands up and down it, after which they rubbed themselves. Then they retired behind the bushes. After a short
time they came on again, this time bringing several sticks
and, in addition, rushing round the other men who stood to
one side. One after another the sticks were fixed upright in
the ground until there were some twenty or more sticks and
stones there. At one stage, when only a few had been brought
in, a special one—the Muraian itself—was produced. The
man carrying it tumbled down on the ground and was followed by the others and they all wriggled and rolled about
in the most grotesque fashion. The Muraian was in the form
of a slightly curved slab of wood, with the representation of
a head at one end, a very short tail at the other, and two
little projections at each side, representing limbs. It was
supposed to be a turtle, to which it certainly showed a considerable resemblance, quite enough to be recognisable, and
the rolling about of the men was supposed to be an imitation
of the movements of the animal itself.

" When all the sticks and stones, many of them elaborately
decorated, some representing yams with strings of gaily
coloured cockatoo feathers wound round them, had been
brought on to the ground, they were arranged in a circle
and the men danced round and round them with their arms
alternately extended and drawn back, while they yelled, *Brau
brau*, that is, ' Give, give.' It was, as the natives told us, a
request, in fact, a demand, to the sacred representatives of
the various animals and plants to provide them with these
same animals and plants that form their food supply.

" Amongst the native tribes of Central Australia I have
seen what Mr. Gillen and myself have called the Intichiuma
ceremonies. These are performed by the men of different
totemic groups, with the idea of increasing the number of the
animals and plants with which the ceremonies are concerned,
but, in the Central tribes, it is only the men of any one totemic
group who perform the ceremony associated with it, and there
is no such thing as any definite request or demand. The
mere performance of the ceremony is supposed to bring about
the desired result. In the Kakadu tribe, and the same is
true of other tribes associated with it, the members of different
totemic groups join together and, though it is difficult to

express, accurately, the difference between the two forms of ceremonies, both of which have the same object in view, that is, the increase of the food supply, it may be said that the Central tribes do not make anything in the way of a personal appeal to any object which is supposed to represent an animal or plant, whereas, amongst the Kakadu, this is most evident. The men of the latter tribe very clearly showed, by their insistent and fierce cry of *Brau, brau,* ' Give, give,' that they were directly asking, even demanding, the representatives of the various animals and plants to provide them with food. Amongst the many ceremonies of this kind that I have seen performed by Australian aboriginals, none have impressed me more than these, as indicating that savage man believes that he is able to control his food supply by means of magic. The way in which the men danced round the ceremonial objects, or rolled over on the ground holding them in their hands, was most suggestive of the idea that, by doing so, they brought about some close connection between themselves and the totemic animals or plants represented by the sacred sticks and stones. All that the men could tell us was that their old ancestors had always performed these ceremonies and that, after they had done so, the animals and plants had always multiplied.

" Altogether we saw about seventy of these sacred stones and sticks which, above all things possessed by the Kakadu and surrounding tribes, are pre-eminently *Kumali* or sacred. They brought just a few at a time to show us, taking the most elaborate precautions lest any woman or child, or even any young man, was in sight. Before they brought them in, they halted under the shelter of bushes and reconnoitred the place to make quite sure that they were safe and that no women were within sight. When a man saw us he would put a finger up to his nose, the sign that they had something *Kumali*. Then, when they were satisfied that everything was secure, they brought them in, wrapped up in fold after fold of paper bark. Whilst showing them to us they only spoke in whispers and, so real was it to them, that we, without thinking about it, felt compelled to do the same.

" They told us that the first of these Muraian objects was found, very long ago, by an old ancestor called Kulbaran.

He saw something strange in the form of a turtle moving about in the water, caught it and discovered that it was Muraian, or rather the turtle told him so. The turtle then described the ceremonies and taught Kulbaran how to perform them and how to make the sacred sticks and stones. He told Kulbaran that they were all *kumali widjeru*, that is very sacred or kumali. He also told him that the old men might eat the Muraian animals but that the young men must not do so. . . .

" Kulbaran, when first he saw the Muraian, said, *Ngeinyimma ameina?* which means, ' What is your name ? ' or ' Who are you ? ' The Muraian replied, *Ngainma Muraian*, ' I am Muraian ' ; *Ngainma jerapo mubilabilla balera*, ' I dance corroboree later on,' and then he danced, lifting up his legs and arms and singing, *Yai, Yai*, as he did so. The old man Kulbaran, said, *onje mubilabilla yama*, ' Which way another dance;' or, ' Is there any other dance ? ' and Muraian showed him some more. Then he said that all the dances that he showed Kulbaran were kumali ; *Jimmidauappa* (a fish) *kumali* ; *Banjil* (a fish) *kumali* ; *Kurnembo iwaiji* (goose egg) *kumali*, and so on, through the whole series.

" The stones that we saw were representatives of the following : Gunumaramilla (a yam) ; Kopereipi iwaiji (emu egg) ; Kulijidbo (a yam) ; Kulori (a yam) ; Kudjalinga (turtle) ; Kudjalinga iwaiji (turkey egg) ; Idabarabara ; Jimeribunna (native companion) ; Purijiliji and Worki (lily root) ; Kopereipi (emu) ; Eribinjori (large crocodile) ; Eribinjori iwaiji (crocodile eggs) ; Alberjiji (whistling duck) ; Mundebenbo (brush turkey) ; Kunjeama (plum) ; Kulekuli (cat-fish).

" The sticks were representatives of the following : Kimberikara (Barramunda) ; Munburungun ; Kulekuli (catfish) ; Tjunara (a yam) ; Jimidauappa (small fish) ; Eribinjori (large crocodile) ; Numereji (a snake) ; Murlappa (a yam) ; Brutpenniweir (Jabiru) ; Jungoan (snake) ; Kudjalinga (turtle) ; Mundebenbo (brush turkey) ; Murlappa (a yam) ; Minjiweya (a yam) ; Banjil (a fish) ; Bararil (a small fish) ; Kimberikara (Barramunda).

" In the case of both the stones and sticks there were, in

many of them, several representatives of the same totemic animals and plants and also distinct stones and sticks representing males, females, and eggs of the same animals.

" The stones of course can be passed on from one generation to another, but the sticks are naturally liable to decay and are renewed from time to time. In a climate such as that of the Alligator River district, it is difficult to preserve, intact, sticks that are continually being greased and painted and are hidden away, wrapped up in paper bark, in damp places, such as those in which the natives secrete them. They are very liable to be attacked by insects, such as boring beetles, and they must be periodically replaced by new ones. When they are used during any ceremony, such as the one we witnessed, the design is more or less rubbed off and, on each occasion, it is repainted. The same design is always used and must not apparently be varied. We several times saw serious consultations taking place amongst the old men as to the drawing of the design on a stick or stone. The white lines are put on with a very crude but effective paint brush, consisting simply of a little twig, about six inches long, one end of which is frayed with the teeth and then flattened out to form a small, thin disc about the size of a sixpenny bit. This is dipped into the white pipe clay which has been moistened with water so as to form a thin paste. It is held between the thumb and fingers, the handle of the brush lying in the palm of the hand in just the same way in which a white artist often holds a brush.

" In addition to its function as an Intichiuma ceremony, the Muraian serves, just as the Engwura does amongst the Arunta tribe, as a *finale* to the initiation ceremonies, during which the older men are shown objects that, in many cases, they have never and, in some, but rarely seen. The same is true of the Engwura, when a series of ceremonies, with men wearing decorations and using ceremonial objects, such as Nurtungas and Waningas, are shown to the relatively younger men. The ceremony is supposed, in both cases, to make the men ' good,' using the word in its native sense ; they must not growl or quarrel. After a man has passed through, or, rather, witnessed, the Muraian, he receives the special status name of *Lekerungen,* just as, in the Arunta, the men who have seen the Engwura are called *Urliara*. It also serves to enhance the importance of the old men and is of service to them in regard to their food supply because, whilst they can eat any of the animals or plants associated with the ceremony, no matter by whom they are captured, the younger men, even when they have seen the Muraian, must not touch anything secured by the old men and must also give the latter a share of any of the Muraian foods that they secure. Also, for some reason that the natives do not know, save that their arms and hands would become very sore if the rule were not carefully followed, the men who have seen the Muraian must, on no account, allow a dog to eat any remnant of their food.

" I have previously referred to the handing down of the sacred stones and sticks. Two examples will serve to show how carefully their history is preserved. In the case of the Emu-egg stone, tradition reports that it has been, in ,succession, in the possession of the following men : (1) Nauundel, who originally found it, (2) Nortmanitj, (3) Pwenguno, (4) Butja, (5) Nanilmango, (6) Nuburungillimaka, (7) Kingunaiya, (8) Yerimain, and (9) Narlinda, who now owns it. . . .

" In the case of an Eribinjori, or crocodile, stick, which the natives regarded as one of the most important, the history is still longer. It was owned in the first place by Kulbaran, who, when he became very old and unable to perform the ceremonies, gave it to (2) Midjail, his younger brother, after whom the following successively received it : (3) Numinbal, (4) Ungoreddi, (5) Alumbawerner, (6) Amunjureri, (7) Bulluoko, (8) Abringillimaka, (9) Ungowilla, (10) Nauukma-witch, (11) Pwenguno, (12) Pordjo, (13) Nauulmango, (14) Kingmanaia, (15) Kerauappa, (16) Naumarak, (17) Mant-jiritj, (18) Yiraman, who died recently, and from whom it descended to (19) Miniamake, its present holder.

" In the Warrai tribe [1] the name for totem is *mumulbuk*. They are divided amongst the classes.[2] One group is associated with the two classes Ajumbitj-Appularan, the

---

[1] The Warrai tribe occupy territory east of the Alligator River, and south of Port Darwin, near the source of the   Adelaide River.

[2] Spencer refers to the four divisions now known as sections.

other with Appungerti-Auinmitj.   Thus Ajumbitj-Appularan have the following : Bulta (eagle-hawk) ; Kinnimill (a yam) ; Gunbelli (small crocodile) ; Norquipito (red ochre) ; Bulp (pipe clay) ; Doito (stone axe) ; Deiurnu (kangaroo) ; Wairdmo (fire stick) ; Jin (leech) ; Gunnigunni (flying-fox). Appungerti-Auinmitj have Murdukul (a fish) ; Yilli (swamp lily) ; Tji (a snake) ; Wit (water) ; Bera (large crocodile) ; Kuala (turtle) ; Niri (dog) ; Gani (night time) ; Wordjal (black plover) ; Ngurin (emu).

" It will be noticed that there are, relatively, a large number of totemic groups associated with objects other than animals and plants, a feature in which this and other of the central tribes differ from the coastal tribes amongst whom, with very rare exceptions, the totemic names are those of edible objects.

" Inasmuch as the totemic groups are divided between the two moieties of the tribe and a man must marry a woman who does not belong to his own moiety, it follows that the totemic groups are exogamic.   The child belongs to a totemic group associated with its father's side of the tribe but not to his father's own totemic group.

" My informant told me that a leech man marries a fish woman and that their children are yam.   A fish man marries a flying-fox woman and their children are leech.   A flying-fox man marries a fish woman and their children are crocodile. . . . Unfortunately, I was unable to gain as complete and minute information as I should have liked. The Warrai tribe is now decadent, having been ruined by coming into contact with the mining fields, and it is always unsafe to rely implicitly upon information in regard to matters concerned with the organisation of a tribe derived from natives who are thus, more or less, demoralised.   Dr. Howitt drew attention to the manner in which tribes had been obliged to modify their old customs in regard especially to marriage, in consequence of the decimation of their numbers.   My informant, called Plainmur by the natives and ' Doctor ' by the white men, in reference to his former profession, was, however, an old man who was well acquainted with the ancient customs of his tribe.   I also had the assistance of a peculiarly intelligent ' boy ' who spoke

English well, so that, I think, the information, so far as it goes, is correct. When their old customs were in force the old man said that the Warrai people never killed their own totemic animal and that if he were to see any one else killing it he would be angry and would ask him, Why have you killed my mumulbuk ?

" In the Waduman tribe [1] the word for totem is Gwaiyan, though some natives pronounce it as if it were spelt Quoiyin or Quoiyan. The following is a list of totemic groups in this tribe : Mudbi (Barramunda fish) ; Ganbin (flying-fox) ; Kumerinji (emu) ; Inumbergo (male kangaroo) ; Undallo (female kangaroo) ; Wallanja (goanna) ; Tjuril (turtle) ; Korondulmi (rainbow) ; Kunadjerri (white snake) ; Kului (red-bellied water snake) ; Tjala or Kunajeraru (cat-fish) ; Pingan (a bony fish) ; Tuaiin (a long-nosed fish) ; Kandaua (moon) ; Butbutbau or Kirriwuk (a bird, the coucal) ; Wallano (a yam) ; Miakka (a yam) ; Kulbijinman (a large venomous snake) ; Miyun (wild dog) ; Biauiak (a small bird) ; Wiyan (water) ; Bulliyan (eagle hawk) ; Mabilli (small wallaby) ; Kadmanning (a small hawk) ; Koallimilla (small turtle) ; Illaluban (carpet snake) ; Errimembo (a venomous snake) ; Ledi (grasshopper) ; five kinds of sugar-bag called respectively Quoiyin, from the top of a tree (the equivalent of Mormo in the Kakadu) ; Gnedbo (a small bag also from high up) ; Luerga (from the base of ant hills) ; Eramalgo or Eramergo (from dead limbs) ; Dielba or Kulmidjin (from the tops of trees).

" In this tribe, as also in the Ngainman, Mudburra, and Billianera [2] tribes, the descent of the class name is in the father's line, that of the totem in the mother's, with the result that the totemic groups are distributed amongst the classes, the same totem group occurring on both sides of the tribe. A man must not marry a woman of his own totem.

" In addition to the main totem each individual has one or more, usually two, accessory totems. The main one is that associated with the totemic group into which he is born. The others are given to him when he is initiated. He is first

---

[1] The Waduman occupy territory near the town of Bradshaw, north of Victoria River.

[2] These tribes inhabit territory near that of the Waduman tribe, south of the Victoria River.

of all, during the initiation ceremonies, told his main totem, which is that of his mother, and, at a later period, the accessory totems. If you ask a Waduman native what is his Gwaiyan he will tell you his main one. He does not usually without further questioning mention the accessory ones, the significance of which I could not find out. As an example of these we may take the oldest Uanai man. . . . His name was Iblongwa and his main totem was Eramalgo, a sugar bag ; his accessory ones are Kandauak (moon) and Tjuril (turtle). His father's main totem was Tjala (cat-fish), with accessory ones . . . two kinds of sugar bag. His mother's main totem was Eramalgo, with accessory ones Kandauak and Tjuril, which happen to be identical with his, though this is not a matter of necessity. As he told us, when he entered his mother, he was Eramalgo ; the other two were given to him later when he was initiated. The different way in which a native regards his main and his accessory totems may be seen from the fact that Iblongwa will not cut Eramalgo out of a tree himself, but will eat it if it be given to him by another man. On the other hand, he will kill and eat Tjuril freely. In the same way, a Quoiyin man will not cut Quoiyin out of a tree himself, but will eat it if it be given to him. The Urella man of the Kulbijinman totem . . . whose name was Waljakula, told us that he would not himself kill the snake Kulbijinman, but would eat it if it had been killed by another man and given to him. On the other hand, he has Biauiak (a small bird) as an accessory totem, and this he kills and eats freely.

" The different totemic groups perform ceremonies for the increase of the totemic animal or plant. The name of these ceremonies is Tjutju, which is quite distinct from the name Pudaueru, applied to the sacred totemic ceremonies, or from Warangin, the name of the ordinary corroboree. The Tjutju ceremonies are the equivalents of the Intichiuma in the Arunta tribe.

" The head man of each totemic group is called Tjungunni. If he dies the next eldest brother succeeds to the post, and so on through the brothers, including amongst these the father's brothers' sons. If there are none of these alive, then the eldest son succeeds. That is, for example, if there be three brothers and the eldest dies, the office of Tjungunni does not descend to the son, but to the elder of the two survivors. If both of them die then it reverts to the eldest son of the first named, even if, in years, he be younger than a son of the second brother. Being the son of an elder brother, he is the ' elder brother ' of all the three brothers' sons, no matter what his actual age may be.

" When performing the ceremony of Tjutju the men of the group paint and dance, and others watching them. After the ceremony of any particular totemic group has been performed the men of all other groups go out and gather some of the animal or plant. If, for example, it be Eramalgo, the latter, after being brought into camp, is taken to the Eramalgo Tjungunni, the men saying, *Me Eramalgo*, ' Here is Eramalgo.' He replies, *Ma angui*, ' Give it, I eat.' It is handed over to him and he puts it in a *pitchi*, mixes it with water, eats a little himself, and hands it over to the other men, saying, *Nun burri*, ' I have finished.' After this they may all eat it. So, in the same way, a flying-fox man will eat a little of the animal, and hands the rest over to the other men who do not belong to the totemic group.

" If a man of any totemic group dies, the animal or plant is taboo to all members of that totemic group until after the performance of a small ceremony called *Orkbau*. The brother of the dead person brings the totemic animal or plant into camp. During the ceremony the members of the totemic group are painted with red ochre. A fire is made and the Tjungunni man passes the body of the animal or the plant, if, for example, it be a yam, through the smoke arising from the fire, after which it may be eaten. All members of the totemic group must put their heads into the smoke of the fire in which the animal is cooked.

" In the Mudburra tribe, whose country adjoins that of the Waduman, the word for totem is *mgalu*, and the head man of each group is called Malugurni. The descent of the totem, as in the Waduman tribe, is counted in the female line. . . .

" The Mudburra natives also perform the Tjutju ceremonies to increase the totemic animal or plant. After securing the latter the men who do not belong to the totemic group bring it up to the head man and hand it to him, the old man saying, ' Give it, I eat.' He takes a little and then hands it back, saying, ' I have finished.'

" The Pine Creek or Wulwullam [1] tribe is now decadent, having for many years, like the Warrai tribe, been in contact with the mining population. One of its oldest men, who could go back to the early days, told me that the totemic groups were divided between the moieties, and that the totem descended in the father's line. A Kangaroo man married a Barramunda woman, and their children were Kangaroo ; a Sugar-bag man married a Rain woman, and their children were Sugar-bag. . . .

" In the Worgait [2] tribe each individual may apparently be associated with more than one totemic group. My informant told me that he belonged to the frog, shark, and sugar-bag totem groups, and that he had inherited them from his father. The first was his main totem, the other two, as he said, ' came afterwards.' His mother was water-snake. A man may not marry a woman of the same totemic name as himself. If a stranger comes into a camp he is asked, *Ninik kuna koga,* ' What is your totem ? ' If, for example, he be a snake (or yam) man, he will reply, *Naidja wunga* (or *wila*) *koga*, that is, ' The snake (or yam) totem.' Further still, my informant told me that if the stranger was an old man and told him that his totem was frog, he, the younger man, would call him *boppa*, the same name that he applies to his father. If, on the other hand, he belonged to the water-snake totemic group, he would call him *kukkà*, the same name that he applies to his mother's brother. There is, so far as I could find out, no restriction in regard to eating the totemic animal or plant.

" In the Djauan [3] tribe the totem groups are associated with the sub-classes, the various pairs of the latter that are known as ' mates,' or *kumaranbun*, having totem groups in common. Thus Ngaritjban and Pungaringba have pelican, kangaroo, and goanna ; Pulainba and Palieringba have

---

[1] Pine Creek is south-east of Darwin, on the railway line.

[2] The territory of this tribe is on the coast, a little to the west of Port Darwin.

[3] The Djauan tribe occupies the territory about Katherine on the Daly River, south-east of Pine Creek and south of the Alligator Rivers.

sugar-bag and lily. . . . A man may marry a woman of any totem group provided she belongs to the proper sub-class, and as the totem groups are strictly divided amongst these it follows that a man cannot marry a woman of the same totemic name as himself. The word for totem is *lunga* and descent is counted in the male line. My informant was a Wamut man of a snake (*tjural*) totem ; he was married to a *Pungaringba* woman of the goanna totem and his children were Kungilla and snake.

" In the Mungarai tribe [1] the totem groups are associated with the sub-classes, the native term for totem being *Namáragua*. Each totemic group has a head man called *Tjugeanandu*. My chief informant, an old man named Wallungwarra, gave me the following list of totemic groups, but it is probable that there are still more ; these, however, were all that he, and two other men with him, could recollect :

" Bat (wallalka), black snake (djungwitj), cat-fish (warba), small crocodile (walbian), crow (waiwagmin), euro (kangilauro), goanna (djerkain), hawk (kamannin), kangaroo (gaauwi), lily (godiak), frilled lizard (wadidji), native companion (dagmin), opossum (widjurt), pelican (abaiya), porcupine (mullulberri), waterplant (ngarait), rain (ngaugo), a non-venomous snake (ngabandi), a poison snake (mimain), water snake (nanjugo), sugar-bag (ngauwap), native turkey (tjambirrina), long-tailed wallaby (walligeru), wallaby or paddy melon (mabiling), dark wallaby (ngirimu), rock wallaby (wunarungun), wind (wailulu).

" The groups are divided amongst the sub-classes [subsections] . . .

" A remarkable feature of the totemic system of this tribe is that while, as usual, a man must marry a woman belonging to a totemic group different from his own, the children pass into one which is neither the same as that of their father or mother, but is associated with the sub-class [sub-section] to which they belong on the father's side of the tribe. The following list indicates a certain number of the marriage arrangements so far as the totem groups are concerned and those into which the children pass :—

---

[1] The Mungarai tribes are on the Roper River, some distance inland from Port Roper.

A Ngapalieri man of the water-plant totem marries a Nakomara woman of the paddy-melon totem and their children are Ngabullan and poison snake.

A Ngapalieri man of the rain-totem marries a Nakomara woman of the rock-wallaby totem and their children are Ngabullan and Euro.

A Nangiella man of the plains-wallaby totem marries a Ngabullan woman of the euro totem and their children are Tjabijin and opossum.

A Nakomara man of the paddy-melon totem marries a Ngapalieri woman of the brush-tailed wallaby totem and their children are Ngaburella and porcupine.

A Ngaburella man of the porcupine totem marries a Ngaritjbellan woman of the frilled-lizard totem and their children are Nakomara and small hawk.

A Ngangiella man of the goanna totem marries a Ngabullan woman of the turkey totem and their children are Tjabijin and lily.

A Ngabullan man of the sugar-bag totem marries a Ngangiella woman of the crocodile totem and their children are Ngapalieri and rain.

A Tjabijin man of the pelican totem marries a Ngapungari woman of the cat-fish totem and their children are Ngangiella and black snake.

A Ngaburella man of the kangaroo totem marries a Ngaritjbellan woman of the wind totem and their children are Nakomara and paddy-melon.

A Tjabijin man of the dingo totem marries a Ngapungari woman of the native-companion totem and their children are Ngangiella and plains wallaby.

" The same curious system is apparently present in the Yungman tribe,[1] into which, however, I had very little opportunity of inquiring. The totem groups appear to be associated with the sub-classes, and the children of necessity belong to a group associated with the father's side of the tribe but with a sub-class to which he does not belong—the sub-class of his father and of his children. Thus, for example, a man of the dingo totem marries a sugar-bag woman and the children belong to the rain totem. The Nullakun term for totem is *Mungaiini*.

" These two tribes appear to differ from their neighbours in having their totem groups divided, not between the moieties, but the sub-classes [sub-sections], so that it is impossible for a child to have the same totem as either its father or its mother. The Mungarai and Yungman are in contact, on the one hand, with tribes such as the Djauan,

---

[1] The Yungman tribe are on the Elsey Creek of the Roper River, west of the territory of the Mungarai.

which has been already described, and, on the other, with the Nullakun and Mara.[1] The organisation of the Djauan, so far as the class system is concerned, is identical with that of the Mungarai and Yungman, and yet the totemic system is practically the same as that of the Mara and Nullakun tribes, from both of which it differs radically in regard to its class organisation. In the Djauan tribe the totem groups are divided between the sub-classes in such a way that those to which parents and children belong have them in common and the descent of the totem is strictly paternal. In the Mara and Nullakun the same is true, though sub-class names are not present. My informant in the former tribe was a Mumbali man and his totem, the native word for which is *Urarakammo*, was a snake called *daual*. His father's totem was *Daual*, and so, also, was that of his children. His wife was a Purdal woman and her totem was *Tjarukual* or Euro ; his mother was a Kuial woman of the *wordabil* or goanna totem. His son must marry a Kuial woman of the *wordabil* totem. Each totem group has its head man who is called *Yunguan*.

" So, again, in the Nullakun tribe descent is counted in the direct male line and the totems are divided between the classes. Thus, the children of a *kulakulungini*, or rainbow man, are *kulakulungini* ; those of a *nanguru*, or large crocodile man, are *nanguru*, and those of a *janambu*, or small crocodile man, are *janambu*. The native word for totem is *mus*, and each group has its head man, who is called *Kujungowangeri*." [2]

North-eastern Arnheim land is a region of the Northern Territory lying north-east of a line extending from Cape Stewart on the north coast to Blue Mud Bay on the Gulf of Carpentaria. The social and totemic organisation of the tribes inhabiting this area have been described as follows by Mr. T. Theodor Webb, Chairman of the North Australia District of the Methodist Missionary Society of Australia :—

" The social organisation of these peoples is marked by a very pronounced emphasis on the importance of the horde,

[1] The territory of the Nullakun lies to the south of the Roper River, and to the east of the territory of the Mungarai. The Mara are situated south-east of the territory of the Nullakun, and some distance inland from the Gulf of Carpentaria. See *Totemism and Exogamy*, i. 237 n., 270, 302 *sq.*

[2] Baldwin Spencer, *Native Tribes of the Northern Territory*, pp. 178-209.

each of which exists as an almost entirely independent unit. These hordes are very numerous ; some of them are very small, and there is definite evidence that several of them have actually become extinct, at least in so far as their patrilineal descent as a separate unit is concerned. With the few exceptions, each of these hordes, no matter how small, has its own particular dialect. In many cases the dialectal difference is small, and in at least one instance would appear to be consciously artificial.

" The two moieties into which the aboriginal society is divided are known as Yiritcha and Dua respectively, and these names are used without variation throughout the area indicated. Each horde is exclusively Yiritcha or Dua, as the case may be, and every man obtains his wife from some other horde of the opposite moiety.

" The two moieties are divided into eight subsections, four Yiritcha and four Dua, and the prevailing form of totemism includes the definite relationship of all members, both male and female, of each subsection (*marlk*), with some particular bird or animal, which is known by the individual as his or her *dʒuŋoin*. These *dʒuŋoin* have, as far as I am able to discover, no association with totem centres. Every member of the same subsection possesses the same *dʒuŋoin*, irrespective of the horde to which he belongs.

" The eight subsections, with their totems, are as follows :—

Subsections		Totems
Male (Yiritcha)	Female	
Ngarit	Ngaritjan	*Kurrt Jumbul ŋorowaray* (slender-limbed kangaroo)
Bulain	Bulaindjan	*Kurrt Jumbul borumŋor* (stout-limbed kangaroo)
Kaijark	Koitjan	*Karrkain* (fork-tailed kite) *Kurrit Jorrk* (large black lizard) *Jiriwi-jiriwi* (wagtail)
Bangardi (Dua)	Bangaritjan	*Urrpan* (emu)
Buralang	Kalian	*Werrti* (agile wallaby) *DʒandiL* (smaller wallaby)
Balang	Bilindjan	*Damala* (white-breasted sea-eagle)
Kamarung	Kumandjan	*Karmaruŋ* (wedge-tailed eagle)
Warmut	Warmutjan	*Warmut* (black-breasted buzzard) *Dulaku* (black-nosed kangaroo)

" The moieties are determined by patrilineal descent, but the subsections by matrilineal descent.

" The regular system of marriage between the subsections, with the subsections of the offspring, is as follows :—

Yiritcha Man	Dua Woman	Yiritcha Children	
		Male	Female
Ngarit	Bilindjan	Bangardi	Bangaritjan
	Kalian	Kaijark	Koitjan
Bulain	Kalian	Kaijark	Koitjan
	Bilindjan	Bangardi	Bangaritjan
Kaijark	Warmutjan	Ngarit	Njaritjan
	Kumandjan	Bulain	Bulaindjan
Bangardi	Kumandjan	Bulain	Bulaindjan
	Warmutjan	Ngarit	Ngaritjan

Dua Man	Yiritcha Woman	Dua Children	
		Male	Female
Buralang	Bulaindjan	Warmut	Warmutjan
	Ngaritjan	Karmarung	Kumandjan
Balang	Ngaritjan	Karmarung	Kumandjan
	Bulaindjan	Warmut	Warmutjan
Karmarung	Bangaritjan	Buralang	Kalian
	Koitjan	Balang	Bilindjan
Warmut	Koitjan	Balang	Bilindjan
	Bangaritjan	Buralang	Kalian

" It will be seen from the above that though eight subsections are recognised, these operate in four pairs, so reducing the organisation in this respect to a four-section system. It should be noticed, however, that normally a man marries a woman of the first-named subsection in the above, *i.e.* a Ngarit man regularly marries a Bilindjan woman, but under certain circumstances may marry a Kalian woman. . . .

" The chief ceremonial object is called *muraian*, and each horde possesses a number. These are, in the vast majority of cases, representations of (*a*) utensils, such as digging sticks (*bartʃu*), dilly-bags (*batti*), clubs (*balata*), etc., supposed to have been used by mythological ancestors ; (*b*) natural species associated in legend with these ancestors ; (*c*) these mythological ancestors themselves or certain of their physical

organs. These *muraian* would, I suppose, be termed ceremonial totems, though it seems an abuse of the term so to
apply it. *Muraian* is the common ' outside ' name for these
objects, while the ceremonial or ' inside ' name is *raŋga*.
Muraian is, on rare occasions, used to indicate anything
sacred or tabu, but correctly the term applies only to these
particular objects, the general term for sacred being *yarin*.
Thus the *muraian* or *raŋga* is *yarin*.

   " The ceremonies associated with these *raŋga* are known
as *nara*,[1] but while there is found an ill-defined system of
local totem centres the *nara* ceremonies are performed at
any suitable place, quite frequently in the territory of another
horde many miles from the totem centre to which it belongs.
Not infrequently both Yiritcha and Dua hordes will unite
for a *nara* ceremony, *raŋga* of both moieties being used.

   " It is upon these *raŋga* that the only real cohesion between the various hordes is based. Certain hordes of the
same moiety, though as widely separated as Elcho Island
on the north coast and Blue Mud Bay on the Gulf of Carpentaria, possess the same *raŋga*, and these are regarded as
belonging to the same *mala*. I leave it to be determined
whether the term tribe, sub-tribe, or some other should be
applied to these *mala*.

   " The horde is usually referred to by the name of the
dialect spoken by the members. The name of the *mala* is
much less frequently used. . . .

   " Though I have been resident among these people for
the past six years I have failed to discover any name which is
applied to any combination of hordes of both moieties.
Neither have I discovered a name for the language of which
the various tongues spoken are dialects. Kopapingo is sometimes used for the various Yiritcha dialects and Jumbarpingo
in the same way for the Dua dialects.

   " As will be gathered, I disagree with Dr. W. Lloyd
Warner in his application of the name Murngin generally to
the hordes of both moieties.[2] As I have shown, the Murngin

---

[1] " It should be noted that the *nara* ceremonies are in no sense increase rites, which are unknown in this region."

[2] *Oceania*, i. 251, 331, and 457 ; also *American Anthropologist*, New Series, xxxiii. 207 ; xxxiii. 172.

is purely a Yiritcha *mala*. All my informants are most emphatic that no Dua man could possibly belong to the Murngin group. It is but one of several Yiritcha and Dua *mala*, the hordes of which are scattered over the same area. I therefore consider Dr. Warner's use of the name to be unfortunate and misleading.

" If a tribe is to be defined as a number of neighbouring hordes which are united by the possession of a homogeneity of language and custom, then it appears that all the people of the area indicated belong to the one tribe, which for the time being must remain nameless.

" The widely separated locations of the hordes of the same *mala* present a puzzling problem. Probably migration, at least in part, accounts for it. An example of this is found in the Daiorrorr horde of the Berrkali *mala*, which within the lifetime of its present members migrated from the south of Buckingham Bay to its present location on the Goyder River. Possibly some evidence of migration is also found in the legends of the people, including the hordes along the northern coast and the islands adjacent thereto. In these legends a very large proportion of the mythological ancestors whose exploits they relate are represented as having lived and laboured and instituted the customs of the people in the neighbourhood of Caledon and Blue Mud Bays. In some cases these ancestors are represented as starting in at that point and travelling right across the country in a north-westerly direction to the opposite coast. These same legends, with local variations, are apparently found throughout the whole area, and the social organisation and the customs of the people are of the one type." [1]

The social organisation of the Aborigines who inhabit north-east Arnheim Land had previously been described by Mr. W. Lloyd Warner, on the basis of the investigations made by him from 1927 to 1929. According to him the aborigines are divided into eight tribes. One of these which he calls the Murngin occupies a territory on the coast of North Australia where the Gulf of Carpentaria joins the Arafura sea. Of this tribe he tells us that " The Murngin are

[1] T. Theodor Webb, " Tribal Organization in Eastern Arnheim Land," in *Oceania*, vol. iii. No. 4 (June 1933), pp. 406-411.

organised into local clan hordes, which are regrouped into the moieties called Yir-i-Tja and Du-a. The clans and moieties possess multiple totems. A number of ceremonies connected with the various totems are celebrated by all the clans during certain seasons of the year." . . .[1]

A child inherits a totem from its father; when the totemic emblem is shown to the boy for the first time, the father or clan leader says : This is your father or your grandfather. The boy will always call it by one of these terms. Most men call their totem " father." Their mother's totem is called " mother," or " mother's brother's son," and the totems of other clans are traced by the nearest relative in these clans.[2]

Where the account of Mr. Warner differs from that of Mr. Webb it is probable that preference should be given to that of Mr. Webb, whose longer residence and labours among the natives entitle him to speak with authority on the subject. The two accounts of the kinship system have been examined and elucidated by Professor A. P. Elkin ; but his discussion of the subject is too technical for reproduction here.[3]

With regard to the kinship and marriage organisation of the tribe, Mr. Warner tells us that " there are seventy-one relatives and seven lines of descent with five generations considered in the Murngin type of kinship structure. The Murngin system has a symmetrical cross-cousin marriage as its fundamental mechanism. A male can marry his mother's brother's daughter but not his father's sister's daughter, while a female marries his father's sister's son but she cannot marry her mother's brother's son." [4]

In the western part of the Northern Territory the Daly River flows in a north-westerly direction into the Timor Sea. In 1932 the tribes of this region were investigated by Mr.

[1] W. Lloyd Warner, " Morphology and Functions of Australian Murngin Type of Kinship," in *American Anthropologist*, New Series, xxxii. (1930) p. 207. Mr. Lloyd Warner's researches were conducted under the auspices of the Australian National Research Council and the Rockefeller Foundation and under the direction of Professor A. R. Radcliffe-Brown.

[2] W. Lloyd Warner, *op. cit.* pp. 207, 208.

[3] A. P. Elkin, " Marriage and Descent in East Arnheim Land," *Oceania*, vol. iii. No. 2 (June 1933), p. 412.

[4] L. Warner, " Kinship and Morphology of Forty-one North Australian Tribes," *American Anthropologist*, xxxv. (1933) p. 73.

W. E. H. Stanner under the auspices of the Australian
National Research Council. The native tribes of this region
were then reputed to be uncontaminated by white influence,
but Mr. Stanner found this to be very far indeed from the
case, for he found that a knowledge of the English language
was widespread among the natives, some of whom spoke it
with remarkable fluency, and most of his communications
with the natives were conducted in English. He spent seven
months altogether among them, including eleven weeks
among the Mulluk Mulluk and Madngella, six weeks with
the Marithiel, and four weeks with the Nangiomeri. On the
whole he had little difficulty in establishing friendly relations
with the natives, except with two tribes, the Marithiel and
Moiil, both of whom really belong to the country between the
Daly and the Fitzmaurice Rivers.

The Marithiel allowed him to witness two complete
circumcision ceremonies, and to be present during stages from
which all but fully initiated men were rigidly excluded. Information as to the sacred life of the various tribes was
communicated only after patient waiting for several months,
during which the natives gradually acquired confidence in
the enquirer.

The remnants of about one dozen tribes now live more
or less permanently within a narrow strip of country, which is
less than twenty miles long, on the alluvial flats between the
middle and the lower reaches of the Daly River. Not all
these tribes actually belong to this region, but have drifted
to it. A few other tribes, which did actually belong to it,
are now either extinct or are broken up and scattered,
although the remnants of one or two remain on the river.

This narrow strip of the river, which was the special field
of Mr. Stanner's researches, is at present and has always been
the centre of practically all settlement since the first invasion
took place, probably about the late eighties of the nineteenth
century. A Roman Catholic Mission station was established
in the country about 1890 or 1891, but it has long been
abandoned.

Among the chief objects of Mr. Stanner's investigations
were the complex kinship systems and social organisation of
the river tribes, and the paralysing fear of sorcery, which

has all tribes in its grip and which afforded him a fund of excellent material. He studied also the domestic and inter-tribal economic systems, which reveal a degree of organisation not usually considered characteristic of Australian tribes.[1]

Among the results of his studies he tells us that the complex sectional, subsectional, or moiety organisation characteristic of so large a part of Australia is not found among the true Daly river tribes. The Nangiomeri, who possess a subsectional system, now live on the Daly, but really belong to the country just north of the Fitzmaurice.

So far as history shows, the Daly River has been an area without moieties, sections, subsections, or any named or unnamed divisions of this kind whatever.

The Nangiomeri are the only natives in the Daly river region who appear clearly to have had a form of totemism before acquiring the matrilineal subsection totemism. It is almost certain that they once possessed a type of patrilineal totemism, but it is too late now to show what precise form it took. Some form of totemism also exists among the Nangor of the northern bank of the Fitzmaurice River. This is possibly dream totemism.

Among the Nangiomeri each subsection is associated totemically with a number of natural species and objects, and a fragmentary list of these given to Mr. Stanner by his best informant carried with it a strong suggestion of the " multiple totemism " of other parts of Australia. But it is membership of the subsections, not totemic affiliation, which governs marriage. According to one of his informants persons of the same totem should not marry, but on this point his information is not satisfactory. Mr. Stanner says that " In the list given me I can find no instance of a totemic object or species being shared between two subsections, not even for the list given for the subsections of a man and his mother's brother, as one would think they should be. All my informants, however, quite frankly admitted that they did not know very much about either the totemic system or the subsection system. There is, moreover, a clear indication that among the tribes from which the Nangiomeri acquired

---

[1] W. E. H. Stanner, " The Daly River Tribes," in _Oceania_, vol. iii. No. 4 (June 1933), pp. 377 _sq._

what knowledge they possess of these new systems, there is some sort of local distribution of the subsections, and of this the Nangiomeri knew nothing, except that in the south-west certain subsections are ' boxed up.'   Even if the Nangiomeri had their complete local organisation still intact, and a kinship system functioning without irregularity, much of the subsection system they have taken over would still be function-less, as it now is.   The eight-subsection system has clearly been elaborated to function in a kinship system very different from the original system of the Nangiomeri, with its orthodox Kariera-type characteristics." [1]   Mr. Stanner's informants knew nothing of ceremonial observances towards the totems, and he adds that many prohibitions against eating certain plants and animals in this area are clearly not totemic, but are temporary prohibitions imposed at certain periods, such as puberty and initiation, menstruation, and pregnancy.

[1] With regard to the Kariera type of kinship system, see below, pp. 54 *sqq*.

CHAPTER IV

TOTEMISM OF THE KARIERA AND OTHER
TRIBES OF WEST AUSTRALIA

KIMBERLEY DIVISION is a large district of West Australia, extending along the coast from Queen's Channel, on the border of the Northern Territory and West Australia to the De Grey River. Adjacent to it is the North-Western Division, occupying the territory between the De Grey River and the Ashburton River. In this district the Kariera tribe was investigated by Mr. (now Professor) Radcliffe-Brown[1] in 1911, with the assistance of Mrs. Daisy Bates, who had for some years been studying the aborigines of Western Australia on behalf of the West Australian Government. The services of Mrs. Bates were generously placed at the disposal of Professor Radcliffe-Brown by the Government.

The Kariera tribe occupies the coast of Western Australia from a point to the east of the Sherlock River to a point east of Port Headland, extending inland for about fifty miles. The tribe is bordered by the Ngarla on the east, the Ngaluma on the west, the Ingibandi on the south, and the Namal on the south-east.

The surviving natives of the Kariera tribe, all of whom speak English, and comprise a total of a hundred or less, are nearly all living on sheep stations that have been established on their tribal territory. They are fed and clothed by the owners of the stations or at the expense of the Government, and the able-bodied men and women work on the stations.

---

[1] A. R. Brown, " Three Tribes of Western Australia," *Journal of the Royal Anthropological Institute*, xliii. (1913) pp. 143-194. Cf. *Oceania*, vol. i. No. 2 (July 1930), pp. 208 *sq.*

The tribe is distinguished from its neighbours by the possession of a name (Kariera, of which the meaning is unknown), a language, and a defined territory. There is no tribal chief, nor any form of tribal government. The fights that formerly took place were not between tribes, but between one part of the tribe and one part of another, or even two parts of the same tribe. Thus there was no unity of this tribe in warfare. The extent of the territory of the tribe is between three thousand five hundred and four thousand square miles. The northern part of their country is mostly level plain covered with grass and scrub with occasional hills of no great height. In the south there are numerous stony hills, with intervening flats. The coast is low, consisting chiefly of sand-dunes and mangrove swamps. The natives have a very large number of geographical names, many of which, if not all, have a meaning that is understood at the present day. An interesting feature of the nomenclature, which often leads to confusion, is that there are often two different places with the same name. Thus, there are two places called Murumbarina, one on the Turner River, and one on the Sherlock River. Murumbari is the name of a species of beetle, which is common, it seems, in these two places. Every geographical feature, every little hill, pool, or creek has its name.

The tribe is divided into a number of local groups, each with its own defined territory. Membership of the local group is determined by descent in the male line ; that is to say, a child belongs to the local group of its father and inherits hunting rights over the territory of that group. These local groups have no distinctive names. To the question, " Where is your country ? " a native will reply by naming one of the more prominent camping places of his local group, or sometimes the place where he was born. Along the coast there are seven local groups, occupying altogether a strip of land about eighty miles long and a little less than ten miles wide. This gives the area occupied by each as about one hundred square miles, or a little more. The inland groups seemed to occupy each a somewhat larger country, between one hundred and fifty and two hundred square miles. This is as might be expected, since the coastal natives have both the land and the sea from which to obtain their food supply. As a rough estimate we may suppose that the tribe consisted of between twenty and twenty-five local groups. It is now impossible to obtain any accurate information as to the former size of the local groups, that is the number of individuals belonging to each. Professor Radcliffe-Brown estimates that each group contained not less than thirty individuals, giving the minimum for the tribe of about seven hundred and fifty, but he admits that this is a very rough estimate.

Each member of a group has the right to hunt over the territory of his group at all times, but he may not hunt over the country of any other local group without permission of its owners. A single exception to this rule seems to have existed where a man was following a kangaroo or emu and it crossed the boundary into the country of his neighbours, when he might follow it and kill it. But in general hunting or collecting vegetable products without permission on the country of another local group was treated as a trespass liable to be punished by death. The respect attached to this law seems to have been so great that infractions of it were very rare. Professor Radcliffe-Brown could find no evidence of the individual ownership of any part of the soil, or any of its products. The whole territory of the group and everything on it appear to belong equally to all the members of the group.

It was impossible for a man to leave his local group and become naturalised or adopted in another. Just as the country belonged to him, so he belonged to it. If he left it he became a stranger, either the guest or the enemy of the people in whose country he found himself. He might pay visits to other groups, and such visits appear to have been very frequent, but his " home " was his own country, the country of his father's father. At the present day the influence of white settlement has altered all this. The country now belongs to the white men, and the natives have to live where they can. But still the attachment of a man to his own country has not been destroyed. Natives often express a wish to die and be buried in their own hereditary hunting ground.[1]

[1] A. R. Radcliffe-Brown, *op. cit.* p. 146.

In their original state the natives never stayed long in one place. They shifted from one camping ground to another perpetually. It does not seem that the whole local group always lived and moved about as one body. A single family, that is a man and his wife or wives and their children, often travelled and hunted by themselves. A single individual, or a family, or several families, might pay a visit to a neighbouring group, during which time they hunted in the country of their hosts. When some particular article of food became very abundant in the country of one group they invited their neighbours to come and stay with them. Thus the inland natives visited those on the coast when fish was plentiful. On the occasion of the performance of a ceremony, members of different local groups might be found camped together often for weeks at a time. There was thus a perpetual movement of population both within the country of the group and from one group to another.

" This state of things," says Professor Radcliffe-Brown, " shows very clearly that the unit of social life in the Kariera tribe was the family, consisting of a man and his wife or wives, and their children. Such a unit might move about by itself without reference to the movements of the other families of the local group. In the camp each family had its own hut or shelter with its own fire. The family had its own food supply which was cooked and consumed by the family. The man provided the flesh food and his wife provided the vegetable food and such things as small mammals or lizards."

A native camp is regularly composed of two parts, the married people's camp and the bachelors' camp. The latter contains all the unmarried men, including widowers ; unmarried women and widows live with one or other of the families of the married people. As the local groups were exogamous, the rule being that a man was not permitted to marry a woman of his own local group, the result was that in the camp of a local group would be found only men and unmarried women and children who belonged to the group by birth, the married women born in the group not living in it, but, with their husbands, in other groups.

With regard to relationship and marriage, the Kariera, together with a group of other tribes occupying with them a large district of south-western Kimberley, are divided into four exogamous sections named respectively Banaka, Burung, Palyeri, and Karimera. No meanings were found by Professor Radcliffe-Brown for these names. To the natives of the present day, they are simply the names of social divisions, and have no further meanings. The other tribes which share this organisation are Ngerla, Ngaluma, Indjibandi, Pandjima, Bailgu, and Nyamal, and probably also the Ngadari, Wirdniya, Targudi, Ibarga, Widagari, and Nangamada.[1] In the Kariera tribe men of the Banaka section may only marry women of the Burung section and a Burung man may only marry a Banaka woman. The child of a Banaka man and a Burung woman is neither Banaka nor Burung but Palyeri, while the child of a Burung man and a Banaka woman is Karimera. The child of a Palyeri man and a Karimera woman is Banaka, and the child of a Karimera man and a Palyeri woman is Burung.

In the Nyamal, Bailgu, Pandjima, and Indjibandi tribes the names of the sections are similar, but the arrangement of the sections is different. Thus a Banaka man marries a Karimera woman and the child is Padyeri, while the child of a Karimera man and a Banaka woman is Burung. So, also, a Burung man marries a Padyeri woman and the child is Karimera, while a Padyeri man marries a Burung woman and the child is Banaka. We find here a condition that recurs in other parts of the continent, in which neighbouring tribes have similar names for the intermarrying sections, but the arrangement of the sections, and consequently the rules of marriage and descent, are different. Marriage between the two tribes is then arranged by regarding a given section in the one tribe as equivalent to a certain section in the other. The equivalence of sections between the Kariera and Nyamal tribes, as shown by genealogies, is—

---

[1] A. R. Radcliffe-Brown, "The Social Organization of the Australian Tribes," p. 35 (*Oceania*, Melbourne, 1931); "Three Tribes of Western Australia," *Journal of the Royal Anthropological Institute*, xliii. (1913) p. 147.

Nyamal			*Kariera*
Banaka	is equivalent to		Palyeri
Burong	,,	,,	Burung
Karimera	,,	,,	Karimera
Padyeri	,,	,,	Banaka[1]

The tribes of the area already indicated have kinship system of the Kariera type, in which a man marries a woman who stands to him in the relationship of " mother's brother's daughter " or " father's sister's daughter." Marriage of actual first cousins is approved and is indeed regarded as the proper form of marriage, though of course it occurs only in a limited number of instances. In all the tribes there is exchange of sisters in marriage, that is, a man's sister is given to his wife's brother in return for the latter's sister.

In this area the individuals born in one horde constitute a patrilineal local clan. Thus in the Kariera tribe in one horde all the persons belonging to that horde by birth will belong to one or other of the couple of sections Karimera and Burung. In another horde the position will be reversed, the persons born in that horde being Karimera and Burung while their wives are Banaka and Palyeri. The local clan is therefore necessarily an exogamous group. A man may not marry a woman born in the same horde as himself.

Each local clan is also, in a certain sense, a totemic clan, having a number of totems. In the territory of each horde Professor Radcliffe-Brown found a number of totemic centres, called *talu* in Kariera, each of which is specially associated with one or more species of natural object. Those natural species for which totem-centres exist in the country of a horde may be spoken of as being the totems of the horde or of the local clan. There is no prohibition against eating or using one's totem. Associated with each *talu* or totem-centre there is a ceremony which is believed to produce an increase of the totem. Thus at a kangaroo centre a ceremony can be performed for the purpose of making kangaroos more plentiful. The ceremony at a given centre is a possession of the clan to which that centre belongs and

[1] " Social Organization of Australian Tribes," p. 34.

is performed by the men of that clan. There is a system of myths which relate how the various totem-centres came into existence as the result of the doings of certain mythical ancestors. It may be noted that a totem-centre is usually a spot in the neighbourhood of which the totem species is very plentiful.

There are traces in these tribes of a system of section totemism. In the Pandjima tribe the euro or hill kangaroo is named *padjeri*, which is also the name of one of the four sections, and it is regarded as belonging to that section. An informant of this tribe stated that the crow and the rock wallaby are Banaka, while the eaglehawk and the plains kangaroo are Burung. In this tribe, and in the Indjibandi, terms of relationship are applied to the animals that are thus associated with the sections. Thus an Indjibandi man of the Padjeri section called the hill kangaroo (*padjeri*) *maiali*, father's father; the eaglehawk, being Burong, he called *tami*, mother's father, and so on.

We have seen that the Kariera tribe is divided into a number of local groups each with its own defined territory, with descent in the male line, and that each local group belongs to one of the two couples into which the tribe is divided. The local group thus forms what we may call a "clan," with male descent, all the male members being "father's father," "son's son," "father," "son," or "brother" to each other.

Each of these clans forms a single totemic group, possessing a number of totems. All the totems of the clan are equally the totems of every member of the clan. For each totem belonging to the clan there is, as we have seen, within the territory of the clan a ceremonial ground or totemic centre for which the name is *talu*. The *talu* is a spot set apart for the performance of totemic ceremonies. Thus the *Pidira talu* is the spot set apart for the performance of ceremonies connected with the *pidira*, white cockatoo. The *talu* belongs to the men of the local group in whose territory it is found, and the ceremonies connected with the *talu* belong to them at the same time. If a *talu* lies within the territory of a certain local group only the members of that local group can perform the ceremonies connected with it.

The totemic ceremonies of the Kariera tribe have been discontinued for many years. Professor Radcliffe-Brown was therefore unable to see any of them performed, and had to rely entirely upon what the natives told him about them. Information of this kind is of course very unsatisfactory. The purpose of the ceremonies is said to be to increase the supply of the animal, plant, or other object with which it is connected. Thus the purpose of the *mungu* or white ant ceremony is to increase the white ants, which are eaten by the aborigines. At many of these totemic ceremonial grounds there is either a single boulder or a heap of small stones and these play a part in the ceremony performed at the place. In some cases it would seem that the stone or heap is struck with clubs or with stones held in the hand. The performers of these ceremonies are painted, and decorated with feathers and bird's down. The women of the clan take part in the ceremonies as well as the men. In some cases songs are sung, in others one of the performers calls out the names of the different parts of the country. The head man of the clan, unless he be too old, takes a leading part in the ceremonies of his clan.

There is no prohibition whatever against a man or woman killing any one of his or her totems, if it be an animal, or against eating it if it be edible. The following is a list of the totems of some of the Kariera clans, as it is given by Professor Radcliffe-Brown, who tells us that " the list does not profess to be complete. It does not include all the clans of the tribe, nor can I be sure that all the totems of any clan are enumerated."

I : KARIMERA-BURUNG

Yiliguji	rainbow.	At Womalana.
Pidira	white cockatoo.	At Balla-balla.
Kurinja	March fly.	,,
Mǎngǎbuga	fish.	
Yatumba	,,	
Pira	conch shell.	

II : BANAKA-PALYERI

Wongali	a lizard.	At Kayingarana.
Tarbun	crab.	
Balanu	fish.	

Banangura	.	.	fish.	At Magalana.
Waragalara	.	.	,,	At Madukurbarana.
Churi	.	.	,,	
Minagalara	.	.	,,	
Kagumada	.	.	,,	At Kagumadana.
Nyumeru	.	.	,,	
Kandara .	.	.	seed.	At Kayingarana.

III : BANAKA-PALYERI

Wanangura	.	.	whirlwind.	At Wanangurana.
Kambuda	.	.	child or baby.	At Pilgun.
Puna	.	.	sexual desire.	At Kalbana.
Wajabi .	.	.	small mammal.	At Wajabina.
Wanangadi	.	.	snake.	At Bambana.
Kulibiri .	.	.	,,	At Kulibirina.
Mungu .	.	.	white ant.	At Mungulina.
Tanamada	.	.	grub.	At Maludarana.
Taiyimara	.	.	honey flower.	At Kaiyuna.
Yigara .	.	.	mangrove.	At Walunguna.
Nyura .	.	.	(?)	
Pindanu .	.	.	(?)	

IV : KARIMERA-BURUNG

Puriya .	.	.	the tide.	At Kurjadagabuna.
Kunya .	.	.	mosquito.	At Chindagalarana.
Kumi .	.	.	sand-fly.	At Kumina.
Ngalun .	.	.	snake.	At Ngaluna.
Mogudi .	.	.	,,	
Yurguliguli	.	.	,,	At Ngaluna.
Tambalambala .	.	bird.	At Chindagalarana.
Namali .	.	.	fish.	At Kabuna.
Ngalara .	.	.	,,	At Ngalarana.
Muraban	.	.	,,	
Waberi .	.	.	,,	At Majanina.
Chindabiri	.	.	,,	
Kalandi .	.	.	,,	At Kalandina.
Manjir .	.	.	flat fish.	At Ngamana.
Kadumada	.	.	medusa (?).	At Kalandina.
Ngalgu .	.	.	root.	At Yarina.
Bagada .	.	.	grass.	At Chindagalarana.
Waru	.	.	seed.	,,

On the list Professor Radcliffe-Brown remarks :—

" Most of the totems are of an edible nature. Among the clans of the coast various species of fish preponderate. There is not a large number of vegetable species in the list of totems. . . . I did not find in the Kariera tribe either a kangaroo totem or an emu totem, nor was there a rain totem, unless we include in this tribe a clan at Pilbara, which more probably belongs to the Injibandi tribe. The absence of these totems in the Kariera tribe is of some interest when we compare that tribe with others, for example, with the tribes on the Ashburton River, to be described later.

" I could not find any prohibition against a man or woman eating his or her own totem if it were edible, or against killing it. Every native that I questioned said that there was no such restriction. A man killed and ate his own totem as readily as he killed and ate any other animal.

" As regards many of the totems, it would seem that the totemic centre or ceremonial ground is in a part of the country where the totem species is naturally plentiful. Thus the ceremonial grounds of the white cockatoo and the March fly are in the creek at Ballaballa, where these two species are plentiful. In a number of cases, not only in this but also in other tribes, I was able to satisfy myself that the totem animal or plant is actually more abundant near the ceremonial ground belonging to it than in other parts of the country. In a large proportion of cases the place where the ceremony is performed is called by a name formed by adding the suffix *na* to the name of the totem. Thus there are two totemic centres for *murumbari* (a beetle), and in both cases the name of the totem centre is Murumbarina. . . . Similar place-names, that is, consisting of the name of some species of animal or vegetable species with the suffix -*na*, are also given to spots where there is no totemic centre, but where the species in question is more abundant than elsewhere. . . .

" It is to be remembered that ' children ' are a totem of one of the Kariera clans, and it is the duty of the members of this clan to perform ceremonies for the increase of children. . . ." [1]

The Ngaluma tribe occupies the coast of West Australia from the Maitland River to the Sherlock River, extending inland for about fifty miles. The neighbouring tribes are the Kariera, the Mardudhunera on the south-west, and the Indjibandi on the south. Ngaluma is the name by which the members of the tribe refer to themselves, and by which they

[1] A. R. Radcliffe-Brown, *op. cit.* pp. 166 *sqq.*

are known to their neighbours. Professor Radcliffe-Brown
could discover no meaning for the name. The extent of the
tribal territory is approximately two thousand five hundred
square miles. It is composed of stony hills with intervening
flats often of considerable area. The chief rivers are the
Maitland, Nickol, Harding, and Sherlock. The pools in
these rivers provide a fairly plentiful supply of fresh water.
There are very few survivors of the tribe, probably not more
than sixty all told. In 1865 they are said to have numbered
from two hundred and fifty to three hundred persons, but
this may have only applied to the neighbourhood of Roe-
bourne and Nickol Bay.[1] The tribe is divided into local
groups in exactly the same way as the Kariera tribe,
and we are told that the description already given of
the Kariera under this heading will apply equally well
to the Ngaluma, and the relationship system of the
Ngaluma tribe is similar in every respect to that of their
neighbours, the Kariera. Again, the totemic system of the
Ngaluma is exactly similar to that of the Kariera. Professor
Radcliffe-Brown was not able to obtain much information
about the particular totems of the tribe ; but he found that
two clans of the tribe had for their totems: *Taiyangul*, a fresh-
water fish; *Piranu*, eel; *Jigura*, a fresh-water fish; *Ngaburain*,
a vegetable ; *Mariangu*, a grub ; *Ngangari*, a seed ; *Jimar*,
a fruit ; *Kalgal*, vomiting sickness ; *Mudu*, cold weather.
Further he discovered that another clan, whose geographical
situation he could not ascertain, had for its totems : *Kalai-
jura*, a bird ; *Walaigura*, pigeon ; *Minarang*, centipede ;
Ngandarimirgura, shark ; *Budabudara*, a fish ; *Puliribuga*,
a fish ; *Win-ge*, a fish ; *Bida-bida*, a fish.[2]

The totemic ceremonies of this tribe have not been performed for many years and the younger men know very little
about them. When the ceremony for producing cold weather
was to be performed the men and women of the clan went
together to the ceremonial ground. There they painted themselves with white clay. Some of the men made a great

---

[1] A. R. Radcliffe-Brown, " Three
Tribes of Western Australia," in
*Journal of the Royal Anthropological
Institute*, xliii. (1913), quoting Curr,
Australian Race, i. pp. 296-303.
   [2] A. R. Radcliffe-Brown, *op. cit.*
pp. 170 *sq.*

break-wind of boughs and grass, and to one side of this a big fire was lighted. The break-wind was so placed that it would shelter the occupants from the south-east wind, which is the cold wind, even if at the time the wind was actually blowing from some other direction. The performers then sat round the fire within the break-wind or shelter and pretended to shiver with cold. After this the weather was sure, they thought, to grow colder in a few days. In some of the ceremonies connected with seed totems, a part of the ceremony consisted of grinding some of the particles of seeds in the way in which they are usually prepared for food, and then scattering the flour in different directions, calling out the names of different parts of the country in which the performers wished the seeds to flourish and ripen. If only these simple savages had omitted the first of these processes, by refraining from grinding up the seeds, they might have discovered that seeds so scattered produce a crop, and so might have discovered the origin of agriculture, thousands of years before its introduction into Australia from Europe. With regard to the totem of vomiting sickness, Professor Radcliffe-Brown learned from an informant that if this ceremony were performed the natives were seized with attacks of vomiting. "Why this ceremony should ever be performed," remarks Professor Radcliffe-Brown, "unless perhaps as a means of annoying their neighbours, it is difficult to see." [1] Perhaps it may have been invented by some primitive Aesculapius to benefit the health of his fellows after a surfeit of food.

The Mardudhunera tribe occupies an area of approximately three thousand five hundred square miles on the lower Fortescue River in western Kimberley. On the south-west the tribe is adjoined by the Nsala, on the north-east by the Ngaluma, and on the south-east by the Injibandi or Korama. The local organisation of the tribe is in all respects similar to that of the Kariera tribe, and their totemism is also similar to that of the Kariera. Each local clan has a number of totems that are transmitted from father to son. The members of the group perform ceremonies, called *talu*, for the purpose of increasing the totem, but there is no objection to a man killing or eating any of his totems.

---

[1] A. R. Radcliffe-Brown, *op. cit.* pp. 172 *sqq.*

CHAPTER V

THE TOTEMISM OF THE KARADJERI AND OTHER TRIBES OF THE KIMBERLEY DIVISION, WEST AUSTRALIA

THE totemism and social organisation of the tribes in this Division of Australia have been investigated by Professor A. P. Elkin. In regard to them he tells us generally, "though Eastern Kimberley, North-Western Australia, has been settled for about fifty years, yet there are sufficient natives left with a knowledge of their tribal institutions to make possible a valuable study of the relationship of totemism to the subsection system which prevails there, and of the relationship of both to the local organisation—a work which badly needs doing. The tribes of this region are all the more interesting, too, because they are joined on the west by tribes with moiety organisation and patrilineal totemic clan-hordes, and on the south-west by tribes with four-section systems. Further, in addition to areas in which the aboriginal culture is breaking down, there are still a number of tribes in which totemic institutions, customs and beliefs are functioning uninfluenced by our invading culture, and are playing their full part in native social and religious life. . . ." [1]

The Karadjeri is the most southerly coastal tribe of the Kimberley Division. Its country stretches from about Nooreen Well on the south, to the southern shore of Roebuck Bay and the neighbourhood of Thangoo Station in the north, a distance of eighty-five miles as the crow flies, and inland about thirty miles in the north and about sixty miles further south. The Nangamade, whose social and totemic organisa-

[1] A. P. Elkin, "Totemism in North-Western Australia," *Oceania*, vol. iii. No. 3 (March 1933), pp. 257 *sqq.*

tion seems to be similar to that of the Karadjeri, joins the latter on the south and south-east. The Yauor, a small tribe around Thangoo Station, with the same type of kinship and totemic systems as the Karadjeri, is the nearest neighbour of that tribe on the north. Two tribes border the Karadjeri on the east, namely the Nygina, about whom we know a little, and on the south of the latter, the Mangala, about whom we know nothing.

The Karadjeri territory is divided into a number of horde-countries called *nura* which are, or were, for the most part patrilineal and patrilocal. A person belongs to the horde of his father and has free access to the countries of his mother and his father's mother. The term *nura*, however, is also applied to a person's spirit-home, the place in which he was "found" by his father; this is usually a part of the horde-country.

Each horde has associated with it one or more totems or *bugari*. As in so many tribes in North-West, Central, and South Australia, the term for totem also designates the long-past time when the culture-heroes and totem ancestors lived on earth, made its natural features, and instituted tribal laws, customs, and rites. Again, as in these other regions the same word has the significance of dreaming.

Where cult-totemism is concerned, the question, "What is your dreaming?" is equivalent to asking "What is your totem?" and is answered with the name of the cult-totem. The ancient time of the heroes is the "dream time," but not the fleeting dream of the night; rather it is the eternal dream-time of spiritual reality to which historical significance is attached. To a native a dream is a real objective experience in which time and space are no longer barriers, and in which information of great importance is gained by the dreamer. This information may refer to the sky-world, if the dreamer be a medicine-man, or to the earth beneath, to his fellow tribesman, or even to his child yet unborn. But the great "dreaming" or dream-time was the age of the mighty heroes and ancestors, who indeed still exist. And so a person's totem links him to that period and gives him a share in it. Again the totem is also *bugari*, dreaming, because it represents the totemite in the dream-life of the present-day men and women. Moreover the totem might well be called " dreaming," since a father becomes acquainted with a child's totem by dreaming of it.   Indeed, according to the theory of conception held by the Karadjeri, and every other tribe of Kimberley, the father " finds " or sees in a dream, or maybe in a waking vision, the child that his wife is to bear.   The country in which he has the dream becomes the horde-country of the child, while a dream associates the child with its totem, its *bugari*.

Karadjeri totemism is a variety of local totemism in that the various *bugari* (totems) are definitely associated with particular horde-countries or localities, and that the father's dream associates the totem and his child, while still a spirit-child, with the country in which he " found " it, which normally should be, or is arranged to be, some part of his own horde-country.   But while fundamentally the totemism is " local," the descent is almost always patrilineal.   Patri-local marriages, that is marriage in which the wife goes to live with her husband, the faith of her children, combined with the patrilineal descent of the hordes, always tends to make descent of the totem, which normally depends upon the accident of conception, birth or " finding," patrilineal.   This is especially true when, as in the Karadjeri tribe, the totems are divided amongst the patrilineal hordes.   Again, where the local totemism is also a cult-totemism, that is associated with secret myths, rites, and sanctuaries, and it is a variation of this in the Karadjeri tribe, a father naturally likes his son to belong to his own totem and to share in its ceremonies. But in the Karadjeri tribe the patrilineal descent on which some of the old men insist is based primarily on the patri-lineal descent of the horde country, amongst which the *bugari* (totems) are divided ;   the chance of " dreaming " the child and its totem outside the father's horde-country is obviated by the sticklers for old beliefs by the fiction that the father must " find " his spirit-child in his own horde-country.   But others, more sophisticated, just maintain that the descent is patrilineal.

There is also the possibility that although a child is " found " in, and belongs to, his father's horde-country, yet a dream will assign to it a totem different from the

father's. In one such case a man of the kangaroo totem
" found " one of his sons in his own horde-country, but
associated with a yam, which then became the boy's totem.
Thus father and son belong to the one " country " but to
different totems.

Usually and normally, the horde-country in which a child
is " found " and born is the same, and is, moreover, the
horde-country of the father. But if they are not the same,
the general principle seems to be to give the place of " finding," that is conception, as the horde-country, though many
regard the place of birth as the horde-country of the individual. No doubt both places are regarded in some
spiritual sense as the person's horde-country, and if the dreaming has been normal the totem of the place of " finding "
becomes the child's totem. In any case the father's horde-
country is also that of his child, no matter where the latter was
" found " or born, for he is brought up in it and is always
free of it.[1]

With regard to associated or multiple totems, there does
not seem to be any obvious principle which governs the
grouping of totems in individual cases. Thus one person
has for his totem two kinds of stingaree (fish), a diver, and
a kangaroo. The last of these does not fit into a salt-water
complex. Another has the sea, cockle, and crab, which are
naturally associated, but his fourth totem is crow. In other
cases the associated totems are rainbow and yam, or fire and
honey, or fire and kangaroo, or stingaree, porpoise, and diver,
eagle-hawk and wattle, or stingaree and human lice, or yam
and bakenia tree. Now those species and objects are associated in dreams, but this is so for they are, in the most
part, first of all associated as multiple totems of horde-
countries, and this is no doubt because, for the most part,
they are found associated in natural life. In other cases
mythology and the evidence of dreams would possibly provide
the explanation.

The totems are exogamous. To this rule Professor Elkin
could find no exceptions, and his informants admitted none
in discussion.

As to the eating of the totem an old man reported

[1] A. P. Elkin, *op. cit.* pp. 266-268.

what was 'probably the general principle, namely that a person might eat his totem, but only if it were killed by a man who belonged to the couple of sections to which the man himself did not belong, that is to the sections of his mother's brother and wife's brother, but not to his own or father's (or child's) section.

The foregoing discussion of hordes and totems applies also to the Yauor tribe, the only difference being one of terms : horde-country and birthplace are called *boru* and totem *dyalnga*. These terms are used throughout Dampier Land, a district of Kimberley immediately north of the territory occupied by the Karadjeri. Almost all Yauor persons have more than one totem.[1]

" In Karadjeri totemism," observes Professor Elkin, " we are dealing not with a variety of social totemism, the primary function of which is to denominate and regulate social groups, but with cult-totemism which gives the individual his place in and share of the ceremonial, mythological, and ' spiritual ' life of the tribe."

Though Karadjeri totemism is primarily a variety of cult-totemism, its economic significance should not be overlooked. The very names and geographical distribution of the totems, together with the existence of ceremonies for the increase of totemic species on which the supply of edible and other socially valuable objects is believed to depend, makes this clear. An examination of the list of totems shows that the totems of a horde-country are species or objects found in it. Of course they may also be found elsewhere, but they are usually specially plentiful, or believed to be so, in the locality of which they are the totems ; moreover, mythology furnishes the reason for this in incidents in the lives of the heroes of the *bugari* (dream) time.

Thus many miles inland, at Mabalngo, one of the great heroes, being hungry, made some holes in the rocks, from which plenty of iguanas came forth. This, obviously an increase ceremony, explains the abundance of iguana at this site now. Being thirsty, the same hero made another hole, and this time fresh water came forth, and has been issuing from the same place ever since as a spring. This is the

[1] A. P. Elkin, *op. cit.* pp. 270-271.

general type of what may be called the local totemic myth, " but my information does not show whether Mabalngo is an iguana increase centre or not, though iguana is a totem of this horde-country." [1]

"The list of totems shows that the vast majority of totems are edible species. Of course spring water as a totem should be included under this heading. Other totems obviously reflect the economic and social importance of the objects concerned : the sea, from which so much of the food of the coastal groups is derived, fire on which the food is cooked, which provides warmth, and is almost the centre of social life, the wattle which provides the wood for the long one-piece spears, the thunder and the rainbow, which are associated with the much-needed rain, and the stars which are the *bugari* (heroes) in the heavenly forms, and so are constant reminders of the history, sanctions, and ideals of the tribe." [2]

The economic as well as the social significance of the totems is demonstrated by the existence of totemic sites at which ceremonies for the increase of the totemic species are performed. The sites, which are usually standing stones or holes in the ground or rock, are commonly found in those parts of the tribal country where the particular species connected with them are plentiful, and normally do increase year by year. There is believed to be a centre for the increase of every species or object which is of value or significance to the tribe. If a centre for a particular species is not found in Karadjeri territory, then one will be found in a neighbouring tribe. A similar belief in the existence of such totemic increase sites for all such species and objects seems to be held by all tribes who possess any such sites.

The rites and centres for the increase of the totemic species may be said to localise and focus the belief in the pre-existence of the spirits of all forms of life and objects which are of value to man and society. This belief applies also to human beings. Spirit-children are believed by the Karadjeri and Yauor to live in trees, stones, fresh water and the sea, and their " finding " is associated, as we have seen, with dreaming, the local country, and totemism.

[1] A. P. Elkin, *op. cit.* p. 281.   [2] A. P. Elkin, *op. cit.* p. 282 *sq.*

Within the time at his disposal Professor Elkin was not able to record many of the rites connected with such totemic centres, but what he did record was sufficient to show that they were of the usual type, to which the term *talu* is now applied. That is, a rite of a prescribed form is performed by a definite group of people, members of the local horde, at the centre which is the dwelling-place or source of the spirits and life of a particular species, the totem, and as a result the species increases. But in addition to the rite, the site, the performers, and the totem, there is usually a myth which records and explains the association of the totem with the site, gives a sanction for the rite, and relates both to the *bugari* (dream or mythical) period. The performers, or at least some of them, are the guardians of the sacred site, the rite, and the myth. That is, they possess, as trustees, that portion of the sacred history, ritual, and sites of the tribe, or, more briefly, that portion of the *bugari*, which is symbolised by the totem concerned, and on which the life and future of the tribe is believed partly to depend.

The performers of rites need not, as in Central and South Australia, belong to the totem. We find that the men of the local horde, in whose country the *talu* site is situated, perform the rite connected with it. Some, perhaps most of them, belong to the totem concerned. There is no reason, however, for doubting that in earlier times the performers not only belonged to one moiety and one local horde, but also to the particular totem, though they might have been assisted by members of other totems. In the Karadjeri tribe the ceremonies for the increase of the totems are divided amongst the patrilineal moieties. Thus men of the Burong-Karimba moiety " own " and lead the rites for the increase of parrot-fish, honey-bees, cockles, garfish, ants, native plums, locusts, pink cockatoo, wallaby, rock-fish, porpoise, crab, and salmon. The men of the Panaka-Paldjeri moiety are in a similar position with regard to the rites for the increase of stingaree, native cat, iguana, crow, flounder, eels, eagle-hawk, pearl-shell, calm weather, opossum, and bandi-coot. The important point is that the rites at the increase site are performed by men of the local horde who belong to one moiety, for any horde or local group does for the most part, perhaps altogether in former times, belong to one moiety. Further the leader, and at least some of the performers, belong under normal conditions to the totem which is being increased and which, incidentally, belongs to the moiety with which the local horde is especially associated.

The performers are fully initiated men, and women and children may not be present. That at least is the general rule. But in spite of this women do play a subsidiary part.

Most of the Karadjeri rites for the increase of the totemic species are performed at definite times of the year, namely, just before the period when the species concerned should normally increase. This is just what happens among the tribes of Central Australia. But some increase rites may be performed at any suitable time or when an increase of the species is specially desired. These latter are connected with species such as the porpoise, or a condition such as calm weather, which are not especially connected with any definite period of the year.

The Karadjeri, like all the Kimberley tribes, divide the year into a number of named seasons, which are distinguished partly by climatic changes, but to a greater degree by the kinds of edible species that are available at the different times. Thus the division is economic as well as climatic, and because nearly all of the increase rites are associated with the definite seasons in which particular species should begin to increase, the division of the year may also be regarded as a ceremonial one, as a sort of sacred calendar.

The Karadjeri seasons of the year are : *wilburu*, a transitional period between the cold south-east season and summer, about September, when equinoctial winds blow and the weather grows hot ; *ladya*, the very hot dry time of the year, about October to December ; *mangala*, the wet season from about January to the beginning of April ; *marul*, another short transitional period, at the end of the rainy season ; and *pargana*, the cold south-east season about May to August.

The season prescribed for any particular *talu* (increase) rite is usually the one just preceding the period, though sometimes it is the actual season, when the species is especially plentiful, or fat, or when its eggs are plentiful. The *talu* centres are situated, as we have seen, in districts where the species concerned do normally increase, and secondly, when the rites aim at increasing the species in districts other than that in which the spirit centre is situated, as they frequently do in the Karadjeri and other Kimberley tribes, only those districts are chosen in which the species does normally increase. In other words, the aborigines are guided by actual economical and geographical facts, and make no attempt to divert the ordinary course of Nature and bend it to any passing desires and needs which they might have. Rather they are concerned with the maintenance of Nature's normal course throughout the seasons. With the regular course of Nature their own life is intimately bound up. And given their philosophy of the pre-existence of spirits and the mythology behind it, their system of *talu* centres and rites for the increase of the totemic species is the logical means of attaining this end. The rites must be regarded as a means of co-operating with Nature in the maintenance of the normal course of events, which should be manifested in the regularity of the seasons and the rain, and the increase of natural species at the usual times. The *talu* system is of course a means by which man expresses his needs, and the rites serve to express and strengthen the unity of the groups within the tribe. In the rites he not only expresses his desires in words and actions, but, as in so many of the rites, he often gives of his own life, that is, his own sacred blood, to the species, through its sacramental symbol, so that Nature, or at least some particular natural species, may continue to live and increase.[1]

We may take as an example the Karadjeri rites for the increase of honey. Men of the Burong section are the principal actors, and are assisted by the men of the Karimba section. Men of the Panaka section ask the former Burong men to conduct the ceremony. The performers go to the hole at the increase centre, which is known as Nangala, and with bushes sweep it and also the rock around the top. They then cause blood both from their arm-veins and from sub-incised penes to flow on the bottom of the hole. Sometimes too the Panaka man who asked the Burong headman to

[1] A. P. Elkin, *op. cit.* pp. 290-291.

" make " honey, that is, to perform the rite, is asked to give some of his blood for the purpose. There is neither singing nor dancing but the Burong men recite certain words. Each of the men present then takes some of the mixture of blood and dust from the bottom of the hole, and puts it in a small hole in a stick. Concealing the sticks in their hair, they go to the different places where bees should be active, and put them in trees. Needless to say, women are not allowed to see these sticks.[1]

Another ceremony for the increase of honey is performed at a spot called Bangadandjading, about two miles from La Grange, where a standing stone about five feet high and one foot in diameter at the top but more at the base, rises out of an outcrop of rock. A small hole at the base, about eight inches in diameter and the same depth, represents a beehive. A Burong man is in charge of the spot, and when performing the ceremony cleans out the hole, rubs off some of the rock into it, and also lets some of his own arm-blood drip into it, uttering words as in the other ceremony for the increase of honey. The bees will then go out and make honey in the trees.[2]

An interesting feature of the increase rites in the Karadjeri tribe is that most of them are associated with a hole in the ground or in rock and that the principal ceremony consists in cleaning this hole. In this way the species are freed to go forth and be propagated. But in most cases an essential ceremony follows the cleaning, namely causing human blood to flow or drip on to the bottom of the hole ; thus the life of the performers is given to, or shared with, the totem, the spirit-centre of which is the hole. Another feature, and one which is essential, is the recital, during or immediately following the blood-giving, of words which express the desire for the increase of the totemic species in the named localities. The transference of a mixture of blood and dust from the honey-totem centre to the trees, is an acting-out of the desire expressed in words.[3]

The totemism of the Karadjeri tribe has also been investigated by Mr. Ralph Piddington, who has given us a

---

[1] A. P. Elkin, *op. cit.* p. 291.   [3] A. P. Elkin, *op. cit.* p. 295.
[2] A. P. Elkin, *op. cit.* pp. 291-292.

valuable account both of the rites performed for the increase of the totems and the myths associated with them. Speaking of their totemism in general, he says that the institution is of fundamental importance in the life of the natives, since it is functionally related to every other element in their culture and determines to a very great extent the attitude towards life of the individuals living in Karadjeri society.

" As far as the writer can judge, the institution of totemism among the Karadjeri has been affected by white influence to a lesser degree than any other element of the culture, probably because of its highly emotional value in the minds of the natives. On the other hand, we must not forget that the culture as a whole has been for many years under the influence of the white man, and we cannot assume that Karadjeri totemism as it appears at present represents exactly the form of the institution as it existed before the arrival of Europeans. However, the more stable elements of the totemic system, such as the increase ceremonies and their associated mythology, may be regarded as retaining the more important of their original features.

" The Karadjeri language has two words for totem, namely, *bugari* and *kumbali* ; however, though one would describe a man of, say, the *wolaguru* (eaglehawk) totem as either *wolaguru bugari* or *wolaguru kumbali*, the two words have somewhat different associations, the study of which is of value in understanding the native view of totemism. The term *bugari*, like the word *alchera* among the Aranda, possesses several meanings. In the first place it connotes that which has a binding force upon the society ; to describe an institution as *bugari* means that that institution has a special sanction which renders it inviolable. This is derived from the fact that all things which are *bugari* were instituted by mythical beings in *bugari* times, that is, in the distant past when the world was created. Thus the most general meaning of the term when applied to a social institution is that it has a sort of categorical imperative associated with it.

" Apart from its reference to the period of the world's inception and the sanction for present institutions derived therefrom, the word *bugari* is also used to denote the totem of an individual ; the connection is fairly clear when we consider that each totemic group is derived from an ancestor or ancestors who in *bugari* times instituted it, and thus in Karadjeri totemism the individual is linked, through his membership of the totemic group, not only with the other members of the group and the associated natural species, but also with *bugari* times.

" Associated with the last meaning is another use of the word to denote dreams ; this again is quite clear in view of the fact that the most important aspect of dreams, in the native mind, is that through a dream a father establishes the patrilineal inheritance of the totem by his children." [1]

" In order to clarify the conception of *bugari* we may consider its relation to two other words, namely *idya* and *mundyu*, which may be translated " true " and " false," respectively ; but whereas *idya* is always contrasted with *mundyu*, it is sometimes contrasted with *bugari*, and sometimes used to qualify it. Thus if a native wishes to convey the fact that an incident which he has described did not occur in the mythological " dream-times " but at some time within the memory of living members of the tribe, he will describe it as *mulal bugari, idya* (*Mulal* means " not "). An alternative way of expressing this meaning is *mulal bugari, dyarla*, the last word denoting present time. On the other hand, *idya* may be used to qualify *bugari*, and is so used to a great extent during initiation when it is impressed upon the novice that the tribal traditions which he is learning are *idya bugari*. We may next consider the relation of the word *bugari* to the word *kumbali*.

" Now *kumbali* means both namesake and totem, so that a man's totem is either his *bugari* or his *kumbali* ; if it is desired to distinguish between the two meanings of the word *kumbali*, the Karadjeri call a man's totem his *bugari kumbali* and his namesake his *dyarla* or *maruŋu kumbali*, *maruŋu* meaning simply man." [2]

" Every Karadjeri man or woman possesses one or more *bugari kumbali*, which are obtained as follows. Before a child is born its father dreams that he sees his own *bugari* together with a *yardaŋgal* (spirit child) ; this must take place in his

[1] R. Piddington, " Totemic System of the Karadjeri Tribe," in *Oceania*, vol. ii. No. 4 (June 1932), pp. 373 *sq.*
[2] R. Piddington, *op. cit.* pp. 374 *sq.*

own horde territory, though he may be absent from it at the time ; the *yardaŋgal* subsequently enters the man's wife, who becomes pregnant. Now a man must dream of his own *bugari* in this way, so that totemism may be said to be patrilineal ; but he may also dream of other *bugari* of his own moiety ; it thus happens that many individuals have three or four totems, and that totems do not belong exclusively to specific hordes, though the increase centres associated with them do, and the increase ceremonies must be directed by a man of the local group in whose territory the centre is situated."

In regard to the killing and eating of the totem there exist quite definite prohibitions. Certain informants stated that they could eat their totem if killed by another man, and one or two that they could both kill and eat it ; these statements, however, are almost certainly the result of European influence.[1]

In this tribe though the director or leader of the ceremonies performed for the increase of the totemic species has full control over the performance of the ritual, he may be helped by other men, and under certain circumstances by women. When the last man of a certain totem dies he bequeaths his title to a man of the same district and not to a member of the same totem belonging to a different country. It thus appears that increase ceremonies are associated primarily with the districts in which the increase centres are situated rather than with the individual members of the totems. Thus, for an example, an increase centre of the parrot-fish totem is situated near Cape Bossut ; some years ago Nyirimba (the last surviving man of the parrot-fish totem) died, bequeathing his office of director of the ceremony for the increase of parrot-fish to Kombil, a Cape Bossut man of the death-adder totem, and Kombil is now the only man who can direct the parrot-fish increase ceremony, though he may, of course, be assisted by other men.

Though the Karadjeri have localised rites for the increase of natural species, by no means all species have increase centres situated in Karadjeri territory. It is, however, essential to note that theoretically (in the minds of the

[1] R. Piddington, *op. cit.* pp. 375-376.

natives) all important natural species have somewhere centres for their increase, and a number of these in the territories of surrounding tribes, even as distant as the De Grey River, can be named as the place where certain increase ceremonies are carried out.

Though the increase ritual is not so circumscribed as it is among, for example, the Arunta (Aranda), there are nevertheless certain prescribed forms. Thus, as mentioned above, the increase ritual belongs primarily to the local group rather than to the totemic group, there being but little solidarity between the members of the same totem living in different countries. Moreover, people of one or other of the two patrilineal moieties are always conceived as directing the ceremony, though they are assisted by members of the other moiety.

Increase centres are generally situated at places where the natural species in question is plentiful. Thus for example Birdinapa Point, which forms the northern edge of Lagrange Bay, is the best place on the coast for any kind of fishing, and here are situated a number of fish increase centres.

Ceremonies for the increase of the totemic species are usually performed once a year, and when a natural species appears at one season only, the ceremony associated with that species is performed just before it becomes plentiful ; on the other hand ceremonies for the increase of foods that are perennial may be performed at any time of the year.

In the Karadjeri tribe an invariable accompaniment to increase ceremonies is a series of instructions uttered by performers as they carry out the ritual ; these are of one general pattern, and consist of instructions to the species to become plentiful. They are continued throughout the ceremonies, various districts being named in succession as places where the totem in question should become abundant. It should be observed that in reciting these lists of districts the natives name only those places in which the species is actually to be found ; at the cockle increase ceremony a performer was corrected by his fellows for naming a part of the coast where cockles are not found. These instructions are associated with the belief that all increase centres were instituted in *bugari* (mythical) times; when a number of spirit members of the species were left at the centres; these come forth under the influence of the ritual and so ensure the increase of the natural species. Sometimes a song associated with the mythical origin of the ceremony is sung.

At the performance decorations are worn : they consist of powdered charcoal, red ochre, white mangrove mud, white down obtained from such birds as the native companion, and human blood obtained by boring a hole in one of the performer's forearms with a pointed bone from the leg of a wallaby ; this last is strictly *rai*, that is to say, it may not be witnessed by women.

Sometimes under European influence these decorations are omitted.

Increase centres are called *ouraka*, that is, clean or tidy places, a term which is also used for the place where the sacred *pirmal* are kept. Increase ceremonies are called *karulbunya*, that is, rubbing.

The increase centre for parrot-fish is situated at Cape Bossut. It consists of an ovoid stone, about eighteen inches in length, partially buried in a horizontal position in the ground. This is said to be a parrot-fish. The headman in charge of the ceremony digs away the earth from around the stone, at the same time saying that parrot-fish are to be increased and asking for a plentiful supply, while as the earth is being dug out it is scattered north and south, while various coastal districts are named and the fish is told to be plentiful in these parts. When a quantity of earth has been removed the stone is taken out and laid on its side near the hole from which it has been taken. It is then addressed as follows, " At low tide you will lie like this." After this the stone is painted with charcoal and also red and yellow ochre mixed with grease, replaced in its hole, and packed around with earth. Branches of trees are then held resting on the tree for a moment, after which they are swept down a pathway towards the sea. This ensures that fish will leave the rock and go down the path to the sea. That ends the ceremony. This rite may be witnessed by women except when human blood is drawn in the way already described. The blood is supposed to make the fish fat. The ceremony is performed during the season that the fish are caught upon the reef at low tide.

About three miles south of Lagrange there is a large stone projecting from the ground at which a ceremony is performed for the increase of wild honey. The ritual belongs to the Burung-Karimba moiety, and women may watch from a distance of about fifty yards. The grass is cleaned away from a circular patch around this stone and also from a pathway of small stones a few yards in length leading away from the stone. The purpose of this is to allow the bees to escape from the large stone and to travel from it down the path of the small stones. Earth is taken from around the base of the stone and scattered in all directions while various districts are named, and the bees are told to become plentiful at each of them. After this some of the smaller stones are taken and thrown against the large one, where they break into small fragments which fly in all directions. The men who throw them at the same time shout " *wah.*" This is said to imitate the buzz of bees, which are represented by the flying fragments of stone. One or two fragments are then broken off the large stone with a tomahawk in order to allow bees to escape. This concludes the ceremony.

The beliefs associated with this ceremony are somewhat difficult to ascertain. Sometimes it is honey that is thought to be increased thereby, sometimes bees, and sometimes bees' eggs are said to be increased. Actually the important thing to the natives is probably the belief that the rite increases their supply of honey. It appears that the first purpose is to increase bees' eggs within the stone ; these then become bees and leave the stone to go into the bush and make honey. This interpretation is borne out by the myth associated with the centre. It is said that two mythical water snakes, man and wife, called Djigurdaing, came from the east and made bees' eggs, as a result of which bees left the stone and made honey. The large stone represents the female Djigurdaing ; her husband is represented by another stone a few hundred yards distant which plays no part in the ceremony. Two stones at the base of the female Djigurdaing represent beeswax.[1]

[1] R. Piddington, *op. cit.* pp. 379 *sq.*

On either side of a small mangrove creek at Lagrange Bay are several heaps of cockle shells. Each of these heaps on the northern bank of the creek represents a shell, and a solitary heap on the southern bank represents the fish inside. The latter is the centre for the increase of cockles, which may be performed at any time of the year. (The cockle-fish is a perennial article of diet.) At the ceremony, which belongs to the Burung-Karimba moiety of the tribe, no decorations are worn, and women may assist. The ceremony is a very simple one, and consists of cleaning out a hole at the top of the mound.

The ceremony was instituted in *bugari* (mythical) times by Djui (bower bird) who, together with his wife, came from the district to the north of Broome. Djui made a nest in a tree and a playground, his diet consisted solely of fish and shell-fish ; the former he killed with a wooden implement which he carried. He made a small yard of stones, and one day, on looking into it, saw a number of fish. He then travelled down the coast making the present native fish traps, semi-circular rows of stones in which fish are caught as the tide recedes. He killed a mullet, the body of which became a stone, which is now the centre for the increase of mullet on the northern shore of Lagrange Bay, and he also instituted the cockle increase centre at Lagrange Bay.

After a while the exclusively fish diet began to disagree with Djui and his wife. They became very sick and at last died, leaving the fish traps, and telling people not to live on fish alone but to eat " nalgoo " and other fruits as well. They also gave the tradition that men caught fish (because the male Djui did so) while women gathered and cooked cockles because the female Djui performed these duties.

At Yardugara, a few miles from Nebrika, there is a local centre for the increase of native cats. The ceremony may be performed at any time of the year, though the best season is *pargana*, since the native cats are fat at this time, when they are tracked to holes in trees or ant beds. Women are not allowed to share in the ceremony, though they may watch it. No decorations are worn ; the performers approach the spot singing a song referring to the eating of men in the associated myth. They clean out the hole, and fling the earth in different directions. This increase centre, which belongs to the Panaka-Paldjeri moiety of the tribe, was established by a *bugari* (mythical) man called Pardjida as follows. Pardjida saw a dead man ; he placed a firestick beside the corpse to cook it ; he then ate the body. This happened a number of times. One day he saw three dead men near Nebrika ; he ate them all except their three heads, which he devoured as he walked along. Having eaten too much he burst, and in this way the native cat increase centre was established.

Near Rolah windmill, about five miles from Lagrange, is a hole in the ground which is a centre for the increase of garfish. Here the ceremony may be performed at any time, but the best season is *marul*.[1] The fish are plentiful throughout the *pargana*[1] season, but are obtainable throughout the year in the mangrove creeks, where they are killed with wooden implements. The ritual is very simple and consists of cleaning out the hole in the ground. No decorations are worn by the performers, and women do not assist at it but are allowed to be present. The ceremony belongs to the Burung-Karimba moiety of the tribe.

The myth of the ceremony runs thus. A headman named Bilyabig of the garfish totem and his wife camped at the spot where they killed a number of garfish ; they died there, leaving the tradition of the increase ceremony to the garfish totem. The woman left here a wooden dish which may be seen as a depression in some rocks near by ; this is a well during the wet season.

Two holes, about twenty-five yards apart, near Nebrika, are a centre for the increase of ants, where a ceremony is performed during the *wilburu*[1] season, both men and women participating. The centre belongs to the Burung-Karimba moiety of the tribe. The performers, men and women, decorate themselves in white down ; the two holes are cleaned out and a pathway cleared between them. The men sit around the hole on the south side and the women at the hole to the north. The latter then crawl along the pathway which has been cleared, to the men's place, where all the performers

[1] For the seasons *pargana, marul,* and *wilburu,* see above, p. 72.

remove their white down and place it in the hole.   It is subsequently blown away by the wind, and so represents the male ant.   This concludes the ceremony, which was established in mythical times as follows.   A number of women used to go in search of ants but could never find any because they had all been taken by Ngalamarara (a goanna woman).   One day the women came upon her singing a song to the effect that the women had no ants because she had taken them all.   The women took Ngalamarara back to their camp, where they treated her as a friend.   Thus was established the ritual for the increase of ants, which are no doubt an article of food for these people.[1]

Near Nebrika is a hole in the ground which is a centre for the increase of the fruit of the native plum tree, and belongs to the Burung-Karimba moiety of the tribe.   The ceremony is performed during the *marul* season, the fruit appearing during *pargana*, though it is not fully ripe until *ladya*.   No decorations are worn, and women may assist. The ceremony consists of pouring water into the hole, producing a brown mud from which balls are made representing the fruit.   These are placed around the hole and left to dry in the sun.   This concludes the ceremony, which was established in mythical (*bugari*) times by a man called Djarumba, who carried a conch shell full of fruit.   He saw a number of people who called out to him, offering food ; when he came close, however, they told him that they had not been calling to him.   This was, of course, untrue.   Djarumba went away, but returned the next day, only to be treated in the same way. The same thing happened a number of times.   One day he met a young man and asked permission to cut his hair off ; he took the hair and rolled it into pellets, which he hung on a native plum tree.   He then picked some of them and placed them in a wooden dish.   Taking this, he went off and found the crowd of people, who treated him as they had always done.   Instead of going away he showed them the pretended fruit, which they ate.   He then took them and showed them the native plum tree, from which they plucked a quantity of fruit.   As it was really pellets of hair, they all died.   Djarumba may now be seen as a native plum tree near Nebrika Well,

[1] R. Piddington, *op. cit.* p. 383.

about a mile from the place where he established the centre for the increase of plums.

On the north-west edge of Injidan Plain there is a centre for the increase of goanna, a kind of lizard. The ceremony is performed during the *wilburu* season, the goanna producing its eggs during *ladya*. The centre belongs to the Panaka-Paldjeri moiety of the tribe. Women may watch it but not share in the ceremony. The performers decorate themselves with stripes of white mud representing goannas. They then clean out a hole in the ground, making pathways along which the goannas are to go to the various districts where they will afterwards be caught. Finally vines are coiled up inside the hole and dragged out along the pathways, thus, it is said, dragging out goannas.

The increase of goannas is associated in the minds of the natives with the ceremonies for the increase of wallabies, which are performed at a place about two miles distant. This association is described in the following myth. Karadaing (a wallaby) used to obtain blood from his arm-veins by scratching them with his claws, a method which he found very painful. He used to place the blood obtained in this way in a bark dish and drink it. One day Karabigi (a goanna) came up and watched Karadaing. Karabigi had a pointed wallaby bone with which he produced blood from his arm. This method was much more satisfactory than that of Karadaing since it was less painful and produced more blood. They drank the blood together and Karabigi gave his pointed bone to Karadaing. As a result of this wallabies now have the pointed bone in their legs, and men know how to produce blood in the correct way. Karabigi established the increase centre associated with this species of goanna, while Karadaing instituted the ceremony for the increase of wallabies.

About two miles from the goanna increase centre on Injidan Plain there is a centre for the increase of wallabies. The ceremony is secret, and may not be seen by women, though they may go near the centre at other times. The ceremony may be shown to a novice during his seclusion in the bush after circumcision, though it does not form a necessary part of the initiation ritual. The rite is performed during

the *wilburu*[1] season, the animals being said to be particularly
fat during the *ladya*[1] season. The men decorate themselves
with charcoal and red ochre, and clean the ground around
the hole in a grove of cadjibut trees, at the same time making
sounds resembling those of the wallaby, and asking that they
may become plentiful in various places. One of the men
allows blood to flow into the hole, and several songs are
sung. These are the same as those told to the novice during
initiation. The ceremony belongs to the Burung-Karimba
moiety.[2]

In the case of the crow and pink cockatoo, we find the
centres for the increase of two natural species situated close
to each other. Between Lagrange Bay and Injidan Plain
is a large dark coloured stone projecting from the ground.
This is a centre for the increase of crows; about twenty
yards distant is a centre for the increase of pink cockatoo.
The two ceremonies are performed together, during the
pargana[3] season, that of crow first. This ceremony belongs
to the Panaka-Paldjeri moiety of the tribe, and the other to
the Burung-Karimba moiety.

The performers clean away any leaves, sticks, or other
litter from around the crow stone. They then lay their
hands upon the stone, stroking it, and asking the crow to
become plentiful. When this is concluded they move on to
the pink cockatoo increase centre, which consists of several
light red coloured stones just projecting above the ground.
These they clean and rub in a similar manner, sitting around
them on the ground.

The mythical origin of this ceremony is associated with
the legend of a crow man, who had two wives, one of whom
was also a crow and the other a pink cockatoo. Of these
two women the former had a black mark on her body and the
latter a pink and white one. For this reason their husband
preferred his pink cockatoo wife, which made the other wife
jealous. Each day the two women went collecting ants' eggs.
They used to work some little distance from each other, and
the crow woman, speaking in an undertone, used to make

---

[1] For the *wilburu* and *ladya*
seasons, see above, p. 72.

[2] R. Piddington, *op. cit.* p. 386.

[3] For the *pargana* season see above,
p. 72.

disparaging remarks about the pink-and-white mark on the other woman's body. When the pink cockatoo woman, not having heard what was said, asked her to repeat it, the crow woman said that she had merely asked if she had obtained clean ants' eggs. This was really a pun on the words *oili* (clean) and *larli* (white). The crow woman had used these words, in a disparaging tone, in reference to the mark on the pink cockatoo woman, but when asked to repeat her words she claimed to have used them in reference to the other woman's ants' eggs, asking whether the food collected was free from the black wax which sometimes contaminates it. One day the crow woman had a large piece of wax in her hand. She threw this at the pink cockatoo woman, breaking her leg and killing her. She then returned to their camp, and when her husband asked her where his other wife was, she replied that she had remained in the bush. After waiting several days the man became suspicious, and on searching he found the dead body. This he buried. Returning to the camp, he said nothing to his wife, but built a large fire into which he threw her. She cried out " *wah* " and so perished.

The tracks of the pink cockatoo woman are represented in the sky by the four bright stars of Corvus. The tracks of the crow women may be seen as the four brightest stars of Delphinus.[1]

At Birdinapa Point there is a centre for the increase of flounders. This consists of a soft patch in the face of the cliff and also several flat stones near by. No decorations are worn, and women may assist. The ceremony takes place during the *marul* season, during which the fish are speared at low water upon the sandy flats near Birdinapa Point. The ceremony, which belongs to the Panaka-Paldjeri moiety of the tribe, consists of scraping the face of the cliff with a cockle-shell and brushing the flat stones near by. There is no detailed myth associated with the centre, which was established by an old man called Birmalang who made a camp near by.[2]

Near the centre for the increase of flounders is a pair of

[1] R. Piddington, *op. cit.* pp. 387 *sq.*
[2] R. Piddington, *op. cit.* p. 389.

long boomerang-shaped heaps of stones. They represent two eels, and the ceremony for the increase of eels is performed there during the *wilburu* or *ladya* season. Men perform the ceremony, but women may watch. No decorations are worn by the performers. The ceremony, which belongs to the Panaka-Paldjeri moiety of the tribe, consists of re-arranging the stones and the cleaning of the surrounding ground.

The ceremony is associated with the myth of Wolabung and Yerinyeri, who made a camp nearby in *bugari* (mythical) times. The eel was one of the forms adopted by Wolabung in frightening Yerinyeri.

Near the Lagrange Bay Telegraph Station there is a centre for the increase of crabs, at which a ceremony is performed during the *ladya* season. The ceremony belongs to the Burung-Karimba moiety of the tribe. The performers are men, but women may watch. The performers are decorated with white mud. The rite consists of cleaning out a hole in the ground. While this is done one man stands with a spear poised in the air, pointing towards the hole. The object of this is that he may be ready to spear the spirit crab as they come from the hole by virtue of the ceremony.

Before concluding his account, which in the preceding pages I have closely followed, of ceremonies which the Karadjeri perform for the increase of totems, Mr. Piddington describes three ceremonies which are not of the usual type, and all of which are performed at Birdinapa Point, the best place on the coast for all kinds of fishing.

To begin with the ceremony for producing calm weather, at the time of the equinoctial tides, natives go " dry " fishing from Birdinapa Point. They wade out upon the reef collecting pearl shells or spearing fish. The original use of the pearl shells was to make pubic pendants and other decorations, but now they are collected in very much larger quantities for purposes of trade. For " dry " fishing still water is desirable, since wind not only creates waves on the surface of the water, but also stirs up mud, and so makes it hard to see under the water. To meet this difficulty the natives perform a ceremony whenever a strong wind interferes with the fishing. This ceremony is designed to produce a condition of calm. The ceremony, which is under the direction of the Panaka-Paldjeri moiety of the tribe, consists of cleaning out a hole and lighting a fire in it. On this are placed bushes. In the meantime the *worara* (old man) Ingardukuran, who established the ceremony in mythic (*bugari*) times, is addressed and requested to produce a condition of calm. Beyond the establishment of the ceremony by Ingardukuran, who subsequently became a tree near by, there is no detailed myth connected with this ceremony.

Near one of the fish-traps in which fish are caught at Birdinapa Point is a stone, visible at low tide only. Here the Karadjeri perform a sacred ceremony during the *marul* season which is designed to increase the supply of fish, particularly salmon, in the fish-traps. During the day while the tide is out men clean away the sand from under the stone. In the hole so formed they bury a conch shell full of human blood and also a bull-roarer which has been smeared with the same liquid. This will, they think, when the tide comes in, attract the fish to the fish-trap where they will be caught.

At Birdinapa Point there is a large rock visible at low tide which represents Djui (the bower bird). Underneath this rock Djui is believed to sit upon a bull-roarer. By rubbing the stone and asking Djui for shell, a plentiful supply can be obtained. The rite differs from ordinary increase ceremonies in that all that is needed is for one man, of either moiety, to rub the stone. This is the usual preliminary to " dry fishing " or " shelling," at the equinoctial tides, as described before. The ritual, and of course the stone, were originally said to have been established in mythic (*bugari*) times by Djui. It should be noted that though Djui belongs to the Burung-Karimba moiety of the tribe, he is said to have died at this place, that is, in the country associated with the Panaka-Paldjeri moiety of the tribe.[1]

With regard to the totemic mythology of the Karadjeri tribe, Mr. Piddington tells us that " of the many Karadjeri myths of *bugari* (mythic) times, the majority are totemic; that is to say, they describe the activities of beings who were neither men nor animals, but exhibited alternately the characters of both of these types of creature. As this is an

[1] R. Piddington, *op. cit.* pp. 391 *sqq.*

extremely common feature of Australian mythology it is unnecessary to deal with it at length.

" Some of the myths, however, concern mythical beings who are not identified with any natural species, and hence cannot be described as totemic. But one must remember that in the minds of the natives the two types of myth form part of an integrated whole—the legendary history of the aborigines. The sacred myths, which may not be told to women, are concerned mainly with cosmogony, and especially with the institution of initiation ceremonies. . . .

" We shall at this stage confine our attention to those totemic myths which have not already been described in connection with increase ceremonies. Very frequently, in concluding the recounting of a myth, informants offer a moralistic interpretation of the story. Where these were given they are appended as traditions established by the myths in question. The most general form of the myths is as follows. The story opens with a certain state of affairs existing ; this is indicated by the natives by describing one day's events and then repeating them for successive days, the series of activities being repeated in exactly the same form over and over again. For the sake of space this has been abbreviated by describing the events as occurring every day or on a number of occasions. Given, then, this existing state of affairs, a *dénouement* occurs, generally resulting in the death of the characters. By this means some element of either the natural or the moral order is established. This is the most general form of the myths, though variations sometimes occur. A common feature of the Karadjeri myths is an association with specific landmarks, stones, hills, creeks, or even trees, the traditional institution of increase centres being a particular example of this principle.

" Among the Karadjeri the mythology of the heavens plays an important part in the beliefs connected with immortality. It is generally believed that the sky consists of a dome of a very hard substance (rock or shell), the stars representing the *bilyur* (spirits) of dead men and women. As to the stars themselves there is considerable difference of opinion ; some say that they are just globes of light, but others believe that they are individual nautilus shells with the fish alive inside them. On the latter view shooting stars are caused by the death of the fish and the dropping of its shell.

" There are, however, two other theories as to shooting stars. According to one of these a shooting star indicates that an important man has died, the direction of the meteor indicating where the death has occurred. The other version is that shooting stars represent fragments of the dead body of Marela (a *bugari* culture hero) falling from the tree in which he was buried. Every star in the heavens represents the *bilyur* of some deceased man or woman, while the more important stars and even constellations represent certain objects and persons mentioned in the myths. . . .

" Not only *bilyur* of the mythical characters are represented among the stars, but also certain of their possessions, such as hitting or digging sticks and, in several cases, their tracks.

" The natives think of the various stars in terms of the time of year at which they are clearly visible (that is, when they appear well above the horizon) during the early part of the night. They realize, however, that they are, generally speaking, actually visible for a total period of several months, and can generally give with a fair degree of accuracy the date of the heliacal rising of any star, showing that their observation of the heavens is not confined to the early evening, though apparently this is the time of the night which is most important to them." [1]

The following stories may be taken as examples of typical forms of legend found in Karadjeri folklore.

Myth of Pardjida and Langgur.—Pardjida (the native cat) cut off the hair of Langgur (the opossum) with a sharp tomahawk. Langgur made a stick for winding wool and using it, proceeding to make opossum wool thread from his own hair. All night he twirled the stick, the noise of which prevented Pardjida from sleeping. Every day Pardjida went out hunting and every night Langgur kept him awake by twirling the stick. One night Pardjida grew so angry that he struck Langgur on the chest with a fire-stick of *bandaragu* wood. This wood is of a yellowish-brown colour. Langgur then took a burning stick of *dyigil* wood and struck Pardjida

[1] R. Piddington, *op. cit.* pp. 393 *sqq.*

with it, the ash marking his body with white spots. The ash of this wood is said to be highly corrosive ; if mixed with tobacco and chewed, it burns the tongue. So to this day male opossums have a brown mark on their chests and native cats are covered with white spots. And to this day the spirit of Pardjida may be seen in the sky as the star Alpha of the constellation Cygnus and that of Langgur as Capella in Auriga. The tracks of Langgur may be seen as several pairs of faint stars between Auriga and Taurus.

The Myth of Djarabalbal.—Djarabalbal (top-knot pigeon) was a woman who used to go out gathering food, but on these excursions she spent a great deal of time tying her hair up into a pointed knot. So she never collected much food, and this caused a good deal of comment among the men at the camp. One day they followed her and saw the way in which she wasted her time. They frightened her and she flew up into the sky, thus founding the tradition that women should not waste their time when they collect food, and also that they should not arrange their hair as men do. The spirit of Djarabalbal is represented by one of the smaller stars in the constellation Auriga.

The Myth of Bardarangalu.—A mother Bardarangalu (snake) was always sick, every day and every night. Every night she died, and her two sons buried her. The boys used to go away and leave her in the ground, and she would shed her skin and follow them to their camp. The old woman's grave was near the water, and one day a frog came out of the water and saw the dead woman in the ground. He sat on the grave and croaked as frogs do several times, at the same time shifting his body about as he sat, and after this the old woman could not rise again. This was the origin of death.

The Myth of Ngulbarlu.—A goanna Ngulbarlu was sharpening his stone axe. He heard a noise, the sound of waves. He went to see what was happening, and found that the salt water had come right up to the bush. He picked a stick and threw it into the salt water saying, " Go back," and the water receded. The man said, " Don't come up here any more, this land belongs to man." So now the tide comes over the land for a limited distance only.

The Myth of Tyanga.—A man Tyanga (oyster) had a

wife who lived in her shell all the time, though he went out every day hunting. At night he used to return bearing food, and ask her to get him water and to make a fire for him. She said nothing, refusing to eat the food which he offered her. As she remained in her shell, which was very hard, all the time, he never could approach her. One night there was a very heavy fog. The woman came out of her shell and went away. She sat under a tree some distance from the camp. Tyanga, having awakened, broke his wife's shell for the first time and found that she had gone. Looking around he saw her tracks and followed them. Presently he heard a sound which was made by his wife sitting under a tree knocking two sticks together. Knowing it was his wife he went to the tree and sat there with her. Now women bustle about and tend to the needs of their husbands, though oysters always remain in the same place.

The Myth of Yindjiyindi.—Yindjiyindi (mantis) used to talk all the time, thus producing *pundur* (south-east wind). The result was that the wind used to blow throughout the year. A number of people wanted to kill him on this account. They used to cut him up into small pieces and leave him to die. But he always recovered and continued to make a south-east wind. One day a man threw a spear at Yindjiyindi's scrotum. The spear struck its mark and killed him. That is why the south-east wind now blows during the cold season only, and not all the year round as before.

The Myth of Rudurudur.—A boy Rudurudur (wasp) used to rest under a tree during a hot summer day, and he would dig at the foot of the tree to obtain water. One day he could find no water and died of thirst; nowadays wasps find water in the branches of baobab trees, and if a blackfellow sees a wasp he knows that there is water in some form near by.[1]

The totemism of the tribes inhabiting Dampier Land has been investigated and described by Professor Elkin. Dampier Land is in the district of Kimberley, West Australia. It is a peninsula, roughly triangular in shape on a southern base about one hundred miles long extending from Broome on the west, to the vicinity of Derby on the east, and with its apex

[1] R. Piddington, *op. cit.* pp. 395 *sqq.*

at Swan Point, just about one hundred miles north of the base. It consists of a comparatively well-watered coastal strip, and of a drier inland region, known as the Pindan, which is in some parts about forty miles or more in breadth. Along the coast there are springs, and water can also be obtained by digging wells, many of which have been made by the natives.[1]

The tribes of Dampier Land are the Djukan in the neighbourhood of Broome; the Ngormbal centring on Barred Creek; the Djabera-Djaber around Carnot Bay; the Nyul-Nyul from Beagle Bay to near Pender Bay on the west and across the peninsula to King Sound, where its northern and southern points are respectively Murdeh Point and the swamp at the mouth of the Fraser River; the Bardi in the northern corner of the peninsula above the Nyul-Nyul; and the Djaui on the inhabitable islands at the mouth of King Sound.

In these tribes the local organisation is of the usual Australian type. Each tribe is divided into a number of patrilineal hordes, each of which occupies a definite subdivision of the tribal territory, called *bor*, the term for camp, and has its headman and " second man." Rules of hunting and trespass apply here as elsewhere. A person is free or not of any particular *bor* according to his kinship relationship to its members. Further, the local organisation plays an important part in the arrangement of marriages: a wife's mother is always sought in a distant *bor*.

The local organisation is associated with the belief in preexistence of spirits. Spirit children, *nagarlala*, sometimes referred to as *rai*, invisible, live in definite centres such as water holes, springs, trees and rocks on the sand and in the sea. The medicine-men are said to know, through dreams, the whereabouts of these places. The entry of a spirit-child into its mother's womb is always associated with a dream in which the father sees or " finds " it. Further, according to Nyul-Nyul informants, the spirit-child tells the father what its name is to be. It also tells the man that he is to be its father, and asks him where his wife is. Having given the

---

[1] A. P. Elkin, " Totemism in N.W.   *Oceania*, vol. iii. No. 4 (June 1933)
Australia (The Kimberley Division),   p. 435.
II : The Tribes of Dampier Land," in

information to the spirit-child, he may then take it in his hand and put it down near his wife, or on her navel. It will enter her womb, though not necessarily at once. At the time of the quickening, the woman tells her husband that a child has entered her womb. He then remembers finding the child in the dream.

The tribes of Dampier Land also believe in reincarnation. Some babies, at least, are believed to be the dead reborn. Such a spirit-child comes to the father in a dream, explaining that it wishes to be born again, this time as his child, and giving the name it previously bore. The father then washes the spirit-child and leaves it in fresh water for three days, after which he puts it near, or sends it to, his wife. This washing is reserved for spirits which are being reincarnated. During the period between incarnations, the spirit sojourns at one of the spirit-centres. Some spirits, however, are not reincarnated ; they are said to go to Loman, from whence there is no return.

The discussion of " spirit-children " beliefs leads on to the problem of totemism in Dampier Land, to which we now turn, but we must first notice that these tribes believe in the existence of local spirit-centres in which pre-existent spirits, and spirits to be reincarnated, sojourn, and to which they may return, that is, if reincarnation is to be their lot. This means that a person belongs to his father's horde because his father " found " him as a pre-existent child, or perhaps we should put it, because he, while still a spirit-child, sought out and appeared to a man of the horde-country in which his spirit-home was situated.

The existence of totemism among the tribes of Dampier Land has been denied by Professor Klaatsch, who investigated the tribes in 1906 and again in 1907,[1] and Professor Elkin came to the same conclusion after spending three months in 1927-1928 among the Nyul-Nyul and Bardi, in the north of Dampier Land. But on his return to Broome in the south of Dampier Land he discussed the subject of totemism with two Bardi men and with several Nyul-Nyul and Djabera-

---

[1] H. Klaatsch in *Zeitschrift für Ethnologie*, xxxviii. (1906) pp. 793-794, and in xxxix. (1907) pp. 636-644.   Cited by Professor Elkin, *op. cit.* p. 440.

Djaber men, and came to the conclusion that so far as these informants are concerned totemism does exist in these three tribes.   I will cite his conclusion in his own words : " The Bardi men definitely associated the ' finding ' or dreaming of the spirit-child with the totem, just as the Karadjeri do. . . . My Nyul-Nyul and Djabera-Djaber informants probably did the same, but I have no definite information on this point. In all three tribes a father ' finds ' in a dream a spirit-child, often, and indeed mostly, in the form of some article of food, fish, animal, and so on.   This species is generally and according to one informant always the totem of the father's local horde-country, *bor*.   Any irregularity is caused by the father being on a visit to another ' country ' at the time he finds the child, who is thus associated with the totem of that ' country.' There seems to be only one totem associated with each *bor*, and so the totem, like the local country, is exogamous ; but there is more in it than this, for according to the Bardi informants, persons of the one totem, though of different *bor* (and apparently more than one local horde can belong to the one totem), cannot intermarry. A special tabu operates in this connection.   Members of the same totem who are at the same time members of the one ' country ' or horde, act towards one another in accordance with their kinship relationship, but members of the one totem who belong to different hordes, have to observe a tabu towards one another somewhat like the parent-in-law tabu.   There must not be any joking between the men of the one *bor* and the women of the other, while the men must not ' growl ' one another.   The function of the tabu seems to be to prevent any behaviour that might lead to the possibility of marital relationships between two *bor* of the one totem, and to preserve the harmony which should exist between totemites even though they belong to different localities.   Thus each horde is a totemic clan-horde, or else is part of a totemic clan.   A child is told what his totem is, and sooner or later he will see it in a dream.   All informants said that there was a tabu on eating the totem. The Bardi added that a man must not kill his totem, but the Nyul-Nyul and Djabera-Djaber said that the totemite might do so." [1]

[1] A. P. Elkin, *op. cit.* pp. 443-446.

" The information which I obtained from the Bardi, Nyul-Nyul and Djabera-Djaber men after my return to the Broome district from the northern part of Dampier Land, shows that as far as they were concerned totemism did exist. This, however, raises a problem : Why did both Klaatsch and myself fail to find it around and north of Beagle Bay ? I am still inclined to think that it was not there, though the spirit-children beliefs are such as one finds in tribes which possess totemism. But if this be so, why should the members of these tribes whom I met later have totems ? The answer may be that they had learnt totemism while associated with Djauor, Nygina, Karadjeri, and Djukan men around and in Broome, and had realized that the totemic beliefs of these men fitted into the pattern of their own spirit-children and *rai* beliefs, and into the scheme of their local organization. If this be so, it would be very interesting to study the process by which the new beliefs have been, or are still being acquired. The whole problem should be tackled in the field, and I believe that if the Bardi and then the remnants of the tribes in order from north to south were studied, more especially making the approach from the point of view of spirit-children and *rai* beliefs, it would be possible to decide whether totemism is an old or recent institution amongst these tribes, and, indeed, whether it really exists at all among some of them." [1]

Passing in a north-easterly direction from the northern point of Dampier Land by way of the Buccaneer Archipelago, we enter Collier Bay. The shore of this bay is occupied by Wurara tribes, whose territory extends from its northern headland to the lower course of the Prince Regent River on the north, and includes the lower waters of the Sale River and all the valley of the Glenelg. The eastern neighbour of the Wurara is the Ungarinyin, which was investigated by Professor Elkin in 1928. The southern boundary of the tribe is the King Leopold Range. The territory of the tribe extends eastward and inland well over a hundred miles, and includes country east of Mt. Barnett and the Hann River, as well as some of the Gibb River valley. On the north it includes the upper reaches of the Sale and the Calder Rivers, and the southern bank of the upper Prince Regent River. This large

[1] A. P. Elkin, *op. cit.* pp. 451-452.

area, probably eight or nine thousand square miles, is occupied by about a thousand Ungarinyin. The country is for the most part very rough, and has not yet been fully explored. In many parts it is inaccessible except on foot, though a few pack-horse tracks have been made. It is, however, a good territory for the native Aborigines, being provided with abundance of fresh water, fish and other denizens of the salt and fresh waters, marsupials, reptiles, birds and various yams and fruits.[1]

The tribal territory is divided into a number of horde-countries, *tambun*. Each horde has its headman, who has the usual powers associated with this position. He can stop fights, even going so far as to break the spears of two men who are disturbing the peace. Visitors who wish to hunt in the horde-country must obtain his leave, and as usual the other elders of the horde consult together when a member of the horde is to be married.

The country of the horde (the *tambun*) is patrilocal, patrilineal and exogamous. The local solidarity of the hordes is so great that the term applied to any one male member of a horde by a member of another horde is applied to all its male members, irrespective of the generation to which they belong, and this is also true of the females of the horde. Hence a person speaks of his relationship (son, father, sister's child, etc.) to a horde rather than to individuals. The question " What is your relation to such and such ' country ' ? " receives for answer a kinship term.[2]

The Ungarinyin possess three sorts of totemism : moiety, local, and dream totemism. This also holds good for the Wurara, whose local organisation, kinship system, "increase" ceremonies associated with rock galleries of paintings, and mythology are similar to those found in the Ungarinyin tribe. In the Ungarinyin tribe the hordes are divided between patrilineal moieties, which are named *amalad* and *ornad*, respectively. The former is also called *yara* or *djulwun*, the hill kangaroo, and *djungun*, a night bird, while the latter's other names are *walamba*, the long-legged kangaroo, and *wotor*, a bird associated with rain. The designations *yara* and *walamba* are the commonest. Professor Elkin thinks

[1] A. P. Elkin, *op. cit.* p. 452.   [2] A. P. Elkin, *op. cit.* pp. 452-453

that the members of a moiety do not observe any special attitude towards the species whose names it bears, but he was informed that a person does not eat any of the totems of the hordes of his moiety that are situated near his own horde. This is an expression of moiety solidarity, which is also evident in arrangements at a large camp where members of the hordes of one moiety are separated by some natural feature, such as a gully, from the members of the hordes of the other moiety. The dual organisation is also manifested in a general fight, members of one moiety taking sides against those of the other moiety, even to the extent of a man's fighting against his sister's son, a thing which he would not do in ordinary camp life.[1]

The name of each *tambun* (horde-country), apart from the usual suffix *-eri*, *-neri*, or *-nari*, is also the name of some animal, plant, bird, or, in a very few instances, of some other object or phenomenon such as rain. When Professor Elkin had obtained the name of a man's horde-country, and asked his informant the meaning of the name he would be given another native name for the species or object designated by the name of the horde-country, or, else a description of it, or, if the informant knew sufficient English, the English name. In a few cases collected by Professor Elkin the name of the animal or other object connected with the "country" is not the name of the horde-country, but probably there is or was another name for the horde-country, which is the name of the object or natural species associated with it. Now the name of the object or native species denotes not only the horde-country but also the members of the horde, or rather those who belong to it by right of birth. In other words it is their totem, their *kian* or mate, as they say. The prefix *bre-* is generally used to make the name of the totem denote the totemites ; thus *gural*, white cockatoo, becomes *bregural*, the people of the white cockatoo totemic clan.

Some horde-countries have more than one totem. This probably explains why such " countries " have more than one name. There are no doubt myths to explain all the cases of multiple totemism, and, indeed, of hordes with only one totem also. Professor Elkin gives examples of both cases.

[1] A. P. Elkin, *op. cit.* pp. 453-454.

Thus to explain the case of multiple totems Professor Elkin cites the story of the grasshopper and the short-tailed iguana. Once upon a time a grasshopper flew from Djaningari, an Ungarinyin horde-country of which it is the totem, to Indalgam, a Wurara horde-country, where it found an iguana, named yadara. He cut off the iguana's hind legs and tail, after which he became a piece of stone about 8 inches long ; this is kept in the secret storehouse, a cave. The myth explains the stumpy tail of the iguana, while the serrated shape of the grasshopper's legs probably suggested that they were suitable instruments for the operation. The short-tailed iguana and the grasshopper are both totems of Indalgam. Again to explain the case of the single totem Professor Elkin cites the story of the corkwood tree. *Yamalba*, the corkwood tree, belongs to Waiangari horde-country, because it was there that it first grew in the *Lalan* or long-past heroic period. The men of the time tried to make spear-throwers out of the *waia*, skin, that is, the bark of this tree, but finding that it was not strong enough, they used the wood instead, and found it suitable.[1]

The totem of the horde is usually a species or object which is very plentiful or, maybe, conspicuous, in the horde-country, such as white stone used for making spear-heads in Unalauni, *marara*, bamboo, in Marara ; *ilwaian*, a water-lily in Ilwaian ; and so on. The totems are mostly edible species ; others are useful objects, such as certain kinds of stone out of which the " laurel leaf " type of spear-points, which are peculiar to Northern Kimberley, are made by pressure flaking ; trees, the wood of which is used for various purposes such as making spear-throwers, shields or throwing-sticks ; bamboo, used in making spear-shafts ; a cane used for lifting honey out of a hole, and certain bushes, *landad*, because they are eaten by emus. A number of heavenly phenomena are included amongst the totems, including the sky, various stars, moon, sun, rain, wind and darkness. It is interesting to notice that with regard to the last class of totems, with the exception of rain, none of them was given to Professor Elkin as what may be called the primary totem of the *tambun*—the totem which gives its name to the " country."

[1] A. P. Elkin, *op. cit.* p. 455.

It is possible to see or imagine that various natural species are especially plentiful in certain districts which, therefore, may be considered to be the hiving-off centres of those species. Similarly, rain may seem to come mostly from a particular region, but generally speaking these heavenly phenomena are totems for all hordes alike. As, however, they are of vital importance to the tribe, they must be brought into its ritual life, and amongst the Ungarinyin, as elsewhere in Australia, this is done on the principle of division of responsibility and the co-operation of the hordes. Thus, for ritual purposes, these celestial phenomena are divided amongst a number of hordes, being added, as it were, to their responsibilities for the increase of *earthly* species and objects.[1]

This brings us to another aspect of Ungarinyin totemism. It is not only a system of naming the hordes, and incidentally of expressing and preserving their strong local solidarity, and a means of binding hordes together, by a co-operation of system of ritual responsibility which is concerned with the maintenance and increase of native phenomena and species; it is also a method classifying Nature. When Professor Elkin made enquiries regarding species not mentioned in any of the genealogies he had recorded, he found that many of them were considered as additional totems of various hordes, either in the Ungarinyin or neighbouring tribes. But if, as sometimes happened, his informants could not assign an object to any particular horde, they would usually give its moiety. Thus everything worth noticing is classified, at least into moieties, and Professor Elkin thinks that if fuller information were obtained it would be found that they are classified into hordes. Such an aspect of the totemism of the tribe accords with the fact that no two hordes have the same totem.[2]

Professor Elkin appends a list of the hordes and totems which he was able to record. They number 45 in all. From among them I will select a few of the more important or interesting. They include turtle, the fish barramundi, white cockatoo, the porcupine, the hill kangaroo, wild dog, emu, water goanna, grasshopper, the crow, the flying squirrel, crocodile; the red fruit of the pandanus, the gum tree,

[1] A. P. Elkin, *op. cit.* pp. 459-460.   [2] A. P. Elkin, *op. cit.* p. 459.

bamboo, the lily, the water-lily, the ground nut, the cane for lifting honey out of holes, white stones used for spearheads, basalt, the shield, the throwing-stick, the wind, the sky, darkness, rain, sun, the moon, and the morning star.[1]

The totems belong to the hordes, that is, they are local, and as we have seen are probably explained by myths. Here it is only important to notice that a person belongs to the horde of his father, and incidentally inherits its totems, its *ungud* or *lalan*, that is, its association with and share in, the long-past mythological age of the culture heroes. But we must also consider local totemism in relation to a belief in pre-existence and theories of conception.[2]

A father always " finds " his child in a dream and in association with water, either in a water-hole or in the falling rain. Even if, in the first instance, as sometimes happens, he " finds " his child in water in waking life, he will see it in a dream later on when he is sleeping in his camp. In his dream he sees the spirit-child standing at his head, and catches it in his hand, after which it enters his wife. If he be away from his camp at the time of this dream, he ties the spirit-child in his hair, and so brings it home to his wife. This takes place at the time of the quickening of his wife's womb. The " finding," however, is not haphazard. It is always connected with different spirit-centres which are *ungud* (mythical) ; thus, spirit-children belong to the mythical age. This is what natives mean when, for want of better command of English, they say that the pre-existent spirits are *made* by *ungud* ; when they are asked for further explanation, they can only deny that this action occurs up above, " on top," on the sky, in spite of the fact that the rain comes down from above, and that the rainbow-serpent, also called *ungud*, is said to bring the spirit-children. They feel that having stated that the matter is *ungud*, nothing more need be said.[3]

Now *wondyad* or rainbow-serpent is also the term for a large quiet edible snake or python, which, however, is also mythical, that is, *ungud*, and as such is said to be the *kian*, or mate of *wondyina*. Now *wondyina*, rainbow-serpent, is the main subject represented in pictures painted by the natives

[1] A. P. Elkin, *op. cit.* pp. 450 *sqq.*   [3] A. P. Elkin, *op. cit.* p. 461.

[2] A. P. Elkin, *op. cit.* p. 460.

in caves which constitute their picture galleries, as will be described later. One of these native picture galleries is situated in each horde-country. In these *wondyina* is always depicted with a nose and eyes and a special head-dress, but without any mouth. Primarily he represents the source of rain, and if his painting is retouched rain will fall, though this should not be done until the beginning of the normal wet season. It does not seem to matter in what horde-gallery the painting be thus retouched; rain will come. But one *wondyina*, the one in the gallery of the Kalarimgeri horde which has for its totem rain, is of special importance in this respect. The headman is able to usher in the wet season by simply dreaming that he has visited this rock-gallery.

Wondyina, however, is causally connected not only with the rain, but also with the increase of natural species, and particularly of the human race. The belief is that if a species, the increase of which is desired, be depicted on a *wondyina* gallery, the increase is assured. But this is not done at haphazard. The species painted on the gallery of any horde are the totems of the horde, and, of course, the painting and retouching is done by fully initiated members of the horde, for the galleries are secret. Thus, the life and increase of any particular totemic species are causally associated with a *wondyina*. Hence the rainbow-serpent (*wondyina*) may be a generalised life-giving power which is symbolised by the special *wondyina* paintings in each cave-gallery. On the other hand, the *wondyina* at the gallery of each horde may be a different culture-hero of the *ungud* (mythical times) to be compared with the various *mura-mura* heroes of the mythical age of the Diera tribe, or the *altchera* heroes of the Aranda *alchirunga*. This point, says Professor Elkin, has yet to be definitely settled.[1]

The female *wondyina* gallery which Professor Elkin visited was said to be definitely associated with the increase of the human race. To touch up the painting results in the going forth of spirit-children to be " found " by fathers and incarnated through the wives. In this case the mechanism for the increase of mankind is the same as for the increase of

A. P. Elkin, *op. cit.* pp. 461-462.

other natural species.   Other *wondyina*, whether classed as feminine or not, are also regarded as sources or guardians of spirit-children.   A particular *wondyina* may be asked in a dream for a spirit-child, or a *wondyina* might offer one to a man as he is dreaming.   Moreover, some *wondyina* are said to be more liberal than others in this regard.   Thus, the pre-existent human spirits are intimately related to the *wondyina* represented on the rock-galleries of the various horde-countries, but only a full knowledge of the tribal mythology will determine the nature of this relationship, whether, for example, *wondyina* brought the spirit-children to the place in the *ungud* (mythical time), or whether they are emanations from him.   However that may be, each person has his *ungud* place or spirit-home, which is near water, and though the place may be some distance from the *wondyina* gallery, yet there is a causal relationship between the two.

An individual, therefore, belongs to his *tambun* (horde) and possesses its totems, because his pre-existent spirit was associated with the *wondyina* of that *tambun*.   Generally his *ungud* place, or spirit-house, the water where his father " found " him, is situated in his father's horde-country, but it might be in another ; in the latter case, a person does not seem to have any claim over this *tambun*, or over the *ungud* centre in it where he was " found."   If this be correct, his connection with the *ungud* time, also called *lalan*, is through the cave-gallery of his own horde, with its *wondyina* and totems which are represented on it, and through the various *ungud* sites of his *tambun*, including his own spirit-home and the " homes " of the spirits of the totems of his horde.[1]

Professor Elkin's informants differed with regard to the existence of a prohibition on killing or eating the totem. The taboo does exist in the tribe, but it seems to be stronger in the northern hordes.   Most informants said that they ate their totem if it happened to be a desirable food. But he was told by a good informant that a person only eats the totem of the hordes of his own moiety, which are situated comparatively far off from his own horde country.   He explained that he could eat white cockatoo, a totem belonging to a horde of his moiety, because it was totem of a salt water

[1] A. P. Elkin, *op. cit.* pp. 463-464.

horde on the Prince Regent River, whereas he belonged to a highland horde at the head waters of the Sale River.[1]

The totems of the horde are depicted on its *wondyina* gallery. Professor Elkin often noticed, especially in the Wurara tribe, that when they were asked for their totems, informants seemed to be thinking of the cave-paintings of their hordes, and to be giving the names of the species or objects depicted there. This is, of course, natural, seeing that it is the duty of the men of the horde to maintain the supply of those species which are its totems, and one way, probably the main way, of doing this, is to paint them on the horde-gallery. The same fact was made apparent when the question concerned the moiety and *tambun* (horde) of natural species. Thus when Professor Elkin was trying to ascertain whether various plants and animals which he had not recorded as horde totems really were such, or whether they were divided between the moieties and *tambun* in any way, he noticed that informants seemed to think along the lines of cave-galleries. For example, on being asked about the kurrajong tree, they said that it belonged to Djeladgi place in Djilia *tambun*, in the southern part of the Wurara Tribe, and that it was painted on the Djeladgi gallery, and so made all kurrajong trees grow.[2]

The increase of the various valuable animal and plant species and the maintenance of the regular operation of various natural phenomena, like the sun, moon, stars, wind, and rain, is assured by means of the paintings in the various *wondyina* galleries. But the Ungarinyin also possess some ceremonies for the increase of the natural species akin to those of the *talu* type, but his imperfect knowledge of the language prevented Professor Elkin from getting much information about them. Thus one totem of the Bangudu horde on the north-eastern border of the tribe is *bangudu*, a small kangaroo. According to a *lalan* or heroic age rule, a hunter having killed one of these creatures must swing it round so that the blood is sprinkled about. This is supposed to produce plenty of *bangudu*. Another ceremony for the increase of kangaroos has been introduced from the south-east. A table-like structure of wood is erected in a secret

[1] A. P. Elkin, *op. cit.* pp. 464-465.   [2] A. P. Elkin, *op. cit.* p. 465.

place out of sight of the uninitiated.   The men then dance round it and sing a song during the afternoon and all one night.   Professor Elkin was also informed of a song which is sung by both men and women for the increase of the honey which is gathered from crevices in the rocks.   As the women are mainly responsible for gathering honey, it is natural that they should take part in the singing.[1]

In the Ungarinyin tribe each person has at least one, and perhaps two or more dream totems, called by the natives *yarin*.   Professor Elkin did not ascertain how a person obtained his dream totem, but he thinks it probable that he obtains it in the same way as the Wurara tribe, where a person's dream totem is the horde totem, or totems of his mother's brother.   This method of descent is very interesting, for it implies a double inheritance of totems.   A man's horde totem is his son's horde totem, but his sister's child's dream totem.[2]

In the division of Kimberley to the east of the territory of the Ungarinyin tribe, is the district of the Forrest River, which flows into Cambridge Gulf.   The following are the tribes and hordes of the Forrest River District, the Yeidji (or Yeithi) tribe on the northern side of the tidal waters of the river and on both sides for some distance about these ; it consists of three large horde-countries or *gra* : (1) Mararan (which means big river), the hilly country just up the river from Forrest River Missions ; (2) Umbalgari, a large plain of about 100,000 acres, now occupied by the Mission ; and (3) Yura, on the east of this plain, between the Patrick and Lower Lyne Rivers and the coast of Cambridge Gulf.

The Arnga tribe on south side of the lower reaches of the Forrest River consists of three hordes.   The Kuru, commencing nearly opposite the Mission landing, the Barangala to the south-east, and the Wolma near the mouth of the river.

The Andedja tribe, called the Kular on the Mission, a word meaning west, consists of a number of hordes, of which the Ulangu and Kilangari on the south of the Arnga and the Almbalu on the west of the Mararan horde, have been closely connected with the Mission for some years. '

The Wembria, on the north side of the upper part of the

<hr/>

[1] A. P. Elkin, *op. cit.* p. 466.   [2] A. P. Elkin, *op. cit.* p. 471.

Forrest River, has four hordes. The Wola, near Mararan, and in order north, the Wona, Wixial, and Alnbo.

The Wirngir is a small tribe or sub-tribe on Malambuna, the corner of land north of the lower Lyne River ; west of the Wirngir is the Wulu, another small tribe, and north of it the Mande. The Bemba tribe is west of these, and outside of the Forrest River district.[1]

The horde-country or *gra* is patrilineal ; a person has the right of residing and hunting in his father's horde-country and bringing his wife to live there, even if his spirit-centre be outside its boundaries. In the latter case, a person has the right of residence in two horde-countries, his father's, and also the one in which his father " found " his pre-existent spirit. The term *gra* is used to denote both the horde-country of a person and his spirit-home, just as the term *nura* is used in the Karadjeri tribe. The spirit *gra* is the place where a person's pre-existent spirit " sat down " beside water, where he was seen by his father, and from which he came when he passed into his mother at the time of her quickening. It is a small natural feature, always associated with water. The father might see the spirit-child in the water when he is walking by, or when he is swimming or fishing. Thus he might spear a fish or a crocodile, but when he brings his catch to land, he sees a spirit-child instead, so he does not take it home, for it is not really a fish or a crocodile. But he might carry the spirit-child home in his hand and put it beside his wife, whom it enters, or it might crawl along like a turtle to the woman who, in her dream, throws dust at it, but does not prevent its entry. The spirit-child always enters the woman while she is asleep, but there is no certainty as to the point of entry.[2]

Each person has three totems : a moiety totem, a clan totem, and a dream totem.

Moiety Totem.—Each tribe is divided into two patrilineal exogamous moieties, or *tun*, named *grauunda*, native companion, and *panar*, turkey. Everybody is either *grauunda* or *panar*, belonging to the *tun* (moiety) of his or her father. As a man's mother's brother always belongs to the opposite *tun*, moiety, and as he must marry mother's brother's

[1] A. P. Elkin, *op. cit.* pp. 471-472.　　　　[2] A. P. Elkin, *op. cit.* p. 472.

daughter, the exogamy of the moieties is automatically observed.   *Grauunda* (native companion) is credited with instituting this law of exogamy between the moieties.   A long time ago, when this bird was a man, he saw a crow-man married to a crow-woman.   He asked the crow who the woman was, and received the answer that she was his sister, not " cousin." *Grauunda* (native companion) then chased them away and made the law that *grauunda* must marry *panar*, thus preventing marriage between brother and sister.   This is apparently the basis of the division of the totem clans between the moieties.   Professor Elkin did not find anyone who had the crow for his or her totem.   Both native companion and turkey are plentiful on the large plain at Forrest River Mission, but the natives say that they very seldom manage to spear the latter, and only occasionally the former.   There is no taboo against killing or eating the moiety totems.   Neither are there any ceremonies to increase these two species.[1]

Clan Totem.—Each individual has a clan totem, called *naragu*, which is the same as his or her father's.   The patrilineal descent of the clan totem holds whether the father first saw the person's baby-spirit in his own spirit *gra*, somewhere else in his own horde-territory, in another horde-country, or in another tribal territory.   Nor does the place of birth make any difference.   Members of the one horde can have different *tun* and *naragu*, that differentiate moiety and clan totems.   Further, two persons belonging to the one spirit *gra* or country can have different clan totems.   The clan totems are divided between the moieties, and are therefore exogamous. A man belonging to one clan may, in theory, marry into any clan of the opposite moiety.

As each horde *gra* or country is patrilineal, and as the clan totems are also patrilineal, we should expect each horde to be a local patrilineal totemic clan, and Professor Elkin is inclined to think that this was formerly the case.   But generally speaking, this is not so nowadays.   The explanation may be that the present hordes are really amalgamations of numerous smaller ones.   Another possibility lies in an occasional instance of matrilocal marriage, that is, the possibility of a man living with his wife in her *gra* or territory ; thus an

[1] A. P. Elkin, *op. cit.* pp. 473-474.

Upper Lyne River man is living with his Umbalgari wife in the northern part of her horde-country, and is likely to be its headman on the death of the present headman, to whom he is related as wife's brother. There has been a good deal of intermarrying between neighbouring hordes and tribes, and therefore such circumstances as these could arise.[1]

Death, especially the death of a man's father, also tends to bring about the same results, for on his father's death a man must leave the paternal *gra* or country until the cold season following the next wet season after his father's death, when he returns for the final burial ceremonies. During the interval he lives, as a rule, in the country of his mother's brother, or in the horde-country in which his spirit-home is situated, if that be outside of his father's horde-country. He might then make that *gra* or territory his own. Incidentally even if he only sojourn there during the period of mourning, he might, during that time, find the pre-existent spirit of his child in a spirit-centre somewhere in it. This child then would have a right to live there and to regard it much as his own, that is, his father's horde-country. In such ways another totem is brought into a horde-country.[2]

The Yari or Dream Totem.—Every person has a dream totem ; it does not impose any restrictions on eating, killing, or marrying. It does nothing directly for oneself by way of warning or in any other way. A child is told by his mother or father what his *yari* (dream totem) is, the parent having dreamt of it. To dream of a person's *yari* means that the person will soon be seen.[3]

Rites for the Increase of the Totems.—These are performed by the headman of the horde in which the spirit-centre of the species is situated at the time of the year the species normally does increase. No one else is present, and, as in many Karadjeri rites, there is no singing. The headman just calls out the names of the places in which the increase of the particular species is desired and can be expected.

The Ceremony for the Increase of Water-lilies.—At the beginning of the rainy season the headman goes to a heap of stones about 3 feet high and 7 feet in diameter at the bottom

---

[1] A. P. Elkin, *op. cit.* p. 475.　　　[3] A. P. Elkin, *op. cit.* p. 478.
[2] A. P. Elkin, *op. cit.* p. 475.

and 3 or 4 feet at the top, at Inderi, on a little hill in Um-balgari country. The heap of stones has obviously been placed there by a man a long time ago. No explanation of its origin is given. The stones are of various sizes, but most of them are about 4 inches or a little more in diameter. The officiant lifts out a few stones from a crater-like hole in the centre of the heap, after first pulling up some grass which has grown there during the previous twelve months. He then throws the stones in various directions, calling out as he does so the names of various spots, water-holes, and billabongs in the tribal territory.[1]

Ceremony for the Increase of Poison-bark.—A similar rite is performed for the increase of poison-bark in the latter part of the rainy season, at a similar heap of stones at Oyamiri in Mararan horde-country. The efficacy of this heap is explained by the following myth : *Dyarmu*, the jaberoo bird, gathered a heap of poison-bark at this place, but *Yumbari*, a white river bird, stole it. A fight between the birds followed, in which burning fire-sticks were thrown about. One of these hit the river bird in the eyes, causing the red mark which is around them, while another that hit the jaberoo made his legs red. After the fight the heap of bark became a heap of stones, which when ritually thrown about causes the poison-bark trees to increase.[2]

Ceremony for the Increase of Rain.—The rain-maker of the Yeidji tribe belongs to the Yura horde. He is now (1933) a very old man, and will be succeeded by his son. He only makes rain during the hot weather when rain is expected. There are two rituals.

(1) With a whitish stone which may vary in size but is not too large to be held in the hand, he rubs a stone of any kind standing alongside of fresh water, saying *burubram*, and then blowing the dust, says, " Plenty rain." This rite is obviously of the same type as those already described for this tribe.

(2) He takes a rain-stone, and mixing it with some of his own grey hairs and some flesh from the abdomen of an iguana, wraps the lot up in some dry grass and puts it under a rock in a fresh water-hole.

[1] A. P. Elkin, *op. cit.* pp. 478-479.   [2] A. P. Elkin, *op. cit.* p. 479.

In both cases the rain-maker camps away from his wife, does not speak, and only drinks dirty water until the rain comes ; this is said to come in two days. The ritual is only performed in his own horde-territory (*gra*). The Lyne River tribes also have a rain-maker, who is a very old man and a headman. If there is too much rain, the rain-maker pulls out some of his grey hairs, and puts them in the fire. He blows the smoke, and thus stops the rain.

These increase rites are clearly associated with the existence of the tribe, but they are not connected with the totemic clans like the *intichiuma* or *talu* ceremonies of the Arunta (Arunda), though they are definitely localised and connected with the horde-country in which they are situated. The headman of the horde performs the rites connected with all the increase sites in his *gra* (territory), though none of the species concerned is his *naragu*, totem. The myth explaining the poison-bark increase site suggests that there is a myth explanatory of every rite performed for the increase of a totemic species. Thus the rites, except perhaps those connected with rain-making, possess all the features of the usual *talu* ceremonies except that there is only one performer, and that his totem is not the species being increased. There is the site, which is the spirit centre of the species, the myth, the action and words, and the species to be increased, but the associated group of totemites is missing, their place being taken by the headman of the *gra* (territory).[1]

The tribes of the Forrest River and the Lyne River of the Kimberley District, which were visited and described by Professor Elkin, were afterwards visited and described in 1934 by Miss Phyllis M. Kaberry, under the auspices of the Australian National Research Council. She spent the months from May to October among the natives. During that time her headquarters were at the Mission Station, except for eighteen days which she passed on a camp roughly sixty miles to the north of the Mission.

Professor Elkin has already described the local distribution of the tribes. On the southern side of the Forrest River are the Kular, Aruga, Ballalangnari and Welyamiri tribes. The two last have an eight-subsection system, whilst all the

[1] A. P. Elkin, *op. cit.* pp. 480-481.

others are divided with moieties alone. Each horde comprises a number of totemic and exogamous clans. The tribes act together in warfare, and members assemble during the " dry " season for large inter-tribal meetings. As a rule, however, quarrels involve one or two hordes of one tribe against a horde or hordes of another.[1]

The horde is the most important unit in the local organisation, and the totemic clans, except for the small part they play in indirectly regulating marriages, are subordinated to the larger grouping. The position of headman is well-defined ; he is spoken of as " owning " the country, its pools, resources, and rock-paintings ; in that capacity he is held responsible for carrying out the ceremonies performed to increase the totemic species. He directs social activities, and visitors must ask his permission before they may camp in the country. He " legislates " for the horde ; one such instance was that of the headman of the Kular *Mamalindi*, ordering that there was to be no more gashing of heads at mourning ceremonies. This order was passed on to the neighbouring headman and the order was observed. Finally, he exercises certain judicial functions. He deals with cases of marital infidelity, and, with or without the help of the older men, sees that the offender is punished.[2]

The social organisation includes the tribe, the horde, the totemic clan, the spirit-homes, and last but not least the family, which in everyday social and economical activities is a clear cut unit. The family or family group occupies the one camp.[2]

Since Professor Elkin has already discussed totemism in North-West Australia in detail, the following account of Miss Kaberry is concerned only with the additional information which she gathered on the subject. She tells us that totemism of this region is not the clearly defined phenomenon of Central Australia, and at first sight the ritual attitude towards Nature is not apparent ; ceremonies for the increase of the totems are not carried out by the totemites ; there is no prohibition against killing and eating the totem ; nor is

---

[1] Phyllis M. Kaberry, " The Forrest River and Lyne River Tribes of North-West Australia," in *Oceania*, vol. v. No. 4 (June 1935), pp. 408 *sqq.*
[2] P. M. Kaberry, *op. cit.* p. 411.

it connected with the bull-roarers. Nevertheless the totem possesses an economic, social, and local significance.[1]

Perhaps the subject may be best approached from the side of mythology. In the remote past, the *winigili* time, animals, birds, and reptiles were men, living a life like that of the blacks to-day. All the totems were human beings except *kundi* (wild plum) and *waina* (sugar bag), which Miss Kaberry never heard referred to as being people, though they existed then. At some point a crisis arose, generally a dispute followed by a fight, and they were all changed into their respective species. The children of these, *e.g. garangula* (native companion) and *wolamba* (kangaroo), or *djidja* (wild turkey) or *wieri* (emu), became *wolamba*, or *djidja* or *wieri* men, that is, men possessing these particular species as their totems or *naragus*. The ancestors were like men in every respect, but possessed certain attributes which enabled them to turn into animals or other natural species.[2]

Of the moiety totem there is very little further to be said. Certain totems such as kangaroo (*wolamba*), blue-mountain parrot (*balinjiri*), poison-snake (*nemera*), belong to the *garangula* (native companion) moiety, while alligator (*jewar*), sugar-bag (*waina*), and goanna (*mangar*) belong to the totem of the opposite moiety *djidja* (wild turkey). The moiety totem thus embraces a wider kinship group than the class totem; it brings into prominence the father's line of descent as opposed to that of the mother. This is clearly shown by the fact that it is sometimes called *alungur*, or by the term for father. The moieties, beyond their indirect regulation of marriage, play no part in social activities, though the latent rivalry or antagonism between the two finds expression in mythology.

Some of the clan totems are common to all the hordes of the tribes of North Kimberley, but generally, if we view a horde's totems collectively, they are seen to comprise one or more elements different from those of another horde. Certain totems—*wolamba* (kangaroo), *jewar* (alligator), *waina* (sugar-bag)—appear in most of the hordes, while *balinjiri* (blue mountain parrot), and *namara* (white cockatoo) figure most frequently in the northern tribes. Exceptions to this rule may

[1] P. M. Kaberry, *op. cit.* p. 425.   [2] P. M. Kaberry, *op. cit.* p. 426.

probably be traced back to intermarriage, and in a few cases to the error of the informant. There is a certain tendency towards localisation of the totems, and Professor Elkin has raised the question whether there was a closer connection in the past. He has pointed out that logically each horde could have been a patrilineal totemic clan. Amongst the Gangalu, Jinanu, Mande, Djuri hordes, *namara* (white cockatoo), *balinjiri* (blue-mountain parrot), *moromborla* or *orli* (kangaroo), and *jewar* (alligator) appear most often. Independently of these results, two of the old men who were headmen of the Lyne River tribes gave Miss Kaberry these as the " *big nagarus* " or chief totems of each horde. If the hypothesis be accepted that the horde was originally a single totemic clan, then it follows that the horde would originally have been exogamous. When Miss Kaberry pointed this out, the old men agreed, and said that a man of the Wirngir horde married a woman of the Djuri horde, and that a man of the Mande horde married a woman of the Gangalu horde. If we accept this hypothesis it establishes a definite relationship between the totemic clans and the ceremonies for the increase of the totem, for the horde carries out the ceremony for its own chief totem.[1]

At present the totemic clans regulate marriage in that they are exogamous, and of course they provide a kinship tie. On the Mission you may frequently hear the expression " Norah's crowd," or " Robert's mob," that is, a group possessing a totem in common.

Lastly we must consider the dream totem. It includes some objects which are never clan totems, such as the rainbow serpent ; certain species of fish, ghosts, pandanus seed, evil night birds and spirits, blossoms, and oysters. Most of these belong to tribes on the southern side of the Forrest River. Amongst the northern tribes a man generally hands on his dream totem to his children, and as a rule it is the clan totem belonging to the opposite moiety. Just as a man's moiety and clan totems establish his relationship with his father's line, so a man's dream totem would in a large number of instances establish a relationship with his mother's line of descent. The former is a recognition of social and ritual

---

[1] P. M. Kaberry, *op. cit.* p. 427 *sq.*

ties, the latter of blood ties. Amongst the southern tribes the dream totem embraces a much wider range of objects, and may be correlated with a different organisation, namely the possession of an eight-subsection system in the Wolyamiri and Ballalangnari tribes. Dream totems which have never been clan totems predominate roughly in the ratio of eighty to sixty-three.

Those objects and species which are not found as totems amongst the Forrest River tribes, for example stars, moon, sun, crab, and so on, are said to belong to tribes situated on the west or east. Finally even non-totemic species were considered by the blacks to stand in a kinship relation to one another and to some of the totems.[1]

To this account of totemism Miss Kaberry subjoins a long genealogy, on which she comments as follows :

" Not only is this illustrative of the drawing of the outside world into the social organization, but on the one hand the association of showers, hailstones, clouds, lightning, and thunder reveal a rudimentary idea of classification or causation ; and on the other it is significant that descent is traced back to firstly the moiety totems, *garangula* (native companion) and *djidja* (turkey), and secondly to the spirits of the dead (*juari*) and to *Wolara*, who was responsible for the institution of initiation and other features of social life." [2]

Ceremonies for the Increase of the Totemic Species.—We have seen that Miss Kaberry has already mentioned the ceremonies performed for the increase of the totems and their co-ordination with the local grouping. She now adds that such important items of food as kangaroo, fish, black plum, lily seed, and sugar-bag have their *talu* or increase centres in most of the tribal territories. An unusual feature of the rites is that the wife of the headman with her sister performs the ceremonies for the increase of lily roots and sugar-bag at Inderi for one year, and her husband does it the following year. She also helps him to perform the rites for the increase of fish, poison-bark, and alligator at Malera. This is an important deviation from the Australian custom, whereby the woman as a rule is relegated to the position of onlooker

---

[1] P. M. Kaberry, *op. cit.* p. 430.   [2] P. M. Kaberry, *op. cit.* pp. 430-431.

at most. More extraordinary still is the practice of the wife accompanying the headman to watch him touch up the painting of alligator with red ochre to ensure an increase of that species. There are two galleries of rock-paintings in the Umbalgari country, one at Jandangi and the other at Wunda. In these galleries there are paintings which represent *juari* or spirits of the dead and totems. They are not taboo to women, though only a few of the old women know their true function. Furthermore Miss Kaberry was informed that at Nyurilu in Gangalu country, old women were permitted to touch up the painting of Brimurer (the rainbow serpent) so that those spirit children who were taken from the pools should be replaced in it. No taboos were observed by the officiants at these rites, but every individual reserved to himself the right to perform ceremonies for the increase of kangaroos, and when he does so he eats no meat at the time, and refrains from washing himself and from sleeping with his wife. Since the women help to increase all the species except kangaroo and possibly white cockatoo, the exclusive right claimed by the men to increase kangaroos does not coincide with the general division of labour between the sexes for which the qualification would seem to be that of age. So far as Miss Kaberry could ascertain, these practices do not obtain amongst the southern tribes, though she was told that among these tribes in *winigili* (mythical) time women used to perform the increase rites along with their husbands.[1]

The headman and his wife perform the ceremonies for the increase of most species at the beginning of the summer, about September or October, and before the rains set in. In most cases the rite is very similar. For wild plum, fish, alligator, wallaby, *wolara* (spirits), reed nuts, and the sun, it consists in rubbing a stone with a smaller one. These stones do not necessarily suggest the shape of the species, though a certain part may be said to represent the eye, tail, or genital organs. Again the site may be a kind of cairn, and the man or woman either digs with a stick, or casts the dirt out or strikes stones together to break them, murmuring " make plenty come up." He names the countries round about

[1] P. M. Kaberry, *op. cit.* pp. 431-432.

where the increase is desired.   No one may eat the species till the headman or his wife gives permission.[1]

Miss Kaberry observes that with regard to the totems thus supposed to be increased by the performance of the ceremonies, " It is difficult to see the value of mosquitoes, evil night birds, and spirits (*juari*), as they seem to be objects either of dislike or fear.   Mosquitoes have a negative social importance, but there is no idea of increasing them for the discomfiture of enemies.   The motive for the increase of *juari* (spirits) does not seem to be connected with the concept of immortality.   Fear of the *juari* (spirits) ensures that all the obligations and mourning ceremonies for the dead are carried out, and fear of them serves as a deterrent to thieving.   Fear of them is thus one of the sanctions behind the maintenance of social life.   Galyidmiri, an old headman, told me that he would not increase mosquitoes again, as there had been too many last year.   And Benmiri said the same thing about alligators, since two blacks had been killed in the previous year.   Probably the influence of the past will prove too strong, but the statements are illuminating in that they reveal how deeply rooted is their belief in the efficacy of the rites.   Wolara is one of the most important spirits, and instituted most of the ceremonies together with initiation.   Although he is in one sense their creator, he is not regarded as standing outside the cosmogony, and the blacks *talu* (perform ceremonies) for him as well." [2]

" The point arises to what extent these practices are magical or religious.   The stipulation that the performer should be either an old man or an old woman indicates the importance of the rite, and perhaps the supernatural or spiritual forces at work.   In so far as the rite appears to bring about automatically an increase in the species, and in so far as the conceptions of sacrifice, propitiation, or petition are absent, there is little to differentiate this ceremony from the garden magic of Melanesia.   But it goes further than this in the recognition that not only do other tribes *talu* (perform rites) for the remaining species and objects, but that some of these include objects which are definitely anti-social, *e.g.* mosquitoes and evil night birds.   If we turn to their mytho-

[1] P. M. Kaberry, *op. cit.* p. 432.   [2] P. M. Kaberry, *op. cit.* p. 433.

logy again we see that all these things existed in Winigili (dream or mythic) times but later changed into stone. It is only by rubbing these stones as Wolara first did, that they will come alive again each season. By this means Wolara provided for the continuance of the natural order in the future, as it were. Underlying everything is the conception that the welfare of the part is inextricably bound up with that of the whole." [1]

With regard to the mythology of the tribes, Miss Kaberry tells us that the myths here as elsewhere provide a background for features of the cultural life of to-day. Some of these have already been mentioned in relation to the increase ceremonies and totemism. Some of them account for daily activities.

In the remote past the great mythical hero Wolara wandered about the country, camping and fighting. He gave men increase ceremonies, circumcision, and hair-belts. At one spot in the Yura horde-country, called Gola, you may still see depressions where he slept with his wife, and flung stones about in a fight. Near this is the site where the increase rites are performed for Wolara. About three miles from this spot are some flat slabs of stone standing upright. They are said to have been placed there by Wolara to point out the direction in which he was travelling. He was also responsible for the phallic-stone at Galbimiri and for the cliffs in the Wirngir horde-country, which he made out of small stones which the spirits had thrown down from the sky. He sent two women up to the sky, where they make turtles that fall into the rivers and pools when it rains. Wolara stole alligator away from the policeman bird and ran away to Wirngir and then plunged into the sea, where he was changed into a stone.

Another mythical being, Yingirmira, stole somebody's wife and was pursued. He threw his fighting-stick from west to east and opened out the hills to make plains. He went to Nulamo and killed a kangaroo, which he tied around his waist. A brown bird, who was a man then, took it and told him how to carry it around his neck. They cooked it, and both died. A similar story is related of two other birds

[1] P. M. Kaberry, *op. cit.* pp. 433, 434.

who were carrying a kangaroo wrongly.   Djidja (wild turkey)
said that they should remove the intestines, so Jadai gave it
to him, his mother's brother, to cook.   They were all changed
into stone.

Some children were naughty, so a wind came along, and
put them in the moon.   They can be seen now.

The rainbow serpent was responsible for the appearance
of all the rivers in *winigili* (mythical) time, and he still makes
the tides and floods.   He told the blacks to paint themselves
with white clay which they found near water, so that they
would be able to find spirit-children.   An old headman
asserted that after a man had repainted the rainbow serpent
in the rock gallery, he would always paint himself with white
clay as well.

Alligator was making water-holes : he took some fire
with him ; blue-mountain parrot snatched the fire-sticks
from him and flew away.   A medicine-man saw a flock of
these birds sitting around a fire ; he stole the fire-sticks and
the birds flew up dropping fire.

The Forrest River myths explain the origin of spear-
making, the preparation of food, the finding of fire, hunting,
and prescribed behaviour towards certain relatives.   The
heroes of the past lived more or less as the blacks live to-day.
There are probably many more stories, but those which have
been quoted have a common currency.   The blacks were
always willing to repeat them to Miss Kaberry and were
eager to show her the places where they had occurred.   They
stamp the *winigili* (mythical) time with an impression of
reality, provide a link with the past, and a sanction for the
life of the present.[1]

In a later article dealing with the beliefs regarding
spirit-children and spirit-centres as these beliefs are found
among the tribes of North Kimberley, Miss Kaberry has
supplemented with some fresh details Professor Elkin's
account of the " finding " of a spirit-child by the father.
Her account runs thus : " A father finds a spirit-child when
he is out hunting or fishing alone.   He may spear a fish or
an animal which is near the water-hole ; this either disappears
or is brought back to the camp by the man, cooked, eaten,

<hr>

[1] P. M. Kaberry, *op. cit.* pp. 435-436.

and sometimes shared with his wife. That night he dreams that he sees the spirit-child playing with his spears or his wife's paper bark ; he thrusts it towards her and it enters by the foot.

" The father may, however, actually see it in the water on the .back of Brimurer, the rainbow serpent. The spirit-child calls out to him and asks for a mother. The man picks it up, places it in a sapling or else in his *mudere* (*i.e.* in his hair, which is drawn tightly back from the forehead, bound with hair string and plastered with red ochre). The next morning the man says to his wife, ' I bin dreamin' spirit-child.' The woman from then on till the birth of the child, does not sleep with her husband and observes certain tabus in regard to the eating of fish and meat. Some of the mission women do not practise these tabus, with the result that their children are said by the others to develop sores." [1]

One reason why these savages so often trace the birth of spirit-children to pools of water may perhaps be found, as Miss Kaberry suggests, in the wild highland nature of the country in which they live. She tells us that the belief of the natives in spirit-children takes on a richer significance and imaginative power because it has for its natural background a country which is intensely vivid in its colouring, and stark in its contours beneath the blazing heat and light of a tropical sun. The spirit centres are certain parts of the river where clefts gash into the face of the red sandstone cliffs that rise sheer from water's edge. They are also the pools of permanent water which are scattered over the land. Many of them have never been plumbed ; they are often fringed with trees of paper bark which rise to a height of 30 or 40 feet, and abound in roots of water-lilies and fish of all kinds. Sometimes these pools may lie 8 miles or more apart, the intervening country being covered with long cane grass, and the hills stony and practically bare of all vegetation. The natives travel from one pool to another, which are camping spots and the scenes of daily life. We need

[1] P. M. Kaberry, " Spirit-Children and Spirit-Centres of the North Kimberley Division, West Australia,"   *Oceania*, vol. vi. No. 4 (June 1936), pp. 394 *sq.*

not wonder, therefore, that as they provide the individual with some of the chief means of sustenance from day to day, they should also be closely associated with the perpetuation of the race. The blacks are bound to these pools, not only by material ties but also by spiritual links, for they are the homes of spirit-children.[1]

The totemic system of the tribes inhabiting East Kimberley has also been investigated and described by Professor Elkin. These tribes, such as the Djerag, Lunga, Djaru, Malugin, Mirung, and others, have the system of eight subsections combined with a kinship system of the Arunta (Aranda) type. Their local organisation is of the normal Australian type. The tribal territories are divided up into a number of horde-countries, each with a headman, who gives leave to visitors to hunt in his " country " and who usually accompanies them in the hunt. Each of these " countries " has its name : thus Wolergi is along the junction of the Mary and Margaret Rivers. Roilu is the adjoining " country " up the Margaret at Eaglehawk Crossing, and Padwadu joins both of them on the east, being situated along the Laura River.[2]

The totemism of this region is subsectional, that is, the totem clans are divided into eight groups, and the descent of the totem depends on the descent of the subsection. A person, therefore, does not belong to a totem of his father's subsection, but to one of his father's father's subsections ; at least, that is the rule in the case of regular marriages. But if a person's parents do not belong to a regular pair of intermarrying subsections, he belongs to the subsection to which his mother's children would belong if she had married according to the general rule. Thus, the father is " dropped." This really means that the descent of the subsections, and therefore of the totems, is indirect-matrilineal.[3]

Since then the descent of the totem depends indirectly on the subsection of the mother, the relation of a man's totem to his father's horde-country becomes somewhat doubtful, especially as we have reason to think that normally each

[1] P. M. Kaberry, *op. cit.* pp. 393, 394.
[2] A. P. Elkin, " Totemism in North-West Australia (The Kimberley Division). The Tribes of Eastern Kimberley," in *Oceania*, vol. iv. No. 1 (September 1933), p. 54.
[3] A. P. Elkin, *op. cit.* p. 55.

locality belongs to one subsection only, and therefore to one or more of the several totems belonging to that subsection. Given patrilocal marriage, that is marriage in which the wife leaves the place of her birth and goes to live with her husband, the father of her children, the type of marriage which normally prevails in Australia, we must picture a man and his son as belonging to the one horde-country, but to different subsections, and therefore to different places in that " country," and again, to different totems, the totems of their respective subsections. The problem would be intensified if, as does happen, a man of the same horde brings in a wife from an alternate intermarrying subsection ; his children would belong to a different subsection and totems from that of either the previous man or his son. Would these children then belong to a different locality in the same horde-country, or to a locality in another horde-country ? This problem has yet to be cleared up, and it might be done by further field work in Eastern Kimberley. The information at present available suggests that a person's locality is the locality of his own pre-existent spirit and, at the same time, is the spirit-centre of his totem. Normally this locality is within the country of his father. When, then, the subsection system is developed or introduced, his subsection becomes attached to his locality, which is that of his totem, while his father's subsection is attached to the father's spirit and totemic locality. Thus it is that a man's locality, or spirit-country, and his totem can be spoken of as belonging to a particular subsection, and normally there will be two subsections in a horde-country.[1]

But how does a person come to belong to a particular locality with its totem and subsection ? The answer is found in the belief regarding conception and child-birth. A man dreams that a spirit-child approaches him announcing that it will be incarnated through his wife. Some time later on he brings some food, such as kangaroo, emu, snake, fish, or bird, to camp, but it is so fat that his wife refuses to eat it. The bystanders, noticing that when someone eats a bit of it he or she becomes sick, say that it is not food, but a baby. The spirit-child enters the man's wife at the time of the

[1] A. P. Elkin, *op. cit.* pp. 56-57.

CHAPTER VI

TOTEMIC ROCK-PAINTINGS IN WEST AUSTRALIA

WE have seen that some tribes in the Kimberley District of West Australia possess what we may call portraits of their totems, painted on the sides or roofs of caves, and that these paintings are made, and from time to time renewed or touched up, for the express purpose of increasing the supply of the edible animals, plants, and other natural or mythical beings thus depicted. The first Englishman to discover and describe these remarkable monuments of savage art in West Australia was Lieutenant, afterwards Sir George Grey, Governor of South Australia. For the convenience of the reader I will quote his description of his first discovery, which was made in the region of the Glenelg River.

" Finding that it would be useless to lose more time in searching for a route through this country, I proceeded to rejoin the party once more ; but whilst returning to them, my attention was drawn to the numerous remains of native fires and encampments which we met with, till at last, on looking over some bushes, at the sandstone rocks which were above us, I suddenly saw from one of them a most extraordinary large figure peering down upon me. Upon examination, this proved to be a drawing at the entrance to a cave, which, on entering, I found to contain, besides, many remarkable paintings.

" The cave appeared to be a natural hollow in the sandstone rocks ; its floor was elevated about 5 feet from the ground, and numerous flat broken pieces of the same rock, which were scattered about, looked at a distance like steps leading up to the cave, which was 35 feet wide at the entrance, and 16 feet deep ; but beyond this, several small branches ran further back. Its height in front was rather more than 8 feet, the roof in front being formed by the solid slab of sandstone about 9 feet thick and which rapidly inclined towards the back of the cave, which was there not more than 5 feet high.

" On this sloping roof, the principal figure which I have just alluded to, was drawn ; in order to produce the greater effect the rock about it was painted black, and the figure itself coloured with the most vivid red and white. It thus appeared to stand out from the rock ; and I was certainly rather surprised at the moment that I first saw this gigantic head and upper part of a body bending over and staring grimly down at me.

" It would be impossible to convey in words an adequate idea of this uncouth and savage figure. . . .

" The dimensions of the figure were—

	Ft.	In.
Length of head and face	2	0
Width of face	0	17
Length from bottom of face to navel	2	6

" Its head was encircled by bright red rays, something like the rays which one sees proceeding from the sun, when depicted on the sign-board of a public-house ; inside of this came a broad stripe of very brilliant red, which was coped by lines of white, but both inside and outside of this red space, were narrow stripes of a still deeper red, intended probably to mark its boundaries ; the face was painted vividly white, and the eyes black, being however surrounded by red and yellow lines ; the body, hands, and arms were outlined in red,—the body being curiously painted with red stripes and bars.

" Upon this rock which formed the left-hand wall of this cave, and which partly faced you on entering, was a very singular painting, vividly coloured, representing four heads joined together. From the mild expression of the countenances, I imagined them to represent females, and they appeared to be drawn in such a manner, and in such a position, as to look up at the principal figure which I have before described ; each had a very remarkable head-dress, coloured with a deep bright blue, and one had a necklace on. Both of the lower figures had a sort of dress painted with red in the same manner as that of the principal figure, and one of them had a band around her waist. Each of the four faces was marked by a totally distinct expression of countenance, and although none of them had mouths, two, I thought, were otherwise rather good-looking. The whole painting was executed on a white ground, and its dimensions were :

	Ft.	In.
Total length of painting	3	$6\frac{3}{4}$
Breadth across two upper heads	2	6
,, across the two lower ones	3	$1\frac{1}{2}$

" The next most remarkable drawing in the cave was an ellipse, 3 feet in length and 1 foot 10 inches in breadth : the outside line of this painting was of a deep blue colour, the body of the ellipse being of a bright yellow dotted over with red lines and spots, whilst across it ran two transverse lines of blue. The portion of the painting above described formed the ground, or main part of the picture, and upon this ground was painted the kangaroo in the act of feeding, two stone spear-heads, and two black balls ; one of the spear-heads was flying to the kangaroo, and one away from it ; so that the whole subject probably constituted a sort of charm by which the luck of an enquirer in killing game could be ascertained.

" There was another rather humorous sketch which represented a native in the act of carrying a kangaroo ; the height of the man being 3 feet. The number of drawings in the cave could not altogether have been less than from 50 to 60, but the majority of them consisted of men, kangaroos, etc. ; the figures being carelessly and badly executed, and having evidently a very different origin to those which I have first described. Another very striking piece of art was exhibited in the little gloomy cavities situated at the back of the main cavern. In these instances some rock at the sides of the cavity had been selected and the stamp of the hand and arm by some means transferred to it ; this outline of the hand and arm was then painted black, and the rock about it white, so that on entering that part of the cave, it appeared as if a human hand and arm were projecting through a crevice admitting light."[1]

Three days later Grey discovered another cave with rock-paintings in the same district. He says : " The cave was twenty feet deep, and at the entrance seven feet high and about forty feet wide. The floor gradually approached the roof in the direction of the bottom of the cavern, and its width also contracted, so that at the extremity it was not broader than the slab of rock, which formed a natural seat. The principal painting in it was the figure of a man, ten feet six inches in length, clothed from the chin downward in a red garment, which reached to the wrists and ankles ; beyond this red dress the feet and hands protruded, and were badly executed.

" The face and head of the figure were enveloped in a succession of circular bandages or rollers, or what appeared to be painted to represent such. These were coloured red, yellow, and white ; and the eyes were the only features represented on the face. Upon the highest bandage or roller, a series of lines were painted in red, but although so regularly done as to indicate that they have some meaning, it was impossible to tell whether they were intended to depict written characters or some ornament for the head. This figure was so drawn on the roof that its feet were just in front of the natural seat, whilst its head and face looked directly down on any one who stood in the entrance of the cave, but it was totally invisible from the outside. The painting was more injured by the damp and atmosphere, and had the appearance of being much more defaced, and ancient, than any of the others which we had seen. There were two other paintings, one on each of the rocks which stood on either side of the natural seat ; they were carefully executed, and yet had no apparent design in them ; unless they were intended to represent some fabulous species of turtle ; for the natives of Australia are generally fond of narrating tales of fabulous and extraordinary animals, such as gigantic snakes, etc."[2]

[1] G. Grey, *Journals of Two Expeditions of Discovery in N.-W. and Western Australia* (London, 1841), i. 201-204.

[2] G. Grey, *op. cit.* i. 214-215.

On the following day " we found two caves in the cliffs, on the right hand, both of which were painted all over, but with no regularity of pattern : the only colours used were red, yellow, and white. The largest of the caves exceeded in breadth and depth any others I had seen, but it was only 3 feet high ; in this one there were several drawings of fish, one of which was 4 feet in length ; these I copied, although they were badly executed. The caves themselves cannot be considered as at all analogous to those I have before described."[1]

After describing the cave paintings which he had seen, and illustrating them with coloured plates, Grey proceeds as follows :—

" As I never, during my subsequent travels in Australia, saw anything at all resembling the painted caves which I have described, I shall here add some observations on the subject, which I could not have there detailed without too great an interruption of the narrative.

" Two other instances of Australian caves, which contain paintings, have been recorded. The first is by Captain Flinders, and the second by Mr. Cunningham in King's voyage.

" The caves found by Flinders were in Chasm Island, in the Gulf of Carpentaria, and are thus described :

" ' In the steep sides of the chasms were deep holes or caverns undermining the cliffs ; upon the walls of which I found rude drawings, made with charcoal, and something like red paint, upon the white ground of the rock. These drawings represented porpoises, turtles, kangaroos, and a human hand ; and Mr. Westall, who went afterwards to see them, found the representation of a kangaroo, with a file of 32 persons following after it. The third person of the band was twice the height of the others, and held in his hand something resembling the *whaddie* or wooden sword of the natives of Port Jackson.' "[2]

" The second instance is taken from Mr. Cunningham's MSS., and is contained in the following extract :—

" ' The south and south-eastern extremes of Clack's

---

[1] G. Grey, *op. cit.* pp. 217-218.
[2] Flinder's *Voyages*, ii. 158 ; G. Grey, *op. cit.* p. 258.

Island (north-east coast of Australia) presented a steep, rocky bluff, thinly covered with small trees. I ascended the steep head, which rose to an elevation of 180 feet above the sea.

" The remarkable structure of the geological features of this islet led me to examine the south-east part, which was the most exposed to the weather, and where the disposition of the strata was, of course, more plainly developed. The base is a coarse, granular, siliceous sandstone, in which large pebbles of quartz and jasper are imbedded : this stratum continued for 16 to 20 feet above the water : for the next 10 feet there is a horizontal stratum of black schistose rock, which is of so soft a consistence, that the weather had excavated several tiers of galleries ; upon the roof and sides of which some curious drawings were observed, which deserve to be particularly described : they were executed on a ground of red ochre (rubbed on the black schistus), and were delineated by dots of a white argillaceous earth, which had been worked up into a paste. They represented tolerable figures of sharks, porpoises, turtles, lizards (of which I saw several small ones among the rocks), trepang, star-fish, clubs, canoes, water-gourds, and some quadrupeds, which were probably intended to represent kangaroos and dogs. The figures, besides being outlined by the dots, were decorated all over, with the same pigment, in clotted transverse belts. Tracing a gallery round to windward, it brought me to a commodious cave, or recess, overhung by a portion of the schistus, sufficiently large to shelter twenty natives, whose recent fire places appeared on the projecting area of the cave.

" Many turtles' heads were placed on the shelves or niches of the excavation, amply demonstrative of the luxurious and profuse mode of life these outcasts of society had, at a period rather recently, followed. The roof and sides of this snug retreat were also entirely covered with the uncouth figures I have already described.

" As this is the first specimen of Australian taste in the fine arts that we have detected in these voyages, it became me to make a particular observation thereon : Captain Flinders had discovered figures on Chasm Island, in the Gulf of Carpentaria, formed with a burnt stick ; but this performance, exceeding a hundred and fifty figures, which must have occupied much time, appears at least to be one step nearer refinement than those simply executed with a piece of charred wood. Immediately above this schistose is a superincumbent mass of sandstone, which appeared to form the upper structure of the island." [1]

After quoting these descriptions Grey goes on to observe that " there is a third instance of a cave with a figure in it, in the district of York, in the settlement of Swan River ; but in this case, the species of circle which is drawn on the cave, or rather scraped into it with a piece of stone, may represent anything or nothing ; in fact, it is no more than any idle or thoughtless savage might have executed, without any fixed design whatever. The only other vestige of drawing contained in the cave is evidently the mere impression of a hand, which has been rubbed over with red paint with which the natives are in the constant habit of bedaubing themselves, and has then been pressed in on the wall." [2]

In 1927–1928 Professor Elkin visited and devoted eleven weeks' study to three sets of cave paintings in North Kimberley. He has described what he saw of them as follows : " One of these galleries is situated on the southern side of Walcott Inlet about seven miles on foot from Munja Station houses. The site is called Beleguldo. The country is very rough, consisting of sandstone ridges, residuals and gullies. Most of the paintings have been executed on the vertical face of the western side of one of the residuals and are sheltered from the weather by an overhanging ledge. The rest are situated on the roof of a low cave which extends back about 30 feet from the wide entrance immediately under the front paintings. The roof of the cave is only from 18 to 24 inches above the floor. The cave paintings are near the entrance. The cave is divided into two parts, that on the left being the deeper. The one on the right has a second entrance, namely, from the south-west. Human bones, painted with red ochre (' to keep them clean '), have been deposited in both parts of the cave. Those in the left side, which extends back from the feet of the large rock-face painting, have almost crumbled

---

[1] King's *Voyages*, ii. 25. Quoted by Grey, *op. cit.* pp. 258-260.
[2] G. Grey, *op. cit.* pp. 260-261.

away, but those in the right-hand division, extending back from the head of the same painting, are much firmer. It is a common custom finally to place the bones which have been dried on the tree-platform, cried over, and then carried about by one of the ' parents,' in a ' picture-cave.' . . .

" As the mass of rock which contains the ' gallery ' is surrounded by other large residuals, the outer paintings cannot be seen until the traveller is within about 15 yards of them. The effect is then very startling. It is easy to understand Sir George Grey's amazement when he first saw similar paintings a little further north. The paintings on the roof of the cave can only be seen by crawling along the floor and then lying down on one's back. Kangaroo ticks add to the memories of such an exploit.

" I shall describe the paintings at this site in three divisions : (1) Those on the rock-face. The most striking of these is a large man, about 13 feet from the sole of the foot to the top of his hair, depicted horizontally along the rock-face. (Figures of this kind are called *wondjina* in the language.) He has eyes and nose but no mouth. His face is partly surrounded by a horse-shoe shaped head-dress. Two small persons of the same type are painted on the body of the large one, representing his children. Two small women, about 2 feet in length, are painted to the right and above the head of the large man. Their head-dress is the same as his. Their breasts and genital organs are clearly depicted. Four more similar figures can still be seen to the right of the main picture. They were about 3 feet long, but have now almost completely faded away. Originally there were also two heads under the large one. The head, breast, and outstretched wings of an eagle-hawk are painted just above the neck of the main figure, and some ' plains wallaby ' feet are also represented. Some small round rings near the feet of the large figure represent a ground fruit, *nalgo.*

" Other features may also be noticed. The breadth across the face, head-paint, and hair of the large figure is 38 inches. What is said to be the beard commences at about the level of the nipples, 31 inches from the nose, and is 22 inches long by 7 inches broad. The left hand and arm have faded out. The right hand is provided with 5 fingers, the right foot with 7 toes and the left with 6. The feet on this, as on one of the smaller figures, are set heel to heel at an angle of 180 degrees, while the toes are represented in childish fashion, as it were, one above the other. The large figure and one of the smaller figures are furnished with belts. In the former case the belt is 4 inches wide ; dots along its centre represent the human hair of which it is supposed to be made.

" The red-ochred band around the head of the large figure represents the custom of applying red ochre and fat over the top of the forehead and frontal part of the head in a strip, and thence down the side of the face. The painting in the picture, however, is not in correct perspective, and suggests that a painted strip of board or other material shaped like a horse-shoe was set round the face. But this was not so. The little lines which project from the outer edge of this head-paint are not the rays of the sun as has been suggested in similar paintings, but represent the hair of the head which is depicted by red lines with black tips. The eyebrows are marked in the same way. The eyeballs are black, being painted with charcoal, most of the nose is red, though the outline is represented by a line of red applied over white (pipe-clay), producing a salmon colour, while the rest of the face and neck is white. The outlines of the body, legs, arm, and feet are made with charcoal. The rest of the figure is white ; this applies also to the smaller superimposed figures, except that there are red dashes on the body of the lower one. The head-paint, hair, eyebrows, eyes, and nose of these are similar to those of the large figure. Like it, too, and all wondjina heads, they have no mouths. In reply to the question why these heads are thus depicted, the natives merely reply in a manner which shows that the representation of mouths is quite out of the question : ' it cannot be done.'

" A figure which is said to represent lightning is painted in red ochre with pairs of parallel lines of white dots running across it, just above the large head. This figure is forked at its upper or right end, and may have originally been forked at the other end also, but the latter is indistinct. It is 42 inches long by 6 inches wide.

' The smaller figures superimposed on the larger one are said to represent the latter's children. The lower of these reaches from the shoulder to the waist of the larger wondjina, its head resting, as it were, on the latter's left breast. It is 41 inches in length. Some of the fingers and toes are missing. There appear to be only 7 or 8 of the former and 6 of the latter.

" The head and trunk of the second small figure lie between the right breast and waist of the large one, while its legs extend along the latter's right leg. Its total length is 68 inches.

" (2) The following objects are depicted on the roof of the right-hand division of the cave : (i) the sun, represented by two concentric circles, the diameters of which are 1 and 2 feet respectively ; the circumferences are represented by red lines representing the rays of the sun. (ii) A woman whose special organs are clearly depicted ; her head is of the usual wondjina type. (iii) A number of white dots which are said to be water-lilies ; the painting of these lilies here as of the *nalgo* on the rock-face is believed to make those fruits plentiful. (iv) A snake ; this is almost hidden under a rock-ledge on the south-western aspect of the sandstone mass.

" (3) A large number of stencilled hands and one stencilled foot appear on the roof of the cave to the left of the large figure. White clay was apparently blown over the hand or foot as the person lay on his back on the floor. A kangaroo is also painted in outline.

" While the kangaroo, the snake, and perhaps some of the other minor figures are fairly modern, some of the rest are certainly very old. Some of the smaller heads are almost totally obliterated by the ravages of time, although for the greater part they are protected from the weather. There is no sign of the left arm of the large wondjina, and the lower limbs of the right-hand child are very indistinct. No attempt, however, is made to restore any of these, though in some cases, especially in those of the large wondjina and his children, the head, head-paint, hair, eyebrows and eyes are certainly retouched and kept renewed. This operation should only be done at the beginning of the wet season, for the re-touching causes rain to fall. As a matter of fact, a black fellow who was with me retouched the eyes of the large wondjina with some charcoal while I was visiting the pictures, and, strangely enough, some light showers fell a few days later in the midst of the dry season. This did much to strengthen the aborigines' faith, and they did not fail to draw my attention to the cause of this unprecedented rain.

" On the floor of the rock-shelter are two smooth stones, each resembling half an emu egg in shape. They are 6 inches high and 4 inches in diameter at the base. One is basalt and the other of sandstone. The two stones are said to represent the testicles of wondjina. They have no doubt been brought from a river-bed such as the Isdell where water-worn stones of both types are plentiful. A number of the Northern Kimberley rivers run along the junction of the basaltic and sandstone formations.

" A second gallery referred to as *wiri modaneri* (*i.e.* a place where a nut called *wiri* or *nalgo* is marked or depicted), which I was able to visit, is situated on a sandstone residual about seven miles east of Munja Station, on the northern side of the Charnley River. There are several masses of sandstone in the vicinity. The one in question has an overhanging ledge and also a tunnel. The western aspect of the lower part of the sheltered edge and the tunnel have been adorned with paintings. The most conspicuous of these are a number of heads of the wondjina type. They are similar to those already described, and like them, lack mouths, but are provided with head-paint. They vary in breadth from 1 to 2 feet. One was evidently furnished with arms and a body, reclining on its right side, but the latter has become obliterated, and indeed, another wondjina head has been painted over it in the region of the abdomen.

" Two of the heads at least are kept ' touched up ' and can be seen from a distance of about 50 yards. Two others in less conspicuous places also appear to be fairly fresh. The heads are said by the aborigines to represent wondjina women. If they are retouched with ochre, charcoal, or pipe-clay, women will have babies. In two places near some of these heads there are a number of more or less round marks, about an inch in diameter. These represent the green plum-like fruit called *nalgo*. The regular supply of this fruit is maintained by painting or repainting representations of it on a wondjina gallery during the wet season. Indeed, even the ' baby increase ' female wondjina are supposed to be retouched only during this same season, when the productive power of Nature is at its height.

"Just inside, on the roof of the tunnel are two outline paintings of large female kangaroos with young in the pouch. Two wondjina heads are painted so as to look at these kangaroos. The latter appear to have been fairly recently painted or retouched. This is said to be done during the wet season to ensure the natural increase of the species.

"The gallery also contains several representations of the sun, said to be a big sun and young suns. Each of these consists of a series of painted rays proceeding outwards from a circle. One of them is provided with what my natives called a beard. It is the inner ring, and is shaped like the representation of the beard on the wondjina of the first gallery, already described.

"A flat-topped block of stone about three feet high stands just in front of the gallery. Four rounded pieces of water-worn sandstone, each about 6 inches in diameter, which rest on top of this are said to be ripe *nalgo*, such as *Ungud* used in the far-off times. The name *Ungud* is sometimes used as though it referred to a person, sometimes as though it referred to a far-off time, and sometimes too, for the rainbow-serpent water spirit. It is also given as the ultimate explanation of such significant things as the obvious artificial arrangement of stones. To the question ' What is that ? ' the answer given is simply ' *Ungud*.'

"In this case, neither the stone table nor the *nalgo* stones show any signs of having been rubbed, as is the case in the Forrest River district. Further, the natives deny that they are rubbed or used ceremonially in any way.

"This gallery, then, is obviously associated with the increase of babies, *nalgo*, and kangaroo, and also has some significant connection with the sun. The association of *wondjina* with babies is not so direct perhaps as in the case of *nalgo* and kangaroo, though it is not wise to be dogmatic. Wondjina is the rain, or the rain-power. Retouching his representation causes the wet season to function normally with its storms and rains. Since *nalgo* and kangaroo then increase, there is some causal connection between the rain and the increase of the species. Babies are connected with the wet season, because a man might ' find ' or see a baby in the rain and lightning which is coming down all around him. A normal wet season therefore increases the likelihood of thus finding a baby. Another version runs that *Ungud*, the rain, carries baby spirits whom he makes on his shoulders. In any case, spirit-babies are always found ' along water.'

" A third set of rock-paintings which I visited is situated high up on the sandstone cliff on the eastern side of a gorge called Bindjibi about eighteen miles from the head of Walcott Inlet. The sides of the gorge are so steep that as soon as a piece of the rock becomes separated from the cliff it rolls down into the valley, the floor of which is consequently very rough. High grasses, pandanus, palms, some eucalyptus and other trees clothe the bed of the valley, along which a stream, small in the dry season, wends its way in a southern direction. A native footpath passes along the bottom of the gorge and out over the head of it leading north towards the Sale River country. The gallery is reached by walking up the steep rock-strewn side of the gorge to the base of the perpendicular sandstone cliffs, which must be at least 300 feet above the stream. The actual cliffs are 100 or more feet in height, above which the land still rises.

" The paintings are found at the base of the cliff. No sign of a beaten track leading up to them was noticed, nor was there any evidence of the rock-shelter under which some of the paintings were found ever having been used for habitation. But the site is obviously visited from time to time for the purpose of retouching some of the paintings.

" The gallery, which is about 30 yards in length, may be divided into four sections, two of which are on the comparatively exposed surface of the cliff, while the other two are protected by a rock-ledge. The first of the former pair is on the extreme left or northern end of the gallery. The second set, separated from this by a few feet, is really a continuation of the third section which is on the perpendicular rock-face under the ledge. The fourth is on the ceiling or ' roof ' of the ledge, certainly about 12 feet from the ground.

" In the interpretation of the paintings I had the assistance of my guide, who belongs to the horde in whose country the gallery is situated, and also of other members of that horde with whom I discussed the pictures on my return to Mundjina Aboriginal Station where they were camping at the time.

" (1) The section on the extreme left included some paintings which were quite out of reach and had apparently been executed when less of the base of the cliff had become detached and rolled down the side of the gorge.

" One of these paintings, which is out of reach, is not unlike an anchor, but possibly represents a human subject or a bird of some kind. Two others depict human beings, one with an object somewhat like an inverted swinging club projecting upwards from the top of the head. The other has a head-dress or perhaps head-paint suggesting rays, and what appears to be a garment extending from the neck to the knees, unless the person was meant to have a very long body and short legs. But as these paintings, which were in red ochre, were somewhat indistinct, no certainty can be reached on such a point.

" A somewhat faded red-ochre painting about 1 foot in length and within reach is a remarkably good representation of a man walking with his arms raised. The nose, chin, and forehead, which are painted in profile, do not suggest the usual aboriginal type of head, but this does not necessarily imply Malay or white workmanship ; it may have been the undesigned result connected with working on the rough surface of the sandstone. It must, however, be admitted that the realistic and life-like representation is certainly superior to that which is usually seen in native galleries.

" This section contains a very strange figure in profile which suggests a human being in sitting posture with a trunk-like or bent beak-like projection on its face. It has, too, what appears to be three legs which are continued round various angles of the rock-face and are eventually made to join together. My guide, however, said that it represented the *barimbarinbua*, a bird which flies along the rocks in the gorges. This picture of it is in an awkward position. It is now indistinct, but the outline and colours—red outlines

filled in with yellow—can be determined with certainty
The length of the trunk, neck, and head is 3 feet, and the
width of the body 8 inches.

" (2) The second section contains a number of the typical
wondjina or *holini* (rain) heads, and also an assortment of
other subjects. The former are similar to those already
described. In some cases, white dots are painted in pairs
of lines across the horse-shoe shaped band of head-paints.
In others this is absent, but as far as I know the dots are only
ornamental and so neither their presence nor absence has
any significance. But the red curved band which is painted
over one head is called *maranana* and is said to represent
malneri, the lightning, as in the large wondjina in the first
gallery. The other subjects include porcupine, water-goanna,
duck, barramundi, fresh-water crocodile (four), goanna
(two), kangaroo (two), rain-bird, snake, and an egg. One
picture seems to represent a man's head and beard in profile.

" (3) On the wall of the rock-shelter. This section
includes in the first place a number of wondjina heads, and
representations of various objects such as the female rain-
bird, a large yam (*terkun*), porcupine, native companion or
duck, a number of rings depicting a fruit, covering roughly
a square of 18 inches by 18, a snake, blossoms frequented
by bees, and a patch of yellow with dark dots representing
a piece of yellow ochre. A number of the heads measure
14 inches by 14, while some are slightly larger. In some
cases, both the face and the surrounding rock are painted
with yellow ochre, and a few of the other subjects are painted,
at least in part, in the same colour. Otherwise the colours
used are red, white, and black.

" The third section also includes three large figures.
One is a full-length wondjina similar to the one seen in the
first gallery visited. He is depicted horizontally as though
lying stiffly on his left side, and his total length is 9 feet
9 inches. The lowest part of the picture is 4 feet from the
floor of the shelter, and almost on the extreme right of the
gallery. The only additional remarks that need be made are
that, as usual, the mouth is not represented, there are only
four fingers on the one hand that is shown, that a definite
division is shown between the legs, making clear that the

being is not wearing a garment, and that some object appears to project from the head-dress. This object is 9 inches long by 2 wide, but I am not sure if it is a head-dress or merely an independent subject drawn near the wondjina. I received the name *taramala* for this, but I do not seem to have learned the meaning of this word.

" Another of the large figures appears just inside on the left of the shelter, on a ledge about 6 feet from the ground. The rocks under it have broken away. It is a horizontal figure resting stiffly on its right side. It is clearly of the wondjina type, but presents a few variations from the more usual form. Thus it is marked by an absence of nose as well as of mouth, the beard commences from near the level of the mouth, instead of from a position some distance further down, and the hairs extend about four times further from the ' horseshoe ' head-paint than in the usual figures. These features gave it on first glance the appearance of an owl. Otherwise it resembles the usual type.

" The face, beard, and belt are painted in white clay, the body and legs in red stripes parallel to the waist, on a white ground. The different parts of the body are marked out in red and the hairs are depicted in the same colour. The absence of charcoal is noteworthy. A wondjina head is painted across the ankles, and one foot is missing, probably because the rock-ledge narrows at that part. The total length of the figure is 66 inches ; the width across the eyes and hair, 18 inches.

" Some of the men whom I consulted concerning this picture said it was *Djandad*, the ' thunder man.' They add, however, that he is not really a man, although they describe him as long and ' skinny.' Medicine-men stop the rain by going in a dream up above, hitting *Djandad* with a stone, killing him, and so stopping the rain. Other informants simply called the figure wondjina.

" The third large figure is a very strange one. At first glance it almost suggests a mediaeval knight with his head and shoulders in armour, and, in addition, wearing a triple-pointed crown and holding a white wand in his left hand. The wand, however, appears to be an extension of his thumb. Moreover, on the same side, not far below the elbow, there is a foot which appears to belong to the figure, and just below this again is what looks like a tail.   It may be that one figure, the mailed head and shoulders, has been superimposed on an older picture.   The so-called armour is depicted in red ochre ; below this is part of a figure in red stripes on a white ground which stops short at the break in the rock underneath where there is a small cave.   Thus, the figure, which is upright, may have formerly been longer.   The outlines of the different parts are in red, while the parts of the face and forehead which are visible, the foot, arm, ' wand ' or thumb, and the crown-like arrangement are painted in white.   The tail is yellow.   The total length of the figure from the top of the ' crown ' to the edge of the rock is 43 inches, the width across the shoulder 16 inches, and across the bottom 17 inches.

" My informants called the figure *Djandad* and *Kolini,* that is, they associate it with thunder and rain.   The wand-like projection of the thumb was interpreted as lightning, and so, too, was the ' tail ' ;   the latter was thought by some to be an arm vein.   The three projections above the head which some thought were ears were said to represent the sky, and the red painting round the face and over the shoulders rain.   The part below this, which appears like a garment, was thought to be the chest, and no further meaning was given to it.

" (4) The ceiling or ' roof ' of the rock-ledge.   The ceiling is 12 feet from the ground, and consists of sandstone. There are a few broken rocks, under the ledge, but they are not in such a position as to have served the painters of the pictures on the ceiling.   In former times the floor of the shelter was apparently much higher than at present.   The lower part of the rock-wall, which is protected by the ledge, consists here of a soft thinly-stratified material, while the upper part is of sandstone like the roof.

" The surface of the roof is now rough, having to a large extent fretted away, but there are still traces of a large wondjina figure which was originally 16 feet in length.   The half of the head which can still be seen is 18 inches wide. Traces of the feet and side are discernible.   The workman-ship and general features appear to have been the same when this figure was painted as in the obviously more recent instances. The condition of this painting together with its position suggest that it was made a very long time ago. It is well protected from the weather, as also is the sandstone face on which it is situated, and yet the latter has fretted away.

" The roof section also contains eleven stencilled hands, some in red and others in black. On the side of the rock-wall, just a foot below its junction with the roof, there are a number of pictures, some of which can no longer be deciphered ; in fact, only four can be made out at all. One of these might be a fish and another a leaf or branch. There is also what appears to be a head in profile, painted in reddish-black, but as the rock has partly broken away, no inferences can be drawn from its apparent shape.

" (5) Stone objects associated with this gallery. A round water-worn pebble inside the shelter is said to be the kidney of *Kolini*, though some informants said that it represented his testicles. There are four similar pebbles just outside the shelter, lying at the foot of the cliff. These have a similar significance. With these can be associated two oval objects like eggs, depicted on the wall of the shelter in black outline, one above the other, with a perpendicular line running together. One informant said these were eggs belonging to rain (*Kolini*), but the general opinion was that they were his testicles.

" Two blocks of stone standing about 10 yards apart on the steep slope below the cliff serve each as a table for a stone slab measuring roughly 24 by 1 by 3 inches, and standing on one end supported by two small stones. These artificial arrangements were said by my guide to be ' rain,' and to have been put there by *Ungud*, that is, by some one in times long past.

" I did not have the opportunity to visit any more of these galleries, but I am of the opinion that almost all, if not all, of the hordes of the Ungarinyin tribe, at least as far inland as Mount Barnett, of the Wurara tribe north of Glenelg, and possibly, too, of the Unambal tribe on the north of the Prince Regent River, have each a gallery." It has sometimes been suggested that these remarkable rock-paintings have been created under foreign influence or even by foreigners instead of by the rude natives themselves, but with regard to this suggestion Professor Elkin concludes : " Omitting the hands and feet of the wondjina figures sketched by Grey there is nothing in the workmanship of any of the paintings, so far as I have seen them *in situ* or in photographs, which is beyond the skill of the present natives, or indeed, of a child. Perspective is mostly absent. This applies to the position of the hands and feet and of the head-dress. The feet are depicted as though the soles were in the same plane as the legs. The number of toes and fingers varies from 3 or 4 to 7 on each foot and hand. What my informants say is the beard commences at about the level of the arm-pits. . . . Therefore, as far as workmanship goes, the natives of the district could have originated this form of art.

" Is, then, the subject one that they could have invented without outside suggestion ? Omitting the robe and the supposed characters on the head-dress of one of Grey's sketches and the armour-like covering on one of the strange figures in the Bingi-bi gallery, there do not seem to be any features in the wondjina and associated paintings that might be supposed foreign to the ideas and practices of the natives. Moreover, the admittedly worn state of the painting may have caused Grey to think that the large figure was clothed in a robe. The armour-like covering, too, which I noticed in one case, may have been the result of a flight of fancy or of the continued process of retouching, though, generally speaking, the original patterns are closely followed and not altered.

" The so-called halo represents the red ochre which the natives paint in a band over the front part of the top of the head and down the sides of the face, and the rays are simply the hairs projecting at the back of this. The white dots applied across the red band are so applied in actual life. Apart from the doubtful robe, some observers think that most of the figures are represented clothed. But it is possible that the stripes, dots, and dashes merely represent the paint applied to a man's body for ceremonial purposes. They do not necessarily suggest a robe or trousers, which is not applied direct to the skin. But, of course, we cannot rule out the possibility that they were originally a copy of men in shirts and trousers."[1]

With regard to the interpretation of the paintings, Professor Elkin observes that " if we cannot solve the origin of these paintings, we can now throw a little light on their meaning and function. The heads without mouths, with the peculiar horse-shoe shaped head-dress, and with or without other parts of the body, are called wondjina or, in some parts, *Ungud*. The heads are the essential part of the figures.

" The first, and perhaps primary, significance of wondjina is that of the power that makes, or which is in, the rain. If a wondjina head be retouched, if wondjina be made ' pretty fellow,' rain will fall, even in the 'dry,' as I have shown. The proper time, of course, for this retouching is at the beginning of the ' wet.' The horde of the Ungarinyin tribe which is especially connected with rain (*Kolini*) is *Kalarungeri*, up the Calder River. Rain is the totem of the horde. If the headman dreams that he has visited and ' touched ' the wondjina painting in the gallery of his horde, he tells everybody about it. They then prepare for the rain which must come. Thus to ' touch ' the picture in a dream has the same effect as ' touching ' it in actual fact. But this may only apply to the headman or other members of the rain horde. As far as I can gather, a wondjina picture in the gallery of any horde will bring rain when retouched.

" Connected with its significance as the power that makes rain or through which rain can be made to come, is the association of wondjina with *Ungud*, in the sense that it is the rainbow-serpent. Sometimes it is said that *Ungud*, a large ' quiet ' edible snake, is the mate or totem of wondjina, and therefore it is painted on a gallery beside a wondjina head. But sometimes the term Ungud is used instead of Wondjina and as such it means rain and rainbow, that is, the rainbow-serpent. One informant said that the rainbow was made by *Wondjad* or *Ungud* moving about. The use of the term *Ungud* also connects the paintings with the long-past culture-giving epoch. *Ungud* corresponds in this sense to the Alchera of the Arunta. *Ungud* carries with it an air of

---

[1] A. P. Elkin, " Rock Paintings in North-West Australia," in *Oceania*, vol. i. No. 3 (Dec. 1930), pp. 257-274.

finality. If a thing is *Ungud*, or made by *Ungud*, there is either no more to be said, or else no more will be said even if it were possible for the informant to do so. The wondjina paintings are therefore efficacious because they are *Ungud*, because they were instituted by *Ungud*, or in the *Ungud* time.

" This leads to the further function of the paintings which I mentioned before, namely, that the retouching or painting of certain of them, the female wondjina, causes an increase of babies, for *Ungud*, the rainbow-serpent, makes and brings spirit-babies down in the rain to the water-holes. A man in the Ungarinyin tribe always finds his baby ' along ' water, and it may be in the rain as it falls. This also applies to the Wurara tribe for some, if not for all, babies. *Ungud* is the term for a person's spirit-centre, that is, the place ' along ' water where his father found him (or her). One Ungarinyin informant told me that wondjina offers a man a baby in a dream, or a man in his dream might ask different wondjina for a baby until he receives a good child. This informant said that some wondjina are mean, but this was not the case with the wondjina of Wilin, Red Bull on the Calder River. Apparently a man puts different values on different wondjina, or perhaps we should say, on different manifestations of wondjina. This belief incidentally associates spirit-babies with the *Ungud* time, and probably behind this there is a myth about some being who brought spirit-babies along to certain spots in each horde-territory. . . .

" The wondjina paintings have still another function. Representations of animals and plants painted on a wondjina gallery, with wondjina, as it were, looking on them, lead to an increase of the species so depicted. If wondjina be retouched and so made active, then the species whose paintings are under his aegis will increase. We would reason that if rain is made, the animals and plants will thrive. The black fellow's reasoning appears to be mystical, but I believe that he recognizes that animals and plants require rain. I am unable to say whether all the animals and plants represented on the galleries are edible. I do not know of any that are not. But such a bird as the rain-bird might be painted as an added means of causing rain. The only other objects which I have seen depicted on these galleries are the sun and a piece of yellow ochre. These are both of great social value, the former for obvious reasons and the latter for painting pictures, spear-shafts, and the human body. I was told by the natives that on a gallery or *banja* in Malandu horde-country, wondjina is depicted carrying fire, probably a fire-stick, an object of immense social importance. Dry grass and a bush-fire, that is, grass on fire, not necessarily a devastating fire, are said to be represented on a gallery in Dura country. Such a fire is of social value, for the natives burn off patches of dry grass as a means of hunting out and stupefying the game hidden in the grass, so that they can kill it easily. The fire in this *banja* is associated with a picture of a poisonous snake, Lenyud, and with a myth according to which this snake when caught in a bush-fire rolled himself along for a con-siderable distance, causing, as he did so, the rough country to become a plain. My informants said that they did not eat this snake because it was too ' cheeky,' savage and dangerous. In other words, it is too difficult to obtain. This is to some extent, at least, an exception to the general rule that all the species represented on the rock-galleries are edible, or are usually eaten. I regret that I am unable to give any meaning of the stencilled hands which adorn some of the wondjina galleries. They are not mutilated in any way. Some of them are of great age. Both white and red are used in stencilling, the colouring matter has apparently been blown over the hand, which was applied to the face of the rock. We may guess that the person who left the mark of his hand on the gallery derived some spiritual benefit, but perhaps the stencilling was merely a pastime.

" I was unable to ascertain if wondjina had any influence over the spirits of the dead, but certainly the rock-shelters which are coloured with his paintings are favourite places for the final disposal of the bones of the dead, which have been previously ' buried ' and dried on a tree-stage. This method of burial and final disposal is very honourable, being reserved for initiated men who are not so old as to be con-sidered ' close-up ' dead. The replacing of their bones in the wondjina *banja* may assure them of a full life in the world above to which the dead are said to go. Their bones, by being kept in such places, are in the *Ungud* atmosphere, and so are in touch with their *Ungud* origin. This may be of significance for the deceased.

" In conclusion, all we can say is that the function of the wondjina paintings is to ensure the regular recurrence of the wet season, the normal increase of edible animals and plants and possibly also of useful objects like ochre, the influence of the sun, and the availability of the supply of spirit-children. Man's part is to retouch, perhaps occasionally to paint anew, the wondjina heads and ornaments, and to paint pictures of the desired object and species on the wondjina *banja* or rock-galleries. The efficacy of the special paintings is associated with the fact that they are *Ungud*, that is, belong to the far-past ' creature ' time. Preservation of continuity with this period is essential for present prosperity ; thus the form of the head must not vary, and the figure, in theory at least, should only be retouched, not painted afresh.

" It is perhaps permissible to regard wondjina as the regenerative and reproductive power in nature and man—a power which is especially associated with rain. I am not sure whether wondjina is really thought of in terms of sex. Some of the paintings are said to be women, while other references to wondjina seem to make them male. Then again he is also the rainbow-serpent, and one of his functions as such is to ' make ' spirit-children. He is apparently a generalised power who can be thought of in different ways according to his different functions, in the same way as the natives talk of different wondjina at different *banja*, and yet admit that these beings are ' all one,' ' all the same.' " [1]

I have given Professor Elkin's description of these re-markable monuments together with his lucid and convincing exposition of their meaning because they throw a vivid light on the life and thought, we may even say the philosophy, of the rude aborigines of Australia. The first need of the inhabitants of Australia, whether black or white, is the necessity for the fall of rain, and to the problem of how to procure it the aborigines have clearly devoted much thought and pains. The centres and the records of their thought and efforts are in these painted caverns, which in a sense may

[1] A. P. Elkin, *op. cit.* pp. 273-279.

be said to correspond to our churches, in which they have given expression to their deepest needs and their desire for communion with those spirits to whose keeping they believe the course of Nature to be committed. To their keeping, too, they commit the mouldering remains of their most distinguished dead, just as with us the most illustrious of English dead are laid to their last rest in Westminster Abbey and St. Paul's. On the subject of these monuments I shall have occasion to touch more at length in the sequel. Meantime I would dwell for a little on the figures of wondjina who, in the character of the rainbow-serpent, would seem to have played so great a part in primitive Australian thought, and who, as the supreme controller of the rain, would seem to have corresponded to the part of Zeus in Greek mythology.

Among the natives of the Forrest River District in Kimberley, to the west of Windham and Cambridge Gulf, the rainbow-serpent is called Brimurer or Ungur, and the rainbow is said to be made by a great water snake in stopping rain. This snake lives in big fresh-water holes, but he is also identified with Lumiri, a large salt-water snake who makes the tides by vomiting water, and causes them to ebb by swallowing the water. He is closely connected with the whirlpools which are caused by the rush of the tide in Cambridge Gulf and Forrest River. Indeed he either makes, or he is himself, these whirlpools. The explanation given for a black fellow being drawn down by a whirlpool is that he has touched Lumiri who has thereupon dragged him under. The phosphorescence seen in these waters marks Lumiri's presence.

Further, the rainbow-water-serpent is the ultimate source of a medicine-man's powers. A medicine-man is "made" by a fully qualified practitioner, who takes the novice with him up to the sky. One way in which he does this is to assume the form of a skeleton and to fasten to his body a pouch in which he places the novice who has been reduced to the size of a very small child. Then sitting astride the rainbow-serpent, he pulls himself up with an arm-over-arm action as on a rope. When he is near the top, he throws the novice out of the pouch on the sky, thus "killing" him. Having reached the zenith, he inserts into the young man some little rainbow-snakes, *brimurer*, and some quartz-crystals which are called *ungur*, the other term applied to the rainbow-serpent. It is doubtful whether the medicine-man finds these magical objects in the sky or has secured them on earth before his ascent ; but certainly it is believed that he can find them on earth at the foot of the rainbow. If he sees a Brimurer in a water-hole, he enters the pool and seizing the snake he obtains the various magical objects which he needs for initiating the novice into his profession. These objects are quartz-crystals, little rainbow-snakes, and also kandila ; these last are said to resemble crooked teeth, and when inserted into the novice, to make him clever.

After receiving these precious objects in his body, the novice is brought down from the sky on the back of the rainbow-serpent in the same way that he went up, namely sitting astride of the rainbow and sliding or pulling himself down hand over hand. The wizard then inserts more of these magical objects into the body of the novice through his navel, after which he wakes him up from his sleep of death with a magic stone. The young man then returns to his normal size and next day practises climbing up to the sky on the back of the rainbow-serpent. Thus the making and powers of the medicine-man are closely associated with the rainbow-serpent, which affords him access to the sky-world. Small snakes of that species are amongst the objects from which he derives his powers, while some of the other magical substances he gets from the rainbow-serpent in a water-hole at the foot of the rainbow. And lest common folk should learn the secret of the medicine man's power, or the " make-believe " on which it may be founded, he forbids them, on pain of death by drowning, to enter the water-hole over which they may see a rainbow passing.[1]

With regard to a belief in the rainbow-serpent among the tribes of South-East Australia, that is, of Victoria and New South Wales, Professor Radcliffe-Brown writes as follows : " In 1920 I published in the *Journal of the Royal Anthropological Institute* a short paper on the rainbow-serpent myth in Australia, in which I pointed out its widespread distribution in many parts of the continent. My studies of Australian

[1] A. P. Elkin, " The Rainbow-Serpent Myth in North-West Australia," in *Oceania*, vol. i. No. 3, pp. 349-351.

beliefs had led me to the conclusion that this particular myth is one of the most important of the mythology, and that fuller knowledge of it is necessary in any attempt we may make to understand the Australian conception of Nature. Recent field researches in the northern parts of Australia have amply confirmed this surmise.

" This myth is a belief in a gigantic serpent which has its home in deep and permanent water-holes and represents the element of water which is of such vital importance to man in all parts of Australia. The serpent is often regarded as being visible to human eyes in the form of the rainbow. The rainbow serpent as it appears in Australian belief may with some justification be described as occupying the position of a deity, and perhaps the most important Nature-deity. In some tribes it is the object of a definite cult either as part of the totemic cult or as part of the cult of the initiation ceremonies. In a considerable number of tribes it is the chief source, or one of the chief sources, of the magical powers possessed by the medicine-man. There is a very widespread association of quartz-crystals with the rainbow-serpent, and throughout Australia quartz crystals are amongst the most important of the magical substances used by the medicine-man.[1]

" So far as our present knowledge goes there is only one region of Australia in which this belief seems to be absent. Mr. Hart was unable to find any trace of it in the Tiwi of Melville and Bathurst Islands. The Tiwi also appear to have no medicine-man, and thus to be unique amongst Australian tribes.

" During recent field-work in New South Wales I was able to obtain a few further scraps of information on this subject. It is unfortunately now too late to study the belief in any detail in the surviving tribes of South-East Australia. The myths of this kind were an essential part of the Bora ceremonies for the initiation of the young men, and were kept alive by being repeated at these ceremonies. Even the oldest men know very little about them, and can hardly be

---

[1] The association of quartz crystals with the rainbow may perhaps be due to the possibility of seeing the rainbow colours (the colours of the spectrum) through these crystals.—J. G. F.

got to talk about them. The Bora ceremonies have been discontinued for many years.

" In Wiradjeri, Wongaibon, and Weilwan the rainbow-serpent was called *wawi*. The rainbow itself is called *yulubirgi* in Wongaibon, but is described as all the same as *wawi*. In the Kanularoi and Jualarai tribes the name was *karia*, the rainbow itself being called *yuluwiri*. The same name *karia* also appears in the Kwiambal tribe. In the Aneuan tribe of New England[1] the rainbow-serpent was called *kabulgan* or *abulgan*. In the Kagai tribe there is a gigantic mythical serpent called *numdanara*, but it is not certain that this is associated with the rainbow. This information, however, was given to me by a woman, and it is probable that many of the beliefs about the rainbow-serpent were known to the men only.

" The rainbow-serpent lives in deep permanent lagoons and water-holes. In the New England tableland it is particularly associated with waterfalls, possibly because at such places rainbows may frequently be seen. Thus I was told that there was formerly one at Walcha in a pool below a waterfall near where the waterfall now stands. There is said to be one in the waterfall at Waterloo.

" Throughout these tribes there is a belief that the serpent will devour human beings who approach its home unless they are medicine-men. An informant in New England compared the *kabulgan* to a shark.

" In all the tribes mentioned it was believed that the medicine-men derived their power from the rainbow-serpent. A man who had already obtained some magical power would go into the pool inhabited by the serpent. I was not able to obtain any account of what was supposed to happen to him there.

" The most interesting point, however, is that a cult of the *wawi* or *karia* was often an element of the Bora or initiation ceremonies of the New South Wales tribes. Many of the sacred Bora grounds had a representation of the serpent in the form of a sinuous mound of earth up to 40 feet or more in length. In preparation for the ceremony the

[1] New England is the name of a district in the north of New South Wales.

serpent was painted. A ceremony took place at the spot and the beliefs about the rainbow-serpent were explained to the younger men who were attending the initiation. . . .

" It is highly unlikely that we shall be able to obtain any more detailed information about the myth from the surviving remnants of the tribes of Victoria and New South Wales. It is clear, however, from the above, that the myth was an important element of the native beliefs in this region. The rainbow-serpent may be said to be the most important representation of the creative and destructive power of Nature, principally in connection with rain and water. It is apparently as such that it played an important part in the initiation ceremonies of some of the tribes of this region." [1]

Before quitting the subject of these remarkable rock-paintings, work of rude Australian savages, I would briefly point to the analogy which may be traced between them and the prehistoric paintings, of a much higher type of art, which in recent times have been discovered on the walls of many caves in southern France and northern Spain. These paintings depict a large number of different animals, mostly edible, sometimes attacked by men armed with bows and arrows or spears. In one of them, for example, we see a wounded bison with three arrows sticking in its flank. In another a hunter armed with bow and arrow faces a stag which defiantly puts out its tongue, while a little above we see a further group where arrows have flown and a stag transfixed limps painfully away. To add to the resemblance of these cave-paintings to the rock-paintings of Australia it should be said that the European paintings are often situated in dark recesses of the caves, to which access is difficult, the enquirer having sometimes to squeeze himself through narrow openings or to crawl on his belly through low passages in order to view them. Various theories have been put forward to explain them, but the opinion to which the best authorities seem now to incline is the one which was first put forward, so far as I know, by my learned friend, the late Salomon Reinach, namely, that the paintings were designed to secure

[1] A. R. Radcliffe-Brown, "The Rainbow-Serpent Myth in South-East Australia," in *Oceania*, vol. i. No. 3 (Dec. 1930), pp. 342-347.

success in the chase of edible animals by means of sympathetic or imitative magic.[1]

It is interesting to observe how primitive man on opposite sides of the world has resorted to exactly the same magical means in order to satisfy the first and most imperious of human wants, the need for food.

To complete the resemblance of the European to the Australian cave-paintings, it is only necessary to add that in both the impression of an outstretched hand, whether stencilled or painted, is a common adjunct of the other pictures on the walls of the cave. It has been suggested by Professor R. A. S. Macalister that the symbol of the hand is a charm designed to counteract any evil magic that might otherwise thwart and defeat the beneficent effect of the other magical paintings on walls of the cave. The symbol of an outstretched hand, whether in flesh and blood or sculptured or painted, is still a very common charm to counteract the supposed disastrous effect of the evil eye in Southern Europe. Symbols of the same sort designed for the same purpose, Professor Macalister tells us, are everywhere to be seen in the peasant villages of Palestine, where they are impressed on the walls of houses, round the doors, on store-chambers and cattle stalls and so forth, and in a modified and conventionalised form tatooed on the faces of women.[2]

---

[1] S. Reinach, " L'art et la Magie," in *Cultes, Mythes et Religions* (Paris, 1905), i. pp. 125-135. As to the European cave paintings see R. A. S. Macalister, *A Text Book of European Archaeology*, i. (Cambridge, 1921), pp. 455-510; M. C. Burkitt, *Our Forerunners* (H.U.L., 1923), pp. 158-224; id. *The Old Stone Age* (Cambridge, 1933), pp. 174-228.

[2] R. A. S. Macalister, *op. cit.* p. 509.

THE evidence as to the totemism and social organisation of the tribes inhabiting the extreme south-western corner of Australia is imperfect, confused, and conflicting. In these circumstances I cannot do better than quote the account of it given by our experienced authority Professor Radcliffe-Brown, who has personally investigated the region and questioned the few survivors of the tribes.

"This area consists of a portion of the south-west of Western Australia, bounded by the west coast, from about Jurien Bay to somewhere in the neighbourhood of Cape Lieuwin, and extending inland in the latitude of Perth for 150 miles or more. The names of the tribes that formerly occupied the region are not known, and little is known with any certainty about the social organization.

"It is difficult to reconcile the statements of the early observers, Sir George Grey and Bishop Salvado, with the later accounts of Mrs. D. M. Bates and with the scanty information I was able to glean in 1910, and there is not space here for a critical discussion.

"Throughout the area the natives were divided into two exogamous moieties named Manitjmat and Wardangmat, after *manitj*, white cockatoo, and *wardan*, crow. (These moieties were first recorded for this region by Mrs. Bates, and were not recorded by Grey or Salvado.) In addition to the moieties there were other matrilineal divisions with names Balarak, Tondarap, Didarak, etc. The number of these cannot be determined with certainty. Mrs. Bates thinks there were really only four, Tondarap and Didarak belonging to the Manitjmat moiety and Balarak and Nagarnuk to the Wardangmat.   But this conflicts with the information given by Grey and by Salvado.

" The kinship system has not been fully recorded, but my own information, which is woefully incomplete, led me to the conclusion that it was apparently not of the Kariera type but might perhaps be near to the Aranda type.

" Since these tribes possessed the normal division into patrilineal hordes, and the moieties and named divisions mentioned above were matrilineal, it follows that each horde contained men of both moieties and of more than one named division. I gathered a little evidence, not conclusive, that the horde was exogamous.

" The named divisions Balarak, etc., may perhaps be regarded as being totemic. Grey says that they derived their names, at any rate in some instances, from animals.   Thus the Nagarnuk were named after a small fish, *nagaru*, and the Balarak after a small species of opossum, *balard*.   Grey also reports statements of the natives that these ' families ' as he calls them had their origin in species of birds transformed into men. Thus the Ngontak came from the mountain duck, the Didarak and Tondarap from two species of waterfowl, and the Balarak from the swan.

" I obtained evidence that natural species were classified under these divisions. Thus the tree used for making spears belongs to the Tondarap division.

" Besides these matrilineal totemic divisions, if we are to regard them as such, there was another system of totemic groups. Mrs Bates states that every person had a totem denoted as *borong* and that the totems were hereditary and that they belonged to the holders of the totems' water-holes, or to the occupants of the land in the vicinity of these waters. As the land was possessed by the hordes and inherited in the male line, it follows that these totems would be patrilineal.

" My own information agrees partly but not entirely with this statement.   There was a system of local totemic centres or totemic districts similar to that which we have noted. The whole country, in other words, contained a number of roughly defined districts, each of which was associated with some particular species of plant or animal which was plentiful in it.

My best informant stated that an individual had as his totem the species associated with the district in which he was born. Thus my informant's father was Manitjmat and Tondarap, and had as his totem the swan. His mother was Wardangmat and Balarak and her totem was an acacia of which the gum is used for food. My informant was Wardangmat Balarak, like his mother. He was born in a *kwamar* (honey-bearing flower) country near Beverley, and this was therefore his totem. It is possible that when my informant spoke of the country in which he was born he may have meant that in which he was *conceived*, but that this might be so only occurred to me when it was too late to pursue enquiries further.

" Though this seems to conflict with the statements of Mrs. Bates, I think it does not really do so. Probably the territory of each horde included several totemic centres or districts, which would therefore all belong to the same patrilineal horde and there would therefore be a sort of patrilineal determination of the totem. It would seem that persons of both matrilineal moieties and of any matrilineal divisions might have the same totem, but even this is not quite certain.

" There is a little evidence, not quite satisfactory, that there were localized ceremonies of *talu* type for the increase of the totem species.

" It is unlikely that we shall obtain any further information about these tribes. We can only affirm that they possessed (1) a division into matrilineal moieties, (2) other matrilineal divisions of a totemic or quasi-totemic character, and (3) a system of local totem-centres, probably with increase rites of the *talu* type, the totem of an individual being normally determined through the patrilineal horde." [1]

---

[1] A. R. Radcliffe-Brown, "The Social Organization of Australian Tribes," pp. 43-45, citing G. Grey, *Journals of Two Expeditions of Discovery*; R. Salvado, *Memorie Storiche dell' Australia* (Rome, 1851), and Mrs. D. M. Bates, " Tribus du Sud-Ouest de l'Australie," in *Revue d'Ethnographie*, vol. iv. (1923) pp. 225-240.

CHAPTER VIII

WORKING under the auspices of the Australian National Research Council, Professor Elkin investigated the social and totemic organisation of the remaining tribes in the state of South Australia. His researches embraced the part, of the State lying north and west of a line connecting Adelaide and Broken Hill, and lasted from February to December 1930. A great part of the area which he examined, while it belongs politically to the state of South Australia, belongs geographically to the centre of the continent. This is true particularly of the tribes about Lake Eyre, including the important tribe of the Dieri, which I have dealt with in my former work, *Totemism and Exogamy*. In what follows I will adhere closely to the lucid exposition which Professor Elkin gives of his own personal researches.

The tribes investigated by Professor Elkin may be divided into two major groups : (1) an eastern or " Lakes " group and (2) a western group, separated roughly by a line drawn from about Charlotte Waters to Oodnadatta, Stuart Range, Lake Gairdner, and Venus Bay. The former group also includes the tribes in the south-western corner of Queensland, while the latter includes tribes in the south-western corner of Central Australia and in the south-east of Western Australia. Further, (3) a southern portion or sub-tribe of the Arunta (Aranda) occupies the country along the Macumba River almost to Lake Eyre, which runs into the Lake at its north-west corner, and so forms a buffer between the northern tribes of the first two groups, and (4) the Naranggu tribe, which formerly inhabited Yorke Peninsula on the south of the eastern groups. In what follows, Professor Elkin gives a brief outline of the social organisation, mythology, and ritual of these tribes.

I. *Eastern or " Lakes " Group*

First as to the eastern or " Lakes " group, the tribes included in this group are, commencing from the north-eastern corner: the Yelyuyendi, Ngameni, and Wongkongaru on the Diamentina and the country north of it ; the Marula, Yauarawaka, Yantruwanta, and Dieri on the Cooper ; the Piladapa on the southern reaches of the Strzelecki and around Lake Callabonna ; the Arabana (Urabunna) and Tirari on the west and south of Lake Eyre respectively ; the Wailpi or Anyamatana on the northern part of Flinders Range ; the Kwiani around the north and north-east of Lake Torrens ; the Pankala on the south and west of the same Lake and on the northern part of Eyre's Peninsula ; the Naua on the southern end of this peninsula ; the Nukuna on the eastern shore of Spencer Gulf between Port Augusta and Yorke Peninsula which was inhabited by the Naranggu ; the Ngaluri on the east of the Nukuna ; the Yadliaura between the Flinders Range and Lake Frome ; the Wadikali between the latter and the New South Wales border ; the Wilyali on the south of the Wadikali ; the Bolali around Broken Hill and the Wilyakali between that town and Tibooburra in New South Wales (the last three were probably sub-tribes of one tribe, which seems to be referred to as the Wilya, and possessed the moiety terms of the Darling River tribes) ; and the Malyanapa, which was mostly in the far north-western corner of New South Wales but belonged to the Lakes group of South Australia.

The main features common to these tribes are : the division into named matrilineal moieties each of which consists of a number of totemic clans.

Certain features of their kinship system, which distinguish them from those of the western group and from the Arunta (Aranda), especially the use of one term for father's mother's brother and mother's brother's son, and one term, frequently the same one, for father's mother and mother's brother's daughter.

The possession, at least by all the northern tribes of the group, of a patrilineal totemism of the *talu* or increase type, and in nearly all cases, combined with this, a matrilineal totemism of the same kind.

Sex totemism and dream totemism.

A type of mythology in which heroes are called Mura-mura. The exploits of these heroes carried them from south-western Queensland to Eyre's Peninsula.

The *wilyaru* rite, the highest stage of initiation, the outward pattern of which is a particular pattern of cicatrisa-tion, consisting of two vertical rows of short parallel scars.[1]

The Moiety System.—The names of the moieties vary in different parts of the area, though the names Matari and Kararu range from the Wonkamala and Wongkongaru on the north to the Ngaluri, Pankala, and Naua on the south. The Yantruwanta, Yauarawaka, Piladapa, Malyanapa, and Wadikali use Kulpuru and Tiniwa as the names of the moieties. The Marula, Yelyuyendi, and Ngulubulu, use Parkata and Wuturu. The Karuwali, according to one member of the tribe, use Matura and Wuturu. Professor Elkin could not obtain sufficient information to enable him to decide whether the Karuwali which joins the Marula on the north-east belongs to the Lakes group or not. The Wilyali, Bolali, and Wilyakali use the moiety names Makwara and Kilpara.

There appears to be only one headman for each moiety. This is definitely the case with the remaining Wailpi. His word is final, especially at secret gatherings or concerning secret matters. The position of moiety-headman passes from a man to his son's son, if the latter be sufficiently old and learned, otherwise a brother of the retiring or deceased headman, ᴠ·some other respected member of the moiety, succeeds him. A man's son is not eligible, for he belongs to the opposite moiety. Such a headman is distinct from the headman of a patrilineal ceremonial totemic clan. The position of the latter passes from father to son.

The moiety organisation functions in initiation and burial ceremonies, in marriage, in a system of settling differences,

[1] A. P. Elkin, " The Social Organ- in *Oceania*, vol. ii. No. 1 (Sept. 1931), ization of South Australian Tribes," pp. 44-53.

called *kopara*, in various secret matters, and in camping arrangements.[1]

Kinship System in the Lakes Area.—Three types of kinship organisation can be distinguished in the Lakes area. (i) The Dieri type is found in the Dieri, Yantruwanta, Yauarawaka, northern Wongkongaru, Piladapa, Yadliaura, and Marula tribes. Its main features are the counting of descent through four lines, whether through males or females, and the use of one term (*kami*) for father's mother and her brother on the one hand, and for mother's brother's (or father's sister's) children on the other. This feature distinguishes the Dieri from systems like the Arunta (Aranda) of Central Australia and the Nyul-Nyul of the Kimberlies, in which the term for mother's brother's (or father's sister's) daughter is the same as for mother's mother's brother's wife. Further, the Dieri lacks the characteristic of many tribes of the Arunta (Aranda) type, in which one term is applied to mother's mother and her brother on the one hand, and to the latter's son's children on the other hand. Instead, in the Dieri system, mother's mother's brother's son's children are classed with brother and sister, or what is much the same, with *yenku*, father's father and his sister. Another feature of the Dieri system is marriage with the mother's mother's brother's daughter's daughter. This, which may be regarded as the typical marriage, is generally put in another way, namely, that the children of two women related to one another as cross-cousins intermarry.

Apart from the exceptions which follow, cross-cousin marriage is forbidden in this north-western corner. But in the Yauarawaka a man may marry his cross-cousin. This, however, may only be the result of the difficulty of finding spouses in accordance with the old law in the present depleted condition of the tribe. The prohibition on cross-cousin marriage has been relaxed as in exceptional cases amongst the Dieri.

(ii) The southern tribes of the Lakes Group possess a kinship system of the Kariera type. Descent is reckoned through two lines only, and a man may marry his own mother's brother's daughter, or his own father's sister's

[1] A. P. Elkin, *op. cit.* pp. 53-54.

daughter, or any other woman classified with her.   In conformity with this, a man's children's spouses are called by the terms for sister's children.   One interesting feature in the Wailpi and Pankala systems which shows their affinity to the Dieri type is that mother's brother's daughter and son are classed respectively with father's mother and the latter's brother, though the terms are changed to those for wife and wife's brother in the event of cross-cousin marriage.

(iii) The Urabunna (Arabana) and southern Wongkongaru in the north-west of the Lakes area, and the Wilyali and probably also the Malyanapa in the south-east, have systems which fall between those of the Dieri and Wailpi.

The tracing of descent, as far as terminology goes, is through three lines, namely father's mother's brother, mother's father, and father's father.   The prohibition of cross-cousin marriage is in force.   Marriage in these four tribes is with the usual four types of second cousins associated with systems of the Dieri and Arunta (Aranda) types, though some Urabunna (Arabana) informants were inclined to think that such marriages were too close.   One term is in use for mother's brother's son and father's mother's brother as in the Dieri type.[1]

TOTEMISM IN THE LAKES AREA.—Five kinds of totemism, distinguished by their function and descent, may be distinguished in the tribes around Lake Eyre and on the Cooper and Diamentina Rivers.   It is now too late to decide whether they were all formerly present in the southern part of the area.

Matrilineal Social Totemism.—Each moiety consists of a number of totemic social groups or clans, which like itself are matrilineal and exogamous, and none of which appear in both moieties in any one tribe.   A person does not eat this totem. It is his flesh, and comes from his mother just as his own actual flesh comes from her.   These social totems are almost all edible.   This form of totemism certainly extended south to the Pankala, if not also to the Naua.

Patrilineal Ceremonial Totemism.—Each man inherits from his father a totem name—usually different from the social totem inherited from his mother—a piece of country with which this totem and a Mura-mura or culture hero were

---

[1] A. P. Elkin, *op. cit.* pp. 55-57.

associated in the past, a myth enshrining the story of this, and a ceremony the performance of which usually brings about an increase of the totemic species concerned, which are only commemorative of the ancient hero. This totem is called *pintara* by the Dieri, *ularaga* by the Urabunna (Arabana) and Wongkongaru, and *nari* by most of the tribes in the north-east of the area.

Each of these ceremonial clans has a headman. The office is hereditary from father to son, provided that the son be old enough, fully initiated and sufficiently well versed in the myth and ritual. The *pintara* (totem ceremony) must be performed by the *pintara* men, though they are assisted by their sister's sons. The former own the *pintara*, though the latter are said to be the " bosses " of the performance, and must see that it takes place. Like the *pintara* men, they have learnt the myth and ritual, and are concerned about the commemoration of the totemic culture heroes, the Mura-mura, and their institutions, and also are vitally interested in rites with which the maintenance of the food supply is associated. The ownership of the *pintara* by the *pintara* men is shown by the fact that after the increase of the species consequent upon the performance of the rite, they must be the first to eat of it, after which they give leave to their " sisters' sons " and then to all others to eat it. Henceforth they themselves as well as others eat freely of it. This point differentiates this *pintara* totemism from the ceremonial totemism in the Arunta (Aranda) tribe as recorded by Spencer and Gillen. Further, a man will not let anyone waste any of the species which is his *pintara*.

Matrilineal Ceremonial Totemism.—This form of totemism was implied in the reference in the preceding section to the " sisters' sons." It is almost the same as the *pintara* type, except for the rule of descent and the somewhat inferior position of the totemite to the totem, its myth and ritual. This totem is called *maduka* amongst most of the northeastern tribes, though the Urabunna (Arabana) refer to it as *abalga*, and the Yantruwanta use the term *amata*. The relation of the two totems is as follows : in addition to inheriting the *pintara* from his father, a man also inherits his mother's brother's *pintara*, which then becomes his *maduka* (or *amata*).

This means that he learns the myth and ritual of the mother's brother's *pintara*, and may visit the sacred site and assist in the ritual as already mentioned. His children do not inherit his *maduka*.

Both men and women inherit *pintara* and *maduka*, but the women have the name only and do not learn the myths nor see the ritual, while the men only do so—according to the old law—after having passed through the *wilyaru*, the highest stage of initiation.

This combined form of patrilineal and matrilineal cere-monial totemism extends from the west side of Lake Eyre into south-western Queensland through the Urabunna (Ara-bana), Dieri, Wongkongaru, Ngameni, Piladapa, Yauara-waka, Yantruwanta, and Marula tribes.

Dream Totemism.—Each person is represented in dreams by some plant, animal, or object, which is his dream totem. To dream of his totem is to know that the person represented will soon appear. This totem is the same as a person's patrilineal ceremonial totem. The possession of a dream totem is common to all the tribes of the group from the Wailpi north.

Sex Totemism.—In all the northern tribes of the group each sex has a plant totem or emblem called by the Dieri and Urabunna (Arabana) *nambu*, and by the tribes further north-east *amama*. The former word means " mate " or " guardian," and the latter " uncle "—" mother's brother." This form of totemism seems to be only a " play " or sportive type. One sex teases the other by pulling its " mate," retaliation follows, if possible, and a fight may ensue. Each sex must look after its " mate " or " uncle."

II. *The Western Group*

The Western Group of South Australian tribes is char-acterised by a remarkable unity of language, mythology, and social organisation. The Aluridja occupy the strip of country along the west of the Finke River from about the South Australian border to Hermannsburg, while the Pidjintara (or Pitjintara) belong to the north-west of the Musgrave Ranges. The Aluridja, Maiulatara, and Pidjintara are really in Central Australia, but their social organisation, mythology, and to some extent their languages justify us in grouping them with the western South Australian group. For the same reasons the natives of south-east central Western Australia may be included in this group.

Only a small portion of the area under consideration is settled by whites, namely a strip of a hundred miles or so in width on the east and along the southern coast. The rest of the area is for all practical purposes waterless. The rainfall is scanty and irregular, and much of the country is sandy.[1]

The tribes of the Western Group are characterised by a number of common features in their social organisation and beliefs, which not only serve to link them together, but also to mark them off from the Eastern Group. These are :—

The absence of moieties or the dual organisation.
The kinship system.
A variety of local totemism in which a person's totem is
    determined by his place of birth.
The mythological theme.
Dream totemism.
Belief in spirit-children.
The pattern of cicatrisation which marks the fully initiated
    man.

The Absence of Dual Organisation.—A casual observer might think that the two terms *Nganandaga* and *Tanamild-jan*, which he would most likely receive in response to enquiries for moiety and section names, denote moieties. This, however, is not so. The term *Tanamildjan* is used reciprocally between persons of one generation and the generations one above and one below—for example, between a man and his father or his son. On the other hand, *Nganandaga* is used between persons of the one generation, and also between a person and others of his grandparents' and grandchildren's generations, for example, between a man and his wife's brother, his father's mother, or his son's daughter. Further, a man's spouse must be *Nganandaga*, and therefore cannot belong to the generation one above or one below himself. Thus in this matter, these reciprocal terms lead to the same

[1] A. P. Elkin, *op. cit.* pp. 61-62.

result as the four-section system.   Indeed some tribes with four-section systems have in addition reciprocal terms for members of the intermarrying pairs of sections and also for the sections of parents and children.   Incidentally the former pair of sections includes a person's grandparents and grandchildren.

The absence of the moiety division is reflected in the kinship system in several features, such as mother's mother's brother's son is called by the term for mother's brother instead of by the term for father, as would be the case in the moiety system ; and again, mother's brother's children are not merely regarded as brothers and sisters as sometimes happens in tribes with the dual organisation when crosscousin marriage is prohibited, but they are called by the terms for brother and sister.

In the Wirangu and in the northern Madutara and amongst the Musgrave blacks, the absence of the moiety system permits the multiplication of " mother's brothers " or possible fathers-in-law, for both the mother's brother's son and the father's sister's son of both mother and father are all four called " mother's brother," instead of two only of these being so called, and two being called " father " as would be the case in a moiety system.   As wife's father is always a tribal or legal " mother's brother," this doubles the number of potential fathers-in-law.[1]

The Kinship System.—All the tribes of the Western Group have practically the same kinship system, and, indeed, use much the same terms.   It is marked by a paucity of terms as compared with the systems of the Eastern Group or of the Arunta (Aranda).   Only two terms are used for all persons of the second ascending generation, and in some of the southern hordes only one term for own son and sister's son, and one term for own daughter and sister's daughter, and cross-cousins are called brother and sister.   But in spite of this descent is reckoned through four lines as amongst the Dieri and Arunta (Aranda).

The marriage rule is similar in some respects to that which operates in the Dieri tribe ; cross-cousin marriage is prohibited, and certain types of second-cousin marriage are

[1] A. P. Elkin, *op. cit.* pp. 65-66.

usually allowed. But there is a difference in the type of second cousin. In the Dieri, children of two women or of two men who are related as cross-cousins, own or tribal, may marry, and no others may do so unless the irregularity be specially adjusted. The type marriage is with mother's mother's brother's daughter's daughter. But in the northern Madutara and in the Wirangu a man may marry the daughter of a man who in terminology is either his mother's or his father's cross-cousin, that is, who is son's daughter of mother's mother's brother, mother's father's sister, father's mother's brother, or father's father's sister. In the southern Madutara and in the Mulatara a man may marry the daughter of a man who is cross-cousin of his mother, or of a woman who is his father's cross-cousin, that is, he marries the son's daughter of his mother's mother's brother or mother's father's sister, or the daughter's daughter of his father's mother's brother or father's father's sister.

The tribes of south-east central Western Australia have almost the same kinship terminology as the Madutara, but they fit it into a four-section system, which has spread to them from their north-west. There are two sets of section names in this region. The first belongs to the district on the east of Laverton, and is Karimara-Burunga, Tararu-Panaka. If Paldjeri were substituted for Tararu, we would have the section names which prevail in the southern Kimberley, with only the slight variation of Karimara for Karimba. The other set of terms belongs to the Mandjinda on the north-east of Laverton, and is Milanga-Burunga, Tararu-Ibarga.

The general marriage rule is that a man marries the daughter of a " mother's brother " from " long-way," and that usually a man does not marry his own second cousin.[1]

Local Totemism.—The totemism which is common to all the tribes of this area north of the East-West Line both in South and Western Australia, is a variety of local totemism. A person's totem depends on his place of birth and the totem associated with that place. Further, this totemism is ceremonial ; the totemite, if he is a fully initiated male, is taught the myth and ceremonies which enshrine the story of the culture hero or heroes associated with the totem, and in

[1] A. P. Elkin, *op. cit.* pp. 67-69.

some cases also, when such exists, the *talu* or increase
ceremony which is supposed to ensure the increase of the
totem.   The *talu* ceremonies do not seem to exist south of a
line drawn west of Oodnadatta.   These ceremonies are, of
course, associated with certain sacred sites.   The southern
hordes merely sing to make the species increase, but the
explanation of this may be that having migrated from the
homes of their fathers in the north, where the *talu* sanctuaries
are situated, they are not disposed to travel back over the
desert for the ceremonies.   Females know the name of their
totem, but neither the myth nor the ceremony.   A person
does not eat his totem, and he feels grieved when he sees
another man kill it.[1]

Mythology.—The tribes of this group at least north of the
East-West Line possess a mythology which is marked everywhere by a common theme.   This is associated with the
totemism of the area and enshrines the exploits of the totemic
heroes of the time long past.   The one term *djugur* denotes
a person's totem and the myth of his particular totemic hero.
Thus, when asked for his *djugur*, a man gives in reply the
name of some animal, plant, or object, or, very occasionally,
merely the personal name of an ancient hero, and then, in
order to complete his answer, goes on to recount the myth
of the hero who also bore the name of the same totem,
travelled about his (the speaker's) horde-country, and probably
performed some exploit or other at or near the spot where he
was born.   A man's *djugur* (totem) is often the same as his
father's seeing that each horde has the same waters and
country, and that a man and his children are very likely to be
born somewhere along the route of the same totemic hero.

This variety of local totemism is similar to the conceptional variety of local totemism of the Arunta (Aranda)
tribe at Alice Springs, in that a person's totem depends
somewhat on chance, and that the members of one totem
tend to belong to the one local horde.   But here the fortuit-
ousness lies in the accident of birth and not conception.
There is no doubt about this in any part of the western
area.[2]

Dream Totemism.—The dream totem in all the tribes of

---

[1] A. P. Elkin, *op. cit.* p. 69.   [2] A. P. Elkin, *op. cit.* pp. 69-70.

the Western Group in South Australia is the *djugur* : that is, if a person dreams of a *djugur* or local totem, a person belonging to that totem will soon come along to the dreamer. But just west of the north-western corner of this state, the dream totem is the species associated with a person's conception.[1]

Spirit-children Beliefs.—All the western tribes of South Australia believe that a definite place (or, perhaps, a few places), called Yualanya, is the abode of pre-existent spirit-children. This has nothing to do with the totem of a child. Children of different totems may all come from the one Yualanya. Having left the spot, some of them are believed to play about on the flowers of the mulga trees. The spirit-home is described as a rock-hole, possibly a cave, containing water, with a sand-hill near by. Women must be very careful how they approach and obtain water at such a place, or else spirit-children may enter them.

In the north-eastern part of the area, the spirit-child changes its sex at incarnation. Thus a woman who dreams that a girl-spirit has entered her womb will give birth to a son.

The tribes of south-east central Western Australia who visit Laverton and Mount Margaret believe that spirit-children enter women in the guise of food. If after having eaten something a woman is sick, and later on dreams of a spirit-child, she believes that when she thought she was eating food a spirit-baby had entered her. Some years after birth the child is informed of its mode of entry into the mother's womb, that is, of the particular article of food (some animal or plant) associated with the mother's first sickness of pregnancy. This animal or plant then becomes the child's dream totem, that is, his symbol in another person's dream. Informants told Professor Elkin that conception could not take place apart from eating " child-food." [2]

Cicatrisation.—The pattern of cicatrisation on the backs of all fully initiated men in this area is the same. It consists of two sets of six or eight slightly curved parallel scars made in an upright position down from each shoulder. Two horizontal scars are raised under each of these two series.

[1] A. P. Elkin, *op. cit.* p. 70.   [2] A. P. Elkin, *op. cit.* pp. 70-71.

This pattern is called *yileri* in the south-western corner of the state, and is a sign of complete initiation.[1]

III. *The Macumba Sub-tribe of the Arunta (Aranda)*

This sub-tribe possesses four marriage sections—Kamara-Pultara and Pananga-Purula.   Each intermarrying pair applies the term Nyurba to the other pair, and the members of each such pair of sections refer to each other as *Unangara* or *Unara*.   These terms are the equivalents repectively of *Tanamildjan* and *Nganandaga*, amongst the tribes of the Western Group.

The kinship terms are slightly different from those formerly used by the Arunta (Aranda) at Alice Springs, but the system is the same.   Incidentally, the prohibition of cross-cousin marriage implies the halving of each section, and this is recognised by the natives.

Each person has two totems.   One is associated with the place of birth.   This local totem, called *inanwa* or *inigwa* and also *aknanindja*, is the equivalent of the *djugur* of the Western Group.   The manner of acquirement, namely, through being born in a certain totemic locality, while it is the same as in the case of the Western *djugur*, is different from that which prevails amongst the northern Arunta (Aranda), where the totem is determined by the place of conception.   Further, the local totemism of the Macumba sub-tribe tends to become patrilineal in transmission, for children are frequently born in their father's *inanwa* country. Again, a man may give his *inanwa* to his sons, or for that matter to other men also, if he needs their help for the ceremonies connected with it.   Sometimes, too, men refer to the *inanwa* species as " father," a sort of ancestor in the patrilineal line.   But in the ordinary course of events a man's children may be born out of his *inanwa* country, and, in such a case, will have different *inanwa* from his, though he may give them his, which they will then possess in addition to their own.

The *inanwa* (local totem) includes the name of a national species, association through a myth with a definite locality, songs, myth, and ceremonies, and in some instances at least,

[1] A. P. Elkin, *op. cit.* p. 71.

talu ritual for the increase of the natural species. In the *talu* ritual the totemite is assisted by other fully initiated men with the same *inanwa* (local totem), and also those whose *altjira*, to be mentioned presently, is the same as his *inanwa*. These *talu* ceremonies seem to have different names according to the particular totems.

Women have *inanwa*, but do not learn the myths or rituals connected with it

The other totem which each person possesses is his *altjira*. This is really the *inanwa* (local totem) of his mother and mother's brother, but becomes, as it were, his secondary totem, linking him to his mother's brother's myth, ritual, and share in the past history of the tribe. It corresponds to the *maduka* of the north-eastern tribes of the state, and gives its owner the right to assist his mother's brother and those who share the latter's local totem, in their *inanwa* ceremonies. The *altjira* is also a person's dream totem.

The totemism of the Macumba sub-tribe has thus affinities with both the Eastern and Western Groups, while its *altjira* mythology and *aknanindja* totemism show its relationship to the northern Arunta (Aranda).[1]

In the foregoing account Professor Elkin has told us that the tribes of the eastern or Lakes Group perform ceremonies of the usual *talu* or *intichiuma* type for the increase of their totemic species, but he has described none of them. However in recent years ceremonies of this type appear to have been witnessed and described by Messrs. G. Horne and G. Aiston for the Wongkonguru and their neighbours, to the east of Lake Eyre, which belong to the Lakes Group of tribes described by Professor Elkin. Their description runs as follows : " The growth of food from seed seemed quite beyond their ken. Ceremonies they have, such as the scattering of certain stones (*murrallacardia*) to make the *wirras* (*Acacia salicina*) grow, or *yelka* (small white stones) were scattered around to give a crop of *yauas* (onion grass) or yams, but no idea existed of planting a seed with the hope of a harvest. True, the seed of the *wirra* was also thrown broadcast, but this seed had first to be crushed, and therefore rendered impossible of fertilisation.

[1] A. P. Elkin, *op. cit.* pp. 72-73.

" These ceremonies are generally performed after a shower of rain has fallen or at any rate seems imminent."[1]

Again, speaking of magic, Mr. Horne says : " I will first describe the stones and ceremony of charming the *wirra* bush to grow. *Wirra* bush is a species of acacia (*Acacia salicina*), and is used by the blacks when chewing *pitcheri*.

" The two stones used in this ceremony are very like miniature hammer stones, which in fact they are. They range in size from some 1½ inches to some 2½ inches in diameter, and are usually worn very smooth through having been carried about. They are passed on from one generation to another, and very possibly they have been in the possession of a family for hundreds of years. It is a very good magic to have them, and the older they are the more valuable they are. This ensures their being looked after very carefully. One that I have is a petrified mussel-shell, and this, I was assured, made it very valuable, for it showed that it had at one time belonged to a moora (spirit), who had turned it into stone, to make it ' more strong.'

" In use these were brought out after a rain and the whole of the initiated men of a tribe gathered at the sandhill where the *wirra* bush was wanted to grow. Each man had two of these stones (they were called *murrallacardia*). A seed of the *wirra* bush was then placed on one of them and hammered with the other, while the performers danced around the spot where the bush was wanted. The performance was kept up till all the seed that had been brought out was used up.

" Another stone that was used in this ceremony was called *kunchera warroo*. It represented the white inside of the seed, and was planted where the *wirra* tree was wanted. It was a small white quartz pebble, usually about 1 inch in diameter, roughly circular, and about ¼ inch thick. These stones are very plentiful around Lake Harry, but are rather scarce in the Wongkonguru country, so they were bartered from the Dieri people or were sometimes given as gifts.

[1] G. Horne and G. Aiston, *Savage Life in Central Australia* (London, 1924), p. 8. Mr. G. Aiston was a member of the Mounted Police of South Australia and resided at Mungaranie for eight years as protector of aborigines in that district. Altogether he had spent twenty years among the aborigines and knew them intimately. He supplied Mr. Horne with much valuable information on the natives.

These were deemed of as much important as the *murralla-cardia*, as without them the plant would not know where to grow.

"Another stone used in plant magic was called *yelka*. This was roughly semicircular, about ¾ inch in diameter across its widest part and about ½ inch thick. It was used to ensure a plentiful supply of *yauas*, a small bulb-rooted plant that grows very plentifully in the water-courses (*Cyperus rotundus*). Half an inch of rain will make these grow, and they are in great favour as food. The ceremony of making sure of a plentiful growth was very similar to the *wirra* bush ceremony, only in this case the seed was not ground. All the men present provided themselves with as many *yelkas* as possible and dancing around a suitable flat in a watercourse, they threw the *yelkas* broadcast in every direction. Directly the *yauas* made a show above the ground the *yelkas* were picked up and saved for another occasion. The song for these two ceremonies was the same :—

Charrili	*Charrili*	*Koppara*	
Roots	roots	plant	
Charrili	*Charrili*	*Koppara*	*Nunta*
Roots	roots	plant	grow

"This was chanted all the time the ceremony lasted." [1]

Clearly these savages took very effective measures to defeat their own ends, first by sterilising the seed which they sowed and next by sowing stones instead of seed.

In regard to the totemism of these tribes, Mr. Horne seems to have discovered a new sort of sex totem similar to that recorded by Professor Elkin in his account of the Lakes tribes. He says : "Whilst my companion was taking photographs on the big sand ridge, I made friends with a little pintie-pintie or wagtail (*Ripidura tricolor*). In ten minutes it became so tame that it would eat flies out of my hand. It followed us for two miles up to the camp. Seeing the pintie-pintie playing round me, one of the men volunteered that it was the women's bird and chaffed me on the subject. When asked if they would eat it they indignantly answered

[1] G. Horne and G. Aiston, *op. cit.* pp. 133-135. The writers do not tell us that the objects for which the increase ceremonies were performed were the totems of the performers, but it seems probable that in fact they were so.

' No.' If, however, a man wanted to tease the women, they said, he would kill one and bring it into the camp on the end of a *kirra* (boomerang), but he must be prepared to fight them. ' *Wadna* hit 'em ' (I would be hit with the digging-stick), was the remark.

" I have not been able to discover a corresponding male totem, if such exists." [1]

With regard to the *mooras* or mythical heroes of the far-past time, to whom the aborigines, as usual, attributed the origin of their institutions, including totemism, Mr. Horne tells us that : " The Wongkonguru group, which includes amongst others the Dieri, Yaurorka and Ngameni, seems to have a sort of ancestor worship, the ancestors being the mooras.

" A moora sometimes appears to have been a master mind who was the first to discover anything, or through whom anything was first discovered or done. They were the first to fashion human beings out of lizards, and they formed the sun. To them is attributed the making of *murdus* or totems, and ceremonies and corroborees invariably have the moora behind them, instigating or appointing, and thus giving them authority. The old men maintain their influence partly by receiving communications in dreams from the mooras. They thus tell where to sink for water and where game may be found. Animals as well as inanimate things, have their mooras, and as Dintibunna said, ' Every man has a moora,' a remark that was another day repeated to me verbatim by Koodnacadie.

" Sometimes one may originate a whole tribe by leaving potential spirit-children in rocks or in trees, whence children are born to women who come in contact with them. For that the father has anything to do with conception is absolutely foreign to the native mind.

" Sometimes two, three or more may be the ancestors of the tribe. This is the case with the Dieri. Rarely has a man a definite moora to himself, as has Dintibunna, ' the maker of the *kirra*,' and in his case the name is handed down through his mother." [2]

---

[1] G. Horne and G. Aiston, *op. cit.* p. 124.   [2] G. Horne and G. Aiston, *op. cit.* pp. 124-125.

Among the achievements which those aborigines attributed to the mythical heroes or mooras was the discovery of fire. The legend of its invention was taken down by Mr. Aiston. He writes as follows : " This is the tale of how fire came to the tribes in this country as it was told to me at Lake Perigundi : I had ridden into the Lake, which was dry at the time, and from the top of a red sandhill I had seen a small white sandhill to the east. I told my boy that we would camp at the white sandhill. The boy was a man of about forty-five years. He did not like that camp, but said nothing. When we got in I unsaddled and hobbled my horse and went down to see if the soak wanted cleaning out. When I came back I found that the boy had pulled the pack saddles off, a couple of hundred yards from the white sandhill. I asked him why, but at the time he did not give any satisfactory reason. After we had had tea he said, ' That hill where moora sit down,' pointing to the white sandhill. I asked him which moora and he replied, ' Moora Moora Paralana.' And this is the tale as he told it to me : ' Long time ago before the white man come to this country a moora come up from down country, and make a camp over behind that big sandhill over to the west. Just about sundown he come over to see the moora Paralana and find him eating raw fish. The down country moora say to moora Paralana, 'What you eat raw fish for? You like him ? ' Moora Paralana say, ' Fish all right ; which way you eat him ? ' Down country moora say, ' Me like to cook them, more better that way.' Then he ask this moora to come over to his camp and he would show him. Over there the down country moora made a fire and put some fish on the ashes and tell moora Paralana to wait a bit. When the fish was cooked the down country moora gave some to this moora and told him to eat him. The moora Paralana eat all that fish and another one that the down country moora cook for himself. He cook some more and at last he fill up this moora.

" ' Then the moora Paralana ask him what he call this thing he use. The down country moora tell him it is called fire. He then ask down country moora to show him how to make it, and when he learn properly how to make fire the moora Paralana kill the down country moora and bring the fire over to this sandhill. He camp here then all the time and make the other blackfellows bring him tucker and young women. By and by he get two young women who do not want to stay with him. They wait till he is asleep and they take a fire-stick and clear out. They show all their people how to keep fire alight and after that they are mooras.' " [1]

[1] G. Horne and G. Aiston, *op. cit.* p. 139. For other Australian myths of the origin of fire see my book *Myths of the Origin of Fire.*

CHAPTER IX

TOTEMISM IN EAST AUSTRALIA

SOUTH-EAST AUSTRALIA embraces the two States of Victoria and New South Wales. This was the first part of the continent to be colonised, hence the native tribes of the region have long been in contact with European civilisation, and under the blighting influence of an alien culture they have so wasted away or totally disappeared that now little or nothing fresh can be learned from the few scattered survivors as to their ancient customs and beliefs. The totemism of the greater part of the area, so far as it could then be ascertained, was described by me in my earlier work *Totemism and Exogamy*, and in this place I shall not attempt to add to the exposition, but shall confine my attention to a part in the northern area of the country which in recent years has enjoyed the great advantage of being personally investigated by Professor Radcliffe-Brown.[1] In particular I shall deal with two tribes, the Yukumbil and Kumbaingeri, as to which he has supplied us with new and fresh information, based on his own researches.

First, the Yukumbil is a large tribe occupying the region of the Richmond and Clarence Rivers in the north of New South Wales and extending over the Queensland border. Their country extends about a hundred miles north and south and eighty miles east and west. The sub-tribe about which Professor Radcliffe-Brown has most information is the Kidjabal of the country at the head of Clarence River. The tribe has a system of four sections with the names Barang, Deroain, Banda, and Bandjura.

[1] A. R. Radcliffe-Brown, " Notes on Totemism in Eastern Australia," in *Journal of the Royal Anthropological Institute*, lix. (1929) pp. 399 *sqq.*

In this tribe, as normally throughout Australia, the most important social group is the local group or horde—this is a small group which owns and occupies a certain defined territory. As normally happens in Australia, these hordes are patrilineal and exogamous.[1]

Throughout the Yukumbil country there are sacred spots at which rites for the increase of natural species were formerly celebrated. Such places are called *djurbil*. Each horde normally had a number of such spots (*djurbil*) in its country. For example we may take the horde which formerly owned a territory of somewhat less than 100 square miles between Woodenbong and Unumgare. In the country of this horde are the following sacred places (*djurbil*)—kangaroo, wattle-grub, native bear, locust, big lizard, opossum, sugar-bag (wild honey), sleep, rain-serpent.

The origin of these sacred places (*djurbil*) is explained by stories relating to a mythical period before man appeared. In Yukumbil this period is described as *Budjeram*, and the mythical beings who lived at that time, and some of whom are still thought to live in the mountains and scrubs, are called by the same name. Each territory of a horde has its own *budjeram* or mythical heroes, and these are friendly to the people of the horde, that is, all the persons born in the horde and all the women introduced from other places as wives of the men of the horde. To strangers, that is persons from other hordes, the *budjeram* of a country are dangerous. A *djurbil* (sacred spot) which is connected with the *budjeram* (mythical heroes) is therefore a dangerous place for all except members of the horde to which it belongs.[2]

Members of the horde to which one of these sacred spots belongs have the power to provide for the increase of the natural species associated with it, by going to the spot and performing a simple rite. To illustrate these rites, Professor Radcliffe-Brown takes a few examples, giving the legends and rites for some of the *djurbil* (sacred spots) of the Woodenbong horde. The first legend relates to two *djurbil*, one for kangaroo, and the other for the edible grub *djubera*.

In the mythical time (*Budjeram*) there was an old woman

---

[1] A. R. Radcliffe-Brown, *op. cit.* pp. 400-401.   [2] A. R. Radcliffe-Brown, *op. cit.* p. 401.

and her nephew, who was a good-looking man. They were living together at the place now known as The Glen. The nephew had a big kangaroo-net, and one day he put up his net. He told the old woman to go and beat up the kangaroo by shouting, and so to drive them into the net, while he stood by ready to kill them when they were entangled in the net. She refused to go, and said that she would stand by the net. So the nephew had to go to drive up the kangaroo, while the old woman stood by the net armed with a boomerang. When the nephew had gone to drive the kangaroo, one very big old-man kangaroo approached the net and became entangled in it. The old woman tried to kill him, but she was not strong enough, and as the kangaroo struggled she also became entangled in the net. Then the kangaroo carried away the net with the old woman in it. As he travelled he soon grew tired, and every now and then he had to rest. At each spot where he rested a swamp was formed, and the swamps are there to this day. Finally he stopped altogether at *Bainmabal*, where the water-hole now is. The kangaroo, the net, and the old woman are in the water. The nephew returned to where he had placed the net, and found the net and the old woman gone. He saw the tracks of the big kangaroo. He followed the tracks. When he came to the water-hole at *Bainmabal* he spoke to his aunt. She told him that she was finished and that he should leave her. He returned to The Glen. Then he started collecting and eating wattle-grubs (*djubera*). As he travelled about the country, wherever he camped a swamp was formed, and these swamps still exist. He reached the swamp called *Djubera* and camped there. He ate too many grubs. His head ached. He rolled about on the ground, and as he did so a water-hole formed, and in that he remained. He is still there.

At *Bainmabal*, which is a water-hole within the township of Woodenbong, rites for the multiplication of kangaroos can be performed. One or more of the performers dives into the pool and stirs up the water. It is said that he could see the kangaroo and the old woman. During the rite the performer talks to the water, saying that he wants the kangaroos to be plentiful, and possibly mentioning places where he wishes them to appear in numbers.

The rite for the increase of the edible grub *djubera* was performed at the pool of that name. The performer dives into the pool and brings up mud from the bottom ; this mud he throws against certain gum trees which stand beside the pool. One man may do this alone, or two or more may carry out the rite together. The performer talks to the water, telling it to make the grubs plentiful. The rite is performed in winter.[1]

The sacred place (*djurbil*) for the multiplication of native bear (*bandjur*) is on the ranges between Unumgare and Woodenbong, and consists of a hole in the rock, but without water. The story runs that in the mythical time (*Budjeram*) the beings of that time were hunting native bears but could not find any fat ones. First, they killed an old-man bear, but as he was not fat they left him ; then they killed a mother bear with a young one on her back. They left them also. The old-man bear came to life again and went up a tree ; the mother bear began to come to life again, and rolled about and turned into stone. She is there in the hole which constitutes the *djurbil*. The rite for the increase of native bear consists of throwing small stones into the hole, talking the while and telling the hole to send out plenty of bears.[2]

The sacred spot (*djurbil*) for locust is near to the last mentioned, and is also a hole or cleft in the rocks. In the *Budjeram* (mythical time) the people of the place used to take their children with them when they went hunting. One day an old woman told the people that they should leave all the children for her to take care of, so that they would be able to collect their food much more quickly, having no children to look after. The people were not inclined to do this, but finally the old woman was able to persuade them. All the people went off hunting, and left their children behind with the old woman. She made a deep hole or cleft in the rock and put all the children in it. There was a very great number. They are still there in the rock, but they are now turned into locusts. The spot is the *djurbil* for locusts.

Locusts are an article of food for the natives. To make them plentiful the performer pulls at a vine which grows up

[1] A. R. Radcliffe-Brown, *op. cit.*   [2] A. R. Radcliffe-Brown, *op. cit*
pp. 401-402.   pp. 402-403.

from the bottom of the *djurbil* place, talking as he does so and telling the locusts to be plentiful. It is said that by a visit to the *djurbil* and talking to it the people to whom it belonged could enlist the aid of locusts. If they wanted to steal a woman or kill a man of another horde, they could arrange with the locusts to make so much noise that any cry for help from the victim would not be heard.[1]

The sacred place (*djurbil*) for *kabai* (honey of the native bee) is a pool in the neighbourhood of Unumgare, near which stand two ironbark trees, while in the same spot there is a yellow stone or rock. The man who wishes to increase honey takes mud from the pool and throws it at the ironbark trees, and also breaks off small pieces from the yellow rock, leaving them lying there. He talks all the time he does this, telling the bees to go everywhere and build their combs in the trees, the stumps, and logs.[2]

The sacred place (*djurbil*) for sleep is of a somewhat different kind from those described above. The men of the horde can go to this spot, and by performing the rite can send a sort of sleeping-sickness to their enemies in any part of the country. The legend is as follows : In the mythical time (*Budjeram*) there was a good-looking man who was looking for *walumban* (a grub that lives in the pine tree). He filled his net bag with the grubs. He camped at a spot near Mount Lindesay. He made a fire, and roasted the grubs and had a meal. After he had eaten the grubs he lay down under a tree and fell asleep. He slept and slept and did not awaken. He is there sleeping still, covered with his opossum skin cloak. His food, the grub *walumban*, is there also, turned to stone. These are certain small stones. There are also at the *djurbil* five stones standing upright in a row.

If a man wishes to send his enemies to sleep he goes to the *djurbil* (sacred spot) and with a sheet of bark hits the ground beside the five standing stones. The *budjeram* (mythical being) stirs in his sleep. The performer then says what he wants, naming the place to which he wishes the sleeping-sickness to go. He may say that he wishes it to attack a person or persons for one or two nights, or he may

---

[1] A. R. Radcliffe-Brown, *op. cit.*
p. 403.

[2] A. R. Radcliffe-Brown, *op. cit.*
p. 404.

send it so that his enemies simply fall asleep and do not awake any more. A short time after the rite is performed there will be a shower of rain, and this is the sign that the rite has been successful and the sleep has gone out to the enemy. It is very dangerous for a stranger to go near this *djurbil* (sacred spot), as he is likely to be attacked by the sleeping-sickness.[1]

Professor Radcliffe-Brown was told that the most important of all the *djurbil* (sacred spots) of the country near Woodenbong is that on the hill called *Banyara* by the natives, which is connected with rain, but his information about this is confessedly incomplete.

In the *Budjeram* (mythical time) there was a snake of the kind called *banyara*. He had wings, and flew from Yulgilbar on the Clarence River and settled on the mountain called *Banyara*. Although the being is thus referred to as a snake, or as having been a snake, it is now referred to as a *warzam*. Professor Radcliffe-Brown could not discover exactly what this word means, but it seems to be the name of some sort of sacred being connected with rain. He was told that *warzam* often makes a noise like thunder in the mountain. If any member of the Woodenbong horde is sick this noise is heard. The *warzam* is friendly to people of the horde but dangerous to strangers. Apparently in this region, where the rainfall is plentiful and well distributed, there was not much need for rain-making ceremonies. The people of the horde could, however, go to this *djurbil* (sacred spot) and talk to *warzam* and rain would fall which would flood all the creeks and valleys.[2]

There is a *djurbil* (sacred spot) for hot weather in the mountains near the Richmond River. Professor Radcliffe-Brown did not hear of any *djurbil* for cold weather in Yukumbil country, but he was told that there is such a *djurbil* belonging to another tribe at Warwick, in Queensland. There is a *djurbil* for wind at a place called *Bululgun* near Roseberry Creek. The legend runs that in the *Budjeram* (mythical time) a man was following a very big bandicoot, which ran into a hole. The man followed the bandicoot into

[1] A. R. Radcliffe-Brown, *op. cit.* pp. 404-405.

[2] A. R. Radcliffe-Brown, *op. cit.* p. 405.

the hole, and travelled along underground until he came to the place where the big wind is shut up under the earth. At the *djurbil* there is a stone covering a hole; if this stone is lifted a cyclone will follow.[1]

Professor Radcliffe-Brown was told of two or three centres at which rites for the increase of children or babies were performed. One is at the place now called Tadam; another is on the Tooloom Range. The latter is a place where there are a number of trees (spotted gums). When the people to whom this *djurbil* belongs wish to make plenty of children, one or more of them will go to the spot, strip a number of small pieces of bark from the sacred trees and throw them in different directions, talking as they do so, and naming the places where they wish the children to increase.[2]

The territory of the Kumbaingeri tribe consists of a part of the coastal region of New South Wales extending from the Clarence River in the north to a point south of the Macleay River. This tribe has the normal local organisation into patrilineal hordes. There is a system of four sections with the names Karbung, feminine Juran; Wambung, feminine Wirgan; Marung, feminine Kargan; and Wirung, feminine Wangan. The arrangement of the sections is

Karbung	Wambung
Marung	Wirung

The kinship system of this tribe is of a type we have not met with before, which Professor Radcliffe-Brown proposes to call the Kumbaingeri type. The classification of kin is to some extent carried out on the same general principles as in the Kariera type. But marriage is prohibited with own mother's brother's daughter, or own father's sister's daughter. A man marries a woman who belongs to the same section and generation as his mother's brother's daughter, and who is, according to the terminology, a relative of the same kind. But she must come from another part of the country, and must not be closely related to him. The normal procedure was described to Professor Radcliffe-Brown as follows. A woman who is " father's sister " to a boy, possibly his own

---

[1] A. R. Radcliffe-Brown, *op. cit.* p. 405.   [2] A. R. Radcliffe-Brown, *op. cit.* pp. 405-406.

father's sister, would look out for a wife for him. Finding a woman who was her " sister," but not closely related to herself or her nephew, she would induce the latter to promise her daughter in marriage to the boy. From this moment, this woman becomes the boy's mother-in-law, and he must avoid her, in accordance with the usual etiquette of Australian tribes. It is, therefore, preferable that he should never have met her before the arrangement is made.

This type of kinship system is clearly related to the Kariera type, but at the same time represents a movement away from that type and perhaps, we may say, towards the Arunta (Aranda) system. It is clearly dependent on the existence of the four sections, and would perhaps be unworkable without them. Its great difference from the Kariera system is in forbidding marriage with near relatives within the marriageable group, that is, within the group of persons classified with the cross-cousins.

All the persons born in a given horde belong to one couple of sections. The horde is, therefore, necessarily exogamous. It seems probable, though the evidence is not conclusive, that a man would not be allowed to marry a woman from his mother's horde. There is also a definite objection to a man marrying a woman from any horde that is geographically near his own. He must seek his wife at a distance.[1]

In the Kumbaingeri language the equivalent of *djurbil* (sacred spot for the increase of species) is *mirer* or *mirera*, and in general the beliefs and practices with the sacred spots so designated are essentially similar to those of the Yukumbil. But while all Professor Radcliffe-Brown's Yukumbil informants agreed that no one would perform increase rites at a *djurbil* except the members of the horde that owned this locality, some of the Kumbaingeri thought that anyone who knew how to perform the rite could do it, even though the *mirera* (sacred place) belonged to a horde other than his own. It is now so long since these rites have been performed, or even talked about, and so long since the local organisation was completely disrupted by the white occupation of the

[1] A. R. Radcliffe-Brown, " The Social Organization of Australian Tribes," pp. 62-63. This exposition of the kinship system of the tribe is given in Professor Radcliffe-Brown's own words.

country, that it is impossible to obtain any quite certain information on a matter such as this. It is clear, however, that there is a very real sense in which each *mirera* (sacred place) belonged to a certain horde and was, if not their exclusive possession, at any rate very definitely their property.

Amongst the *mirera* (sacred places) about which Professor Radcliffe-Brown was told, there were two or three for the increase of kangaroos, two for opossum, and others for the increase of emu, kangaroo rat, dingo, crab, cod fish, perch, oyster, and a species of shell-fish. The only vegetable species for which Professor Radcliffe-Brown heard of increase rites was a vine with edible fruit called *girguru*.

An interesting point with regard to the kangaroo is that in one part of the country there is a place for the increase of old-man kangaroo only, while elsewhere and belonging to a different horde there is a *mirera* (sacred place) consisting of two water-holes, one connected with the female kangaroo and the other with the little kangaroo of either sex. There are therefore separate increase rites for male kangaroos and for females and young. The rite in each case is similar—striking the water of the sacred pool and talking to it.[1]

Two unusual *mirera* (sacred spots) are connected with two diseases : *gunandi*, a form of diarrhoea, or perhaps colitis ; and *bilir*, apparently dysentery. By performing rites at these spots, a man could send a visitation of sickness upon an enemy. If a man were attacked with *gunandi* he would try to think of some one of the horde to which it belonged whom he might have offended and who might therefore have sent the sickness, and he would then go and ask to be pardoned for his offence and healed of his illness. For a cure he would be taken to the *mirera* (sacred spot), and the man who took him would talk to the place, saying that the patient was now to recover. A little sand from the sacred spot would be rubbed on the sufferer's body. After that, the natives say, the sickness would go.

The *mirera* (sacred places) for tiger-snake and for the death adder seem chiefly to have been used for sending

---

[1] A. R. Radcliffe-Brown, " Notes on Totemism in Eastern Australia," in *Journal of the Royal Anthropological Institute*, lix. (1929) p. 406.

these snakes against enemies. A man could go to the tiger-snake *mirera* (sacred spot), and striking the water there, and throwing it in a given direction, and talking to the water, he could send tiger-snakes to kill his enemies in that quarter. Similarly with the *mirera* (sacred place) for the adder, which is a round water-hole on the top of a mountain with a number of stones spotted like the adder in the neighbourhood. The performer throws some of these stones into the water, and throws water in the direction in which he wishes the snakes to go and attack his enemy.

An unusual *mirera* in the Kumbaingeri country is one for ghosts near Coramba. The Kumbaingeri explanation of the *mirera* is that they were formed in the mythical period, but it is impossible to obtain the legends in any fullness.[1]

Professor Radcliffe-Brown tells us that the Dangali, Ngambar, and Ngaku, three other tribes of this region, appear to have had customs very like those of the Kumbaingeri in regard to rites for the increase of natural species. They occupied in the past territories on the middle and lower portions of the Macleay River, and on the Nambuccar River. The remnants of them are now living together and are discussed together in this account.

Professor Radcliffe-Brown could not discover any word in their languages exactly equivalent in use to *djurbil* or *mirera*. They have however, or once had, exactly similar sacred spots, and in a number of instances the name of the place is formed by adding a suffix to the name of the natural species with which it is connected. Professor Radcliffe-Brown's enquiries, though hasty, were sufficient to demonstrate the former existence in these tribes of localised increase ceremonies of the same sort as those described for the tribe further north. Thus in the Ngaku tribe there is a spot near Crescent Head, where increase rites for the jew-fish can be performed. There is a deep hole in the middle of a swamp : the performer thrusts a spear into this hole, splashes the water, and talks to the place, telling the jew-fish to be plentiful.[2]

In these three tribes, however, Professor Radcliffe-Brown

[1] A. R. Radcliffe-Brown, *op. cit.*   [2] A. R. Radcliffe-Brown, *op. cit.*
pp. 406-407.   p. 407.

came upon a problem. Here every individual has a special connection with some species of animal which is his *bagar*. A person may kill and eat the animal so related to him, but when he dies all his nearer relatives must abstain from eating that particular food for a certain period. The period of abstention is different for different species of animals. The longest is that for porcupine, so that when a man whose *bagar* is porcupine dies, all his nearer relatives abstain from porcupine flesh for three years. The period for some foods was much shorter, sometimes as short as three or four months.

An enquiry as to how the *bagar* was acquired elicited the statement that it was inherited from the father, but this statement was modified later, and Professor Radcliffe-Brown was told that a man gets the *bagar* of his father and a woman that of her mother. He adds that he thinks it is quite certain that a man always has the same *bagar* as his father, and that it is at any rate possible that a woman takes that of her mother's brother.

. The problem thus presents itself whether there is any connection between the *bagar* and the increase rites. The instances are too few, says Professor Radcliffe-Brown, to enable us to draw any certain conclusion, but they do suggest the possibility that a man's *bagar* was always some species of animal which was connected to the horde to which he belonged, by reason of the existence of a place for increase rites for that species within the country of the horde. It has thus been possible to trace the former existence of localised rites for the increase of natural species through 200 miles of the coastal strip of New South Wales. It may yet be possible to follow up these enquiries for another 100 miles southward as far as Port Stephens, but from that point southwards it is now too late to obtain any information, as all memory of former native customs has entirely disappeared. There are a few indications that lead one to suspect that a similar cult may very well have extended right through the coastal region of New South Wales and possibly into Victoria.[1]

Summing up the foregoing investigations, Professor Radcliffe-Brown observes : " The characteristics of the cult of

[1] A. R. Radcliffe-Brown, *op. cit.* p. 408.

these coastal tribes may be enumerated as follows. The sacred spots at which increase rites are performed are marked by the presence of a water-hole, some peculiar feature of rock or stone, or by trees. A majority have a water-hole. Only very few have sacred trees without either a water-hole or some rock formation. Amongst the sacred stones there are some which are said by the natives to resemble in shape the species with which they are connected. Thus at *Wandjimirera* (*wandji* = dog), near Coramba, there is a rock which is said to have the shape of a bitch. At *Wiranaia* (*wira* = duck), near Colombatti, there are stones shaped like ducks. In a number of instances I was able to satisfy myself that the animal or other natural species is, or formerly was, actually abundant in the neighbourhood of the spot where the rite for its increase was performed. Throughout this region the performers of the increase rites do not paint themselves or put on any special decorations, nor do they dance or sing as part of the rite. The performer talks all the time he is carrying out the rite, but there are no set forms (spells of prayer) that he repeats. He just tells the animal, or whatever it may be, to become plentiful, and mentions special places where it is to become abundant. The rites themselves are very simple in form—splashing water, throwing stones or mud, knocking fragments off a rock, and so on. In describing the rites to me in Dangati two words were repeatedly used as descriptive of the rites themselves : one *giregerin*, seems to mean to poke or stir up ; the other *mangin*, means to catch hold of a thing, therefore to get or obtain.

" Throughout this area there is apparently a legend in connection with each of the places at which increase rites can be performed, and such legends all refer to the mythical times at the beginning of the world and to the beings who then existed." [1]

" In the Yukumbil tribe, there is a classification of natural species as belonging to the four sections of the community. It is impossible to obtain now anything like a complete account of this classification, so that the following table only gives the classification of a few species which my informants were able to recall during a short discussion of the subject.

[1] A. R. Radcliffe-Brown, *op cit.* pp. 409-410.

Deroain	Barang	Bandjur	Banda
kuruman	*kurunara*	*tandur*	*narain*
male kangaroo	female kangaroo	male wallaroo	female wallaroo
nuban	*wagan*	*bulaban*	*magoin*
eaglehawk	crow	female rock-	male rock-
wagun		wallaby	wallaby
scrub turkey		*kuman*	*kiraban*
nurin		female padi-	male padimelan
emu		melan	
nagam		*kagun*	*wurgulum*
dingo		laughing jackass	magpie
namal		*panandjurgan*	
goanna		a small bird	plain turkey
		bandjur	
		native bear	
		burnin	*bilin*
		porcupine	bat

" It may be noted that animals of the kangaroo kind are treated differently from others.   Thus the male kangaroo is called *kuruman* and is Deroain, while the female kangaroo, called by a different name *kurunara*, is Barangan.   Similarly with such animals as the wallaroo, padimelan, and wallaby. When the male animal is in the one section the female is in the section with which the first intermarries. . . . There is no prohibition in the Yukumbil tribe against eating the animals belonging to one's own section.

" So far as I could determine, there was no interrelation between this classification of natural species under the four sections and the system of local increase ceremonies.   It is of course possible that an intensive study of the mythology (which it is now too late to carry out) might have revealed some connection.

" I was unable to discover any evidence of similar classification in the Kumbaingeri or in the tribes further south, but I am not prepared to say that it did not formerly exist.   In these broken-down tribes it is almost impossible to obtain certain evidence of the former non-existence of any custom or institution. . . .

" These tribes of New South Wales also provide us with examples of what has been called sex-totemism.   In the Yukumbil tribes the bat belonged to the men and the night-hawk belonged to the women. If any woman killed a bat there would be a fight between the men and women ; and, *vice versa*, if the men were annoyed with the women, they would kill a night-hawk and there would be a fight.

" In the Kumbaingeri, Zegera, and Dangati tribes the bat was the representative of the men, but it was a species of woodpecker that was the representative of women. There is a legend that it was this bird that first taught women how to climb trees. The bat is described as being ' clever,' *i.e.* skilled in magic. A native pointed out to me that the bat and the woodpecker have this in common, that they both live in holes in the trees. . . .

" This little strip of New South Wales coast therefore affords us examples of localized increase rites, of classification of animals under the sections, and of sex-totemism, all three of which are widespread institutions in Australia. In addition it gives us the *bagar* of the Dangati tribe, a form of totemism that has not been recorded before." [1]

<hr>

[1] A. R. Radcliffe-Brown, *op. cit.* pp. 412-415.

CHAPTER X

TOTEMISM IN QUEENSLAND

IN recent years a system of totemism has been discovered by Miss Ursula McConnel in the Wik-Munkan tribe of Cape York Peninsula, the most northerly point of Queensland and of Australia. Her description of the system is excellent, and I will follow it closely.

The Wik-Munkan is the largest and most important of a group of tribes in Cape York Peninsula, characterised by names formed with the word *Wik*, signifying "speech," which occupy a stretch of country along the Gulf of Carpentaria, thirty to fifty miles wide, through which flow the Watson, Archer, Kendall, Holroyd, and Edward Rivers. The territory of the Wik-Munkan begins below the junction of the Coen and Archer and the Pretender and Holroyd, and extends to the mouth of the Archer and the junction of the Kendall and Holroyd. It touches the Watson River in the north and the Edward in the south, and covers an area, roughly speaking, of three thousand square miles. The Wik-Munkan do not come in contact with the sea, for a strip of land along the coast varying in parts from two to ten miles wide is inhabited by kindred coastal tribes. Of these the Wik-Natera or Wik-Kalkan occupy the coast for sixty or seventy miles south of the Archer River, concentrating chiefly on two inland arms of the sea called Yoinka and Arimanka ; the Wik-Natanya or bush-rat people inhabit the corner of the coast between Arimanka and the Kendall—a distance of ten miles, and the Wik-Nantjara occupy the coastal country between the Kendall-Holroyd and the Edward.[1]

[1] Ursula McConnel, " The Wik-Munkan Tribe of Cape York Penin- sula," in *Oceania*, vol. i. No. 1 (April 1930), pp. 97-98.

The Wik-Munkan and kindred tribes have a similar social organisation. In every case the tribe consists of a number of patrilineal clans, each claiming descent from common ancestors and possessing rights of hunting over a certain territory. The Wik-Munkan includes about thirty such local clans, of which a few are practically extinct, the majority have from one to five members, a few from five to ten members, whilst others, as the carpet-snake, native companion, crocodile, and ghost clans have from ten to twenty members. As all these clans were probably at one time equally large, it may be assumed that the Wik-Munkan tribe must have originally numbered from fifteen hundred to two thousand people.[1]

The members of a clan hunt chiefly on their own grounds, to which they are deeply attached. · Each local horde or camp consists of members of the local clan, together with women of other clans who have married into the clan, but without the women of the clan who have left it to marry into other clans, for the clans are exogamous. The numbers in a camp are often or sometimes increased by visits from relatives from other clans. When food supplies are scarce in any district or a variety of diet is desired, members of one clan may visit their relatives in other clans whose hunting grounds provide other sources of supply. At special seasons, when food is plentiful in any district, members of the clan in charge send out invitations to their relatives to come and join them. In this way large camps gather periodically on favourite hunting grounds—panja swamps, water-lily lagoons, and reaches of the river where fish are plentiful.[2]

Each clan has a number of totems of varying importance which are common to all members of the clan. These totems are mostly drawn from objects of utility round which daily interest centres, and in the case of natural supplies, from those found in the district occupied by the clan. The totems of these people thus reflect their economic interest. For example, the totems of the coastal tribes include dugong, sea turtle, sharks, oysters, crabs and shellfish, bony bream, and ·big salt-water fish such as barramundi and white-fish ; also

[1] U. McConnel, " The Wik-Munkan Tribe : Part II : Totemism," in *Oceania*, vol. i. No. 2 (July 1930), p. 181.· [2] U. McConnel, *op'. cit.* pp. 181-182.

" thunder," which heralds the north-west monsoon season ; the " high tide," which brings in food ; a " small bird," which is believed to guard the fishing operations of a clan ; bark canoes and spear-handles so necessary to fishing expeditions and the hunt ; pelicans, geese, pigeon and scrub-fowl, flying-fox, bush-rat, wallaby, and the " fresh young grass " on which they feed, as also arrowroot and yams. Besides objects of utility and those of utilitarian association totems may include dangerous and disagreeable things, such as " crocodiles " and " flies," which possess a negative social interest in that they cannot be ignored but may be increased for the discomfort of enemies and strangers. Other totems again are derived from objects of social significance such as " fire," which apart from its general utility for warmth and cooking is the centre of family life and associated with the disposal of the dead, the " bull-roarer " which is given to young men at their initiation ceremony, and the " shooting star " or meteor which is believed to signify the death of a relative. The " baby," " sweet-heart," and ghost totems reflect the chief phases of human life—birth, mating, and death, which are the basic interests of social life. In every case the totem has thus a social value, direct or indirect. Personal names of members of the clan are derived from characteristics of the clan totems or reflect their social value to the clan. Members of the " shooting star " totem, for example, are called *Aka-battana* (*aka* = ground ; *battan* = hits), those of the iguana totem are called *Pantamo'a* (iguana runs up a tree), and those of the kangaroo totem are called *Panpointjalama* (kangaroo sniffs the air and smells a man). Clan names of men and women sometimes reflect their respective occupations in association with the totem : for example, men take their names from the spear-handle totem (Wik-Natanya) and women from the fishing-net and dilly-bag totem, it being a woman's work to make and use dilly-bags and a man's work to make and use spears.[1]

Totems and the personal names derived from them are passed to the children from the father's family. When a woman is about to bear a child she goes into the bush with her mother. The child is not seen by its father till the navel

[1] U. McConnel, *op. cit.* pp. 181-182.

string has come away. It is seen first by the mother's younger brother, and laid face downwards on his body. Later it is taken by the mother, together with an offering of fish and yams, and is placed in her husband's arms. From that time he assumes responsibility for it, and it receives a name from one of his clan totems. It is usual for a brother or sister of the father, according as the child is male or female, to assign a name to the child, who then belongs to that totem. If a man has several sons or daughters they generally receive names from the father's brothers and sisters in order of their age. Sometimes a name is taken from the father's father, the father or the elder brother. According to the Wik-Nantjara a man cannot give his own name to his son during his lifetime, as this would endanger the life of the child. After death, the name of the deceased may not be spoken nor passed on, until the period of mourning is over.

If a child receives its name from its mother's clan it is commonly because it has no acknowledged father, or because its mother comes from a strange tribe, so that its connection with its mother's people may be preserved. In that case it may belong to both its father's and mother's totems. Names may be passed from one clan to another so long as the clans belong to the same moiety. This is sometimes done, for example, when members of one clan are dying out and there is no one left to take the name of a certain totem. For example, a woman of the bone-fish clan was given a name belonging to the bush-nut clan because there was no woman left in the latter. It is possible that at one time personal names were attached to all totems, being required by the number of people in the clan. Now that numbers have dwindled, only those names belonging to the most significant totems remain.[1]

The Wik-Munkan word for totem is *pulwaiya*. *Pul* or *pola* is the term used to distinguish the father's father or a forbear in the male line. *Waiya* is sometimes used with kinship terms to signify old. There is an intimate personal link between a *pulwaiya* (totem) and its clan people. If a man is sick or injured he may attribute the malady or the hurt to an injury inflicted by someone on his totem.

[1] U. McConnel, *op. cit.* pp. 183-184.

The *pulwaiya* (totem) has a sacred place of origin, its *auwa*, where it resides and whence it issues forth.   These *auwa* or totem centres are sometimes the nests and breeding-places of the birds, animals, and plants concerned, and are always situated on the hunting-ground of the clan to which they belong, where the totemic species is abundant.   Each *auwa* (totem centre) has its own peculiar characteristics. Trees, bushes, rocks, naturally or artificially arranged, ant-beds or holes in the ground in the neighbourhood of the *auwa*, are sacred to the totems.   There is always water near by in the shape of river, creek, lagoon, water-hole, swamp, or well at the bottom of which the *pulwaiya* (totem) resides and into which the dead of the clan are believed to go.   They are said to play about their *auwa* in the shape of their totem. That may be why plants or animals are protected near the *auwa* (totem centre) of their representative totem and why the killing of an animal or the injuring of a plant near its *auwa* (totem centre) is not only strictly forbidden but is believed to be attended by grave consequences.   It is to these ghosts or spirits that appeal is made during the ceremony performed at the *auwa* to ensure a plentiful supply of the totemic object.   That the clan should feel its economic dependence upon its ancestors is natural, since it is from them that the knowledge and skill required for the pursuance of economic activities have been handed down.   This aspect of totemism is illustrated in the ghost clan, where the *pulwaiya* (totems) are human beings who are said to have taught men the arts of building the dams and fish-traps and cooking the fish in ant-bed ovens.[1]

The ceremony for the increase of a totem is performed by the leading men in the presence of other members of the clan.   Strangers may be admitted to the ceremony, in which case sweat from the armpits of the leaders is rubbed over their faces and chests so that the totem will smell and know that they " belong " to the totem and no harm will befall them for their intrusion.   The leading men paint themselves for the ceremony with white clay to represent the totemic object. The ritual differs with the various *auwa* (totem centres). Trees may be struck, the ground stamped upon, the tops of

---

[1] U. McConnel, *op. cit.* pp. 185-187.

the ant-beds may be hit off, the ground swept with bushes and mysterious sounds made, the totem being instructed to " come up plenty," and to go in all directions for the use of man. It is as if each clan made itself responsible for the origin, sufficiency, and continuity of those objects of social and economic value associated with its daily needs, so that among the various local clans most human wants are met. It is reasonable to suppose that rites for the increase of the totems were performed at all totemic centres where an increase of the totem was desired. It is possible that many rites have fallen into disuse because no one is left to renew them, the totems alone being remembered. In some cases even the totems are remembered only with an effort. An attempt is usually made to keep up the most important totem centres when their disappearance is threatened by depletion of the clan strength. They are generally in this case taken over by a neighbouring clan, for example the native companion clan has taken over the carpet-snake totem centre on the Tokali River, of which the original clan or tribe is now extinct.[1]

The totemic cult of all the other Wik tribes is similar in the main essentials to that of the Wik-Munkan. The Wik-Nantjara have a yam *auwa* (totem centre) where yams are said to originate, consisting of a water-hole in a little creek which always remains sweet. The spirits of the dead are thought to go down into the water-hole to stop the salt water from coming in to spoil the yams. Every year when rain begins, the ceremony of smoothing out the mud in the water-hole takes place. Mud is thrown about the sides of the water-hole and the place is tidied up. This is believed to ensure a good crop of yams in the coming season.

At the crab and barramundi *auwa* (totem centres) ceremonies are also performed for the increase of crab and barramundi.[2]

The following survey will show how close is the correspondence between the clan totems and the objects of economic value in the districts over which these clans have hunting rights. The personal names of the clan members will be seen to reflect in a picturesque and striking manner the

[1] U. McConnel, *op. cit.* pp. 187-188.
[2] U. McConnel, *op. cit.* p. 188.

characteristics of the totems, or their value to the clan, whilst the myths and legends reflect laws, beliefs, and customs of the people with regard to their totems.

In the lower reaches of the Archer River, the banks of which are lined with mangrove, is the *auwa* (totem centre) of the black mangrove, the seeds of which are eaten after special preparation. On the other hand, the fruit (*mai po'am*) found higher up the river has its *auwa* (totem centre) there. The totem centre consists of some hollows in the ground and the ceremony performed for its increase consists of the cleaning out of these hollows to the accompaniment of mysterious sounds. Various species of palm trees with edible fruit have *auwa* (totem centres) in those parts of the country where they are chiefly found. The pandanus has an *auwa* on the Holroyd River consisting of a dried-up swamp in the vicinity of which are many pandanus trees heavily laden with fruit. The kernel of the fruit is good to eat, though difficult to extract. Another palm (*mai koinkan*) found on the Upper Archer River has its *auwa* (totem centre) there. In the heavily timbered forest country of the Kendall River is the *auwa* of the flowers of the messmate and blood-wood trees, which are one of the main sources of the honey supply. The *pulwaiya* (totem) lives in a water-hole in a creek beside which are many messmate and bloodwood trees covered with marks made by tomahawks of all ages during the ceremonies performed to ensure the growth of the trees. The personal names of the clan, *Ku-ungana* (messmate in bud), *Patjabunta* (messmate in flower), and *Maipatjaka* (*mai* = food, *patja* = flower), signify that the main point of interest is the flower which holds the honey. It is believed that when the last man of this clan dies and no one is left to perpetuate the custom of chopping at the trees the supply of honey from messmate and bloodwood trees will cease throughout the Peninsula. Honey is a staple food and satisfies the craving for something sweet. The *auwa* of the honey totem is on the Edward River.[1]

There are several varieties of water-lily. One small blue lily is plentiful on the lower Archer River and has an *auwa* (totem centre) there at a place called Taimanir. Two other

[1] U. McConnel, *op. cit.* p. 189.

species of water-lilies have *auwa* (totem centres) at Taiam
and Potjauwa in the lagoons of the Archer River, where
these water-lilies grow.   No lilies may be gathered from the
sacred lagoon of Potjauwa.   No information was available as
to the ceremonies associated with the water-lily totems on
the Archer River, but on the Holroyd River lagoons a small
sweet water-lily had an " increase " ceremony associated with
its totem-centre.   At the beginning of the water-lily season,
the roots and seeds were gathered and cooked in large
ceremonial ant-bed ovens on an open space near the lagoons.
After these had been cooked they were left to be washed away
by the flood waters of the following wet season and so carried
into the lagoons and creeks.   This it was believed would
ensure a good crop of water-lilies in the following year.
After this ceremony had been performed water-lilies could be
gathered and eaten.   In a little creek running into the Archer
at a place called Panam, is an *auwa* (totem-centre) for bush-
nut.   This little edible root grows in the swamps into which
the creek overflows in the wet season.   The creek has a rocky
bed, under which the water disappears to emerge again
lower down, being visible here and there through holes in
the rock.   In these mysterious-looking holes is the bush-nut
auwa (totem centre).   Stones are thrown down into the water
to attract the attention of the *pulwaiya* (totem) to the needs
of the people for a fresh supply of bush-nuts.   The rite is
accompanied by strange sounds and movements of the hands
over the holes.   The personal name *Kumama* (*mama* means
" pick up ") refers to the gathering of roots out of the swamp
mud.   The woman's name *Tipnguta* (*tip* means " root ")
refers to the way in which the women mash up the roots for
food.   An interesting identification of the totem with the
dead occurred at the ceremonial burning of the body of a
dead man belonging to the bush-nut clan.   The women
mourners as they danced and sang stooped over the body,
stretched out their hands towards it as if picking up bush-
nuts from the swamp, and lifted them to the dilly-bags
suspended from their heads as though placing the nuts in
them.[1]

    Above the water-lily lagoons the Archer River runs in a

[1] U. McConnel, *op. cit.* p. 190.

clear shallow stream through a sandy river-bed.   Here the stately long-legged jabiru picks his way about the sand and dives his beak beneath the water for fish.   The clan names reflect this picture.   For example, *Manwuna* means the jabiru plunges his neck below the water to spear the fish. Here the jabiru and storm-bird have their *auwa* (totem centres).   The *auwa* of the storm-bird was formerly in a well beside which it nested   A deep channel in the bank made by the water after rain is pointed out as the path by which the *pulwaiya* (totem) came.   Now the storm-bird has shifted its *auwa* (totem centre) to a hole further off.   The *auwa* of the plains turkey is in a lagoon south of the Archer River in which no one may swim.   Legend tells of a man who disregarded the taboo and fell dead on coming out of the water. The native companion *auwa* (totem centre) is in a small swamp on the northern bank of the Archer River.   Half-way down the bank is a hole which at the increase ceremony was cleaned out to the accompaniment of mysterious sounds, and in the river bed some holes in the rocks were approached in a mysterious manner.   The native companion clan is the largest now extant in the Wik-Munkan tribe.   In a little creek running into the Kendall River is the *auwa* (totem centre) for bream.   The remark, " Fish there all dead himself" (they die after breeding), suggests that this is the breeding-place of the bream with which the Kendall River abounds. Close by the creek, small ant-beds have been arranged in a circle with lines of· ant-beds going east and west from the circle as if coming up from the *auwa* (totem centre).   These ant-beds are said to be bream.   While Miss McConnel was there the spot was tidied up, fallen ant-beds were replaced and others were added to the group to make more bream, whilst the fish were bidden to go in all directions to fill the creeks and rivers.[1]

One of the most interesting totems is the fire *(tuma)* totem.   *Tumauwa*, the fire totem centre on the banks of the Archer River, consists of some very old logs against which are growing some small bushes.   At this spot, it is said, fire " makes itself."   It is also said that at one time the body of a dead man—an ancestor of the clan—was burned there.

[1] U. McConnel, *op. cit.* p. 192 *sqq.*

The plucking of leaves from the bushes is strictly taboo, because it is believed that the sacrilegious act would cause a fire to break out, and to spread far and wide. This prohibition against touching the *auwa* (centre) of a dangerous totem is an interesting antithesis to the process of stirring up the totem which takes place at those centres where an increase of the object is required. A water channel leading into the river was pointed out as the path made by the *pulwaiya* (totem) when he came looking for a place to settle and went down into the river. On the river-bank are rocks of a reddish colour suggestive of fire. It is dangerous to pass under these rocks, for the *pulwaiya* (totem) would be angry and cause the water to surge up and upset the canoe. In passing the spot, the canoes keep to the other side of the river. Another dangerous totem is the salt-water crocodile, which is very much feared. Its *auwa* (totem centre) is in the swamp near the mouth of the Archer River. Some men profess to be able to " make " the crocodile and to send it out after an enemy. It is dangerous, therefore, to make a crocodile man angry. The crocodile magic is as follows. The crocodile man takes a lizard or iguana, draws blood from his arm, puts it in the lizard's mouth and then ties the lizard up in grass with its legs and tail protruding, and lays it in the sea, calling it his " son," and bids it grow into a crocodile. When the man's mouth is sore he knows that his son the crocodile has grown big enough to eat small fish ; when his mouth gets sore again the crocodile is big enough to eat large fish. The man then forgets about his " son " and tells no one what he has done. He goes back to his camp with a stick over his shoulder, which signifies that he has done something, but no one asks what it is. Later he goes fishing and sees a ripple on the water. The crocodile sees him. When it does nothing the man knows that it is his " son " whom he has made. Putting sweat from under his arm on a stick he lays it in the water where the tide will carry it to the crocodile. The crocodile then follows him and he puts sweat on its face and in its mouth and cleans its teeth with a straw, taking care not to touch its back, for that would make it angry. The crocodile then recognises him as its " father." The man sends his " son " into the lagoons and rivers to round up fish and send them towards him. When the man catches plenty of fish he knows it is because his " son " the crocodile has sent them to him. If he has an enemy he sends it after him. The crocodile will go everywhere till he finds the enemy and will bring him to his father. A man cannot kill his own " son," the crocodile, and if any one else should kill the crocodile the man will become sick— he will weep and be sorry for his " son " who has been killed.

In a neighbouring clan the fly totem may be increased at its *auwa* (totem centre) for the discomfort of strangers. Possibly, like the fly, the leech may also be increased with the same object. Women dread the leeches when they go into the lagoons and swamps to gather water-lilies, and some swamps are so badly infested that no one can be persuaded to go into them. There are several snake totems, but the carpet-snake totem on the Tokali River has a wide reputation and is much feared. The carpet-snake totem affords an interesting comparison with other animal totems. The emphasis upon one big snake, more important than the others, is more pronounced than in any other clan.[1]

Thunder is said to be the voice of the carpet-snake (*Oingorpan*), who growls on the approach of strangers He lives in a hole under a big rock overlooking the Tokali River. From this rock he can see the approach of strangers along the river or from the opposite shore and so can go down under the water, upset their canoe, and take the occupants to his hole under the rock. This hole, it is said, connects by an underground passage with the big feasting-ground where the strangers were eaten by the snake. A heap of bones is pointed out as the remnant of the snake's feast. Investigation proved them to be the bones of emu, bullocks, and other animals. Besides the chief snake there are many others, some of which inhabit rocks by the river and help the chief snake to keep watch, but most of them live in fig trees in the vicinity. These trees are sacred: bark may not be peeled from them to make string, and should any one pluck a leaf a big snake might come up and consume him. Snake-holes are pointed out in the trees, also the tracks of these reptiles

[1] U. M⸱-Connel, *op. cit.* pp. 195-196.

into the holes and branches of the trees on which they sun themselves.

No snakes may be killed or eaten near this spot. Near by is a swamp where the snakes come to drink at night. If any one attempts to step into the swamp, which is naturally boggy, the snake will drag him down under the water and take him to his hole, which has an underground connection with the swamp.[1]

The most significant of all the totemic clans is the ghost clan, which contains all the essential aspects of the other clans, and since in this case the totem is human, it throws a valuable light upon the meaning of the various animate and inanimate totems of the other clans. *Ornyauwa*, the ghost totem centre, is situated towards the middle of the Wik tribal area on a string of lagoons to the south of the Archer River, which are probably a continuation of the Archer River and Yoinka River lagoons. The economic aspect of totemism is not lacking in this clan, for the fish plays an important part. It has an *auwa* (totem centre) on the creek between the lagoons at *Ornyauwa*, in which are a series of fish-traps and dams in varying stages of desuetude. These are pointed out as having been built by the *pulwaiya*—obviously the clan forbears. Near by are extensive ant-bed ovens, also said to have been made by the *pulwaiya*, who taught men this art. Ant-beds standing near the fish-traps and ovens are said to contain ghost women who guard the fishing-activities—the big ant-hills are the elder women and the small ones the young girls. The tops of the ant-beds are struck off and the ground is swept with branches. This latter act brings an increase of fish; the former, of sweethearts. Care is taken not to strike the ant-beds too hard, for fear of causing trouble. The women keep aloof during this rite to avoid suspicion Near the fish-traps is the *auwa* (totem centre) of a small bird which is said to guard the fish-traps.

The big lagoon—*Ornyauwa*—is the *auwa* (totem centre) of the male ghosts, and a smaller one—*Pantiauwa*—is the *auwa* of the female ghosts, of which the most interesting are the young girls. Romance centres around *Pantiauwa*. Ghosts from the two lagoons meet in the space between.

[1] U. McConnel, *op. cit.* pp. 196-197.

The ghosts live at the bottom of the lagoons. No one may enter the lagoons nor fish in them. If one should try to swim in *Pantiauwa*, the women ghosts at the bottom of the lagoon would poke the intruder with their yam sticks. Sometimes the ghosts emerge from the water and walk about, but they disappear quickly when any one approaches. The ghost girls come up out of the water and sit on the logs of the lagoon sunning themselves.

Sometimes the women ghosts come up out of the lagoon and roam about looking for yams and honey. A story tells of a ghost girl who, being sorry for a man that could not find any honey, caused a big piece of honeycomb to fall at his feet. These girl ghosts sit by the camp fires and guard them while a man sleeps or goes hunting, that is, if he belongs to the ghost clan; but they steal from the camps of strangers, taking their spears and so forth while they sleep. A legend tells how a man stole a girl from the ghost clan and how on returning with her later the couple were speared to death. This legend appears to explain the origin of the ghost totem. Another legend records the punishment meted out to a man who broke the taboo of the ghost clan at *Ornyauwa*. A man was passing these lagoons on his way back to Kendall River from " the bamboo place " with a bundle of bamboo spears on his shoulder. As he came near the lagoon he heard singing. Coming up quietly he saw a bevy of ghost girls disporting themselves in the water. Quickly he went back and laid down his bamboo spears, picked out a good one and, holding a branch in front of him, stole back to the lagoon as if stalking an emu. He came up close, chose the girl he wanted and threw his spear, wounding her in the arm. In consternation the ghost girls dived under the water, but wading in he secured the wounded one. He put his sweat on her, saying, " You are my woman." Then taking blood from his arm he smeared it on her and rubbed her to make her warm. She was very frightened and struggled, but finally went with him. He took her to his camp and everyone wanted to know where he had found her. He told them—" in a lagoon." After a while he brought her back to *Ornyauwa*, but when they came up to the lagoon they both fell dead. When people came they found the two, the lover and his lass, lying dead by the lagoon.[1]

A short distance from *Pantiauwa* is the baby *auwa*. Milkwood trees are struck for girl babies and gum trees for boy babies. Women who desire babies take part in the ceremony and as the trees are struck their names are called out. Women who do not want babies keep away from this ceremony, and are afraid to swim in the lagoon or to drink the water lest they should become pregnant.

Another interesting totem is the bull-roarer which is used in connection with the young men's initiation ceremony. It is presented to the young men and they see it for the first time at their first initiation and are taught how to swing it. The *auwa* (totem centre) of the bull-roarer is at *Kulepan* on the Watson River. A legend tells of the original finding of a bull-roarer in this place, and points the moral as to the evil consequences of breaking the taboo imposed upon young men during the initiation ceremony according to which they may not speak to women nor eat meat. The legend runs as follows : Some young men left camp before the end of their initiation and took their spears with them (two old men saw them go). They went up the Archer River to a flying-fox camp, and there the boys saw some young girls swimming in the water. They sat down and prepared their spears, then set off for the flying-fox camp. They speared the flying-foxes and brought them back, the girls helping to cook them in ant-bed ovens. They then returned for more flying-foxes, each taking some girls with him. When they returned the flying-fox in the ant-bed oven had come to life and spoke to them. They were very frightened. They then looked up and saw a cloud of flying-foxes above them. These swooped down, seized the young men and carried them away, and they were never seen again. This was their punishment for ignoring the laws of their tribe. The girls too were frightened and sank beneath the water, but one girl was left behind. As she went she saw something lying on the ground, a bull-roarer, and swung it. Then she too sank beneath the water, leaving the bull-roarer behind. It was found afterwards by a man, and since that time no woman has ever been allowed

[1] U. McConnel, *op. cit.* pp. 198-200.

to see or use a bull-roarer. Men keep them for themselves and do not show them to the women.[1]

The dingo or dog is an important asset to the daily life of the people. It guards the camp, hunts game, and is trained not to eat its quarry. It is prized as a domestic pet, some clans giving totemic names to their dogs. Men will build a special shelter for a dingo bitch with pups, and women will carry the pups from one camp to another no matter how heavily laden they may be, whereas they will eat the pups of wild dingoes. The dingo totem centre is one of a string of deep lagoons running back from the Archer River towards the coast. It is said that if anyone should try to fish in this lagoon the dingo at the bottom would cut his line and take the hook. Near by is a water-hole where the female dingoes dwell and between the two is a flat space levelled by the water, where the male and female dingoes come up to play at night. Away to the south of these lagoons the open melon-hole country stretches towards the Kendall River. On the edge of this country, which is the natural habitat of the kangaroo, is the *auwa* (totem centre) of the kangaroo. Probably this swamp is where the kangaroos come to drink, water-holes being scarce in the melon-hole country. Members of the kangaroo clan seem to belong equally to the dingo and bream clans and form a link between the Archer River and Kendall River groups. The emu totem has an interesting legend which describes a brawl between two emu and native companion men, who belong to opposite moieties, and accounts for the origin of the emu and native companion by the transformation of these men into their totemic animals after death. This mythological identification of the dead with the totemic animal which represents the clan is but a logical extension of the belief that the ghosts of the dead appear in the form of the totemic animal in the vicinity of the *auwa* (totem centre), their presence in this spot being incidental to the part taken by them as mediators between man and Nature in the " increase " ceremony. The emu *auwa* (totem centre) consists of a shallow hole or nest under the trees by the edge of the Kendall River. There were once two eggs in the nest which the *pulwaiva* (totem) has now removed because no

[1] U. McConnel, *op. cit.* pp. 200-201.

one has cared for the nest. The only remaining man of the clan has not been near the ground for years. On top of the bank was another nest which also had eggs in it at one time. There is a waterway from the nest on the bank to the one by the river, which is said to be the pathway by which the emu *pulwaiya* (totem) came down to drink. An emu man and his wife had plenty of children. He hid all but two of them. These two played beside him as he slept by the nest. The others played on the bank above. A native companion man came with a big mob of children. The emu man said, " You have a lot of children, I have only two ! " and he killed the children of the native companion man. Whilst he slept the native companion man took gum from the ironwood tree, heated it in the fire, and smeared it on the emu man's back. The emu man woke up yelling and jumping. As he jumped he made holes where his feet touched the ground and water oozed up in them like well-water. These formed the big water-holes and lagoons in the vicinity. He then got gum from the grass tree, heated it in the fire, and burnt the head of the native companion man. His wife meanwhile had gone to find the crow doctor up at the head of the Kendall River and brought him back with her. The crow doctor sucked the emu man and treated him, but in vain—he swelled up and died. At his death he changed into an emu with a mark behind where the native companion had burnt him, and went down under the water taking with him his wife whom he had killed for neglecting his children. From them came many emu. This caused the water to rise higher and higher till the lagoons and water-holes joined together and formed the river. The other man died from the wound on his head and turned into a native companion with a red mark on his head where the gum had burnt him. It was the crow doctor who thus caused them to turn into native companion and emu. This legend is like so many other Australian legends which account in this manner for the origin of animals and certain natural features of the country. These stories are simply myths of " beginnings " that deal not with creation as a whole, but with those local portions of it with which the clan is personally concerned.[1]

[1] U. McConnel, *op. cit.* pp. 201-203.

The survey of the totemic system of the Wik-Munkan and allied tribes may be briefly summarised thus :

(1) The totems are drawn chiefly from objects of social value, particularly from objects of *economic importance*, upon which the clans depend for their subsistence. The complimentary nature of the clan-totems reflects the economic interdependence of the clans and the unity of the tribes.

(2) The totems, thus identified with its interests and sentiments, come to represent the clan as a kinship group and symbolise its unity, and so in this indirect manner to govern the marriage laws.

(3) The sentiments of the clan are naturally linked with the clan ancestors who form its traditions and who, endowed with miraculous powers by the mystery of death, are deemed able to regulate the forces of Nature which benefit mankind, and who are thus intimately associated with the totemic objects required for the welfare of the clan. It is but a short step for the totem which represents the clan to become identified with the clan ancestors. Myths and legends forge a closer link by making of the ancestor a kind of creator responsible for the origin of the totem, usually in terms of a transformation legend according to which the ancestor turns into the totem at death.[1]

The Wik-Munkan kinship system for the most part resembles that of the typical Australian tribe in that it recognises—

(1) exogamous and localised (patrilineal) clans ;
(2) division of the tribe or tribes into two exogamous moieties ;
(3) (junior) sororate and levirate ;
(4) cross-cousin marriage (with modification) ;
(5) an all-embracing classificatory terminology.[2]

The Wik-Munkan system differs from the average Australian type in not using a four- or eight-section system—and in its peculiar modification of the cross-cousin marriage.

The Wik-Munkan make a distinction in terminology be-

---

[1] U. McConnel, *op. cit.* p. 203.

[2] U. McConnel, " The Wik-Munkan and Allied Tribes of Cape York Peninsula, Part III. : Kinship and Marriage," *Oceania*, vol. iv. No. 3 (March 1934), p. 310.

tween the mother's older and younger brothers and between their offspring. A man's wife is the daughter of his mother's younger brother, and a woman's husband is the son of her mother's elder brother.

Correspondingly, the Wik-Nantyara and Wik-Natanya, besides distinguishing between mother's *older* and *younger* brother, distinguish between father's *older* and *younger* sister as well.[1]

" The eldest son of a family has a right to, and usually does, marry the eldest girl or two in a family. If he does not take advantage of this claim, it passes to his younger brothers in order of age. But once the claim has been passed over it can never be renewed, nor can an older sister be passed over in favour of a younger one. This custom, which is known as the junior sororate, works well, for it prevents rivalry and disputes between brothers. A man may often pass on one of his wives so obtained to a younger brother or clan brother if the latter is still unmarried. A man is under an obligation to take care of his older brother's widow and children. As with the sororate, so with the levirate, a widow passes always to a younger brother of her husband, never vice versa.[2] This law, the junior levirate, is clearly reflected in the kinship terminology. A woman addresses her husband and her husband's younger brother, or prospective husband, by the same terms, *monja*. But she addresses her husband's older brother, whom she may not marry, as *pinyawa'a*. A strict taboo protects brothers from misunderstanding regarding each other's wives. A man never approaches his older brother's camp whilst his older brother's wife is present. Should he do so and speak to her, he might create suspicion in his older brother's mind by appearing to be interested in a woman who is to be his wife on his brother's death. On the other hand, since no such possibility exists between a woman and her *pinyawa'a*, a man may approach and speak to his younger brother's wife without suspicion." [3]

The customary or most orthodox marriage is that which takes place between the children of " blood " brother and sister. A man marries his mother's full brother's daughter—

---

[1] U. McConnell, *op. cit.* p. 311.
[2] That is, the widow never passes
to an elder brother of her late husband.
[3] U. McConnel, *op. cit.* p. 327.

he marries back into his mother's clan, into which his father married before him. A woman correspondingly marries her father's sister's son. A man must give his daughter to his sister's son if she is of the right age. A man marries into his mother's clan, his sister marries the son of her father's sister who is likely to be married into the mother's clan.[1]

"Ties of blood have a steadying influence upon the marriage contract. The tendency to marry back into the mother's clan is backed by strong sentimental preference, and such marriages are likely to be more successful than those contracted between less intimately related and more distantly located clans. The link between brothers and sisters persists after they grow up and form new family ties of their own. As a widow, a woman looks to her brother's protection and seeks the shelter of his camp. He is responsible for her and her children until the mourning for her husband is past and she remarries. During her years of widowhood she will dissociate herself entirely from her husband's family, observing rigid food taboos regulated by her husband's brothers. Her brothers will help her in the care of the corpse and in the final disposing of the body. For months her brothers and sisters will assist her in collecting the necessary food, which is then offered to her husband's relatives, to the accompaniment of a mourning song and dance. After the final ceremony is over her head is shaved, food taboos are lifted, and she is expected to take her normal place in society again by marrying her husband's *younger* brother, or his equivalent. If she does not do this her brother may exact a penalty. A case was reported to me of a man who had killed his sister because he was ashamed of her unwillingness to fulfil her social obligations. A man is answerable for his sister's actions, and if she offends the social code he is responsible for her correction. A man will, however, defend his sister's rights in a just quarrel against the family and clan into which she has married. If it is his mother's clan, conflict is not so likely to occur because of the close bonds of sympathy between these two clans. If a man's wife and his sister are exchanged between more distantly related clans or tribes, trouble more easily arises."[2]

[1] U. McConnel, *op. cit.* p. 332.   [2] U. McConnel, *op. cit.* pp. 332-333.

" Although a woman leaves her father's local group on her marriage, she does not sink her identification with her own clan. Her older brother's children are the *nenka*, her younger brother's children are her *pinyaya*. It is she who calls the name for her *kami* (brother's son's daughter) and *pinyaya* (brother's daughter) in infancy when adopted into the clan. This child, who bears the same totemic name as herself, may become her son's wife. It is common to find a man's wife and mother bearing the same totemic name as members of the same clan. A woman will visit her own clan grounds whenever possible, bringing her children with her. Her brothers will interest themselves in her children and take an active part in their upbringing, initiation and marriage settlement. The mother's brother is something of a male mother to his sister's sons. In giving his daughters to them in marriage he is providing for their future as well as that of his daughters. A woman is no less interested in obtaining for her daughter a place in her own clan on her marriage. With this end in view she will instruct her daughters in her own clan lore, so that they may the more easily make their home there later on.

" These mutual arrangements seem to be the key to the happy family situation found so often in an Australian aboriginal camp. Strong attachments are forged between intermarrying clans, and it is a definite custom to go on intermarrying into the same locally adjacent clans. The ghost clan on the Archer River, for example, intermarries with the neighbouring kangaroo and dingo clan, and also with the native companion clan on the other side. The emu clan on the Kendall River intermarries with its neighbour the native companion clan, and so is on the same social footing towards it as is the ghost clan. The Wik-Natanya bush rat clan on the Holroyd River intermarries with the Wik-Nantyara barramundi clan across the river, and also with its coastal neighbours the Wik-Natera spear-handle clan. It is as if intermarrying families had settled near each other for convenience (as the parents-in-law in camp life for the same reason camp conveniently near, but aloof from, their sons-in-law) and had established rights over the locality in which they settled, exchanging wives and reserving these rights for their children in the male line. Two locally adjacent clans which continuously intermarry form together a 'company' and are as it were on ground with interchangeable hunting rights. That is, a man has a right to hunt on his wife's ground, and offers in return the hospitality and privileges of his own to his wife's people. . . ." [1]

"Although each occupied area provides certain food facilities over which the resident clan has established rights and control, food supplies vary in different areas, and reciprocity of sharing food supplies is secured. It is generally recognized that though a clan has hunting rights over its own area, the control of the food supply by 'increase' ceremonies is not for its own benefit alone, but causes abundant supplies in all other areas. Not only so, but it is generally understood that areas specially rich or unique in raw materials should send out word to relatives in other clans when the supply is ripe for consumption. The clan in charge must always initiate the first and ritualistic taking of food, after which all are permitted to tap the supply.

"Thus whilst it is usual for clans to hunt on their own grounds in small groups which follow their own bent and maintain a certain privacy, it is usual when special foods are available in certain areas for people to come from far and near to share in the hunting advantages of their relatives. Such propitious spots as 'panja' swamps, water-lily lagoons and river reaches where fish abound, are recognized meeting places for all and sundry. These big camps afford a fitting occasion for the holding of initiation ceremonies for maturing youth, for the discussion of affairs of social importance, for the rediscovery of old ties and the forging of new ones. Relatives newly acquired are introduced and their social position reconstructed. Courtesies, compliments, gifts and gossip are exchanged freely. It is a time of gaiety, of renewal of old friendships, as well as marriage settlement and exchange.

"In any large camp met together for economic or ceremonial purposes, tribes will take up their position according to the direction whence they come, N., S., E., or W. Similarly, within the tribal camp families will group them-

[1] U. McConnel, *op. cit.* pp. 333-334.

selves nearest those most intimately related, usually by clan
ties. Throughout the camp there extends from one camp
fire to another a chain of kinship, more intimate between
some families than others, closer between some clans than
others, and between some tribes than others. This relative
intimacy largely corresponds to the local proximity of intermarrying clans and tribes on their own grounds." [1]

Wik-Munkan Mythology.—The myth is a recital of the
original creative activities of the *pulwaiya* (totemic clan
ancestor and hero) and the inauguration in the beginning of
the ritual which forms the precedent for its present practice.
As the *pulwaiya* " went down " into his appropriate *auwa*
(totem centre) he assumed or " caused to be " the form of the
totemic object with which he is associated. The ritual is not
a mere recital of the original creative activities of the totemic
hero, but reflects chiefly the relationship between the totemic
hero and his clansmen of the present day. The ritual is
sacramental in that by this means they enter into contact
with their *pulwaiya* (totemic ancestor) who comes out at
their request and perpetuates for their needs the objects for
which he is responsible. Myths often have a currency as
legends or stories, but real inner meaning of the myths in
relation to ritual is known only to a few, and is the special
property of a clan. One man said he had " dreamed " the
ritual of which he was in charge, but that his father had also
dreamed it before him. The ritualistic procedure is apparently handed down from one generation to another relatively
intact, but it seems that a man " re-dreams " the ritual and so
acquires the necessary mystical qualifications for carrying it
on.[2]

The myth and ritual of the bonefish and bull-roarer totems
throw an interesting light upon these practically
universal aspects of Australian aboriginal culture, the
" increase " ceremony and the cult of the bull-roarer. In
recounting it Miss McConnel tells us that her object is to
draw attention to the close link between myth and ritual and
the inner meaning which these reveal.

The Bonefish.—The bonefish *auwa* (totemic centre) is in

<hr/>

[1] U. McConnel, *op. cit.* p. 335.   Wik-Munkan and Wik-Natara Tribes,"
[2] U. McConnel, " Myths of the   in *Oceania*, vi, 1 (Sept. 1935), p. 66.

a small creek up the Archer River, in which the bonefish breeds, and below which in the river reaches the bonefish is hunted at night-time with special spears in canoes by torch light.

The myth describes how Wolkollan the bonefish once lived as a man at Adeda with his brothers the ironwood and bloodwood trees, and how he went northwards to visit his sister Mai Korpi the mangrove. Quarrelling, he hit her on the head with his spear, which is now the stalk standing up out of the seed of the mangrove, and she struck him on the back with her yamstick—the mark which she made may still be seen on the bonefish. Mortally wounded they made peace. Mai Korpi (mangrove) went down in a flat place where mangrove grow. Women gather the fruit of the bean-pods for food. Wolkollan joined his brothers again at Adeda, and bidding them farewell, went down under the water there, promising as he did so that bonefish would come out in plenty for men to spear for food whenever they came to this place to chase them out.

In the ritual the bonefish-god (as Miss McConnel calls him) comes out of a bloodwood tree covered with red clay and riddled with spears (it takes several to kill a bonefish). He is both god and bonefish. At his feet kneels the suppliant who fans into life the phallus of the god which appears to rise of itself in response. Finally the fan is removed and the hand of the suppliant is seen to support the phallus—an act of disillusionment which is common in ritualistic procedure. This fanning of the phallus is apparently the inner meaning of the hitting of trees, stamping of the ground and sweeping of the *auwa* (totem-centre) which usually accompanies the stirring-up of the *pulwaiya* (totemic hero) in increase ceremonies at the totemic centre. Beside the bonefish-god stand his wife and partner in creation, who went down near by and is to be seen in another ritual covered with white clay, also riddled with spears. The white clay is perhaps symbolic of the milkwood tree which is usually associated with women, as the red clay of the bonefish-god is symbolic of the bloodwood tree.

Elsewhere Miss McConnel gives us another description of the same ceremony, in which she tells us that the phallus used in the rite was made of wood. A photograph that accompanies the article shows that the bonefish hero or god, as she calls him, is personated by a living man, and that both the phallus and the spear are attached artificially to his body. In any case the ceremony seems to show that the Wik-Munkan are acquainted with the nature of physical paternity.[1]

This ritual is the possession of the bonefish clan (Wik-Munkan tribe) and is performed especially at the *Wintyanam* or second initiation ceremony, when the initiates, now men, are introduced as it were to the secrets of the clan. The bonefish ritual was performed for the first time for many years when the last young man of the clan recently came of age.

The Bull-roarer.—The bull-roarers are of four different types. Two of them, called the *moiya* and *pakapaka*, belong to the Wik-Munkan (bonefish clan), and two others, called *moipaka* (male and female), belong to the Wik-Natara tribe.

(1) The *moiya* represents a young girl just entering the age of puberty. It is a small leaf-shaped plain piece of wood attached to a string and stick, and is swung by young initiates at the end of the first part of the *Utyanam* or first initiation ceremony.

(2) The *pakapaka* represents a girl who is fully mature. It is a longer and broader tongue-shaped piece of wood, painted red and white and fastened to a string. It is swung by initiates at the close of the Utyanam ceremony.

These two bull-roarers are associated in a myth with two young *utyana* (initiates) who at the end of the *Utyanam* ceremony break taboos by eating flying-foxes and sharing their food with girls. As a punishment flying-foxes carry off the initiates, and the girls are swept by the tide down the river on to a rock, where most of them " go down," but two find a bull-roarer and swing it with great interest, singing as they swing, " What is this swinging into the clouds that is forbidden ? That we two downstream are swinging ? " Then with the words " It belongs to us women really, we have found it ! But no matter ! we leave it for the men ! It is they who will always use it ! " they place it in the crack of a bloodwood tree and go down under the water. This is

---

[1] U. McConnel, in *Oceania*, vol. vi. No. 4 (June 1936), p. 460.

the *auwa* (totem centre) of the *moiya* and *pakapaka* bull-roarers and of the young girl. The bull-roarer is now taboo to women.

The ritual shows the girl swinging her *moiya* (bull-roarer). To one side sits Mai Korpi, the mangrove, who belongs to the same clan, making her mangrove food. This ritual is part of the Utyanam or first initiation ceremony.

Another rite shows the two initiates standing hand in hand while the girl swings the *pakapaka*. The white clay on the girl's breasts is symbolic of womanhood. The red clay on the initiates represents the red of the flying-fox and the white clay represents the mud with which the initiates bedaubed themselves to prevent the flying-foxes from seeing or smelling them when they sneaked up to spear the flying-foxes in the mangroves. This pattern is the conventional one used for initiates in the *Utyanam* or first initiation ceremony. This ritual is only shown to a privileged few.

The *moipaka* (male and female) are said to be husband and wife. The male *moipaka* is shaped like a phallus and the female *moipaka* is like a larger *pakapaka* (girl bull-roarer) and is said to be a grown-up woman. They are both painted red and white. The *moipaka* is swung to attract the attention of a married woman. If it is swung outside the camp, she will come out of curiosity to see what it is. The swinger then quickly hides it, for should a woman see a *moipaka* she would no longer be curious and the charm would not work. It can only be swung by *mantaiyan*, that is, "strong men," who are married.

One myth tells of two *mantaiyan* (married men), elder and younger brothers. They made a *moipaka* and kept swinging it in turns. Finally they placed it in the crack of a tree and "went down" into their *auwa* (totem centre). (This legend is very suggestive of others in which the elder brother makes a woman of the younger, who becomes his wife, the ritual of which shows two male *moipaka* one of which is said to be a woman.)

The ritual of the *moipaka* shows a line of men lying on the ground with arms outstretched and their hands touching. One of these is a "woman" and has a *moipaka* lying on her abdomen. This is said to represent the married woman who has as yet no child. Another ritual shows a line of men similarly lying, with hands clasped (symbolic of continuity). One in the middle represents a woman with a baby (made of beeswax) lying on her abdomen. Those on the left of the " woman " are men who were growing old. Then came woman and birth. Those on the right are the children who came after as a result of sex and birth. At the end of the line stands a man who swings the (female) *moipaka*. The ritual symbolises the continuity of life by means of sex and birth. (Another myth, which belongs to the baby totem, describes the making of the first baby which the *pulwaiya* then placed inside a woman.[1])

The bull-roarers thus reflect the various stages in the development of sex-relationship, from the awakening of sex interest at the age of puberty (*moiya* and *pakapaka*), to the sex life of young married couples and the acquiring by them of children by this means.

TOTEMIC HERO CULTS IN CAPE YORK PENINSULA

The totemic culture of the relatively undisturbed and dominant Wik-Munkan tribe, which is akin to that of the neighbouring eastern and western tribes, may be regarded as a " norm " for the tribes occupying a very large area in Cape York Peninsula, extending right across the Peninsula and for a hundred to two hundred miles up and down it. The totemic stones at the rock-cod *auwa* (totem centre) in the territory of the Kandyu tribe, near Coen, are comparable to the totemic ant-beds at certain of the Wik-Munkan *auwa* (totem centres). From all accounts the " story-places " and " story-stones " of the eastern coastal Koko ya'o and Yan-konyu tribes are of a similar type.[2]

After making a careful study of the Wik-Munkan tribe in 1934, Miss McConnel was able to compare and contrast its culture with that of the coastal tribes north of the Archer River, which possess phonetic, linguistic, and kinship systems distinct from that of the Wik tribes. In contrast, the totemic

[1] U. McConnel, *op. cit.* pp. 68-70.
[2] U. McConnel, " Totemic Hero-Cults in Cape York Peninsula," in *Oceania*, vol. vi. No. 4 (June 1936), pp. 452-463.

culture of these northern tribes seems to be similar to that of the Wik-Munkan, though one may detect a somewhat different mood. The heroes of the northern tribes seem to " wander " rather more restlessly, and to be more *humanly* active than the Wik-Munkan heroes, as they walk about " looking for a place to settle." The Wik-Munkan *pulwaiya* (totem) seem to wander over more restricted areas, and to go down rather more unexpectedly and suddenly into their respective " story-places " (*auwa*).[1]

A new motive occurs in the myths of the northern tribes in that when their hour is come and they are about to leave the world they " share out their grounds " before they disperse, and then proceed " to look for a place to settle." Nevertheless, they *do* eventually settle in appropriate areas, choosing a spot suitable to the natural characteristics and habitat of the totemic objects into which they emerge. Like the Wik-Munkan heroes (*pulwaiya*) they also are ancestors (*ulai* or father's fathers) of the clans which occupy the territory on which the respective " story-places " are now found.

Miss McConnel has the impression that the coastal people, and the animals also perhaps, are less established in the narrower northern end of the Peninsula and so wander rather more restlessly than do the inland Wik-Munkan who occupy a very good region and seem to be more deeply rooted to the soil.[2]

Myths of totemic heroes are a curious blending of human and natural characteristics and reflect not only the human and social interests and activities of the people to whom they belong, but also the characteristics of the objects into which they are transformed.

The wanderings of totemic heroes usually reflect the roamings of men of to-day on their hunting expeditions. A myth told by the Leminiti, a northern coastal tribe, is an example of this restless type. The native companion, opossum, mudshell, white-crested pigeon, and crayfish *ulai* (totemic ancestors) were, according to this myth, holding an initiation dance. The native companion seems to have been the leader, possibly on account of his dancing gifts. When the dance was over they " shared out their lands," and then

[1] U. McConnel, *op. cit.* p. 463.   [2] U. McConnel, *op. cit.* p. 463.

began to scatter to their respective homes, which were allocated to them. The native companion told the mudshell to go up Norman Creek and the crayfish to follow down Windawinda Creek, whilst the opossum was to go up 'Possum Creek. The native-companion chose a place near the sea and " made a nest " there ; and the " eggs " (stones) are to be seen to this day. As the opossum, crayfish, and mudshell wandered looking for a place to settle they collided with each other on the fringes of their respective grounds. When the opossum remonstrated with the others because the ground was *his*, the crayfish and mudshell politely retreated down their respective creeks, leaving the inland country to the opossum. The crayfish made his home in an appropriate spot on the Embley River near the mouth of the creek. As the mudshell retreated towards the sea, he found all the crested-pigeons camping near the sand-beach, cooking and eating " red fruit." The jackass came up to the camp, had a look at it, and then went and reported to his friends, who were the enemies of the pigeons. All of a sudden the camp was surrounded and raided. The pigeons picked up their children and fled towards the sea, leaving behind them clubs, spears, dilly-bags, and fire-sticks. There they all " went down into the sea " and the mudshell " went down " in the creek. These are now the totemic ancestors (*ulai*) of the clans which occupy these sand-beach grounds.[1]

Similarly in another myth the swamp turtle, ducks, iguana, and Torres Straits pigeons. " shared out their grounds." The duck put stones and made a nest, saying " I'll go down here." But the Torres Strait pigeon said, " I'll go further north and stay there ", so he " went down into the sea." The disappearance of the pigeons down into the sea northwards is interesting in view of the migration of the pigeon northwards each year.

In a myth of the Ndra'anit, another northern coastal tribe, the hero, Mbu the ghost, was going for a " walkabout " on the sand-beach with his wife. They paddled their canoe up a creek, then went back down the creek and followed up the main river, fishing as they went. When they met Mbu's brother, Tyit the fish hawk, they went back to the sand-

[1] U. McConnel, *op. cit.* pp. 464-465.

beach to hunt sea-turtle. Mbu suspected his brother Tyit
of hawk-like greed in devouring the turtle he had been
charged to carry back to the camp. So they quarrelled and
Mbu was mortally wounded in the fight. After " sharing
out their lands " Mbu bade a last farewell to the land of his
ulai (father's fathers), and gave parting instructions to his
brother as to the disposal of his body and the great dance
that was to be held in his honour around his corpse. Accordingly, the body of Mbu, whose incarnation is the ghost, was
prepared in the manner now used all over this area, by
disembowelling, drying, wrapping in tea-tree bark or placing
on forked sticks. In this way Mbu aptly assumes the rôle in
mythology of patron of ghosts and of rites for disposal of
the dead and of the tribal mourning song and dance. The
attribution of these burial rites, which have more cultural
affinity with the customs of the neighbouring Papuans than
with Australian usages, is interesting as a hint of a possible
culture connection with New Guinea. Nevertheless Mbu,
the ghost, is a genuine totemic hero of the mainland pattern.
Given that these customs exist on the mainland of Australia,
they must be accounted for in mythology, as are all other
social customs, ideas, and beliefs, by attributing them to
some culture-hero. The incarnation of Mbu as a " ghost "
and his association with rites for the disposal of the dead is a
natural consequence of the belief that the spirits of the dead
assume the form of ghosts.[1]

Two mythical heroes of the Wik-Natara tribe, coastal
neighbours of the Wik-Munkan, were accredited with such
extensive wanderings from the direction of the north that
Miss McConnel was at first inclined to suspect them of being
migratory heroes, particularly as a material incarnation was
not immediately revealed. Mythology describes these two
heroes as older and younger brothers who came travelling
from afar out of the north-east and as wandering on southwards down the Gulf coast, inventing spears with stingray
barbs, and spearing stingray as they followed along the sand-
beach, creating also as they went the tidal rivers and the sea.
Clearing all the scrubland that is said to have stood where
the Gulf now is with a boomerang, they journeyed out over the

---

[1] U. McConnel, *op. cit.* pp. 465-466.

Gulf taking the tides with them and "went down" in the west.

This myth has so many points in common with a moon myth of the Koko-yalunyu tribe on the Bloomfield River on the east coast, which describes the throwing of the boomerang (new moon) out over the sea, the moon's first creation of woman, and his institution of marriage, and so forth, that Miss McConnel was forced to abandon her suspicion that these Wik-Natara heroes were migratory, and to identify them as the moon and the morning star, the journey of which bodies across the sky from the direction of the north-east in the dry winter season, when the coastal people are camping and fish along the sand-beach, is reflected in the wanderings of these heroes. The voyage out over the Gulf reflects the setting of the moon and morning-star in the west, the road they took is the silver track of the moon in the water of the Gulf, and the tides follow these heroes as they do the movements of the moon. A dance which is said to have been invented by these heroes is now associated with a sand-beach clan. The movements of the dance depict the gradual development of a more intimate relationship between the two brothers. The elder one gradually assumes a masculine rôle, making clubs and spears, and generally dominating the younger, who in his turn gradually assumes the rôle of the woman, gathering wood, laying the camp-fire, cooking the fish in ant-bed ovens, and so forth. The elder finally makes a woman of the younger and marriage is instituted.[1]

The wandering of the sand-beach moon-hero is an interesting contrast to the stationary moon-hero of the inland Wik-Munkan, who, according to tradition, dwells at the bottom of a deep water-hole, in which the reflection of the moon appears. The moon-hero also is a clever fisherman. But he does not use a spear with stingray barbs, he poisons the water as is the custom in this region, and so makes men jealous of his ability thereby to catch so many fish.

The association between moon and fish may be related to the liveliness of fish on moonlight nights.[2]

The Kawadji or Sandbeach people of the east coast of Cape York Peninsula represent a very distinct type of Australian aborigine. They are essentially fishermen and

[1] U. McConnel, *op. cit.* pp. 466-467.   [2] U. McConnel, *op. cit.* p. 467.

dugong hunters, and unlike most Australian aborigines are often great seafarers. All the Sandbeach men are skilled canoe builders and navigators, and make adventurous voyages among the coral reefs and sand banks of the Great Barrier Reef, in search of dugong and turtle, and the eggs of turtles and sea birds. To those whose acquaintance with the Australian aborigine has been confined to the natives of the interior, the contrast is a striking one. Kawadji (the people of the east) is the name given by the Kanju and other inland people to these salt-water natives, who comprise several distinct tribes. They are still nomads—hunters and collectors —but as they obtain their chief food supply from the sea with the long harpoon and the multiple-pronged fish-spear, their wanderings are less constant than those of the inlanders. While they sometimes know hard times, their lot is never so severe as that of the tribes of the interior of the continent. It is true that they have long fasts and great gorges, but real drought, with its attendant hardship, is unknown, and food is in general fairly abundant. With the first rains of the north-west monsoon season the hordes move camp on to the open sea-front outside the line of the sand dunes, well above spring-tide level, to escape the floods, and the mosquitoes which come in thousands. There the natives remain stationary for several months. Food is abundant, and there is little doubt that the initiation ceremonies, with their elaborate ritual, were formerly carried out at this season. When food is plentiful the natives are in the best of spirits. Food supply is the limiting factor in most of the activities of primitive man, and in hard times even the best-tempered savages become dour and sullen, even morose. Such, then, are the Kawadji; the Koko Ompidamo of Running Creek, and the Yintjingga of Stewart River, Princess Charlotte Bay; the Ompela or Katanyu, whose territory extends from Break-fast Creek near Claremont Point to Cape Sidmouth; the Yankonyu from Cape Sidmouth to Cape Direction; the Koko Ya'o, whose territory extends from Lloyd Bay to the Olive River, and the Wutati of Margaret Bay.[1]

[1] Donald F. Thomson, " The Hero Cult, Initiation and Totemism on Cape York," in *Journal of the Royal Anthro-* *pological Institute,* lxiii. (1933) pp. 453-458.

These tribes were investigated by Mr. Donald F. Thomson, Bartlett Research Scholar of the University of Melbourne, with the help of a grant from the Australian National Research Council, in the years 1928–1929. In his first expedition he met with the Koko Ya'o tribe on the Lockhart River, and spent four months with the tribe. He has given us a valuable account of their totemic system, which in the sequel I shall follow closely.

The Koko Ya'o are a typical salt-water people. Both in material culture and in social organisation they are fairly representative of the Kawadji group of tribes. The dual division is well marked, the tribe being divided into two moieties, called Koiyana and Karpeya respectively, which, with the totemic clans, are the only exogamous groups. The clan is the land-owning group. There are no chiefs, and no central authority in the tribe, the small nomadic groups, popularly known as "camps," for which the name "horde" has been proposed, being independent, self-governing units ; but it is evident that the Hero Cult has acted as a modifying influence in establishing tribal centre or capital at Tolnonoma (Upper Pascoe River) and so providing the basis for tribal, as distinct from clan, solidarity. This, with the peculiar type of totemism, described later, probably resulted in a greater freedom of intercourse between hordes than exists in most other parts of Australia. The regulation of conduct is in the hands of the old men, recognised by the possession of special knowledge and experience. All the Cape York natives have the greatest respect for age and grey hair, and no man who is not entitled to the honorific "*Tjilbo*" (the grey-headed one) would think of raising his voice during a discussion of tribal affairs.[1]

This account of the influence exercised by old men in the Koko Ya'o tribe furnishes a good instance of the common Australian form of government to which I have given the name of *gerontocracy*, or the rule of old men.[2]

The Koko Ya'o are patrilineal, tracing their descent in

---

[1] D. F. Thomson, *op. cit.* p. 459.

[2] I am glad to learn that the word *gerontocracy* that I coined for this purpose has now been incorporated in the English language by its inclusion in the *Shorter Oxford English Dictionary*.

moiety and clan through the fathers. Thus each horde occupies the territory owned by the clan to which its male, but only some of its female, members belong, that is, those who entered it by birth and not by marriage. The horde was formerly the war-making group, and the intermittent fighting that was till lately carried on, was between the hordes of the same or another tribe, but generally of the opposite moiety. The opposition between moieties is strongly marked on Cape York, and is an important factor in the social life of the people. This is well shown at the boundary between the Koko Ya'o and Yankonyu tribes near Lloyd Bay. Here the linguistic distinction is not an important one, and the question of whether a horde on the border line belongs to the Koko Ya'o or the Yankonyu tribe is regarded as of less importance than whether it belongs to Koiyana or Karpeya moiety. The actual names of the moieties, Koiyana and Karpeya, extend beyond the bounds of these tribes, through the Ompela and Kanju tribes, and are found in only a slightly altered form, as Koiya and Karpi in the Yintjingga and Ai'ebadu tribes.[1]

Mr. Thomson was unable to discover any meaning for the names Koiyana and Karpeya, but the natives always claimed to be able to distinguish physical differences in the eyes, face, skin, and hair. In the Koko Minjen tribe of the Lower Mitchell River on the Gulf of Carpentaria, the moieties were called Pam Lu'l and Pam Bi'b, meaning straight-haired people and curly-haired people, respectively.

Mr. Thomson had an interesting example of the opposition or rivalry that exists between the moieties at the Mission Station at Lockhart River, in which most of the remaining members of the Koko Ya'o, Yankonyu, and Ompela tribes have now been collected. There the favourite pastime of the younger people was a kind of football. Members of these three tribes joined in the games, but the opposing sides were invariably Koiyana and Karpeya, so that the members of each tribe were divided against one another, the bond between members of the moiety being stronger than that between members of the tribe. This opposition also finds expression in the mythology of the Koko Ya'o, which tells

[1] D. F. Thomson, *op. cit.* p. 459.

that Koiyana moiety once had a monopoly of fire and Karpeya a monopoly of water.

In the Koko Ya'o tribe the classificatory system of relationship is found, two types of marriage being permitted, that is, either with a classificatory mother's brother's daughter or father's sister's daughter, and with a sister's son's daughter, respectively, *with whom no blood relationship can be traced.* Marriage with an actual cross-cousin is prohibited. The division of the tribe into four or eight exogamous sections which occurs so·commonly amongst Australian tribes, is not found in the Koko Ya'o tribe, nor in the Ompela, Yankonyu, Yintjingga, Kanju and Dia'yuri tribes, and Mr. Thomson was unable to discover any traces of them in other parts of Cape York Peninsula.[1]

I'wai (the crocodile), the Culture Hero of the Koko Ya'o, was the leading figure among the Yilamo or Wulmpamo, the ancestors of the present race. These " Big Men," as the natives call them in English to-day, were mythical ancestral beings who invented the present culture and traditional stock of knowledge. They lived at a time in the dim past, generally called by the somewhat nebulous term *omonoma*, literally, " in the beginning, at first," the favourite word on which to commence the telling of a legend. One of Mr. Thomson's informants, an old man of the Ompela tribe, which is closely akin to the Koko Ya'o, told him that the mythical heroes or *Yilamo* were succeeded by the Middle People, who in their turn were followed by the present generation, who have seen the arrival of the whites.

In the days of Yilamo, *minya* (animals) were men. Mr Thomson's informants told him that to this rule there were some exceptions, and that the dingo (*Apanya*) was never a man. Implicit in the mythology and Saga of I'wai (the crocodile) is the belief that I'wai, as well as the other Yilamo (mythical heroes), were once mortal, not supernatural beings, although they were endowed with powers not possessed by men to-day. I'wai himself is regarded as having the form of a man, at least at the beginning of his legend, although many of the attributes that he possesses in the Saga seem to

[1] D. F. Thomson, *op. cit.* p. 460.

be those of a crocodile, particularly when he swims with his
initiates on his back.

Among the Yilamo (mythical ancestors) I'wai alone can
be regarded as a Culture Hero. It was I'wai who invented
the initiation ceremonies, the others were merely spectators
or " helpers." It was he who called meetings of the other
Yilamo to watch him " play," and the songs in the present-
day ceremonies are those of I'wai. The belief of these people
in the ancestry of the present race is particularly interesting.
Like all primitive people who are dependent on memory and
tradition alone, they have no definite ideas of the antiquity
of their race ; the present order fades away into the dim past
only a little further than the memory of the oldest of the old
men extends. Beyond that were the " middle People "—
the human ancestors who followed the Yilamo and who
bridge the gap that they feel to exist between the Yilamo and
the present day. The Yilamo (mythical ancestors) handed
down their stock of knowledge to the Middle People who have
passed it to the present race. The old men in each generation
are the guardians of traditional knowledge, which they pass
on to the succeeding generation at initiation, in the form of
songs and legends. No Koko Ya'o man would ever think
of doubting the reality of the Yilamo (mythical ancestors),
for every day he has proof of their existence, in his totemism
and *kintja* (taboo) as well as in every natural feature of the
country, which he knows like a book, and each part of which
is indelibly associated with the Culture Hero and the Totemic
Ancestors. From his earliest childhood he has been accustomed to meeting evidences of the doings of I'wai, and each
day he is constantly seeing physical features in his own land—
boulders, headlands, and islands—left by I'wai on his
Odyssey, giving optical proof of the reality of I'wai, and the
deeds recounted in the Saga of I'wai that he has heard the
old men, whom he had every reason to revere, tell and retell,
with flashing eyes.[1]

The full Saga of I'wai has been recorded by Mr. Thomson,
largely in the native language, but need not be given here.[2]

The Koko Ya'o have totem centres of the usual kind,

[1] D. F. Thomson, *op. cit.* pp. 460-   [2] D. F. Thomson, *op. cit.* pp. 463-
463.   467.

at which they perform ceremonies of the common *Intichiuma* or *talu* type for the increasing of the totems. These centres were left behind by Yilamo, typical Australian totemic ancestors, mythical beings who first appeared in the form of men and later assumed the form of animals. These Yilamo performed extraordinary deeds, the scenes of which are often marked by stones ; sometimes the totemic ancestors were themselves turned to stone ; but directly or indirectly they gave rise to the " story stones " or totem centres of the present day.[1]

The totemism of the Koko Ya'o, in common with the whole of the Kawadji group of tribes, while it retains in some respects a typical Australian form, has a number of new and interesting features, particularly in the personal totemism, as well as in the *Intichiuma* rites, first described in the classical work of Spencer and Gillen.

Every adult member of the tribe possesses two distinct kinds of totem which may be classed as follows :

(1) The personal totem, called *nartjimo norntadji*, which he does not inherit at birth, but which comes from the mother's moiety, and sometimes from her clan. Conceptional totemism is absent, and the natives have a knowledge of physiological paternity.

(2) Clan totems called *pola* (father's father), of which each individual has several, shared by all members of his clan, and handed down from generation to generation in the patrilineal line. These are associated with Yilamo (mythical ancestors), and are centred about totem centres or " story stones," at which ceremonies for the increase of the totem of the *Intichiuma* sort may be carried out.

(1) *Personal Totemism of the Koko Ya'o.*—The personal totemism is of a singular type. Although the Koko Ya'o are strictly patrilineal, the personal totem, of which each individual possesses one only, comes, not from the father, nor yet from the father's moiety, but from the mother's moiety, and is determined by augury commencing soon after birth and culminating in the removal of an upper central incisor tooth The personal totem is associated with a spirit called *norntal*, and, unlike the *pola* (clan totem), it carries the strictest *Kintja*

[1] D. F. Thomson, *op. cit.* p. 492.

(taboo). All the *pola* (clan totems) of the mother's and mother's brother's clans are called *nartjimo*, but there is no special personal relation between a man and these *nartjimo* until one of them becomes associated with his *norntal* at the rite of tooth avulsion. He is not forbidden to kill or eat any *nartjimo*, with the exception of the one associated with his *norntal*.

In order to understand fully the ceremony of tooth avulsion, and personal totemism, some account must be given of the belief of the Koko Ya'o in the life after death, which is so closely linked up with the personal totem and the dream life.

Every person, at birth, possesses two spirits. One of these, the *norntal*, is that which pulsates on the head of an infant (the fontanelle). It resides in the body only during early childhood and with the closure of the frontal suture goes to a place in the mother's country called the *nartji norntadji*, the place of the *norntal*. The other spirit, the *mipi*, or " ghost " as it is most frequently translated, remains in the body until death, when it goes to join the *norntal*, with which it has remained in intimate association during the dream-life of the individual.

The intermittent sharp indrawing of the breath that occurs frequently when an infant is playing or " crowing " is called *ka'anta*. The *ka'anta* is regarded as associated with the *norntal*. When this occurs the mother tries to stop it by putting a broad band of white ashes across the baby's chest. If she does not succeed she takes the child's right elbow between her teeth and " bites " it, at the same time calling out the names of her younger brothers and sisters, own as well as distant, who are *kala* and *papa* respectively to the child. If the *ka'anta* ceases when the name of one of these relatives (most frequently the *kala*) is called, the man is said to take the *ka'anta*, and the *norntal* of the child goes to his *nartji* (clan territory). A special relationship is established between the child and this relative, although he does not appear to be distinguished by a special name. The *pipi* (father) and *papa* (mother) of the child may not speak to him until they have made ceremonial presentation of food, and when the child is well grown, but before the avulsion of the tooth, he and the *kala* (relative) must make a ceremonial exchange of presents. Until this exchange has been carried out they may not speak to each other.[1]

The operation of tooth avulsion is generally performed about the age of puberty, or a little later. In the case of a boy it is usually performed in the period after initiation and before marriage. The operation must be performed by a member of the mother's and not of the father's moiety. Only one tooth is removed ; in the great majority of cases it is the right upper central incisor, rarely the left. The operation of tooth avulsion is not *kintja* (taboo), but is carried out publicly in the ordinary camp, and is performed upon both sexes. The individual to be operated upon first washes his or her mouth with clean water, then spits into a vessel full of water, placed before him. The *Wulmpamo* (big men) look and try in the words of the natives, to " make it out," to detect a resemblance in the form of the spittle to an animal, plant, or other object, from the *pola* (clan totems) of the *kala* or *papa* (relatives) to whose clan territory the *norntal* (spirit) of the child has already departed. If the spittle moves freely about in the water it suggests either an animal or man. But if the spittle remains stationary, and merely spreads out a little, it is thought to take the form of a vegetable, or of some inanimate object. This search for omens is repeated again before the tooth is knocked out, but it serves merely as a guide to the old men and does not finally determine the totem of the subject. Not infrequently a female relative, a *papa* (mother, mother's younger sister) may aid in interpreting the omen. In the case of Ataparradi, younger brother of Pornjogobi, the old men saw " blood all over," *i.e.* the blood-stained spittle was diffused freely through the water. They cried at once " *Porta !* " (red ochre). After the examination of portents the operation is completed by placing a stick against the tooth and striking it with a stone until the tooth becomes loose and finally breaks away. Meanwhile the names of the *minya* (animals), *mai'yi* (plants), *nartji* (clan territory) and personal names of the relative associated with the *ka'anta* are called. The animal or plant named at the moment the tooth comes out is the personal totem of the subject. If,

---

[1] D. F. Thomson, *op. cit.* pp. 492-494.

as often happens, the tooth breaks as the personal name of the relative is called, this man gives one of his *pola* or clan totems to his *mampa* (elder sister's son) as his personal totem. If the tooth hangs after being struck, all is well, but if it jumps out from its socket, the victim has not long to live. The end of a fire-stick is finally heated by friction and thrust into the hole from which the tooth was knocked out.

The relation of a man to his personal totem is very different from that to his clan totem, and many strict taboos are associated with it. A man may not kill his personal totem if it is an animal, and he is forbidden to eat it whether it is an animal or plant. He may not speak the name of his personal totem and either calls it *yukai*, a word used for a proper name when it is taboo, as in the present instance, or for a period following the death of a person who bore it, or he refers to it by a more or less elaborate circumlocution. If a man were to kill his personal totem he would be sick. If another man kills his personal totem when he is near he is said to shiver and become " cold sick." A woman whose personal totem was *ka'oma* (Echidna) told Mr. Thomson that she had twice eaten her personal totem and had " heaved up " afterwards. The personal totem of Ataparradi was *porta* (red ochre), a clan totem of his mother's territory. He was not prohibited from using red ochre altogether, but he was not allowed to take it from Ortortinon, his mother's actual territory, although others were free to do so. But from other places he could take red ochre. Again, it is the practice when employing red ochre on a small scale to place it in the mouth and moisten it, and then use it with the thumb and finger. But Ataparradi would not put it in his mouth at all [1]

Apart from the strict taboo on killing or eating it, a peculiar relation exists between a man and his personal totem. He acts as his guardian and protects him, as for example when he is camped alone. Sometimes when he is on a journey he may awaken to find two " devils " standing near him. One of these exhorts the other to leave him alone, crying " Poor fellow, let him sleep." That is his personal totem.

To the relative (*kala*) whose totem he has taken falls the

[1] D. F. Thomson, *op. cit.* pp. 495-496.

task of carrying the tooth to the territory to which the *norntal* (spirit) of the young man (or woman) has already gone.   Generally he will leave this tooth at the totem centre of the personal totem, most frequently in water, or in a tree, according to the nature of the totem.   The *kala* wades into the pool carrying the tooth, and throws it between his legs into the water.   After it has been thrown into the water the ·man to whom the tooth belonged may never drink from this place, although others may do so freely.   The *norntal* (spirit) is intimately associated with the dream-life, and the totem place is also called the dream place.   It is therefore immaterial whether a man asks " Where is your *norntal* ? " or " Where do you dream ? "   Throughout life, when a man dreams, his *mipi* (ghost) goes to his totem place to join his *norntal*. For this reason he may not be awakened from sleep except by calling his name from a long distance.   The natives' conception of sleep is very close to that of death ; in each the *mipi* (ghost) leaves the body to join the *norntal*.   If a man has a lagoon or water-hole as his totem place he may dream that he is swimming there with his personal totem.   If his personal totem is a bird he may dream that he is flying with it.[1]

With tooth avulsion, a special relation is set up between the young man and the operator on the one hand, and the *kala* or *papa* (relative) at whose name the tooth came away on the other.   Once more the young man must make ceremonial presentations of food to each of these people before he may speak to them.   In the case of the *kala* or *papa* whose totem he has taken, and to whom has fallen the responsibility of taking the tooth to the totem place, the obligation is reciprocal.   Not only may the young man not speak to his *kala* or *papa*, but he may not smile or show the place from which the tooth has been removed until the mutual presentations have been made.

If the tooth has not been removed the *mipi* (ghost) will be compelled to drink foul water—water containing maggots —after death.

When they see a " shooting-star " the people know at once that somebody is dead.   If, as of course most frequently

[1] D. F. Thomson, *op. cit.* p. 497.

happens, the star merely passes across the heavens, they say that somebody from another district has died, but if a report is heard, the watchers cry " *Mumpa!* " They know that somebody is dead, and this his *mipi* (ghost) has come to join his *norntal* in their own country.[1]

To this account of the personal totem Mr. Thomson adds :. " Although at the outset I spoke of the rites *ka'anta poiyan*, and of tooth avulsion as ' auguries,' they are obviously· subject to considerable manipulation, and are under the full control, in the first instance of the mother, in the second of the operator and his assistants—all members of the mother's moiety. For this reason it is probably of little moment whether the totem is obtained direct when the tooth is avulsed, or is given indirectly through a mother's brother or sister. In either case the result is the same— the personal totem of the individual comes only from the mother's moiety. Indeed, it is a foregone conclusion that the personal totem must come from a mother's moiety, its very name, *nartjimo*, mother's father, indicating this, and I think that it is really to be regarded as a relic of a previous matrilineal condition that has now been completely super- seded. The only apparent purpose served by the· use of ' augury ' seems to be the outward appearance that it gives of the influence of portents in the selection of the personal totem, as if the operators—who are themselves members of the mother's moiety—felt that less violence was done thereby to the patrilineal principle."[2]

(2) *Clan Totems of the Koko Ya'o.*—The clan totems are called *pola* (father's father) by the members of the clan, and where it is not clear from the content whether a man is speaking of his human *pola* or his clan totem, he will often say *minya pola*, literally " animal's father's father." Al- though the names *pola* (father's father) and *nartjimo* (mother's father) applied respectively to the two types of totem suggests a belief in descent from the totem, no such tradition exists. The natives do believe, however, that in the days of the Yilamo (mythical ancestors) the *minya* (animals) of the present day were men.

When Mr. Thomson questioned his informants about their

[1] D. F. Thomson, *op. cit.* p. 498.   [2] D. F. Thomson, *op. cit.* p. 499.

relation to their *pola* (clan totem) they replied, " *Pola* like a brother," but strangely enough, and in striking contrast with the severe taboos associated with the personal totems, there is no prohibition whatever upon the killing and eating of the clan totem. We have seen that the Koko Ya'o are organised into local totemic clans in which descent is patrilineal. The number of totems possessed by each clan appears to be extremely variable, and may be from six to twelve, or a much greater number. Mr. Thomson found no evidence of a chief totem, but in each clan there is no doubt that some of the totems are more important than others. In a number of instances the clan territory bears the name of one of the *pola* (clan totems) of the group, but in none of these cases is there any evidence to support the suggestion that these are principal totems.[1]

Again we have seen that exogamous sections are not found in this tribe, but that two exogamous moieties are present. All important plants, animals, and other material objects have been brought within the scope of totemism. The totems are divided between the two moieties, and when a man knows what another's totems are, he also knows to which moiety he belongs. As the moieties are exogamous, it follows that no man can marry a woman with the same clan totems.

It is a common practice among the Koko Ya'o and the neighbouring tribes to name their dogs after their clan totems, but never after their personal totems, and indeed most of the names of the dogs are those of totemic animals and plants.

Although not in any way associated with the life after death, as are the personal totems, the clan totems are also intimately bound up with the dream-life. If members of his group dream of a man's clan totem during his absence on a journey, they know that he is about to return.

Many of these clan totems are associated with " story stones " connected by mythology with the Yilamo or totemic ancestors. At these stones rites of *intichiuma* or *talu* type may be performed for the increase of the totemic species by old men of the clans to which they belong, but they do not appear to be performed as regular season rites, as in those

---

[1] D. F. Thomson, *op. cit.* p. 500.

described by Spencer and Gillen and in many other tribes. Such rites for the increase of the totems are not performed for personal totems. A man named Pornjogobi belonged to a clan whose territory centred about Mosquito Point, from which it took its name. At this spot the dugong " story stone." was situated. If the people noticed a falling off in the number of dugong, a ceremony to increase dugong was performed at this stone by the old men who claimed the dugong as a clan totem. The stone was approached slowly. The men then took leaves with which they struck the stone, spitting and hissing through their lips, as they cried, " You come plenty ! Come plenty ! Come plenty ! " In the same clan territory was situated also the " story-stone " of the large edible crab. Increase ceremonies were also carried out here when these animals were scarce. As in the ceremony previously described, leafy branches were gathered, and the old men struck the stone with them, walking around and splashing it as they cried, " Crab, you come plenty ! Come plenty ! " Finally the leaves were thrown into the water.[1]

In the territory of the clan Porn'yinon on the Middle Pascoe River, there are a number of very important totem centres, including that of Pai'yam the Rainbow Serpent. He frequents a lagoon, the water of which is said to be black in colour, and hot, and is believed to be the urine of Pai'yam. Mr. Thomson's informant told him that he had seen the water shoot up from the place of Pai'yam. Sometimes Pai'yam leaves this lagoon and goes inside a great stone at a place called Api. Pai'yam is said to resemble a snake ; he has marks of many colours on his body and a great crest on his head. Members of his clan, but no others, might swim in the black lagoon, and the natives told Mr. Thomson of a man who had gone to that place, and whose *mipi* (ghost) was taken by Pai'yam. Mr. Thomson was not able to discover any evidence of a totemic cult associated with Pai'yam.[2]

" The most unusual of all totems is *wolmpilgobi*, sexual licence, which is associated with the ' woman story stone ' at Tolnonoma. If they ' flash ' the ' woman story stone ' at Tolnonoma, left by I'wai, they declare that the woman will ' go *wolmpilgobi* ' (lewd or loose). My informants said that

---

[1] D. F. Thomson, *op. cit.* p. 501.　　[2] D. F. Thomson, *op. cit.* pp. 501-502.

this story thing was once ' flashed ' by a man who had been pushed (coerced) by another who wished to obtain an ' outside ' woman, *i.e.* a woman from another place, for women were difficult for a young man to obtain. He put on *porta* (red ochre), *matan* (white paint), and *normpa* (charcoal) and a special *keni* (medicine) used to attract women. The women all went *wolmpilgobi* and ran after the man. . . . Now they have stopped flashing this stone. This abstract *wolmpilgobi*, which possesses the women as a consequence of the painting of the totem centre, is also a totem of the clan of Tolnonoma.[1]

" There is strong evidence for the belief that the cult of I'wai (the crocodile) came into Australia through Torres Straits. It is non-totemic and has been superimposed upon a totemic culture in which it belongs not to one clan or to one moiety, but to the tribe as a whole. The cult associated with it is practised by all the clans of the tribe, and thus forms a basis for tribal, rather than clan solidarity."[2]

The territory of the Yir-Yoront tribe is that part of the western coast of Cape York Peninsula which includes the mouth of the Coleman River and the three widely separated mouths of the Mitchell River, its coastal extent along the Gulf of Carpentaria being about fifty miles, its inland extent between thirty and forty miles. This area lies about three hundred and fifty miles south of Cape York, and is bisected by the fifteenth parallel of latitude south. The geography of the area is in general similar to that of a region lying to the north which has already been described by Miss McConnel.[3]

The tribe was investigated in 1933 by Mr. Lauriston Sharp, under the direction of Professor A. P. Elkin, of the University of Sydney, and under the auspices of the Australian National Research Council, on the recommendation of Professor A. R. Radcliffe-Brown and W. Lloyd Warner. He devoted the months from June to December to the investigation.

The tribe numbers at present over two hundred individuals, but it seems to have been formerly considerably larger. The

[1] D. F. Thomson, *op. cit.* p. 503.
[2] D. F. Thomson, *op. cit.* p. 504.
[3] Lauriston Sharp, " The Social Organization of the Yir-Yoront Tribe, Cape York Peninsula," in *Oceania*, vol. iv. No. 4 (June 1934), p. 404. For Miss McConnel's description of the country lying to the north, see above, pp. 188 *sqq.*

decline in population has not disorganised social and ritual life, about which little had been known and reported before Mr. Sharp's investigation.[1]

The Yir-Yoront are entirely surrounded by Koko-speaking tribes. To the north are the Koko-Taiyor, some of their clan lands extending north of the Edward River. They are the least disturbed tribe of the Peninsula. They are very closely allied with the Yir-Yoront by intermarriage and common custom, having the same patrilineal moieties and the type of kinship system. South of the Yir-Yoront, and extending to the Nassau River, are the Koko-Bera and Koko-Papun tribes, with a Kariera type of kinship and with patrilineal moieties which are named as are those of the Yir-Yoront. Inland of the Yir-Yoront are the Koko-Wanggara, south-east of the Alice River ; and Koko-Mini from the upper Palmer River, and Koko-Olkol from the upper Coleman River also stray into this region. These tribes have kinship systems of the Kariera type with four exogamous sections.[2]

The protection afforded by the Mission and the reserve has maintained the integrity of the tribes in this region to a surprising degree. The name of the Yir-Yoront tribe is derived from their language, for the word *Yir* means speech.

The kinship structure of the Yir-Yoront is characterised by—

(*a*) Unilateral or asymmetrical cross-cousin marriage. A man must marry his mother's brother's daughter, that is, his matrilineal cross-cousin, or some other woman denoted by the same kinship term ; he may not marry his father's sister's daughter. The rule prohibits the exchange of sisters between two men ; a man may not marry the sister of the sister's husband.

(*b*) The tracing of the descent through three primary lines, which leads to the recognition in terminology and behaviour of five patrilineal lines of descent. The conventional five generations are distinguished.[3]

The Yir-Yoront have a normal type of Australian patrilineal cult totemism. The patrilineal clans of the tribe are grouped into two patrilineal moieties, named *Pam Lul* and

---

[1] L. Sharp, *op. cit.* p. 405.
[2] L. Sharp, *op. cit.* pp. 406-407.
[3] L. Sharp, *op. cit.* p. 412.

Pam Bib, which are the same divisions found in the tribes to
the north and south.   Among the Yir-Yoront all the men of
the *Pam Lul* clans marry into the other moiety ; but only
men of certain *Pam Bib* clans marry into *Pam Lul* clans,
the others marrying into clans of their own *Pam Bib* division.
The moieties accordingly cannot be correlated with the
kinship system and they do not function to control marriage,
nor do the natives think of them as associated with the
marriage rule.   The natives can give no meanings for the
names of the moieties.   Each moiety in the different tribes
has as its own peculiar totem a bird, *talar*, a night-hawk for
the *Pam-Lul*, and *min-lulu*, a small night bird, for *Pam Bib*.
The *Pam Bib* night bird is numbered among the totems of
one of the *Pam Bib* clans ; but another *Pam Bib* clan counts
the *Pam Lul* night hawk among its totems, so that the totem
of a clan in one moiety serves for the totem of the other
moiety.   An explicit rule prohibits a man killing or eating the
totem of his own moiety, but normally these particular birds
are not eaten anyway.   As usual in a dual organisation, the
moieties function ceremonially.   Occasionally a member of
each moiety insults the other moiety by killing its totem and
hanging it up in a public place.   The men of each moiety
then contribute various personal ornaments for the decoration
of their dead totem, and throw harmless reed spears at the
man who killed it.   The dead birds are thrown away, buried,
or burned without ceremony.   The moieties are also opposed
to each other in ritual combat in certain of the clan totemic
rites.   Other characteristics of the moieties are derived from
the clans which compose them, and their solidarity is thus
chiefly derivative.   The association of the clans in the moieties
appears entirely fortuitous.[1]

The Yir-Yoront clans are further grouped into " Coastal
People " and " Inland People."   There is no correlation
between these divisions and the moieties.   There is also a
ritual opposition between these geographical divisions in
some of the rites.

There are twenty-eight extant Yir-Yoront clans, the
largest numbering over thirty persons, while others are on

[1] L. Sharp, " Ritual Life and Economics of the Yir-Yoront," in *Oceania*,
vol. v. No. 1 (Sept. 1934), pp. 19-20.

the verge of extinction. The various clans are ranked to a slight degree, their prestige depending on the tribal importance of the clan's ancestors, on the importance of the men in the living clan, on the size of the clan and its domain, and on the relative strength of the clan's position in the kinship structure. One or more of the older men in each clan is recognised as a leader, being termed " head man." Together these " head men " constitute the community gerontocracy or senate, to which men are elevated in part by their relation to the clan, in part by their personal abilities as generally recognised by the tribe.[1]

Several clans may be associated in one exogamous patrilineal descent line of the kinship structure. These different clans of one descent line do not have a common origin or common ancestors ; their separate lineages extend backwards into the mythical ancestral times without confusion like Euclidean parallel lines. The ancestors of such clans may have acted together in some of the great events of tribal mythology, thus providing sanctions for the peculiar alliance of the clans themselves. These mythological sanctions are especially strong when the associations of different clans follows natural lines, as when the " Rainbow Serpent," " Water Snake," and " Fresh Water " clans, or clans whose countries are near each other, are allied within one patrilineal line. However, many clans are associated without apparent sanction or reason. This linking of different clans by the kinship system has important effects in the general clan organisation.

The following factors contribute to the solidarity of any clan : a common patrilineage which includes a group of clan ancestors who lived at the beginning of time and continue their existence as spirits into the present and future to the special benefit of the clan ; a common country or countries, made up of places associated with past, present, and future activities of the ancestors and which, with their natural resources, are under the exclusive guardianship of the living clan, aided by the ancestors ; personal names which belong to the ancestors or which pertain to things, places, or activities associated with them, and which are borne ex-

[1] L. Sharp, *op. cit.* p. 20.

clusively by members of the clan and their dogs ; common multiple totems, things or activities particularly associated with the ancestors in the past or present environment, one of which serves as a clan name ; that portion of the sacred and profane tribal mythology which describes the doings of the clan ancestors and relates the totems to them, and thus to the living clan which has the special, but not exclusive, guardianship of these myths ; representations of the ancestral activities and totems by the adult men of the clan in the tribal ceremonies which serve ostensibly to introduce the young men of the tribe to their ancestral heritage ; the increasing of certain totems, not necessarily belonging to the clan, by individual men and women of the clan, at certain spots within the clan domain.[1]

There is no special name for the remote ancestral time, but it was very long ago. The ancestors of the mythical times, with few exceptions anthropomorphic but endowed with extraordinary powers, lived on the whole as the natives live to-day. They created the chief topographical features of the country, usually by throwing their belongings about in a careless manner. They performed a number of Promethean feats for the benefit of mankind, they established sacred sites, and delimited clan countries and totems. Certain individuals among the ancestors transgressed tribal custom, copulated with their sisters or with menstruating women, and so on, but these are significantly known as " crazy," and are analogous to the " crazy boy " culture heroes of some other primitive peoples, who antithetically exemplify what should not be done. The ancestors exist in the present world as spirits, an order distinct from the spirits and ghosts of the common dead. They are now entirely beneficent, to the tribe in general and to their own clan in particular, aiding the sick and distressed, favouring members of their own clan, but never directly injuring others. The present members of the clan reflect the past of the ancestors in names, personal characteristics, and relationships. An individual has his " own " ancestor, a kind of *alter ego*, whose name he bears, who physically resembles him, whose wife is his wife and whose children are his children. A man calls his ancestral

[1] L. Sharp, *op. cit.* pp. 20-21.

twin " young brother " ; he also thinks of himself as his own
" younger brother," apparently unaware of the philosophical
subtleties involved. The modern individual is not a reincarnation of the ancestor, they have no " soul stuff " in
common, nor has the " spirit-child " from which a man
develops any connection with the ancestral double.[1]

A majority of the Yir-Yoront clans have multiple countries
which are not contiguous, and which vary from an acre or
two up to a number of square miles in area. These several
countries are found in a rough north-south band, so that
there is little differentiation in the character of a clan's
countries. The countries of a clan, with their natural resources, are owned by all clan members in common, the
ownership being sanctioned by the common tribal mythology
in which certain activities of the clan's ancestors are located
in the clan countries. The right of exclusive use of the land,
which is distinguished from ownership, is extended to the
children of clan women and to members of clans associated
in the same patrilineal line. People gather and hunt ordinarily
in whatever country they will. Thus there is practically a
standing permission which opens a clan's countries to all, but
this permission may be withdrawn by the clan in special cases.[2]

For each clan there is one watery spirit-centre situated on
the clan domain in a lagoon, creek, or arm of the sea. Here
a particular male or female ancestor of the clan resides, whose
province it is to send out all the " spirit-children " which will
be born into the clan. These spirit-children derive from an
inexhaustible store, are transformed into some active natural
object such as a leech, snake, small fish, whirlwind, or turtle,
which can enter the body of the mother after it has been seen
or " found " by the mother herself or by the real or classificatory father, who transmits it to the mother. There is no
dreaming associated with conception, nor is any ritual
attitude adopted towards the supposed natural agent of conception, which may or may not be one of the multiple totems
of the child's clan. The natives say that children are sent out
from the spirit centres only when people have intercourse ;
but it is not the intercourse, but rather the immigration of
the " spirit-child " which causes a pregnancy. " Spirit-

[1] L. Sharp, *op. cit.* p. 22.　　　　　[2] L. Sharp, *op. cit.* p. 23.

children " are sent out without consideration of the regularity
or irregularity of the parents' marriage. When a woman
discovers that she is with child, the circumstances of the
" finding " of the natural agent, which may have been
several months before, are remembered by the mother or
by a father. Since the responsible ancestor sends " spirit-
children " only of his own clan to the countries of his own
clan in his own tribe, the resultant offspring is affiliated to the
clan in whose country the natural agent was found. With
the aid of various obvious fictions the spirit-child is usually
" found " in the clan country by the child's real father. But
a child is sometimes " found " in the clan country of a
classificatory father, that is, in the country of a clan which is
associated with the real father's clan in a patrilineal descent
line of the kinship system. In this event the child is excluded
from its real father's clan, but is brought up by its own family,
with the result that a family may include several children of
the father's clan and several children of different but associated clans. The position of a given man's children is
thus fixed as regards the kinship system, but variable as
regards the clans. A person belongs to his father's clan, but
it may be the clan of the real father, or the different clan of a
classificatory father. In any event, it is clear that the fixed
patrilineal kinship group serves as the limiting factor in clan
descent, whatever may be the reasons which determine affiliation to a specific clan within this group.[1]

When a child is a few days old, the father accepts it,
and he or a classificatory father gives the child a " big
name," which is definitely associated with an ancestor of the
clan to which the child belongs, and thus publicly affiliates
the child to its clan. This name may at the same time belong
to an older male or female relative of the child. At teething
age a child receives a " little name," which is also associated
with the clan, and by which the child is generally known.
This ordinary name may derive from a relative or may have
been made up by the father. Every person receives at least
these two names. But since older persons bearing these same
names may die, and the names thus become taboo, a third or
fourth name is often required.[2]

[1] L. Sharp, *op. cit.* p. 24.　　　[2] L. Sharp, *op. cit.* p. 25.

Everything in the Yir-Yoront environment is associated with one or more clans as a totem, and is thus brought into relationship with the human society. This apportionment of all nature among the different clans follows the principle that whatever was particularly associated with the ancestors of a clan, or whatever may in some fashion be linked with these ancestral associations, now belongs to the clan. Because the white man is called " ghost," all things pertaining to him are attributed to the " Corpse " clan to which all ghosts belong, since the white man and his culture have not yet been associated with any ancestors in the tribal mythology. Some of the totemic associations appear to be fortuitous, but for others a natural or economic basis of classifications may be found. Coastal clans number coastal phenomena among their totems, inland clans, inland phenomena. All totems of a clan are common to all clan members and some may be shared with other clans, especially those in the same patrilineal descent line. Except for the two moiety totems, there is no taboo on killing or eating the totems. It is believed that a man pressed hard by his adversary may escape by changing himself into any one of his clan totems. A man may sometimes think of totems in terms of the kinship system as these terms would be applied to human members of the same clan. It is apparent that there is little formal recognition of the totem apart from the ritual and mythology, but a knowledge of these is sufficient to enable an adult man to give without hesitation the clan affiliation of almost any object. A clan derives its name from what might be considered the chief totem of the clan. This totem is prominent because it plays an important rôle in the ancestral mythology, with the result that many of the clan personal names are associated with it. But no special attitude towards the chief totem differentiates it from the other totems of the clan. The ancestors are not totems, but because of their extraordinary powers they are sometimes confused with totems. The totems of a clan are associated with the moiety to which the clan belongs, but the association is obviously secondary. Clan totemism is the only type found among the Yir-Yoront : they have no sex or individual totems.[1]

[1] L. Sharp, *op. cit.* p. 26.

As the daily technical activities and kinship behaviour of the Yir-Yoront reproduce the ordinary life of ancestral times, so the totemic group ritual reproduces the extraordinary doings of the tribal ancestors. The ritual life of the group may best be described in terms of the sacred rites and rites with which the tribe is intimately associated, as far as these have been recorded, the record not being necessarily complete. There are at least twenty-five " sacred grounds." These are monuments commemorating some ancestral event which happened at the spot where they are situated, and they are named after some feature of this event. The monument consists of one or more stones ; all stones, except a poor conglomerate which is not used for this purpose, having to be imported, and so lending additional value to the site. Ten of these monuments are " little sacred grounds " and have no taboos or rites connected with them, and are generally uncared for. These, and the myths connected with them, are openly known to all members of the community. Fifteen " big sacred grounds " are taboo to women, children, and all men not properly introduced to them. The stones of these latter sites are considered dangerous in themselves, and associated with them is a tabooed area of varying size. Some of the myths accounting for the establishment of the sites in ancestral times are secret. The clans in whose territories the sites are found own them and the associated ceremonies ; they have special charge of keeping up the sites, enforcing the taboos, and introducing the uninitiated, but they are aided by all tribesmen who have been properly introduced. At six of these " big sacred grounds " the rites consist of a simple introduction, following the ancestral example, to the stones and to two or three different kinds of food found near the site ; thereafter the initiate may enter the tabooed area and hunt or gather the tabooed food there, though over-indulgence leads to dire physical disabilities. The introduction to these six rites may be made at any time of the year. The tabooed foods are not necessarily totems of the clans in charge, and there is absolutely no associated idea of increasing these foods. A ceremony which is purely historical, but which includes the introduction of the uninitiated, is performed at three other sites. This rite is of general tribal significance, but while the clan which owns the site is in charge, members of other clans represent their own clan ancestors in the many episodes of the ceremony. At the six remaining " big sacred grounds " group increase ceremonies are performed, all men who have been introduced to the ceremony participating. These rites are also historical in character. But it is expressly affirmed that they increase certain things, and these things play a prominent part in the myths of the rite, although nothing is expressly said or done during the ceremony about increasing them. In three cases the things increased (sweethearts and children, children and turkey) are associated as totems with the clan which owns the site and ceremony ; in the other three cases (diver ducks twice and wallaby) there is no association between the totems and the clans in charge.[1]

Thus of the twenty-five recorded permanent sacred sites, only six are ostensibly associated with increase ceremonies. It should be noted, however, that the stones of a large majority of these sites, " big " and " little," are believed to represent, in order of frequency, eggs of birds, after which many sites are named, the organs of generation, and excrement.

The Yir-Yoront participate in at least ten other group ceremonies, but these are associated with different sites, which are not permanently sacred or tabooed. The areas where the secret parts of these rites are performed year after year are tabooed only for the duration of the ceremonies and for a short period thereafter. Five of these ceremonies are purely historical : three similar rites, dealing with the " Rainbow Serpent," are held in three separate countries of that clan ; another is held in " Corpse " clan country, and deals primarily with that subject, but the fifth, dealing with crocodiles, is not held in the " Crocodile " clan country. Of these ceremonies not connected with sacred grounds, three are increase rites, two of them for the increase of wallabies are exactly similar to that mentioned above, which is associated with a sacred ground, and, as in that case, the officiating clan does not number wallaby among its totems, nor is the animal especially prolific near the places where the rites are performed. The third ceremony in this category

[1] L. Sharp, *op. cit.* p. 27.

is for the increase of turtle, which is a totem of the clan in charge.

This somewhat numerical presentation, which has perhaps indicated the complexity and confusion of the variety of ideas lying behind the group rites of the Yir-Yoront, may be summarised from a slightly different point of view. The Yir-Yoront participate in nine group ceremonies, which are believed to increase six different things, which are totems of the clan in charge of the rite in only four cases, and the rites are held at permanent " sacred grounds " in only six cases. The objects to be increased are not especially abundant in the region where the rites are held. There are eight purely historical rites, three (which are the same) being held at " sacred grounds."[1]

The ceremonies which have been mentioned are group rites in which the different clans participate together. A very different type of ritual is the individual increase ceremony. It is this type of ceremony, rather than the group increase rites, which seems the closer analogy of *talu* or *intichiuma* rites, so commonly performed by the Australian aborigines. Dotted all over the Yir-Yoront territory are numerous " holes " named for various things, chiefly for fish, vegetables, animals, birds, and insects, sometimes at a place where these things are naturally abundant, sometimes not. These things are not necessarily totems of the clan in whose country the " holes" are found. These sites are depressions in the ground, sometimes associated with trees, but never with stones. They are not sacred, and their names, situation, and purpose are known to the community in general. Only eighty of these, representing some fifty different things, have so far been recorded, but there are undoubtedly many more. Annually, during the rains or the season following, one of the older men or women of the clan in whose country this particular " hole " is found performs alone, but not secretly, a simple ceremony to increase the thing associated with the site. The operator cleans out the depression and then, variously, jabs it repeatedly with a digging stick, or knocks a spear-thrower or stick against the associated tree, or throws dirt out in all directions, the while muttering, " plenty, plenty," or singing out place-

[1] L. Sharp, *op. cit.* p. 28.

names of his own and sometimes neighbouring tribal territory, but omitting names of places where the object is not naturally found. There are variations of this procedure, and the same object may be increased in different ways at different sites by the same person. Each site was established in the mythical times, when an ancestor associated the thing in question with the particular spot of his clan's country, though there is no evidence that the ancestor instituted the increase ceremony itself. Beliefs concerning the present increase of objects are fairly clear. " Images " of the object which exist in the site are " made " or " brought alive " by the ceremony. The ancestors do not explicitly aid in this process, they are not called upon, nor did they necessarily place the " images " in the site. Merely for the sake of description, and with numerous obvious reservations, the " images " which pre-exist in the Yir-Yoront increase holes might be termed primitive, Australoid analogies of the Platonic " ideas." The rite simply materialises these " images " or " ideas." The operation is recognised as distinctly different from that which makes or controls rain, lightning, and crocodiles. A survey of the various things increased shows that many of them are economically important ; but other equally important things are omitted, and are not known to be increased by clans of other tribes, but simply " grow by themselves." A good many things which are of no apparent social concern whatsoever are also increased, as well as things which are definitely anti-social. The native does not believe that he must increase runaway wives, diarrhoea, poisonous snakes, hornets, mosquitoes, and so on, for the continued welfare of society or because he must " support Nature." The inconsistencies of the system are difficult to explain, though it may be superficially concluded that the native is simply partially recognising and perhaps co-operating in the inevitable processes of Nature in his environment.[1]

" In this discussion of clans and the totemism associated with the clans," observes Mr. Sharp in conclusion, " nothing has been said of hordes. The typical Australian horde hardly appears as a separate entity in the Yir-Yoront social

---

[1] L. Sharp, *op. cit.* pp. 30-31.

pattern. It is most nearly approximated by the patrilineal clan, which is the autonomous land-owning unit, and exogamous. Because of factors resulting from the division of a clan's land into separate lots, and because an individual is not necessarily in his real father's clan, the Yir-Yoront clan-horde assumes a somewhat aberrant form. The camps comprise fragments of many different clans, the individual members of which shift about from one camp and country to another, some being associated with one large portion of the tribal territory which is considered their range, others with another. Even during the rainy season, when the community splits up into very small camps, the men of a clan are separated and do not live together in their own territory as a horde. This does not vitiate the sentimental ties which attach a clan to its own particular ' home ' countries, which if not often or regularly lived in by a clan member, are frequently visited. In the arrangement of the larger dry-season camps, tribes live separately if more than one are represented, but within the tribal grouping the clans are divided and mixed.

" In concluding this discussion, the importance of the ancestors, of the social past, must again be emphasized. From the point of view of the native, the ancestors are the centre about which so much of his life revolves. The customs and beliefs associated with the ancestors provide a mechanism which relates the individual to the group and, with the group, to Nature. They are the chief factors in the solidarity of clan, tribe, and race. They provide the sanctions and explanations of the native's world." [1]

TOTEMISM IN OTHER TRIBES OF QUEENSLAND

The last tribes of Queensland which I shall notice consist of a group of tribes which formerly occupied a large territory in south-eastern Queensland bounded by an imaginary line drawn from Bowen to Cloncurry, thence to Thargomindah and across to Brisbane. The tribes are now broken up and dispersed, but fragments of them are collected in the Settlement at Cherburg, near Murgon, where they were

[1] L. Sharp, *op. cit.* pp. 31-32.

examined by Miss C. Tennant Kelly during about four months in 1934. She tells us that all the tribes included in this area possess the marriage organisation in four sections, with two moieties which are exogamous, with matrilineal descent. The names of the moieties and sections change as the language changes, but over a considerable area the sections are termed Wungo and Kupuru in the Wuturu moiety, Banbari and Kulgila in the Yangaru moiety. This is so all along the coast from Bowen to Bundaberg, where they change entirely and become Barong and Balkoin in the Kapyne moiety, Dharwoin and Bunda in the Dhilbye moiety. Despite the changes of the names of the sections and moieties, the members of all these tribes living communally on the Settlement were able to identify their right sections in another tribe and language. The most commonly used words for the moieties are Wuturu and Yangaru. Miss Kelly is convinced that there is no meaning for either moiety or section terms throughout this area.[1]

The division of natural species between the moieties is not consistent for the whole area, although the list will probably be identical for several adjacent tribes. Thus opossum is always to be found in the Wuturu moiety except in the tribes from Bundaberg south to Brisbane, but right along the coast from Brisbane to Bowen, and right through to the west, and among the Kalali of Thargomindah this is the case. Fresh water is Yangaru along the coast, but in the west it changes to the opposite moiety.[2]

The Kuam people of the Nebine River say that when a man dies and goes to the spirit world his own *yuri* or totem meets him and introduces him to all his relations, that is, the natural species which are included in the same moiety. These people also said that the reason why the frog was in the opposite moiety to the opossum was because the frog was the opossum's father; for there was a resemblance in the way they hopped. According to the kinship system one's father was in the opposite moiety. When Miss Kelly's informants worked out lists of totems contained in each moiety

---

[1] C. Tennant Kelly, "Tribes on Cherburg Settlement, Queensland," in *Oceania*, vol. v. No. 4 (June 1935), pp. 461-464.

[2] C. Tennant Kelly, *op. cit.* p. 464.

they invariably reasoned along these lines : trees and the birds which made their nests in them were in the same moiety ; trees which grew alongside creeks, or in water-holes and swamps, were in the same moiety as water, fishes, water-fowl, lily-roots.[1]

Sometimes her informants would give the name of one natural species for both lists, as in the case of the Kabi Kabi (Maryborough), where the carpet snake is in both moieties, but there are four kinds of skin markings recognised, and two of them go to each side. The Wierdi (Clermont) give the grey kangaroo as Mapin (Wuturu) and the red kangaroo as Dhabim (Yangaru), but in battle the men of these totems would not fight each other. The Wierdi people say that certain natural species belong to fire and others to water ; opossum, bee, and sand goanna are said to " own fire," while carpet snake, scrub turkey, lizard and porcupine " own water." It was claimed that long ago " we (the Wierdi) were a people who had fire and no water, and these fellows who lived in the scrub had water, so we joined up. They gave us water and we showed them how to make fire. They had a clever man who knew the ' talk to bring water.' "[2]

Another interesting feature of this tribe is that each totem is specially related to a tree, and at death a forked piece of the correct tree is placed in the ground at the final resting place of the deceased's bones. Thus emu is said to own box tree, porcupine and eagle-hawk own brigalow, opossum owns kidji. Soft woods were in one moiety and hard woods in the other.[3]

Although the moieties are known and recognised, they are seldom mentioned in conversation unless information is sought about them ; on the other hand the names of sections are used in everyday conversations. The greatest emphasis, however, is placed on the totem. This establishes a person's relationship beyond doubt. This totemic emphasis is also seen in the burial rites. For example, at the funeral of a member of the Kabi Kabi tribe which Miss Kelly witnessed, the deceased's father went ahead of the cortège waving his arms in a beautiful swooping movement in imitation of the eagle-hawk, then again he would kneel and scratch in the

---

[1] C. Tennant Kelly, *op. cit.* p. 465.   [3] C. Tennant Kelly, *op. cit.* p. 466.
[2] C. Tennant Kelly, *op. cit.* p. 465.

sand, like a scrub turkey, the totem of the deceased, and then he would make curious twisted markings in the sand to represent his own totem, carpet-snake. The man's wife (deceased's mother) was scrub turkey. The right marriage for this man would have been with an eagle-hawk woman. Therefore the father performed the ceremonies for the deceased as if he had been a child of a " right " marriage. The eagle-hawk rite was performed in order to ensure that the deceased's father's father might recognise his grandchild as he entered the spirit world.[1]

Still in the more western parts of the area the moieties also function in burial rites. Thus among the Kangalu of Emerald the body of a deceased person was carried for a time, the Wuturu facing the sunrise and the Yangaru facing the sunset. At a funeral of a member of the Kuam tribe the relatives were " smoked " by the members of the opposite moiety to which the deceased belonged.[2]

Miss Kelly obtained numerous accounts of the ceremonies performed for the increase of the totems, but only gives a summary description of her results. A man of Kungabula (Warrego River) described for her the rites for the increase of kangaroos. Every such rite took place at a certain spot of great sanctity, and these places were always most vividly described.

Among the Kabi Kabi rain was " made " by a " clever " man. Accompanied by some other old men he ascended Mount Ural at Miva near Tiaro. Near the top of the mountain is a cave at the door of which a rare vine grows, not to be found elsewhere. The stem of this vine when cut contains a watery substance. Taking portions of the vine stem to the very top of the mountain, the " clever " man talks to Biral (all-Father), shows him the dryness of the land, and mentions neighbouring friendly tribes who are suffering for lack of rain. Cutting the vine into as many pieces as the number of tribes mentioned, he throws a piece in the direction of each tribe's territory, calling out the name of the tribe as he does so. Miss Kelly's informant has seen the rain come down in torrents almost immediately after this ceremony.[3]

---

[1] C. Tennant Kelly, *op. cit.* p 466.   466-467.

[2] C. Tennant Kelly, *op. cit.* pp.   [3] C. Tennant Kelly, *op. cit.* p. 467.

The Kuam (Nebine River) say that the first " sugar-bag " (bee) was made by the bat, who found a sticky milky weed which he glued on to a few cockatoo feathers ; it then flew away.   He chased it all around the country owned by the Kuam until it came to a big cave called Ungwari ; but now it was a bee.   Afterwards the rites for the increase of bees were always performed at this cave.[1]

A similar system of personal names existed throughout the area.   Three names are given to both men and women. First the Yamba name, which indicates the spirit home of the bearer.   At his death his spirit will return to this place.   Old people on the Settlement many miles from their own country longed to go back to their own tribal territory before they died in order to ensure their spirit's safe return to its home. Secondly, the Kujal name.   This is held in common with brothers and sisters.   Strangers can know you by this name. Thirdly, the Kyi name, which is a personal and secret name rarely told to anyone except a close relation.   The second and third names are derived from the father's totem.   Thus a woman who was opossum (inherited from her mother) was named for emu, for that was her father's totem.   Her Yamba or spirit home name was Butilbaru (a sandy creek-bed " back home "), her Kujal name meant " emu moves its neck this way and that," and the Kyi name meant " old emu walking up and down." [2]

Importance was attached to dreams in which totemic symbols appeared.   If a man dreams of a carpet-snake and this is his wife's totem, then he knows he will soon have a visit from a close relation of his wife's family.   The dream is interpreted thus : an old male snake means the wife's mother's brother.   If it is wounded the wife's mother's brother is sick and wishes them to go to him.[3]

Right through the area there seems to have been a taboo on eating one's own totem.   Sometimes the entire tribe refrained from eating a certain animal or bird.   The Kalali observed a strict taboo on porcupine, which was believed to be an evil spirit stuck all over with spears with which their ancestors had brought him to subjection.   It was considered

[1] C. Tennant Kelly, *op. cit.* pp. 467-468.

[2] C. Tennant Kelly, *op. cit.* p. 468.

[3] C. Tennant Kelly, *op. cit.* p. 468.

a breach of good manners to kill the totem of a person in his presence. Usually the owner of the totem would turn away and hang his head as if in mourning until the hunter had gone out of sight with his catch.[1]

A Kupuru man marries a Kulgilayan woman and the children are Banbari, and so on. This is the ideal marriage, and in addition the woman should be of the same totem as the man's father—which, therefore, brings the man's children back to his father's totem. One or two of Miss Kelly's informants said that to marry " wrong " in the olden times would have been punished with death, but on investigation " wrong " marriages proved to have very definite rules governing them. They were never contracted (*a*) with a woman of the same totem, (*b*) with a woman in the same marriage section as one's self, and (*c*) with a woman of " close blood." The children of these so-called " wrong " marriages always take the same section as would have been theirs had the mother married correctly. Further, a person receives his totem from the clan of his mother and mother's brother. It is the latter who sponsors a youth through the Bora or initiation ceremony, and who plays an important part in the marriage ceremonies of his sister's daughter. He is, indeed, at all times the most important man in the lives of his sister's children. Moreover, this relationship is not affected by the " wrong " marriage of his sister. The children are of the same totem regardless of their father's section.[2]

All these rules are significant, since they prove that the " wrong " marriage was condoned by society and had definite laws to control it. It would seem that the totemic clans and kinship and not the sections were of primary importance in marriage and descent. True, the section system does group together brothers and sisters in one section, thus by its rule of exogamy preventing incest, but it is the totemic grouping which is fundamental. Informants said that if persons of the same totem married, a man's father would be of the same totem as himself and therefore stand to him in the mother's brother relationship. This, of course, would be " incestuous " and would anger the totemic spirit, with the result that

[1] C. Tennant Kelly, *op. cit.* pp. 469-470.

[2] C. Tennant Kelly, *op. cit.* p. 471.

there would be no further increase of that particular totemic species. Hence society takes precaution to protect itself from such a calamity by placing all people of the same totem in the one moiety and emphasising the brother-sister relationship of the men and women in the same section. These precautions are prompted by fear of the totemic ancestors and the withdrawal of their favour in the form of food. The sections are an added safeguard, though tribes without them manage just as well. Nor do the sections function ceremonially ; throughout the transitional and mortuary ceremonies it is the moieties and clans which constitute the groupings and set the rules for the behaviour of all concerned.[1]

It is of interest to note the extent to which totemism is retained in the life of the Settlement. Both full-blood and half-caste natives, provided they were reared as children in the native camp, have a very real belief and interest in the totemic ancestors. Contact with the official and the missionary have made them chary of openly discussing these matters. They fear the ridicule of the white man, but at the time of death one can observe how deep-rooted is this belief, and in their grief mourners who previously seemed completely under mission influence return to the older forms as if they had never ceased to practise them. This is all the more remarkable seeing that all funerals are conducted by the missionaries.

A very general custom is for the father or, in the present disintegrated society, any other male relative to proclaim aloud to the spirits the good qualities of the deceased who is now on his way to meet them. This was done by the father of a girl whose baby died. He called out each night for about an hour, until a new moon appeared. He called on the totemic ancestors and then on all the people who had died during his own memory, and who were any relation to the baby.[2]

In conclusion Miss Kelly observes that " in such a tangled society as that on the Settlement there is very little hope of moiety or section organization surviving. Various tribes have totems which appear in different moieties, thus adding to the chaos, and sections do not seem fundamental in the native organization. Also there is definite white influence

[1] C. Tennant Kelly, *op. cit.* p. 471.   [2] C. Tennant Kelly, *op. cit.* p. 472.

operating on the ritual and social life which takes no account of either moiety or section.

" But as yet there is no sign that the totemic clan system will cease to function. The totem as a personal possession survives. The important thing to-day is—' What skin are you ? ' ' I am 'possum,' is probably the reply. ' I too am 'possum, we are brothers.' . . .

" The older people guard their religious secrets very jealously from the young men and women who have been reared since birth with white people. The young men are not initiated and are therefore not suitable recipients of the tribal lore and totemic secrets. They will, however, strive to prevent the marriage of two of these young people who are of the same totem Sometimes their warnings are heeded, but in other cases white influence aids the younger generation in its defiance. These marriages are always termed ' unclean ' by the older people." [1]

[1] C. Tennant Kelly, *op. cit.* pp. 472-473

CHAPTER XI

THE totemic and social organisation of the tribes of Central
Australia have been described once for all in the classic works
of Sir Baldwin Spencer and F. J. Gillen, to which subsequent
research appears to have added very little, though we have
seen that Professor Elkin in 1934 was able to give us, from
personal observation, an account of the Macumba sub-tribe
of the Arunta.[1] In 1926, long after the publication of his two
great works on the Central and Northern Tribes, Spencer
paid a final visit to the Arunta for the purpose of revising,
with the help of the few remaining old men of the tribe, his
former reports of their customs and beliefs. He was able to
verify the general accuracy of his earlier description of the
tribe, and to supplement it with some fresh and interesting
details. The new information is fully set forth by him in his
book *The Arunta, a Study of a Stone Age People*, published
in 1927, and is given by him more briefly in his last work,
Wanderings in Wild Australia, which was published in 1928.
From this last volume, which contains his final conclusions,
I will extract what he tells us of the totemic system of that
tribe, which may be regarded as the centre or pivot round
which his great researches revolved. He writes as follows :—

" It was not until 1926, when revising our work amongst
the Arunta, that I learned more fully the meaning of certain
of the Engwura performances dealing with the Alchera
beliefs and what may be called the cult of the *Churinga* in its
association with the *kuruna* or spirit part of each individual.

" There are four terms that are of special importance in

---

[1] See above, pp. 167 *sqq.*

connection with the fundamental beliefs of the Arunta—
alchera, knanja, churinga, and *kuruna.*

" The term *alchera* is one of somewhat vague and wide
import which it is difficult to define with anything like
absolute precision.   It is not applied to any being, human or
superhuman, mythical, or regarded as actually existing, but
it is intimately associated with the far past times in which his
totemic ancestors came into existence, lived, wandered about,
and died.   Each individual has his or her *alchera,* and here
we come in contact with the second term, *knanja.   Knanja* is
the native word for totem ; that is, the particular animal or
plant between whom and every individual a very special
relationship is supposed to exist.   In many cases the native's
ancestors are supposed to have been transformed into human
beings out of the totemic animal or plant.   The term *alchera*
includes it, and with it the original ancestors of the totemic
group, the natives' association with them, everything they
possessed, everything they did, and the times in which they
lived.   If you ask a man the question, *Iwunna Alchera unta ?*
' What is your Alchera ? ' he will answer, *Alchera nukwa
Achilpa,* ' My *alchera* is wild cat,' or whatever his totem may
be.   A man's *alchera* and his totem and totem group, or
knanja, are so closely interwoven in his thoughts that they
are practically inseparable.   So much so is this the case that
the reply to either of the questions, *Iwunna Alchera unta* ? or
Iwunna Knanja unta ? will be the same, simply the name of
his totem.   The word *alchera* can be used both as a substan-
tive and as a qualifying term.   Sometimes the word *alcher-
inga* is used ; *ringa* meaning of or belonging to, but, most
often, the natives simply say *alchera.* . . .

" The word *alchera* is, however, not only used in this
sense, but is also the one commonly used for dream, as in the
following :—

" *Ingwendama, inwulla* ;   *Alchera, erlia, ta eruka*—
Sleep, last night ; dream, emu, I saw.

" *Ingwendama, inwulla* ;   *Alchera, atnitta nukwa, kurna,
ta eruka*—Sleep, last night, dream, my stomach, bad, I saw.
That is, last night I dreamt I was bad inside or I felt bad
inside.   Seeing and feeling are very closely akin to one
another in the native mind.

" From the above it is very evident that the *alchera* is not applied to any individual and, further, that one of its fundamental meanings is dream. As a matter of fact it is significant to find that natives who can speak, as many of them now can, a little English, when referring to a man's·*alchera* and everything associated with it, always call it ' his dreaming.'

" The third and fourth terms, *churinga* and *kuruna*, are closely bound together. The *churinga* are, one and all, connected with the totems. At the present day the whole country occupied by the Arunta is divided into a very large number of larger or smaller areas, each of which is associated with some special totem, kangaroo, emu, Makea tree, and so forth, and in each such area there is a sacred storehouse, often a cleft in the rocks or the hollow stem of an ancient gum tree, in which the *churinga* of the group are safely preserved under the charge of the head-man of that local totemic group. These storehouses are called *Pertalchera*, from *Perta* a rock and *Alchera*. No woman, of course, ever ventures near to one of these, and no man dare touch the *churinga* that they contain without the consent, and almost invariably in the presence, of the head-man who is in supreme control, not only of it but of the most important ceremony associated with each totem group, the object of which is to ensure the increase of the totemic animal or plant.

" The fourth term, *kuruna*, is the name applied to the spirit part of each individual member of the tribe. Each of them has his, or her, special *churinga*, and between this and his, or her, *kuruna*, there exists a most intimate relationship. Originally the *kuruna* came out of the *churinga* and, when a native dies, it goes away to the *Pertalchera* where its *churinga* is stored, and there it remains until such time as it chooses to undergo reincarnation. As the result of a splitting in the early *alchera* days, each kuruna has also a double or another self called *Arumburinga* which always remains associated with the *churinga*.

" The earliest traditions of the Arunta deal with the origin of the ancestors of the various local totemic groups in the *alchera*. There are various traditions in different parts of the tribe, which occupies a great extent of country, but they all deal with one or more great superhuman Beings called

Numbakulla, a word that means ' self-existing,' or ' out of nothing.' They it was who did everything in the early *alchera* times, created the country, or at least its main features, made *churinga* and the *kurunas* associated with them, founded the totem groups, gave and taught the natives everything they now possess and know.

" The Arunta is a very large tribe and so there are many differences in traditions in different parts, but, in all of them, a Numbakulla is associated in some way or another with the origin of men and women. According to one tradition no actual men or women existed at first in the *alchera* but only incomplete creatures, half human, half animal. The Arunta savage has worked out for himself a crude theory of evolution. According to this tradition, he believes that, in the *alchera*, the whole country was covered with *Kwatcha alia*, or salt water, which was drawn away to the far north by people who always wanted to get it and keep it for themselves. It is a curious coincidence that this tradition reflects, in general outline, what geological evidence indicates to have been the case, so far as the existence of a great inland sea, once covering the country now occupied by the Arunta, is concerned. In those early days there were only groups of what are called *Inapatua*, or incomplete human beings, who dwelt on the shores of the salt water. They had no distinct limbs and ate no food but looked just like human beings, all huddled up into rounded masses, in which only the outlines of the different parts of the body could be seen. It was supposed that some of them were being changed into men out of lizards, others out of rats, kangaroos, snakes, emus, parakeets, Makea trees and so on Far away, in the *Alkira aldorla*, that is, the Western sky, there lived two great Numbakullas. Coming down to earth, armed with great stone knives, they took hold of the *Inapatua*, one after the other. A few cuts released the arms and legs ; fingers and toes were added by making four cuts at the end of each limb ; the nostrils were bored by the fingers. A slit on each side separated the eyelids and a cut with the knife made the mouth, which was pulled open several times to make it flexible. Thus, out of animals and plants, arose the original groups of human beings who, when they were formed, were naturally associated with the same animals and plants. The particular one with which the human ancestor was thus closely associated, out of which he was supposed to have been evolved, is spoken of as that individual's totem or *Knanja*, and thus we see the earliest origin of totemic groups amongst the Central tribes, or rather the savages' idea in regard to their origin. To the Arunta man of the present day, the connection between him and his totem is a very close and intimate one, in fact the totem of any man is regarded as himself. As a native once said to us, when we were discussing the matter with him, ' That one,' pointing to his photograph, which we had just taken, ' is just the same as me ; so is a kangaroo (his totem).'

" According to this tradition, when once they had come into existence, these ancestral people, or at least many of them, started to walk across the country—lizard people along one track, kangaroo people along another, frog people along another and so on, right through the various totem groups. Every one of these ancestors possessed, and often carried with him, or her, a sacred *churinga*, with which the spirit part of the individual was supposed to be intimately associated. As they wandered over the country they made all the natural features—mountains, valleys and plains, creeks, clay pans, water-holes and gorges—that are now familiar to the natives. At certain places they halted to perform ceremonies, and there certain members of the different parties died, or, as the natives say, went down into the ground ; that is, their bodies did, but their spirit parts remained above in company with the *churinga* and stayed behind when the party moved on, remaining in some rock or tree that was ever afterwards sacred to them and was called that individual's *Perta knanja* or *Rola knanja*, that is, his totemic rock or tree. It very often arose to mark the spot where the ancestor died.

" When all their wanderings are plotted down on a map, it looks just as if the whole Arunta country were crossed by an intricate network of railway lines, with hundreds of stations representing the stopping-places of the different totemic groups, where the spirits have remained, forming what are called *knanikillas*, or local totem places, and at each one of these there is the secret hiding-place, where the *churinga* are kept, which is called a *pertalchera*.

" The old men know all about these things and what spirits inhabit different places—kangaroos in one, wild cats in another, emus, rats, snakes, fishes in others, and so on. When a child is born it is simply one of these old ancestors who has undergone reincarnation, and thus every individual in the tribe gets his, or her, totem name and belongs to the same totemic group as did his ancestor. In most Australian tribes the totem of a child is inherited from either its father or its mother, but in the Arunta this is not so.

" The Arunta firmly believe that a child, in spirit form, if it chooses to do so, can enter any woman who comes near to its *Knanja* tree or rock." [1]

This concludes my survey of the more important discoveries that have been made in Australian totemism since the publication of my book *Totemism and Exogamy* in 1910. The evidence which I have adduced in that and my present work may be regarded as sufficient to prove that among the rude aborigines of the Continent totemism has been of universal prevalence and great antiquity. Of its universal prevalence the facts which I have cited are testimony enough : of its great antiquity the natives themselves are witnesses, for they unanimously attribute the origin of totemism to certain great mythical or superhuman beings, their remote ancestors in that dim past which is the most distant time to which their traditions and memory go back.

Exogamy, the fundamental law of the whole marriage system of the aborigines, is itself no doubt ancient in Australia, but seems to have been later in origin than totemism, for some of the natives have a tradition of a time before its introduction, when the sexes enjoyed complete freedom of intercourse without any restrictions whatever, and even the nearest relations cohabited without compunction or shame.[2] But by comparison with the venerable age of totemism, exogamy itself might almost seem to have been a modern innovation ; at least this is strongly suggested by the observation that in its more complex forms of the division of a tribe into four or eight exogamous sections, the institution at the present day is still spreading among certain of the tribes,

---

[1] B. Spencer, *Wanderings in Wild Australia*, i. pp. 278 *sqq.*

[2] *Totemism and Exogamy*, i. 350 *sqq.*

some of whom find considerable difficulty in fitting the new rules into their former and much simpler systems of marriage.[1]

Of all the features of Australia totemism the most important and striking are the ceremonies which the natives perform for the increase or multiplication of their totems. Most of their totems are edible or otherwise useful objects, hence by performing the ceremonies they believe that they provide themselves with all the necessities and with many of the conveniences of life, and their faith in the efficacy of the ceremonies appears to be absolute. In themselves the rites appear to be purely magical.[2] For they think that by their performance they can compel Nature to do their bidding, and so to supply all their wants. It is true that in reporting the rites the white observer occasionally says that the natives ask or request the totems to go forth and increase ; but in thus reporting they always use the indirect form of narration. Wherever they report the very words of the natives, these always, so far as I remember, take the form of a command addressed to the totems, " Go forth and increase ! " or some such words. This is characteristic of magic as opposed to religion. Though rites performed for the increase of the totems have not been reported for all the tribes of Australia it is probable that they have actually been practised by all. If the whole aboriginal population of Australia, who rank with the most backward of mankind, thus trust, or have trusted in the past, to magic rather than to religion for the supply of all their wants, it may be thought to tell in favour of the hypothesis which I long ago put forward, that in the early history of humanity the age of religion has been preceded by an age of magic. It is not surprising that the clearest evidence in favour of the hypothesis should survive in

---

[1] See above, pp. 51 *sq.*

[2] I am aware that Prof. Elkin appears to doubt or deny the magical nature of the ceremonies performed for the increase of the totems. But with all respect for his high authority I venture to think that in this he is mistaken. The rites in question appear to me, if I may judge by the descriptions of them given by competent observers, to be purely magical. That they were magical was the opinion of Sir Baldwin Spencer, than whom no one had a better opportunity of judging of the nature of the rites, which he witnessed so often. See above, p. 33. Cf. A. P. Elkin, " The Secret Life of the Australian Aborigine," in *Oceania*, vol. iii. No. 2 (Dec. 1932), p. 133.

this, the smallest of all the Continents, which, with its archaic types of fauna, flora, and humanity, may almost be described as a museum of antiquities, which Nature herself has set apart from the rest of the globe on purpose to satisfy the curiosity of later ages as to the early history of the world.

BOOK II

TOTEMISM IN MELANESIA

CHAPTER I

TOTEMISM IN NEW CALEDONIA

MELANESIA is the name given to the long chain of islands which skirts the eastern shores of Australia and New Guinea, from New Caledonia in the south to New Britain and New Ireland in the north. The name is derived from the black or swarthy complexion of the natives, who stand at a much higher level of culture than the rude aborigines of Australia with whom we have hitherto been concerned, for they occupy permanent settlements and houses and subsist chiefly by the diligent cultivation of the ground. With perhaps a few exceptions the natives appear to belong to one race, and to speak a common language. The main stock is believed to be Papuan, mixed with elements brought by immigrants from and through the East Indian Archipelago.[1]

The natives of New Caledonia, the largest and most southerly of the Melanesian Islands, appear to possess a system of totemism, which has been described for us by the experienced French Protestant missionary, M. Maurice Leenhardt, but though he gives us a long list of totems, his description of the system is somewhat vague and lacking in precision.

He tells us that the totemic system is seldom thrust upon the attention of the observer except in the refusal of tabooed foods.[2]

" The wooden sculptures on the big house are not simply ornamental, they are memorials or symbols. The decorative

[1] R. M. Codrington, *The Melanesians* (Oxford, 1891), p. 1 ; A. C. Haddon, *The Races of Man and their Distribution* (Cambridge, 1924), p. 17.

[2] M. Leenhardt, *Notes d'Ethnologie Néo-Caledonienne* (Paris, 1930), p 179.

art is not yet separate from religion, which concentrates its thought in a symbol or an image. The thought is that of perpetuating the ancestor and conserving his protection. In the ceremony (*pilou*) at the end of mourning they say to the deceased, ' Return now to thy maternal kinsfolk in the forest, leave us. We loved thee, we have made thy portrait.' By portrait they mean the sculptures they have made. The duty of the portrait is to watch over the descendants and ensure them the favour of their ancestors. . . . The sculpture on the ridge-pole, the most important of the sculptures, is directly associated with the totem ; for the totemic herb is placed in the highest conch-shell of the spire ; and in prayers for the long life of an infant they swear by ' the totem up on high.' . . . In front of the house are great stones in which the spirits of ancestors reside. Behind the house is the favourite haunt of the totem. The space behind the women's house is very strictly forbidden or tabooed, for their totem is the most feared." [1]

He tells us that in general the totems are chosen from the less conspicuous and formidable aspects of Nature, but he mentions as exceptions to the rule, the totems of thunder, the wind, and the shark. He adds, however, that everything in the system has a bearing on human existence (*appartiennent aux parages de l'homme*).[2] From his long list of totems, about forty in number, we may take the following : thunder, rain, several species of lizards, hairy caterpillar, cricket, shark, field-mouse, *ue* (a species of grass or herb), mullet, wave, worm, octopus, eel, bubble of air.[3]

The natives regard the totems as their ancestors, and the old men are unanimous in declaring that the totems claimed by the clans as their ancestors are very often the maternal totems, whose traditions the women are able to impose upon their sons. The paternal totems play no part in the social life of the tribes, which M. Leenhardt attributes to a belief of the natives that the father has no share in the transmission of life to his offspring. In the long and intricate line of maternal and paternal descent, which conforms to the classificatory system of relationship, the natives hesitate to distinguish

[1] M. Leenhardt, *op. cit.* pp. 10, 22.   [3] M. Leenhardt, *op. cit.* p. 178.
[2] M. Leenhardt, *op. cit.* p. 201.

which is the true totem, the paternal or the maternal, where
that of the father counts for less and that of the mother's
brother (*kanya*) plays an intimate and profound part in the
life of the paternal group.[1]

With regard to particular totems we are told that the long-
haired caterpillar infests the family domain, the house, the
altar, the field, and the bush or forest which furnishes the
family with the means of subsistence. When they see it they
do not crush it, but ask, " What are you doing here ? " and
they request it to go away. In speaking to the insect they
use the polite plural as in addressing a maternal uncle or
elder brother. They think that the insect promotes the
growth of the crops, particularly the roots of the *soa*, which
require a long preparation to make them edible. At the same
time the caterpillar is supposed to guard other edible plants.
Living on the crops from which the people derive their subsistence and promoting the growth, the insect is deemed to
be the supporter or nourisher of the family. When anyone
has offended it the caterpillar is believed to punish the offender
by inflicting him with madness at the hour of twilight.

There are altars to the caterpillar, which are in the charge
of the younger branch of the family. The priestess is a
mother of the family, and her son is the *kavu* or Master. At
each of these altars pointed poles are set up, or roots of *soa*
are pricked. And round about the altar are planted wild
edible plants, over which the caterpillar is believed to keep
guard. No burnt sacrifice is made on the altar, but on it
they place an offering consisting of cakes of *soa*, and at it
they pray that the crops of the family may thrive. When
girls of the caterpillar clan marry into another group they
take with them their totem, and find an altar to the caterpillar
in their new home. The caterpillar is the totem of the
Boerhexau and Nei clans, two of the most ancient clans in the
valley of Honailon, but the members of these clans say that
the caterpillar totem came to them through the women. The
insect is believed to contain in its body stones which are the
petrified soul of an ancient warrior.[2]

---

[1] M. Leenhardt, *op. cit.* pp. 202-
203, and for classificatory system of
relationship, see *id.* pp. 63 *sqq*

[2] M. Leenhardt, *op. cit.* pp. 181-
182.

The lizard is a totem all over New Caledonia, but it is not always the same species of lizard. Four different sorts of the reptile are recognised as totems. In the North-West the natives regard with great respect a large stone, a natural rock near the crops, and in the season the *kavu* or Master, after offering a sacrifice, invites the lizard to follow him, and leads the creature up to this stone which it is supposed to enter and to dwell in until the time of harvest. The lizard meets us again in indirect form in the small sacred stones which are preserved at the entrance to the house. These stones are believed to be at the same time the petrified spirits of the ancestors of the family. In all the domestic groups or clans of the lizard totem, when a death has taken place and the priest is about to catch the soul of the deceased, the soul presents itself to him in the form of a lizard. The lizard is the great protector of the crops, and the guardian of women in childbed, to whom he ensures a safe delivery. It is, in a word, the strength and the life of the clan that respects it. The totem of the small lizard (gecko) is supposed to render people sad, silent, and dejected : it engenders hypochondria. Yet it is the guardian of the house, and shows by its agitation when some misfortune is about to befall the family. As a totem the large lizard is thought to cause emaciation, water on the brain, scrofula, and consumption. For these diseases remedies can be applied in the shape of certain herbs, the secret of which is possessed by the Master of the totem (*kavu*). The large lizard is " protected " by the wives of the junior branch of the group or clan and their sons. This is the native way of saying that these wives and their sons are the priestesses and priests of the lizard as the totem of the clan. These persons guard the altar of the great lizard totem with the same pious care with which the caterpillar clan guards the altars of the caterpillar totem. Down to recent years a dance of the lizard totem was performed at a place on the west coast, in which the lizard was represented by a dancer, loaded with ornaments like a great chief. The persons who shared in the ceremony daubed their bodies with clay in imitation of the marks on the skin of the lizard.[1]

Another totem is a species of large sea serpent, in French

[1] M. Leenhardt, *op. cit.* pp. 183-185.

plature, which at low tide lives in crevices in the rocks, or on trees. It goes down to fish at high tide and may also be encountered in deep water. In the coastal regions it plays the same totemic part as the lizard in the interior of the country. Like the lizard, this sea-serpent is charged with the duty of promoting the growth of the crops, and members of the totem mimic the tortuous progress of the reptile in the path which they trace in order to lead it to the arrow-root. The serpent is believed to cause rheumatic pains in the knees, the head, and the back, and lack of sleep. The Master of the totem (*kavu*) possesses a herb which is an antidote to these maladies, but Pastor Leenhardt has not heard of any altar erected in honour of this totemic sea-serpent. Not but that such altars may not have existed in the past, but the clan has not kept up the tradition, and the altars have fallen into desuetude. However, members of the clan still make offerings to their totem, the sea-serpent, at the time when they break up the taro roots before planting them. They lay a plant of taro on a small hillock which serves instead of an altar, with a sacred pole beside it. And they repeat the same ceremony when the crops are ripe.

Members of the clan hang up images of the serpent in the fields to ward off thieves. The serpent is greatly feared, and people strictly respect the surroundings of houses which it guards in its capacity of totem. Certain rites attest a worship of the sea-serpent. Thus in order to attract trade winds at the time of the young arrow-root people at Canala hoist a black and white striped flag to a pole. The stripes on the flag are intended to imitate the stripes on the serpent's body. Again, at Gomen, a dance called *hia* is performed, in which men who represent the dead descending to the spirit-land, advance holding in their hands wood carved and painted to mimic the sea-serpent. They hold the serpent's head in their mouths and pretend to eat it, which is thought to complete their resemblance to the spirits of the dead, because the sea-serpent, the lizards, and all the other totems are the food of the dead, and that is why human beings may not eat them.[1]

The mullet is the totem of several clans in different parts of the island. When a member of these clans dies, and they

---

[1] M. Leenhardt, *op. cit.* pp. 185-186.

see a mullet pass in the river, they call it the " father " of the deceased.   They think that the spirit of the deceased (*ko*) is in the fish, which is their totem.   They do not distinguish between the spirit of the dead and the totem, which for us are so different.   When the mullet appears in shoals, they call this the *boria* of the dead.   The *boria* is a complex ceremony in which the gods receive the dead in a dance.   A shoal of mullets appearing at the moment of a clansman's death recalls this dance of the gods.   Members of the mullet clan exalt the glory of the mullet in mimic dances.   When this dance of the mullet clan was performed for the last time a rifle-shot rang out at the close, at which the dancers fell as if dead to the ground, the report of the rifle signifying at once the explosion of dynamite among the fish, and the extinction of the mullet clan by civilization.[1]

The shark is the totem of numerous clans in the island. In the north two sharks belonging to two different families are equally famous.   They have each a name, one being called Yevavang and the other Moajilien.   These names seem to be the names of ancestors, and the families pray to these sharks at the altars with the sacrifice of cooked arrow-root, exactly as they do in honour of ancestors.   The name of the shark called out to a warrior in battle is a symbol of virility and redoubles his strength.   When the name of the totem is pronounced by a man in the presence of a woman who belongs to the corresponding fraternity, and is therefore his classificatory sister, the hearers are covered with confusion, which seems to imply that the shark has a sexual significance.

The shark is supposed to live in mud and filth, hence ordinary people of the shark clan are careful to keep their houses and surroundings very clean, lest their totem the shark should come to revel in it, bringing with him the diseases that follow in his train; but on the contrary, the Master (*kavu*) of the shark totem, in order to keep his totem by him, lives in a state of perpetual filth, never cleaning the ground about his house or altar, and not even retiring to a distance to satisfy the needs of nature.[2]

The worm is an important totem on account of the damage it does to the taro plantations.   There are different

---

[1] M. Leenhardt, *op. cit.* p. 188.   [2] M. Leenhardt, *op. cit.* pp. 189-190.

kinds of worm totems. The merit of the worm totem consists in bringing water, and maintaining humidity and
verdure, a source of riches to the clan. Its danger consists
in its habit of burrowing in the ground, thus causing the
water to escape and the soil to collapse. Hence in the clan
at Koerhon, the people of the worm totem perform a dance
during the growth of the taro and sing a song in praise of
their totem the worm, believing that thus they prevent the
worm from devastating the water channels. The song only
contains the names of ancestors and of the places of their
crop where they wish the worm to bring the water.[1]

Thunder is a widespread totem in New Caledonia. There
is a Thunder-stone in which the ancestral spirit is enclosed.
At the ordinary altar of the clan (*ka moaro*) is a sacred pole
which is the wood of the thunder. This totem is not supposed
to have any influence on the crops. It does not cause any
illnesses. Its great merit consists in its outbursts of thunder
and lightning, which are not clearly distinguished, but are
much dreaded. Hence in the clan Neare, when one of the
last masters of thunder died, and when his clan was taking
his skull to the Calvary or place of his ancestors, the people
of the clan held a great assembly in order to show their
respect for their thunder totem. They feared to excite a
great thunderstorm should anyone show any want of reverence for their totem. And they carried away the skull to the
top of a distant mountain, where a thunderstorm, if it broke
out, would do no harm.[2]

With regard to kinship and marriage, a woman's proper
husband is the son of her mother's brother. The father ranks
with his brothers : the idea of fatherhood not being clearly
developed. All cousins on the father's side are called
" brothers." There is little conversation between brothers
and sisters. " Brothers " in the classificatory sense fall into
two distinct " fraternities," according as they are children
of the father's brothers or of the mother's brothers; the former
belong to the paternal clan, the latter to the maternal clan.
Brothers and sisters of the same clan show great deference to
each other : incest between them is strictly avoided.
Marriage is an exchange of cousins - german between a

---

[1] M Leenhardt, *op. cit.* p. 191.   [2] M. Leenhardt, *op. cit.* pp. 197-198.

CHAPTER II

TOTEMISM IN THE LOYALTY ISLANDS

THE Loyalty Islands are a group of islands lying to the east of New Caledonia. Lifu, the largest island of the group, measures some fifty miles in length by twenty-five in breadth. The natives are Melanesians. The existence of totemism among them is recorded by Mrs. Hadfield, who resided as a missionary on the island of Uvea for many years.

Her account of the evidence, though somewhat vague and popular, is best given in her own words. She writes : " Each tribe had its own particular totem. In one tribe it took the form of a lizard ; in another, that of a rat ; whilst everyone agreed that the kingfisher—*Ciciete*—was a bird of ill omen and the incarnation of wickedness. To the present day he is regarded with ill-favour, and indeed his boldness and wicked knowing looks suggest all kinds of devilry. However hungry a Lifuan may be he can never persuade himself to eat either a kingfisher (*ciciete*), a white owl (*men*), or a lizard (*thu*).

" Some time ago one of our cats caught a kingfisher but refused to eat it. I pointed out the fact to a native who was about the house ; but he showed not the least surprise, his remark being equivalent to saying, ' Do you suppose your cat, or any other well-regulated cat, would dare to devour a *ciciete* ? '

" Supposing the totem of a particular sorcerer to be an owl, the sorcerer was supposed to know and quickly recognize the individual member of the species which acted as his special medium ; but as other members had not the same powers of discernment, all the individuals of the three species

enjoyed a happy immunity from wilful slaughter ; for everyone feared to destroy any of these birds ·or animals lest it
should prove to be the incarnation of some powerful spirit.
They believed too that the death of one of these mediums
also meant the death of the sorcerer who controlled the
spirit embodied in it.

" The appearance of a kingfisher did not always augur
the same event. To a man, of whose tribe he was the totem,
his appearance was a certain premonition of death ; whilst
to a woman belonging to another tribe, and with a different
totem, he brought good news; for his peculiar whining note
told her that there was some fish at her home needing her
attention ; and so thoroughly did she believe this that she
at once left her plantation and hurried home to prepare the
fish for the evening meal." [1]

[1] E. Hadfield, *Among the Natives of the Loyalty Group* (London, 1928),
pp. 156 *sq.*

CHAPTER III

TOTEMISM IN THE NEW HEBRIDES

MALEKULA, which was formerly called Mallicolo, is the second largest island of the New Hebrides group, about forty-five miles long, lying to the south of Espiritu Santo, which is the largest island of the cluster. In 1926 the natives of the island were carefully investigated by Mr. A. Bernard Deacon, and he has given us a valuable account of the principal results of his researches, though his premature death prevented him from putting his reports into a final form. He discovered the existence of totemism in several parts of the island. His account will be best given in his own words.

" Totemism is a word which has been defined in a variety of ways, or used in a vague sense to cover almost any relationship between men and animals or plants which has a ritual aspect. If we accept as a definition that totemism is a special ritual relation between a group of human beings on the one hand and a species of animal, plant, or natural object on the other, then it may be said that the people of at least parts of Malekula are totemic. Most of the data on this subject comes from the south-west districts (Seniang and Wilemp), from Mewun and from Lambubu. Concerning the other districts there are only very brief notes, but these are sufficient to suggest that totemism is to some extent a feature of all the coastal Malekulan cultures, and very possibly of those of the interior as well.

" In Seniang and Wilemp it is found that every clan is associated in a definitely ritual way with some plant or animal species, most usually with a variety of some edible plant, or some tree, or some bird, or some mammal such as a pig or

rat.   The exact nature of this association varies, but respect
for every representative of the totemic species is always
present, and save where the totem is some edible root, this
respect commonly takes the form of abstaining from injuring,
killing, or eating it.   For instance, the *nimbile* bird is un-
molested by the people of Lu'ha, Tivulemp, and Tunggor,
the reason being given that it has the power of killing men.
A man of Evun Ambus may not cut the tree *nambus* lest
he die. . . , nor might the people of Tomman Island (in the
days when that islet was still inhabited) kill or eat the dove
nivimar.

" Sometimes there is a closer bond between the members
of a village and such a totem, and the lives of the men are
regarded as linked with the lives of the animals.   The people
of Looremew may not shoot the small bird *nevilala*, and if a
flight of these alight on the house of a man of this group it
is a sign that he will shortly die.   The locust, *naambei*, holds
the same position for the people of Ndawu.   If people see a
lot of locusts lying about, or exceptionally active, they know
that a man of this village has died.   It is explained that the
creatures' activity is the result of the spirit of the deceased
having entered into them.   The locust is not touched by the
people of this clan, nor is it killed by them, for it is held that
should this happen then a man of Ndawu will die.

" Further, the parent village of every clan has its sacred
place in which almost always there is a sacred stone in which
resides a spiritual being.   These are mostly concerned with
the *neerew* or ' harvest festival ' of the clan, but in some
villages at least the indwelling spirit is that of the totem. . . .

" Certain villages not only respect their totems but claim
origin from them, and it is possible that if we had more data
we should find this to be an universal belief in these districts.
The men of Tenemet and Lembwilavi are, for instance,
descended from a pig ; the ancestors of Loorlanggalat came
forth from the nettle-tree which split open, and members of
this group avoid cutting it therefore.   Similarly the people
of Maur trace their descent to a *naur* tree, of which the pith
was full of men—the tree burst, the men came out and
married with women of other clans. . . .

" Perhaps the most complete account of totemic beliefs is

recorded from the village of Iumloor, and is probably typical of those held in Seniang and Wilemp. The inhabitants hold themselves to be descended from a female rat, and hence no member of Iumloor or of its daughter villages may kill or eat a rat. It seems that this respect for the rat leads men of Iumloor to resent the killing of rats by others, for it is said that should a man of a descent group other than Iumloor unwittingly kill a rat, the people of Iumloor compel him to eat it. If he refuses to do so or evades it, then they seek an opportunity to kill him. Further, the connection in death of a man with his totem is exemplified by the Iumloor beliefs. The spirit of a man or woman of Iumloor enters a rat at death. The conception appears to be that all rats form one entity into which the spirit of the deceased enters or merges somehow. Thus if the rats become unusually active and destructive in the villages of other clans, the people thereof say : ' Someone must have died at Iumloor, the rats are busy again.' . . .

" As has been mentioned, the respect of men for their totem takes the form, common to other totemic peoples, of refraining from eating it, if it be edible, or if it be inedible from killing, cutting, or in any way injuring it. In everyday life a man only observes these restrictions towards the totemic species of his father's (and hence of his own) clan, but should he visit and stay in the village of his mother's clansfolk, then he will observe also the totemic restrictions relating to it. This is, however, probably only one example of the general rule that a ' stranger ' staying in a village observes, out of courtesy, the restrictions which are observed by his hosts. The same holds true for a woman, but in addition she must, if she be married, behave in respect of her husband's totem, according to the same rules of avoidance that she observes towards her husband's parents. Thus a woman married to a man of Benaur may not say the word *nikakal,* nor may she eat it ; and one married into the clan of Iumhahlilong may not say *nionibant* (' the owl ') but uses a metaphor to express her meaning. There is in this district no record of a man observing any similar tabu towards the totem of his wife, though in Mewun he appears to do so. Such ritual attitudes towards the totems seem to be enforced for the most part by ritual sanctions, though the evidence for this is very scanty. Thus if a man of Ndawu were to kill a locust a man of that village would die, and if a man of Evun Ambus were to cut a *nambus* tree he would perish. . . .

"It would appear that one object may be the totem of more than one clan. Thus the bird *nimbile* is respected by the three independent villages of Luha, Tivulemp, and Tunggor, while the *nikakal* is the totem of Bendur, Leneven, and Teleleu. . . . On the other hand, there is also evidence that the villages of one clan may sometimes have different totems. . . .

"Besides the totem which most if not all clans possess, many have also the power of 'making' or 'increasing' some essential foodstuff or a widespread natural phenomenon. Those clans which have power over a foodstuff celebrate annually at the time of the yam harvest a kind of harvest festival called *neerew*, *naarew*, or *noorow*, the aim of which is to make plentiful the plant or animal concerned. The *neerew* of each clan takes its name after the foodstuff which it controls, as, for instance, the *Neerew Mbetep* (' *Neerew* of the bread-fruit '), or *Neerew Nimbaai* (' *Neerew* of the yams '). The rites are performed by one specialist for the whole clan, and the fruits of his labours benefit not only his own people but the whole district. Such a specialist is called the *nimbatin nowor*, and there is always one, and apparently one only in every clan. The name may perhaps be translated ' head magician.' His office is essentially a public one, and in the normal course of events would pass from a man to his eldest son, to whom the necessary instructions would be given. It appears that this instruction comprises not only the rites which must be performed for the *neerew* ceremony, but also the secret or " true " names of a large number of objects such as bananas, the sea, the sun, and the moon. What the purpose of these ' true ' names may be, or on what occasions they are used, there is nothing to tell us, but they are evidently held to be very sacred, for no *nimbatin nowor* may even reveal them save to his successor. . . .

"The chief or ' parent ' village of every descent-group is associated with a sacred place, called in Seniang the *newut tisamp* and in Wilemp the *newut bilian* or, alternatively to both these, the *nembrmbrkon*.   All subsidiary villages have apparently the same one as their parent village.   Such a place is the charnel-house of the clan, and is also usually regarded as the residence of a maleficent ghost who is by tradition associated with the group.   This ghost has generally as its particular abode a sacred stone which is usually the principal object in the *nembrmbrkon*. . . . The sacred stones themselves often form the centre of a *neerew* ceremony, and it would seem that they are considered to be potent because of the *temes* (ghosts) which reside in them, but the rites do not appear necessarily to include any invocation of these beings.   Thus the *neerew* object of Looru is famine, which is caused by the simple casting down of the ' stone ' of famine (*Nevet Namar*). . . . The names of a few of the stones have been recorded.   Thus we have the *Nevet Lelembel* of the clan *Lelembel*, the *Nevet Nemosi* and *Nevet Nevul* (the Star Stone and the Moon Stone) of Rahulemp village, and the *Nevet Namar* (the famine stones) of Uraau, Mbwilmet, and Looru.   These three villages are all of different clans, but they have this in common, that in one way or another they can produce famine in the district.   In Uraau and also in Mbwilmet famine is also regarded as the totem of the clan, and by the men of the former village the famine stone is (called ?) their ancestor, for it was out of the *Nevet Namar* that the *nivinu mbon* tree grew, whence sprang the first men of the Ndindinemer clan." [1]

At the village of Benaur when the harvest festival is to be celebrated for the increase of foodstuffs, a space is cleared near the village, and certain plants are planted round it.   In the centre the earth is banked up to form a kind of circular basin.   This is lined with leaves of the kind used for wrapping up puddings and filled with water.   Certain leaves are then wrung into the water, after which some stones, resembling the *nikakal* tubes in shape, are put into it, and the formula " May the *nikakal* bear, may its roots be many," is muttered by the head magician.   Young children and babies are then brought and bathed in this water, after which the seed-tubers of the *nikakal*, which are to be planted, are also dipped into it.

[1] A. Bernard Deacon, *Malekula, a Vanishing People of the New Hebrides*,   ed. by Camilla M. Wedgwood (London, 1934), pp. 588-598.

They are then distributed and planted. Similarly at the village of Rahulemp at the harvest festival for the increase of yams the head magician made a concoction similar to that described and poured it over a basket of seed-yams, which were then distributed among the villages of the district and put into the gardens of each clan. For this yam ceremony a sacred stone is used. Its name is not recorded, but the story runs that once at midnight a man perceived a stone flying through the air, much like a *nivinggoum* bird. He shot it, and it fell to the earth and it became the abode of " the ghost of the yam fertility ceremony." It is always in the possession of the head magician of Rahulemp, and is used in some way not specified to ensure the fruitfulness of the yams.[1]

Pigs were apparently increased by a rite very similar to that performed for yams. A special liquid was prepared in the sacred place of the village concerned, and was then either poured over certain pigs or into certain pieces of the sacred prehistoric pottery which are preserved in the sacred places of many clans which have ceremonies for the increase of pigs.

There are several clans which do not perform any ceremony for the increase of foodstuffs, but which have control over such phenomena as famine, wind, and war. These, too, perform a ceremony which, however, is not annual but may take place at irregular intervals. Why war or famine should ever be brought about intentionally is not clear. It seems improbable that antagonism towards neighbouring clans would lead to it, for, as with the ceremony for foodstuffs, the results appear to affect the district as a whole. It must, however, be appreciated that the clans which can make war and famine can also work their opposites—peace and plenty —just as the clans which can raise wind can also still it.[2]

Concerning totemism in the district of Mewun the data are very scanty. Here, as in Seniang, each clan appears to be associated with some plant, animal, or natural object from which it traces its descent. The names of only three such totems, however, have been recorded.

The people of Alou village are descended from a *ninduo* tree which split open and produced a man. This man

[1] A. Bernard Deacon, *op. cit.* pp. 602-603.

[2] A. Bernard Deacon, *op. cit.* pp. 603-604.

married a woman who was the daughter of a certain species of snake.   The inhabitants of this village behave, therefore, with respect to both the *ninduo* tree and the snake.   The former may not be touched or cut, and this, since it is a wood much used in carving, is a serious prohibition.   The snake may not be killed and is believed to be friendly towards its human relatives.   These will not speak its name but refer to it by the term used for mother-in-law.   The taboo on speaking the name of the totem appears to be the same here as in Seniang, so that a woman who is the wife of a man of Alou refrains from saying the name of the tree *ninduo*, since it is said to have the same status as the husband's parent, and this restriction is, in Mewun, also extended to a man who is the husband of a woman of this group.

" The people of Loutagha are descended from a *newongke* bird which was in turn given birth to by a stone.   They refrain from killing all birds of this species and respect them. All women who have married into the village regard the *newongke* as a parent-in-law and refrain from using its name.

" The only other totem mentioned from Mewun is the tree *nimismes*, which belongs to the Melpmes clan.   This tree sprang from the head of the wife of the mythical creator Butwanabaghap after her death ; it burst and brought forth the people of Melpmes.   If those near Melpmes should cut this tree, or even should its branches or leaves be torn in a hurricane, dysentery is believed to break out and cause many deaths.

" Each village has, too, a ceremony by means of which it increases a certain foodstuff.   Such a ceremony is called *nogho* in Mewun, and from the data available it is clear that it is the same as the *neerew* of the southern districts. . . .

" The *nogho* are celebrated in the sacred place or *logho* of each clan by a clan fertility-magician, the *nemugut nogho* (' the man of *nogho* ') whose office, like that of the *nimbatin nowor* of Seniang, passes from father to son.   The *logho* corresponds closely to the *nembrmbrkon* of Seniang, for it is the clan charnel-house and, so far as is known, is always associated with a stone which is the residence of a *temes* (ghost), from which it derives its potency." [1]

In the district of Lambumbu Mr. Deacon found that the

[1] A. Bernard Deacon, *op. cit.* pp. 607 *sqq.*

totem of the village Lowag was the cabbage, but beyond
that he gives no information as to the existence of any beliefs
concerning descent from or respect for any particular species
held by any clan. " There is, moreover, definite evidence
that in Lambumbu, as in Mewun and Seniang, most, if not
all, descent localities have a sacred place, *wut moul*, and
perform a ceremony to increase a certain foodstuff. This
ceremony is the *nogharo*; thus there is a *nogharo* of the
yam at Lembelag, Timbini, and Piri; of the bread-fruit
(*Nogharo Nembet*) at Tambinbon, Lowag, and Tivlamp; and
the clan Ran Nembew performs the *nogharo* of pigs (*Nogharo
Nimbuah*). It is perhaps significant that the totem and
nogharo object of Lowag are distinct. Of the nature of the
nogharo rites we are ignorant save for a short account of the
Nogharo Nimbuah. A bamboo vessel, kept specially for the
ceremony and handed down from each clan magician to his
successor, is taken to the stream called *nowei narug* and
filled with water. The leaves of *nisivung* and *nimumwengk*
are then squeezed into the water and the bamboo carried to
the middle of the dancing-ground. Here, standing between
the gongs, the magician pours the infusion on to the ground
while muttering the words : ' The sows' bellies swell up ;
the sows become they great, bear they pigs ! '

" It will be noticed that in this account there is no mention
of any invocation of a *temes* (ghost), nor is there any evidence
that *temes* are associated with the *wut moul* (sacred place)
at all, though since the information concerning Lambumbu
is very incomplete, such negative evidence is of little value.
There is, however, a brief note concerning *nogharo* ceremonies
as a whole which states that many of them are worked by
means of spells (and, presumably, the performing of certain
rites) muttered over stones resembling the species to be
increased. Thus bananas are multiplied by acting upon
stones resembling bananas; for bread-fruit (*nembet*) there are
certain stones in the *wut moul* of the clan which performs the
nogharo nembet. There are also in this same tabu-place
certain pots. . . . To increase the bread-fruit the stones
are taken and placed inside one of the sacred pots to the
accompaniment of spells. . . .

" It may be inferred from the foregoing account of the

Nogharo Nimbuah that each clan has its special clan fertility magician, but the title of the office and all details concerning it are lacking. There is one interesting statement, however, about the magicians of the clan Ran Nembew who perform the *nogharo* of pigs. In order to guard the pigs of the district against disease, these men receive on their death different burial from that of ordinary people. It is true that their bodies are placed in the ground in the usual way, but their heads are left projecting, for it is greatly feared that, should the earth come into contact with and rot the head of a pig-magician then universal sickness of, or misfortune to, the pigs will follow ; they will die, or their tusks will break and will not grow long. The cheeks of the magician are burnt away with fire, then the head is covered with a leaf, cut off from the body and put up in the men's club-house, not in the charnel-house as is done for ordinary folk. Sometimes the fear that the earth will come in contact with the head is so great that the body is not buried, but is put into an old gong which is set on a rough trestle in the charnel-place, out of the reach of the dogs and pigs. It is said that a gong is only used because it is a ready-hollowed tree, and that where there are canoes one of these would be used, it being the same thing. When this form of disposal is employed, the skull and bones are not removed after the body has rotted.

" The *nogharo* differs from the *neerew* or *nogho* in one important respect : it is not an annual ceremony, but has an eight-year cycle. All *nogharo* are not performed during the same year, however, so that in any one year there will probably be one or two such ceremonies taking place." [1]

"With regard to the district of Lagalag in the south-west we are told that the records of totemism are of the vaguest, but among these people there is clearly a series of ceremonies which correspond to the *nogharo* of their neighbours to the west. These are called *naambi*, and mention is made of the *naambi nen nindum* (the *naambi* of the yams). . . . At the village of Lagandu, too, specimens are found of the sacred prehistoric pottery, here called *nughumbe*, and they are associated, as in Lambumbu, with the rite of increasing bread-fruit performed apparently by an official called *mugh*

[1] A. Bernard Deacon, *op cit*. pp. 611-613.

is nen nembet. It is mentioned, also, that yams are increased with the aid of certain black stones, and this suggests another close parallel to the use of stones in the *nogharo* of Lambumbu."[1]

" Thus, we see that of the districts in the west of Malekula, those of the south-west, Mewun, Lambumbu, and Lagalag, are united in the custom of performing at certain stated intervals a ceremony for the increasing of certain food-stuffs. Further, this rite is carried out for each foodstuff by one special magician in each separate clan, and may be said to be owned by that clan. This is also probably true for the inland district of Nesan, but the evidence for this region is less reliable than it is for the districts mentioned above. It is reported that fertility rites exist similar to the *nogharo* of Lambumbu, but called *nilian*, and that even in this part of the country prehistoric pottery is found which, again as in Lambumbu, is used in connection with the *nilian nembet*, the fertility ceremony for bread-fruit. There is no mention, however, of any special clan-magicians in this district. Among the Big Nambas nothing is recorded of any fertility rites, but it is clear that many of the clan villages believed themselves to be descended from and have a respect for certain animal and plant species. Thus the first two men of Mawei were brought forth by the pigeon *mbilig*, and this is to-day neither killed nor injured by members of this village. Again, a creeper *vimil* gave birth to five men and one woman. The latter was handed over to the people of Tevter village, and in exchange one of the sons of the *vimil* married a Tevter woman. From this couple are descended the people of Batarmul. By them *vimil* is described as ' all same mamma belong all,' and it is forbidden to cut this creeper in the vicinity of their village. Another plant, the *nive*, bore the men of Botvovwu. Whether all of this species are respected is not recorded, but the original plant is still to be seen in this village; the men's house has been built over it, and the skulls of the dead are put up in its branches.

" Quite apart from these clan fertility rites for the increase of food, however, there is another important ceremony akin to them which provides a further cultural bond between the

[1] A. Bernard Deacon, *op. cit.* p. 613.

districts of the south-west and the north. This is the very sacred ceremony of ' Making Man.' The name by which it went in the south has been lost, but it was celebrated formerly in the now extinct village of Iumoran on Tomman Island. In Mewun it was known as the *Nogho Tilabwe*, or ' Great *Nogho*,' and in Lambumbu as the *Nogharo Nomur* or the ' *Nogharo* of man.' Whether it ever existed among the Big Nambas we do not know, but in Lagalag and Nesan it is not to be found, and for its absence we have positive as well as negative evidence, the indications being not that it has disappeared as a result of depopulation, as has happened in the south, but that it never existed in these two districts.

" The names *Nogho Tilabwe* and *Nogharo Nomur* suggest that this rite is of the nature of one of the ordinary clan fertility ceremonies, but it differs from them in certain respects, notably in the fact that, though owned and primarily performed by one village, it concerns intimately the whole district and is apparently attended by persons from all villages. In Seniang and Wilemp there were, further, two fertility rites, called respectively *Neerew Rahulemp* and *Neerew Mbatiar*, which combined the functions of a harvest festival and a commemoration of the dead ; and which were almost certainly closely allied to the ceremony for ' the making of man,' though they do not appear themselves to contain any obvious rites for human fertility."[1]

Some scanty and doubtful evidence for the survival of clan totemism in Tanna and Aniwa, two islands of the Southern New Hebrides, has been recorded by Mr. C. B. Humphreys, who prefers, however, to speak of symbolism and symbols instead of totemism and totems. I will give the evidence which he adduces in his own words. Thus, speaking of Tanna, he says : " Of clans, as usually understood, there is no direct evidence. Wherever one goes, however, one constantly finds unexpected evidences of what, in other parts of the world, would be called clan symbolism. Many of my informants believed that certain people are descended from certain birds. For example, the wagtail or flycatcher (*takaskisi*), the long-tailed tit (*garafi*), the hawk (*melikom*), the black hawk (*mianuhu*) are acknowledged to be birds

[1] A. Bernard Deacon, *op. cit.* pp. 614-616.

from which people descended at one time, though the present knowledge of just who are these descendants of bird ancestors is entirely lacking. Kuokarei told me of an instance where a group used to belong to the banana people and the eating of that fruit was taboo in a certain number of villages in the vicinity of the Mission at Whitesands. To-day there is no sign of this prohibition. The banana is eaten freely by all people everywhere as far as is known, and most certainly in this particular locality. Kuokarei added that the people of the villages where the banana was taboo used to exchange the banana for a fruit which they might eat, making the exchange with villages where there was no prohibition against the fruit in question. This exchange form of totemism has no connection with the double form of the custom found in Fiji and elsewhere. In Enophulus, a few miles from Whitesands, there is evidence that such things as bread-fruit, wind-and-rain, and other natural phenomena have been used as clan symbols. More definite is the informa-tion as to fowls in this connection. Many natives bore testimony to this. There is reason to believe that fowls existed in the New Hebrides prior to the arrival of the Spaniards. Indeed, Turner insists that they have always been there. More probably they came in from Indonesia with one of the many movements of people from that area. In any event, the precise locality where fowls occurred as clan symbols is not known to-day, nor if they might be eaten by the people who claimed them. It is curious that no evidence of clan symbolism can be found existing to-day. In making the enquiries on this point, it seems at first that, perhaps, the exact meaning of the question was not under-stood by the man then being questioned. But, when all the men interrogated insisted strenuously that there is no such thing nowadays, the testimony was too strong to be ignored. Nor can reticence about a matter which is of a very personal and private nature to the native entirely explain this denial. With the consensus of opinion given against clan symbolism by a large number of the more intelligent males in the community, one must admit that it does not exist to-day. It is probable that the breaking down of old customs and traditions which is so evident in all Tannese culture has

made particular havoc in the old clan organization   Beyond
the belief that at some time in the past a system of clan
symbolism existed in this island, one dares not go." [1]

With regard to totemism in the island of Aniwa, Mr.
Humphreys observes, " Serpent worship was practised in
Aniwa, according to Kuokarei, and the sea-snake is the totem
of some of the people there." [2]   Again, summing up the
evidence for the former existence of totemism in the New
Hebrides, Mr. Humphreys observes : " We have seen that
the existence of totemism in these islands is of the most
nebulous sort, but that there are certain objects in Tanna
and Aniwa which are closely akin to, or derived from, a
system of clan symbolism, with a more or less clearly defined
belief in descent from the symbol itself and, in some quarters,
a certain reluctance to eat it.   Now clan symbolism is rare
in Polynesia, although it exists in Tonga and Samoa and
is very strong in Tikopia, with its Polynesian culture, but
it becomes increasingly common as one proceeds north-
westerly through the New Hebrides and the Solomons to the
Shortlands and the Melanesian islands to the north.   The
only simple explanation of its practical disappearance in
the islands we are considering is that the influence from the
north-east which came in with the kava folk brought little
of this element of culture, and it finally became what it is
to-day—only a memory of its former power as a taboo and a
genealogical explanation at the same time.   Considering the
strength of totemism in certain parts of the Solomons,
notably in the coastal regions of San Cristoval, it is possible
that the kava folk who introduced totemism in its pure form
came south-easterly through the Solomons to the New
Hebrides, while those who reached the Southern New
Hebrides by way of Tonga and Samoa were less impregnated
by totemistic ideas and practices.   Fox distinguishes between
a bird totem people in San Cristoval and a people who were
probably earlier but whose totemism can hardly be called a
pure form, and it is possible that we have here the explanation
of the variation in totemistic beliefs throughout the Pacific." [3]

[1] C. B. Humphreys, *The Southern New Hebrides* (Cambridge, 1926), pp. 14-15.

[2] C. B. Humphreys, *op. cit.* p. 121.

[3] C. B. Humphreys, *op. cit.* p. 179. As to Mr. Fox's evidence, see below.

CHAPTER IV

TOTEMISM IN TIKOPIA

TIKOPIA is a small island of the Pacific, measuring only some three miles in length by a mile and a half in breadth. It lies between the New Hebrides on the south and the Solomon Islands on the north, and it therefore belongs to the chain of islands to which the name of Melanesia is given ; but the natives are not Melanesians by blood and language. Racially, linguistically, and culturally, they belong to the Polynesian stock. They have been carefully investigated by Mr. Raymond Firth, Reader in Anthropology in the University of London, who spent just a year among them, from July 1928 to July 1929. I will quote his general description of the people : " Rarely visited by Europeans and with no white residents, Tikopia lies in the extreme east of the British Solomon Islands Protectorate, and is inhabited by twelve hundred healthy and vigorous natives. Homogeneous in speech and culture, they are a unit of what may be termed the ' Polynesian fringe ' in Melanesia, their closest affinities being not with the people of the Solomons region but with those of Samoa, Tonga, and even more distant groups to the east. Almost untouched by the outside world the people of Tikopia manage their own affairs, are governed by their chiefs, and are proud of themselves and their culture. They are primitive in the sense that the level of their material technical achievement is not high, and they have been affected in only a few externals by Western civilization ; at the same time they have an elaborate code of etiquette, a clear-cut systematic social organization, and they have developed very strongly the ceremonial side of their life. They still wear only their simple bark-cloth, they live in plain sago-leaf thatch huts,, they carry out the traditional forms of mourning, marriage, and initiation.   *Mirabile dictu,* a large section of them still worship their ancient gods with full panoply of ritual, a condition almost unique in the Polynesia of to-day." [1]

The natives of Tikopia have a system of beliefs and rites relating to certain species of animals and plants, and the question whether this system deserves to be called totemism has been carefully investigated by Mr. Firth.   It bears on the general question whether totemism has been an institution in Polynesia as a whole or not.   On this disputed question I may refer the reader to what I have said in *Totemism and Exogamy.*[2]   Here it may not be out of place to quote some of the special evidence which Mr. Firth adduces in discussing the problem for Tikopia.

" The social organization of this community," Mr. Firth tells us, " consists of four large patrilineal kinship groups, which for convenience may be termed clans, though they are not necessarily exogamous in marriage relations.   Each of these is governed by a chief (*ariki*) who, in his capacity of religious head of the group and performer of the principal *kava* rites, stands in a special relation to the gods (*atua*). These comprise the spirits of his ancestors, the dead clan chiefs in order of precedence, headed by a number of major deities, sometimes distinguished as *tupua*, who have never lived on earth as men.   Each chief has as his council and assistants in religious affairs a small number of *pure matua*, elders, who hold their rank by virtue of their position as heads of the most important families in the clan.   Each elder has his own *atua* to whom he performs ceremonies, but in a more limited sphere than his chief.   There is to some extent a parallelism between the arrangement of social groups in the community and the arrangement of deities in the religious scheme.

" The nature of Tikopian totemism can be understood only after reference to the attitude of the people towards the living objects of their natural environment as a whole.   To the native, the primary matter of interest, apart from the

[1] R. Firth, *We, The Tikopia* (London, 1936), p. 5.   [2] *Totemism and Exogamy,* ii. 151 *sqq.*

classification into animals, plants, etc., is the distinction between things which are eaten and those which are not eaten.

" The diet of this island people consists almost solely of vegetable products and fish, but within these limits is extremely varied. There appears to be very few species in either domain which, though edible, are not utilized for food. Of the great majority which figure on the bill of fare nothing need be said here ; the four chief vegetable items, however, demand consideration—the yam, the taro, the coconut, and the breadfruit. Each of these is affiliated with one of the clans of the island and is regarded as being in a sense their special property. Following the native mode of speech in which the term *fakarono*, meaning primarily ' to listen,' or secondarily ' to obey,' is employed to denote this relation, it may be said that the yam ' obeys ' sa Kafika, the coconut ' obeys ' sa Tafua, the taro ' obeys ' sa Taumako and the breadfruit ' obeys ' sa Fangarere. The rôle of controller is often assigned in ordinary conversation to the chief of the clan. Thus as an alternative statement it may be said that the yam ' obeys ' or ' listens to ' the Ariki Kafika—and so on ; the meaning is the same in both cases, since in all ceremonial matters and in much else as well the chief is the representative of his clan. The term *fakarono* as used in this connection implies no conscious obedience on the part of the plant, no imputation of personality, but simply that jurisdiction is exercised over it by the particular chief in question. This control relates primarily to religious ritual, the chiefs of Kafika and Taumako having certain very sacred and important duties to perform in connection with the seasonal planting of yam and taro respectively, while the Ariki Fangarere celebrates ritually each crop of breadfruit as it comes to maturity. The Ariki Tafua has no such definite obligations or privileges connected with the coconut, which is probably to be correlated with the fact that this palm has no well-marked fruiting season, but bears almost continuously throughout the year, several different stages of the nut being represented in its crown at any one time. . . .

" There is no restriction of any kind on the growing of these foodstuffs by members of a clan other than that which

exercises special jurisdiction over them.   Every man of the
island community has his patches of taro, usually, though not
invariably, his clump of yams, and always his breadfruit and
coconut trees.   But when the appropriate time comes it is
left to the members of the affiliated clan, headed by their
chief, to perform the due rites. . . .

" The association of each clan with its food plant rests in
native belief on the relation between the plant and the principal clan deity.   Each of the four groups has its main god,
who is regarded with great reverence and is termed sacred
(*tapu*) in the highest degree.   He possesses a variety of
names ; one or two of these are widely known, but the others
are supposed to be the property of the chief alone.   To meet
the needs of ordinary reference the descriptive terms ' Te
Atua i Kafika,' ' Te Atua i Tafua,' The Deity in Kafika, The
Deity in Tafua, and the like are employed.   Often, again,
euphemisms are in vogue, as ' *Ko ia e nofo i te vai* '—' He
who lives in the water,' for the God of the Lake, represented
by the freshwater eel. . . .   A more accurate statement
then from the native point of view is that the yam, taro, and
other food plants belong primarily to the chief *atua* of the
respective divisions, and that it is through this that the clan
and chief exercise their interest in them.   Hence the seasonal
ceremonies mentioned above have a very definite aim : they
induce the deity to continue his policy of productivity and to
send once again the crops by which his people live.   The
association of the clans with the principal food plants of the
island and the performance of rites to ensure a continuance of
their fertility is comprehensible in that the importance of these
foodstuffs is thereby maintained in the eyes of the people,
their cultivation is invested with a certain religious sanction,
and their economic interest is thus reinforced.

" The specific social partition, however, whereby each
clan is definitely responsible for one type of plant, rests on
different grounds.   In the native belief it has its foundation in
an incident, in reality of a mythical nature, which is held to
have happened in the distant times when men were gods and
gods were men, and when the principal deities themselves
were the clans in the land.   The story in the best known version is that an *atua*, by name Tikaran, came to the land of

Tikopia from foreign parts. On his arrival a feast was made, and a huge pile of food, *te ana*, was set up in the marae (sanctuary or temple) of Rarokola in Uta. Emulation then began between the local deities and the visitor as to who would be the victor in trials of strength and speed. According to the usual tale, a hopping match was instituted, and a circuit of the lake was begun. The contestants had passed round the seaward side, left Namo behind, and had entered on the path through Te Roro, when Tikaran slipped and fell. He made pretence of having injured his leg on one of the rocks which strewed the way, and began to limp. Suddenly, however, he made a dash for the glade of Rarokoka, where the provision for the feast lay, and grabbing up the heap, fled to the hills. With the Family of gods in close pursuit he made for the crest, but arriving at the spur of Marepa he slipped and fell once more, so that a deep groove in the hillside at the present day is known as ' The Place of Falling of Tikaran.' The Family of deities, coming up, were just able to grab, one a coconut, another a taro, another a breadfruit, and others a yam, before their opponent, gathering himself up, bolted to the edge of the cliff, and being an *atua*, launched himself into the sky and set off for the far lands with his ill-gotten gains. He retained the bulk of the feast, but the Family had been able to save for Tikopia the principal foodstuffs, and transmit them to posterity. Thus the Atua i Tafua had seized a coconut, whence his clan now control that fruit ; the Atua i Taumako had grasped a taro, which is now the vegetable of that clan ; the Atua i Fangarere had gripped a breadfruit, which is now controlled by his group, while Pu ma, deities of Kafika, had obtained the yam, which is now under the jurisdiction of this clan.

" The tale is thus a myth of a type common to many primitive peoples. Its general function is to provide a foundation for existing socio-economic relations.

" The partition in sphere of interests to which it refers, to be understood clearly, must be studied in conjunction with the whole religious system of Tikopia. There it is seen that in every important aspect of life there is a division of function among the four clans, each headed by its chief, having its own part to play in the total scheme. It is not easy to frame a satisfactory generalization, but after an intensive study of the culture of these folk the present writer is drawn to the conclusion that the small size of the island and the dense population, in association with the intricate ceremonial so characteristic of all Polynesians, and the conflicting interests of the major groups have done much to favour the minute division of social and religious duties and privileges which one observes. On the other hand, the need for social unity within this limited area has tended to promote also the rather remarkable complementary functions and interlocking ties which link clan with clan.

" One problem which may arouse interest is the definiteness of the clan association with the principal food plants, and the absence of such specific linkage with the chief species of edible fish which have no such clan affiliation. This is probably to be correlated with the greater fixity of the plant species, the fact that their propagation, their growth and their harvest are more under human control, and that they are clearly localized at all times; fish, on the other hand, are much more liable to variation, and are present to human ken, as a rule, only in immediate connection with their capture." [1]

" None of these plants are in themselves considered as sacred, nor are they ever termed *atua*. They are controlled by the principal *atua* of the respective clans, and figuratively are spoken of as being the bodies or portions of the anatomy of these supernatural beings, but they are not *atua* in themselves. No Tikopian ever termed an edible food plant an *atua* even when speaking of it on the magico-religious or mythic plane. . . .

" The relation of the four principal plant food-stuffs to the social order is in quite a different category from that of animals. In the latter case it is not the edible, but the inedible elements which are associated with supernatural beings. The facts are clear. The taro, the yam, the coconut and the breadfruit are of great importance in the native life. They are closely and directly linked with their respective clans, a complex series of rites is performed in each case to ensure their productivity, and the members of each clan, as of the others, may eat the clan plant. With birds and sea creatures

[1] R. Firth, *Totemism in Polynesia* (*Oceania*, 1931), pp. 3-10.

the converse is the case. Species used as food are linked with no social group, and any increase rites are of a more generalised type. It is the inedible kinds which are associated with clans and clan gods, they have little attention paid to them and, naturally enough, are not the subject of any increase ceremonies. Even when one of the creatures is killed, no ritual procedure is carried out to avert ill results. If we are to speak then of these phenomena as constituting totemism it must be acknowledged that there are in Tikopia two distinct types of the institution—the positive, relating to plant food-stuffs, with emphasis on fertility; the negative, relating to animals, with emphasis on unsuitability for food.

" There is no question of association of plant and animal species in any form of ' linked totemism ' ; they are on entirely different planes of religious interest.

" The animals and marine creatures which enter into the ritual relation embrace a variety of species, and certain corresponding differences of behaviour towards them are exhibited by the natives. These may now be considered in detail.

" The simplest relation occurs in the case of certain crabs, lizards, insects and such ' small deer.' This class comprises creatures such as the *kaviki*, the ghostly pale little land crab, which lives in burrows in the sand, often under the house floor, whence it emerges by night and stalks rustling over the coconut matting, to engage in battle or love affairs, to the annoyance of the humans whom it disturbs. The *kalamisi* or *karamisi* is a kindred animal, a crab of a reddish-brown or yellowish hue, somewhat hairy-legged, the favourite residence of which appears to be the crotch of a branch of a tree. Both these species of crustacean are termed *atua*, being inedible. At times it is thought they are entered by itinerant spirits, often of the malignant disease-bringing kind, against whom man has continually to be on his guard. When such a ghostly being is thus its denizen the crab is noticeable for its interest in human beings. An actual native statement will illustrate this point. . . . The significance of this is that the disease-bringing spirit is thought to enter for its own purpose the body of the crab, which thus animated, crawls over to the sleeping man and pinches him with its claw. The man awakes, reaches out for the creature, grasps it and drawing it to him, maims it. . . ." [1]

"The term *ata* is frequently used to describe the relation of the supernatural being to the animal which is its manifest form. In its most concrete sense *te ata* is the *shadow*, as of a person cast by the sun. . . . It is also used of a *reflection* as of an image seen in a pool of water. The appearance of a spirit in material animate form is also described as its *ata*, which is best translated in this connection as its *image* or *simulation*. . . . The word *ata* is used only when the concrete materialization is that of a living creature ; in other cases the spirit may have as a permanent resting-place an object such as a war club, a spear or the sacred centre post of a clan house. These are alluded to as *fakatino*, embodiments of their respective deities. The *fakatino* is a permanent concrete symbol of the supernatural being, a definite individual object of known locale ; the *ata* is the form which he simulates at will, and may be any individual of a given species. . . .

" Natives say that in Tikopia all birds and animals are *ata* of various *atua* which appear in this form to mankind. To this general statement there are certain exceptions since a few kinds of bird are not regarded as serving *atua* as a vehicle for manifestation, and are eaten freely. The great majority of species, however, are associated with supernatural beings.

" But not all animals of the one kind are so characterized. Some may be acting as media or materializations of the spirits, fraught with religious interest and perhaps with peril, while others of the same species remain simple and harmless creatures. The problem then arises of how to distinguish the one type from the other—to separate the spirit in animal shape from the mere animal. This problem has had to be faced by the native and an attempt made at its solution, since, while on the one hand it is impracticable for him to respect and give licence to every member of every animal species which he encounters, it is imperative from the point of view of religious belief to observe a becoming reverence to such creatures as may be possessed by super-

[1] R. Firth, *op. cit.* pp. 12-14.

normal attributes. The broad test is based in a rational manner on the behaviour of the animal itself. If it behaves strangely in a manner not characteristic of its species, then it is an *atua* in animal guise; if it acts in normal fashion, then it is an ordinary individual and may be treated as such. . . . The point of this statement is that if a person walking through the woods sees a startled bird fly away from him or a swamp-hen run, then it is simply a creature in natural form ; if, however, it comes towards him and exhibits none of the fear which is to be expected in the circumstances, or if it hovers near him and keeps up a continuous cry for no apparent reason, then it is held to be inhabited at the moment by a supernatural being. So also with fish, into which spirits also enter on occasion, and which betray their nature by abnormal conduct."[1]

" The same applies to the bat, which is common in the island. Being a fruit eater it is looked on by the people as a great pest, but probably as a reflex of the same circumstance, is regarded as a creature of the gods, in particular of the clan of Tafua. Sometimes when encountered it is a manifestation of the *atua* ; more often it is merely the animal itself. . . . The *peka* (bat) is not eaten by the Tikopians, and they express great distaste at the idea. . . . Its characteristic odour is unpleasant. . . . The bat ordinarily is treated with scant ceremony, and though not usually harmed by adults is often pelted with stones by children and occasionally brought down in triumph. Reproof from elders may follow, but only of a mild nature. A man who by intention killed a bat would be regarded as having committed an unwise action but not necessarily a sacrilegious one. . . . The bat is a thieving animal and as such has little sympathy in its misfortune. But for this reason it receives, on the other hand, some consideration. When a man finds a bat eating fruit in his orchard or gnawing at a coconut, if he be a cautious person he does not endeavour to kill it, but merely scares it away, apostrophizing it under the name of *Pu* (ancestor) as it flaps off, to go to other districts and obtain food. He treats it gently lest, being possibly an *atua* masquerading in animal guise, it resent harsh treatment and retaliate by returning again and again to his crops."[2]

[1] R. Firth, *op. cit.* pp. 16 *sqq.*   [2] R. Firth, *op. cit.* pp. 19-20.

" It is believed by the Ariki Tafua and by the community at large that he has special control over the actions of the bat, and that if he is offended by some action of the populace he can by reciting an appropriate appeal, induce the creature to go and damage their coconut crops by severing with its sharp teeth the stems of the immature nuts. As a corollary to this belief, when the people see in their orchards evidence of unusually severe depredations by bats they attribute this to the ill-will and the recital of spells on the part of the chief against them. . . .

" The deference of the people of all clans to the bat appears to indicate that this creature owes its ritual importance primarily to its economic notoriety, its powers of destruction of food, and that the link with the specific clan *atua* is of secondary interest.

" Somewhat the same attitude exists in the case of the *sivi* (parroquet) and *karae* (swamp-hen). The parroquet is destructive to coconut and other tree fruits by reason of its promiscuous nibbling, which causes wastage of food even when the quantity consumed is not great. As with the bat, however, violent action is not usually adopted, being replaced by methods of suasion. A man sitting in his house and hearing the cry of a parroquet in his orchard near at hand will call out—

> ' Go, Ancestor ! to set up your sacred beak
> On the crests of the hills
> And leave this place here
> For the preparation of a food gift for you.'

These words politely invite the bird to betake itself to the mountain heights, and allow the spot which it is raiding to stay vacant in order—so it is assured—that the crops thus left to mature may form an adequate food present for it at some future date. On hearing this, it is believed, the parroquet is under compulsion to fly off and feed in another locality.

" For the *karae* (or swamp-hen) a similar procedure is adopted. A person will utter the formula—

> ' Go, Ancestor ! and set up your sacred beak here
> On Maunga Faea or in Soso
> To eat a large taro root for yourself
> And a great stem of bananas for yourself.'

Here the bird is induced to go by mention of the prospect of large crops in other places. . . . The swamp-hen is perhaps the greatest animal pest known to the natives. It is extremely voracious, and taro and banana suffer heavily from its incursions. . . . Because of its persistent thieving habits the *karae* or swamp-hen is very unpopular, and though recognized as the *ata* of a clan deity is nevertheless sometimes killed."[1]

" The standard of judgment as to whether one is encountering an animal or an *atua*, however, being empirical, is admittedly subject to error. It is understood that a man may sometimes mistake the spirit for an ordinary creature, and by lack of caution involve himself in mischance. This is illustrated by an incident which happened some years ago, in which a party of men ate of a kind of crab known as the *paka foran* and died in consequence. This animal is believed to be one of the forms in which the Female Deity, Te Atua Fafine, manifests herself, but on this occasion the folk imagined that they were dealing with the *ata*, the physical simulation, and not the spirit. Their tragic fate, however, was evidence of their mistake. . . . One of the party only refrained from eating; he dropped the morsels of food between his legs when invited to partake and so survived. . . .

" The idea in regard to the injuring, killing or eating of such creatures as are believed to be *ata* of *atua* is that any action of this kind which is apparently followed by no ill-results has involved the animal alone ; but if any misfortune should occur soon afterwards, then this is held to be proof that the *atua* was in possession at the time. This is merely a special case of the general principle that the presence of an *atua* is to be deduced from the behaviour of an animal—if eating it makes one ill, then it must have harboured a spirit. . . .

" The basis of identification of the presence of a supernatural being varies somewhat with different species. Thus the black lizard which frequents the native houses and is common throughout the island is believed to be an *atua* if it presents a peculiar shining appearance. . . .

" The *moko* (lizard) is regarded as being the *ata* of Atua i

[1] R. Firth, *op. cit.* p. 25.

Raropuka. The crocodile, known as *moko toro* (crawling lizard) is held to be the *ata* of the same god. . . .

" As a rule the animal which is thought to serve as the *ata* of a deity is not eaten, though it may be killed on occasions. The swamp-hen, for instance, is never utilised for food. . . . With the pigeon the case is not quite parallel. Normally it is not eaten. . . . Though this bird is not eaten by Taumako, it may, in some circumstances, be used as food by persons of the other clans, though such action is rare, and would not be performed by *tama tapu* of Taumako clan, *i.e.* people whose mother is of that stock. One informant gave me a ruling on the question of eating the pigeon—as follows : ' If a woman of Taumako marries a man of Tafua, then she refrains from eating the *rupe* (pigeon), and her *muaki tama*, the eldest son does also. Her younger children may eat of it. Her husband used to eat thereof, but when his wife comes and they dwell together, it is *tapu* for him then. When the eldest son marries, then his children may eat this bird ; they eat then, because their own mother is different.' The *tapu* is not incumbent on the grandchildren, even on the offspring of the eldest son—unless, of course, their mother also is of Taumako, in which case they too will refrain. The licence allowed by this rule is largely theoretical ; in practice hardly anyone in the entire population appears to eat the pigeon, and though plentiful, it is not regarded by the natives as an item in the food supply. On the other hand, natives of Taumako clan are quite eager that this bird shall be shot, giving as a reason that it consumes *voia (Canarium* nuts) and other useful forest fruits. . . ."[1]

" The restriction of the prohibition on eating an animal associated with a clan deity to the children of the eldest born only, is paralleled by the custom observed with regard to the *tukuku* and *panoko*, two fish which are *tapu* to sa Kafika. They are not *ata* of *atua* on earth, but according to native belief have a special function to perform in the afterworld in connection with the dead of Kafika. For this reason ritual abstention is observed, but only by the eldest son and eldest daughter of each Kafika family. Moreover, when women of Kafika marry husbands of Taumako, Tafua or Fangarere,

[1] R. Firth, *op. cit.* pp. 30-32.

their first-born likewise do not eat of these two fish, though the later born do. . . .

" Other birds, in addition to those already mentioned, serve as media or simulacra for important deities. Such are the *sikotara* (kingfisher) which is the *ata* of the Atua i te Uruao, the God in the Woods, the principal deity of the Porima family. The *kareva*, the long-tailed cuckoo, which is sometimes seen in the island, is an *ata* of the same *atua*. The *sivi* (parroquet) is sacred to sa Taumako, being utilized as a material medium by the chief *atua* of that clan. . . . A few birds are entirely free from any restriction in the matter of fitness for food." [1]

" More interest is displayed in marine creatures, and the distinction between edible and non-edible species is clearly marked. . . . The *fai* (sting-ray) and the *ririno* (also a ray) of which there are said to be three varieties, red, black, and white, are all *ata* of the *Atua Fafine*, the Female Deity of Kafika. . . .

" Most of the fish known to the Tikopians are used as food, and are not regarded as being associated with spirits or deities, but a few of them are so classed. The *sakura* and *takua*, types of swordfish, are used as *ata* by the Atua i Taumako—they are called his *tino*, his body, signifying his material manifestation—and so are sacred for the clan of that name. Special interest attaches to the *marana*, which is apparently of the dolphin type. One variety of this is known as the *marana sa Korokoro* since it is supposed to have special affinity with the family group of Korokoro, which belongs to the Tafua clan. If this creature is found stranded, as occasionally occurs, then an offering of green food—taro plants or breadfruit, and fresh coconuts—is set beside it by the family mentioned. This is called *putu*, a term which is used also to denote an offering set on the grave of a person recently dead. After this ritual deference has been paid to it the dolphin is taken away and cooked. The flesh is divided among the four clans of the island according to a definite traditional rule. . . . The portions are known as *rau*, the conventional name for a ' ceremonial share ' and each is the *rau* of the principal deity of the clan to which it is presented.

[1] R. Firth, *op. cit.* pp. 30-33.

The gift is taken in each case to the chief of the clan as representative of his people, and is eaten by him and such of his family and clansfolk as he chooses.   The people of sa Korokoro group do not eat of the dolphin at all.   *E tapu*— ' It is prohibited '—for them.   This is due to the belief that this creature is a form of materialization of their principal *atua*.

" It may be noted that here is an especially clear case in which an animal species is affiliated with a family group, but not with the whole clan of which this group is a member— the situation is one of ' family totemism,' not ' clan totemism.'

" The whale is known also to the Tikopian people, and is termed by them the *taforo* in common speech, or in an honorific phrase, *te Uru Pon o te Vasa*—' The Head Post of the Ocean Spaces.'   At rare intervals a whale is driven ashore, and its huge bulk attracts considerable attention. Great numbers of people of all ages and both sexes assemble, and as the men of the community go to join this crowd they each grasp a weapon and on arrival at the scene brandish it fiercely. . . . Though the actions are in mimicry of fighting no actual disorder takes place.   This is termed the *fakaveve* of the whale.   The idea is that the creature is the material form of an *atua* which has come to land, and there is a possibility that it may be a bringer of disease, since to the Tikopian the onset of an epidemic is always associated with influences, mainly supernatural, from outside the island, The threatening gestures of the *fakaveve* are intended to frighten off any such evil-minded *atua* and so preserve the health of the land.   In addition to this a *putu* of green food is carried from the orchards and placed by the carcase, as is done with the *marana*.   This is by way of offering to the *atua* so that by the dual attitude of placation and threatening he may be induced to behave favourably to the people. . . ." [1]

" The octopus and the various species of eel appear to be in a different category from the creatures already discussed in that here the *atua* is more closely related to the animal itself, being in fact a personification of the species.

" The octopus is regarded as the embodiment or the actual form of the Atua i Faea, a male, his personal name

[1] R. Firth, *op. cit.* pp. 74 *sqq.*

being Feke. Usually the deity seems to be zoomorphically rather than anthropomorphically conceived. . . . This *atua* is identified with the sun, the rays corresponding to the splayed tentacles of the octopus. . . . In addition to his own proper shape, Feke also enters into or simulates certain other creatures. One of these is *una*, the small red hermit crab. Another is *toki*, the giant clam, which is also regarded as an *ata* of the *atua*. . . . The position of the octopus in the religious scheme of the natives is thus somewhat involved. The *atua* Feke is a personification of this animal species ; he is able also to materialise in the form of the hermit crab and the clam, which implies considerable powers of transmutation. Moreover he is represented also by a mountain *massif* with its springs of water, and by the sun with its beams, an identification which is based on a general factor of similarity— a central body and a number of divergent rays. Again, as a deity of the Tikopian pantheon Feke is married to Nau Fiora, goddess of Tafua clan, has children by her and on certain ceremonial occasions of the chief of Tafua is conceived as performing the appropriate duty, on the spiritual plane, of coming to tend the oven with his bundle of firewood on his shoulder, as all good husbands do on earth. The exact degree of abstraction, the precise relation which the spiritual being Feke is imagined to bear to his material form the octopus, the sun, the clam, or the mountain crest is difficult to define ; it apparently varies according to the circumstances.

" The position of the eel is very similar. Eels fall into two divisions—those of the lake and those of the sea. The former have no specific name beyond that which is applied to the Eel-god himself—' Tuna,' the term ' te Atua i te Vai,' ' the Deity in the Water' being the common mode of reference. Occasionally one type is distinguished by the description, ' the deity possessing ears,' since it has apparently ear-like protuberances at the sides of its head. The commonest of the marine eels is the *rafua*, a sandy-grey speckled creature with a flat cruel head. . . . The *rafua* is also spoken of as 'Te Atua i te Tai.' 'The Deity in the Sea,' in contrast to its fellow of the lake. It is regarded as being the material embodiment of one of the most important deities of the

Taumako clan. The *natinia*, a species of sea eel banded in brown and white, is associated in particular with the Fangarere people, since it is the *ata* of the *Atua i te Ava*, the Deity of the Channel, who is invoked by them. . . .

" None of the species of eel is eaten under any circumstances. It is a creature for which the natives express the greatest repulsion—*e fakakinokino*, 'it is disgusting,' they say. The eel of the lake in particular arouses this aversion. . . . Perhaps the sentiment of aversion to it and the prohibition against eating it—a prohibition which, unlike others, is never disregarded—can be correlated with the myth as to its origin. There is not space to give the full text here, but in brief, the story is that the various species of eel in the guise of their respective *atua*, were formed from the *membrum virile* of the Atua i Tafua, being cut therefrom by a female deity and flung, one portion into the salt water to become the reef eel, another likewise to become another sea eel and another into the lake to become the denizen of the fresh water." [1]

Summing up the evidence for traces of totemism in Tikopia, Mr. Firth observes : " In the first place the ritual attitude towards natural species does not bulk largely in Tikopian religion, either on the part of individuals or of groups. Elaborate ceremonies are conducted to promote the fertility of the chief plant food-stuffs, but for the animals associated with spiritual beings and social groups no specific ceremonies exist, no offerings are made to them, and they receive little formal attention. Their interest, in native eyes, is indirect and subsidiary.

" This is the result of the belief that individuals of the natural species—apart from the food-stuffs mentioned above—are simply vehicles or manifestations of gods, ancestors, or other spiritual beings, and a distinction is drawn coherently by the natives between an individual of the species so controlled or simulated by a supernatural being, and one which is a purely normal creature.

" It is evident also from this why the idea of the identity of the natural species or individuals of it with the social group or with any person thereof is entirely lacking. The ' totem '

---

[1] R. Firth, *op. cit.* pp. 38 *sqq.*

animal is neither a representation nor an emblem of the human group, nor is it a member of the group. Interference with the creature, or the killing or eating of it, is regarded as a hostile act, not towards group property or a fellow member, but towards the deity who may be in possession of it at the time, and who will punish the sacrilege. The material object is then differentiated clearly from the spiritual being who employs it in manifestation. It is the *atua* who is of constant importance, who is invoked in many ceremonies ; his *ata* is of interest only on random occasions. Moreover, there is no belief that the social group or any portion of it is descended from the animal with which it is thus connected. Origin may be traced through the *atua*, the supernatural being, though this concept of descent from the higher deities is not clearly formulated, and may even be denied by some informants. The common belief is that each social group traces its origin to an ancestor, endowed with supernormal qualities, but conceived as a human being, who lived and died as such." [1]

On the whole, we may say that though the Tikopian system of beliefs and rites concerning animals and plants which has been so well described by Mr. Firth is not totemism in the ordinary sense, yet it may have been developed out of an earlier system of totemism, the old totems being replaced by gods and goddesses. If that is so, the Tikopians may be said to occupy an intermediate stage in the progress from totemism with its magical rites to religion with its worship of divinities.

[1] R. Firth, *op. cit.* pp. 43 *sq.*

CHAPTER V

TOTEMISM IN THE SANTA CRUZ GROUP AND IN THE
SHORTLAND ISLANDS

THE Santa Cruz group is a cluster of islands lying to the
north-west of Tikopia, and to the east of San Cristoval,
one of the Solomon Islands. The natives have a system of
totemism of the most regular pattern, as it is described by the
late W. H. R. Rivers. He says : " The part of Melanesia
in which we have the clearest evidence of genuine totemism
is the Santa Cruz group. We know so little of the culture of
this region that the matter may not be so simple as it seems,
but on the available evidence this group possesses the institution of totemism of the most typical kind in the form of
exogamous clans, the members of each of which are bound
together by the possession of a common totem, usually an
animal. When the totem is an animal it may not be killed or
eaten by the members of the clan ; when it is a plant it may
not be eaten or even touched ; and when, as in Vanikolo,
the totem is an object of an unusual kind, there are definite
restrictions on its use. Members of the grass clan may not
walk on the grass, and those of the bowl clan may not eat food
cooked in a bowl. Further, there is a definite belief in descent
either from the totem or from some one connected with the
totem ; thus, members of the bowl clan trace their descent
from a woman who floated to the island in a bowl.

" In Vanikolo we seem to have a condition unusual in
Melanesia in that each clan possesses only one totem, but it
may be that only the names of the chief totems were given to
me, and that there are here, as elsewhere, other and subsidiary
totems. In the main island of Santa Cruz and in the Reef

Islands, on the other hand, each exogamous clan has associated with it several animals which may not be eaten, and in most cases there is no evidence that one of these is more important than the rest." [1]

Further, Rivers found a system of totemism in the Shortland Islands. On this subject he says : " In the Shortland Islands there are exogamous matrilineal clans (*latu*), with each of which two totems called respectively *tua* and *tete* are associated, the former meaning grandfather or male ancestor, the latter grandmother or female ancestor. Only some of these animals are forbidden as food and those so treated are called *tabu* or *tabutabu*, the former being used with the possessive suffix (*tabugu*) and the latter with the possessive noun (*sagu tabutabu*). It may be noted that there was general agreement about the totems called *tua*, only one being assigned to each clan, while the accounts of the *tete* were more uncertain, one animal being given at one time or by one informant, and another or others on other occasions." [2]

[1] W. H. R. Rivers, *The History of*
Melanesian Society (Cambridge, 1914),   ii. 75 *sq.*
[2] W. H. R. Rivers, *op. cit.* p. 77.

CHAPTER VI

TOTEMISM IN THE SOLOMON ISLANDS

In Arosi, the north-western district of the island of San Cristoval, a large island of the Solomon Group, the natives possess a regular system of totemism which has been described as follows by the experienced missionary, Dr. C. E. Fox.[1]

" From this short account of Arosi itself I pass on to the social organization of its people. They are divided into exogamous clans with matrilineal descent (except in one or two cases to be referred to presently), and each clan has a totem which is generally a bird. The clans are not named after these bird totems, but there is a universal belief that the people of each clan are descended from their totem. The totem bird is treated with great respect, neither killed nor eaten, and was apparently sacrificed to. There are two interrogative pronouns in the Arosi language, one used exclusively for persons and the other for everything else ; a *tei* for persons, *taha* for things ; but if you enquire about a man's clan it is common to use the former : *A tei burunga mu* ? Who is your clan ? and the bird is given—eagle, hawk, kingfisher, etc., and *burunga*, one of the words for clan, means also remote ancestor, and is used by Christian natives for Adam and Eve. In several cases, too, there are definite stories of the origin of the clans from women or girls who turned into birds, as in the case of the owl clan, whose ancestor was the girl who changed herself into an owl to escape from her mother. As for the taboo on eating or killing the totem bird, it certainly was strictly enforced, though there

[1] C. E. Fox, *The Threshold of the Pacific* (London, 1924).

may be more laxity at the present time. I have not heard of any religious ceremonies connected with the totems, and probably none are observed nowadays ; but there is some evidence that sacrifices were once generally offered in the existence of the *dara manu,* sacred bowls, literally ' bird bowls.' These are carved and very highly prized food bowls in which sacrifices are even still offered. One of those figured[1] has a snake carved in the middle of the bowl, and is the *dara manu* of the snake clan in which sacrifices are offered to the snake, of which only the men belonging to the snake clan can partake. The bowl, with a bird holding a fish in its mouth, had sacrifices placed in it when the people went fishing, the fishermen eating them. . . .

" The clans were (and still are) exogamous with matri-lineal descent, but it must be remembered that schools and civilization have for many years been breaking down the clan system in Arosi. Natives are now to be found who do not know to what clan they belong. This is partly due to the fact that Christianity has been breaking down the clan system as it regulated marriage, for the earlier missionaries either did not know of the existence of the clans (even Dr. Codrington did not) or perhaps deliberately ignored them and encouraged marriage within the clan ; lately a conference of native teachers decided to forbid a man to marry a woman of the same clan, but this rule was not allowed by the synod of the diocese. Formerly the clans were strictly exogamous, and though marriages within the clan took place, at the least a heavy fine had to be paid by the offender. An exception should perhaps be made of the clan of the chiefs (Araha) as pedigrees show many marriages of Araha men to Araha women. It is chiefly in the coast villages that the clan regulations have become laxer, and it is in these villages that the taboo against killing the totem is more lightly regarded, yet even there it is still respected. A Tawatana man lately told me he certainly would not kill either the totem of his father (eagle) or that of his mother (crab), but especially the latter ; he said that if one of the crab clan were murdered he, with all other crab people along the coast, would feel bound to punish the murderer ; but if an eagle man were

[1] The bowl is figured in Dr. Fox's book.

killed he would only be ' a little angry.'   There is certainly respect for the father's totem." [1]

" Probably it is true to say that there is now very little religious meaning attached to the totems ; and the clan system is purely a social organisation.   A member of a clan can always appeal to all the other members of his clan for help and protection and can never be destitute.   Wherever he goes in Arosi he will find clansmen who will give him hospitality, and even beyond Arosi, but curiously enough, not so much in Bauro as in Guadalcanar or Malaita, and especially in Guadalcanar ; the clans have different names there, but are identified (by the lines on the palm of the hand) with the Arosi clans.   Some Guadalcanar men lately arrived in Arosi, having run away from a plantation in Guadalcanar, eighty miles distant, and were at once received and helped by the people of the Arosi clan corresponding with their own. An Ulawa man going to Guadalcanar to a village two hundred miles from his home, found people of his own clan (he was told he was Lakuili).   A white trader in San Cristoval was told, after his labourers had examined the palms of his hands, that he belonged to a certain clan, and found much advantage from it." [2]

Totemism is also found in the small island of Santa Anna, lying off the south-east coast of San Cristoval.   There are only two villages, one on the lee and the other (the original settlement) on the weather side, but both these villages are very large as Melanesian villages go, much larger than any on the mainland.   The village on the weather side is now the larger, containing between four and five hundred people, but according to native tradition the· older village was very much older than this.   It is the original village, called Finnatogo, which is here described.   Down the middle of this ran a road about three-quarters of a mile long, and the houses were built on each side.   Three of the five clans into which the people were divided lived on one side of this road, and two on the other.   They were further divided into pairs. Atawa and Amwea, living opposite one another, shared a burial ground ; Agave and Garohai, the next pair, also had a burial ground in common, while Pagewe lived alone.

---

[1] C. E. Fox, *op. cit.* pp. 10 *sq.*   [2] C. E. Fox, *op. cit.* pp. 12 *sq.*

Agave, however, had a small subdivision, Pwapwaroro, who lived with them.

These clans are named after animals. Pagewe is the shark, Agave the crab, Pwapwaroro the firefly, Garohai the turtle. The members of the clans believe they are the descendants of the animals after which the clans are named ; stories are told of the original animal ancestor of the clan : no member may eat of the animal from which his clan takes its name ; and sacrifices and prayers are regularly offered by the members of clans to their animal ancestors. Thus totemism seems here to have developed into a worship of ancestors, only the ancestors are animals, not human beings. In the case of the Garohai or turtle clan, the story of the animal ancestor runs as follows. In very ancient days, before Santa Anna existed, a turtle lived on the neighbouring island of Santa Catalina. This turtle had two children, a boy and a girl. The children noticed that the turtle used to take coconuts and bananas and plant them on a certain spot at the bottom of the sea, not far from Santa Catalina, and by and by they asked their mother her reason for planting these things at the bottom of the sea. The turtle, in reply, told her children to make a hook from a piece of her shell, and when they had done this they got out their outrigger canoe and paddled over to the spot where the turtle had been busy planting useful trees underneath the sea, and there they cast their hook, which the turtle fixed on to a rock below, and the children pulled lustily, but the rock broke. However, the turtle fastened it to another rock which was firmer, and the children hauled on the line, and up came Santa Anna, all ready prepared and planted. And as for the truth of this story you have only to go to the east side of the island and there before your eyes is the broken rock on which the hook failed at the first attempt. The names of the children of the turtle were Waikariniparisu and Kapwarinaro. The girl Kapwarinaro bore children, and it is from them that all the turtle people come. They throw into the sea money, nuts, and food of various sorts to turtles. None of the turtle clan may eat any part of a turtle, and the consequence of breaking this rule, even in ignorance, is death. The turtle clan is the chief clan on Santa Anna, since to their ancestress the people owe the island itself.   They have a peculiar privilege.   At the eastern point is the stone that broke, and there beside it the two children of the turtle turned into two rocks.   When boys and girls in Santa Anna come to a certain age they go through a ceremony called *Haaraha, i.e.* " making great " or " becoming a chief " (" Apparently all perform this ceremony in Santa Anna ;   in Arosi it is only done by members of the Araha clan ").   At the final feast the boy or girl is placed on a platform and decorated with ornaments, and then a boy of the Garohai (turtle) clan goes to the sacred rock-children and covers them over with coconut leaves, and on the day fixed for the *Haaraha,* the candidate goes to the Garohai boy and gives him money, which his father has provided him with, and they go together to the place, and the Garohai boy then uncovers the two stone children to the gaze of the boy or girl, who now becomes *araha.*[1]   It is a time of great feasting and merrymaking, and any Garohai boy may act as master of the ceremonies, some boy probably who wishes to make a little money for himself.[2]   Mr. Fox does not tell us whether the clans in Santa Anna are exogamous, but on the analogy of the totemic clans in Arosi, which are certainly exogamous, we may perhaps assume that the totemic clans in Santa Anna are so also.

Elsewhere Dr. Fox tells us, " The totemism of Santa Anna is typical totemism of its kind, especially as regards its two clans called Garohai (Turtle) and Agave (Crab).   It seems to have been added to a dual organization, Atawa and Amwea, which existed there before the totem people reached Santa Anna."   Further he says that " the totemism of Arosi must be connected with that of Bougainville and the Short-lands, in that the totems are birds, and also because it is associated with cremation.   Cremation is also found in Guadalcanar.   Bird totemism has not been described there, but one may be confident that it will be found there also. Bird clans occur in south-east Malaita." [3]

With regard to the existence of totemism in Bougainville and Buka, the two most northerly islands of the Solomon group, we have the evidence of Miss Beatrice Blackwood,

[1] In Arosi this name *araha* designates the clan of chiefs.

[2] C. E. Fox, *op. cit.* pp. 71 *sqq.*
[3] C. E. Fox, *op. cit.* pp. 350-351.

who spent a year in the islands in 1929 and 1930. " On Buka and North Bougainville there are two main divisions. Naboin and Nakarib. Their relative importance is determined by the one to which the chief belongs taking precedence over the other. They are frequently referred to by the names of their respective totems. The totem of Naboin is invariably *manu*, the large brown eagle. That of Nakarib varies in different districts. On Buka it is *kekeleo*, which, curiously enough, is the domestic fowl, an importation. That this is a relatively recent innovation seems indicated also by the fact that on Bougainville the totem of Nakarib is *karib*, the tree-rat.

"These divisions must be described as clans and not as moieties, because in many villages there are one or more others, which, though they have but few representatives and may be on that account of less importance, are nevertheless independent in status, and are never regarded as subdivisions of the two just mentioned. These smaller clans vary in name and number in different localities ; the largest number known to me in any one village is nine. Any of them may be unrepresented in a given village for a long time, and may be reintroduced by marriage. Descent is invariably matrilineal. But by mutual agreement a member of one clan may be adopted into another, though this is not a common practice. On the whole, the clan division seems to play a less important part in the life of these natives than it does in other Melanesian communities." [1]

Marriage is normally exogamous, and man and wife belong, as a rule, to different villages. There are no enjoined marriages. Unions between relatives, including parallel and cross cousins, are forbidden. There is, however, a certain amount of slackness in the observance of these prohibitions at the present time. There is a strict rule of avoidance between a woman and her sons-in-law. She must always have within reach a long hood of pandanus leaves stitched together, with which to hide her face on the approach of her sons-in-law. They, on their side, must avoid coming into

---

[1] Beatrice Blackwood, " Report on Field Work in Buka and Bougainville," in *Oceania*, vol. ii. No. 2 (Dec. 1931), p. 213. Buka is an island some thirty miles long lying immediately to the north of Bougainville.

close contact with their mother-in-law. There are no restrictions on social intercourse between a girl and her husband's·parents, with whom she usually spends a great part of her life between betrothal and the consummation of the marriage.[1]

[1] B. Blackwood, *op. cit.* pp. 214 *sq.*

CHAPTER VII

TOTEMISM IN ONTONG JAVA

ONTONG JAVA comprises about one hundred small islands arranged in and around a lagoon thirty-five to forty miles long by twenty broad at its widest point. It lies to the north-east of the Solomon Islands at approximately latitude five degrees south and longitude one hundred and sixty degrees east. The northern tip of the island of Ysabel, one hundred and fifty miles to the south-west, is the nearest point of the Solomon group. All the islands are barely above the reach of high tides, and are entirely of coral formation. There is no soil beyond sand and coral detritus mixed with decayed vegetation, and the variety of the flora is extremely limited.[1]

The social and totemic organisations of the islanders have been investigated and described by Mr. H. Ian Hogbin, who spent about a year in the islands, from November 1927 till November 1928. Of the natives he tells us that they speak a dialect of Polynesian, and, as is usual with these dialects, we find a regular consonantal change. In appearance the islanders also show definite affinities with the Polynesians. They are light in colour, ranging from copper to brown, and the hair of the majority is wavy. There are, however, quite a number with straight hair and others with woolly mops resembling the Melanesians of the Solomon Islands.

There are two tribes at Ontong Java. The territory of the more important runs from the island of Pei in the north of the atoll, right around the lagoon to the island of Kape'i in the north-west. The remaining islands, all in the north,

[1] H. Ian Hogbin, "The Social Organization of Ontong Java," in *Oceania*, vol. i. No. 4 (Jan.-March 1931), p. 399.

belong to the other tribe. These two groupings of people shall be spoken of as the Luaniua and the Pelau tribes respectively, after the two main villages.[1]

With regard to the social division of the natives they have, besides individual families, wider groups which Mr Hogbin calls joint families. These include normally all the persons who trace their descent through males back to a common ancestor who lived as a rule about six generations ago. Sometimes it may also include some individuals who trace their descent from this ancestor through females, but this is exceptional. The group has a " manager," who is always the eldest member. He may be spoken of as the headman ; in him all the landed property is vested. There is no mechanism to provide for the division of joint families. They do divide, for very few count descent from a common ancestor who lived more than six generations ago, but there is no ordered scheme by which the subdivision is effected.[2]

If we describe a totem as an object, generally, but not always, an animal or plant, with which a group of people have a ritual relation, then all the wealthy joint families at Ontong Java have a totem, and some of them two or three. In the ordinary course of events the child takes the totem of his father, but if he belongs to the joint family of his mother, then it is hers that he will take. The accompanying list gives some of the more important groups with their totems :

Keila	*u* (coconut crab).
Kiloma	*leia* (Nicobar pigeon) and *malau* (the jungle fowl).
Kepae	*moa* (common fowl).
Kemalu	*mano* (shark) and *'omeke* (food bowl).
Oko	*pakupaku* (mussel) and *hano* (a species of tree).
Akaha	*pakuahau* (an unidentified fish) and *ua* (a species of tree) and *unu* (a centipede).
Kenolei	*hiaka* (white eel) and *'ohuki* (black eel).

Other totems include the *'alali* (parrot fish), the *mokumoku*

[1] H. Ian Hogbin, *op. cit.* pp. 403 *sqq.*   [2] H. Ian Hogbin, *op. cit.* pp 407 *sq.*

(banded demoiselle fish), etc.   It will be noticed that one of the totems of Kemalu is not a natural object.

Edible totems may not be eaten.   If someone does accidentally eat his totem, for no one would do so purposely, there are almost certain to be fatal results, though if the offender is a woman, she may be sufficiently fortunate to escape at the expense of bearing an albino child.   The penalty when a man of Oko touches a *pakupaku* (mussel) is curious.   It is said that a razor-fish will come up to him when he is swimming and tickle him until he opens his mouth to laugh.   He will then swallow so much water that he will drown.   The more common penalty for infringing the taboo of the totem is death caused, it is believed, by one of the species entering the body of the culprit and consuming his bowels.

There are also prohibitions when the totem is not edible. If it is a species of tree, then the rule is that the timber may neither be used in house-building nor may it be burnt.   The most·extraordinary totem is the food bowl.   At Kemalu this utensil may not be placed on top of a sleeping-mat nor may it be carried outside the house unless it is covered.

There is no definite obligation for a man to respect the totem of his mother, unless, of course, he is adopted into her group.   A vague idea exists, nevertheless, that it is bad to break the tapu, and it is generally avoided.

Poor joint families do not possess totems.   The probable reason for this is that the group is loosely bound together when it has only the minimum of property interests.

Ontong Javanese do not regard themselves as in any way descended from the totems nor do they think they are of the same substance as themselves.   The totems, it is said, were chosen by the first priests at the command of the culture goddess Ke luahinge.   They consequently have a mythical origin, but it is quite a different one from the mythical origin of the people themselves.

It is believed that the totems exert protective powers, though generally these are not very clearly defined.   Folk tales tell of fishermen whom they have rescued from drowning, and there are traditions of other people being given aid when they were in critical situations.   The relation of the Kemalu people to their shark totem is rather different. If they are forbidden to eat shark, so also are sharks forbidden to eat them.

" One is familiar with ceremonies the object of which is to increase the totem species, but I believe that up to the present they have never been recorded either in Polynesia or Melanesia. Such ceremonies took place regularly at Ontong Java. They formed part of the *sana* festival, but were only performed by the priests on behalf of their own totems." [1] Unfortunately space did not allow Mr. Hogbin to describe any of these ceremonies for the multiplication of the totems.

---

[1] H. Ian Hogbin, *op. cit.* pp. 420 *sq.*

CHAPTER VIII

TOTEMISM IN THE LOUISIADE GROUP

THE Louisiade group is an archipelago lying to the south-east of New Guinea. The natives belong to that branch of the Melanesian race to which Dr. Seligmann has given the name of Massim. The natives of the D'Entrecasteaux Archipelago, of the Trobriands, and of the south-east extremity of New Guinea, belong to the same branch of the widespread Melanesian race.[1] Of the Louisiade Group the most easterly part is the isolated island of Rossel. The social and totemic organisation of the natives of Rossel have been investigated and described by Mr. W. E. Armstrong, formerly Government Anthropologist in Papua, who spent two months in the island in 1921.

The island is small, about a hundred square miles in area ; its greatest length is about twenty miles, and its greatest breadth is about ten miles, and it has a native population of about 1500 persons. It is surrounded by a coral reef, which encloses a large lagoon that measures about a hundred square miles at the western end, and one of about twenty square miles at the eastern end. The island is of volcanic formation, the highest mountain rising to a height of nearly 3000 feet. It is thickly wooded throughout, and contains the usual economic plants of this part of the tropics. The villages are mostly situated in the interior, many of them at a height of over a thousand feet.[2]

The natives of Rossel are divided into clans, which

[1] C. G. Seligmann, *The Melanesians of British New Guinea* (Cambridge, 1910).

[2] W. E. Armstrong, *Rossel Island* (Cambridge, 1928), pp. 1 *sq.*

may, without appreciable error, be regarded as exogamous. There are about fifteen, or possibly a few more, clans on the island, some of which are widely dispersed. Descent in them is matrilineal. Each clan is characterised by three linked totems, plant, bird, and fish, of which the plant is the principal. The Southern Massim have four linked totems, bird, plant, fish, and snake, of which the bird is the principal. Although the usual questions as to the totems only elicit in Rossel three totems, further enquiry shows that there is a fourth totem of a different order, and this is the snake, the fourth totem of the Southern Massim clans. In the case of the latter this snake is merely a species of snake, which is not rigidly avoided. The snake totem of a Rossel clan, on the other hand, may be described as a god—it is sometimes regarded as an individual, sometimes as a species. Moreover, those snakes that function as totems are avoided and feared equally by all clans, irrespective of their totems. The three primary linked totems, on the other hand, do not seem to be the subject of avoidance or respect by any of the clans, though it is possible that a person would not kill or eat the bird totem of his father's clan. Avoidance of the father's bird totem, and to a certain extent of all his totems, is usual among the Southern Massim and even more pronounced than avoidance of their own totem. The primary totems of the Rossel clans are frequently food plants. One important clan has the sago as totem, and Mr. Armstrong came across no individuals for whom sago was taboo—it seems unlikely that the most important food on the island would be taboo for any one clan.[1]

An interesting feature of Rossel religion is its systematic nature ; something of the orderliness of the native monetary system seems to have crept in to their theology. Rossel Island has, quite definitely, a supreme deity known as *Wonajo*. He, most appropriately, resides on the top of Mount Rossel, the highest mountain on the island, for the creation of which he is responsible. Although, originally, Wonajo and his people seem to have been human in form, on Rossel he is supposed to take the form of a snake by day and assume his human form only at night. Most of the gods have this

[1] W. E. Armstrong, *op. cit.* pp. 38 *sq.*

double character, alternating between the human form and that of a snake. Curiously enough the creator Wonajo is not the ancestor of the race ; for the inhabitants of Rossel are descended from a god, *Mbasi*, whom Wonajo expressly invited from Sudest, the nearest island, to be their progenitor. The origin of a number of elements of culture is ascribed to Mbasi rather than to Wonajo.

This snake god Mbasi wedded a girl, Konjini, said to be of fair skin, whom Wonajo found on the island and wooed in vain. From their union came an egg, and from the egg issued the first two human beings, from whom all the people of Rossel are descended.

At this early stage of history, the division of the people into clans and the rule of their exogamy were instituted by Wonajo and Mbasi, who gave each clan its specific totems. Totemism appears to have been already in existence among the gods. The plant totem of Mbasi was *ndua*, a kind of banana. Wonajo, oddly enough, has two of each of the three linked totems, two plants, two birds, and two fish.

The origin of one of the totems of Wonajo is given in a tale that describes him as wandering in the forest on his way to Mount Rossel, the Olympus of the island. He discovers a beautiful flower, which is supposed not to exist now. This he puts in his hair and adopts as his totem, composing a song about the flower.

Matrilineal descent was established after all the totems had been distributed. With the plant totem of a god, which was assigned to one of these mortals, the other totems—bird and fish—were associated. A clan has, therefore, its three totems and an intimate relation to a certain god ; and when a clan is now asked for its totems, the god is often given as a fourth totem. But the name of the god is given as if it were a species of snake, just as the other totems were given as species and not as individuals. Furthermore, Mr. Armstrong was told that snakes of these species were sometimes encountered, and when recognised, were avoided.[1]

[1] W. E. Armstrong, *op. cit.* pp. 126 *sqq.*

CHAPTER IX

THE D'Entrecasteaux Archipelago lies off the east coast of New Guinea. As we have seen, it is inhabited by the Massim, a branch of the Melanesian race. The natives of the northern islands of the archipelago have been investigated and described by Mr. D. Jenness and the Rev. A. Ballantyne, of whom the latter had resided for eight years as a missionary on Goodenough Island, while Mr. D. Jenness spent about a year in the archipelago in 1911-1912, under the auspices of the Committee of Anthropology of the University of Oxford.

After describing the marriage system of the natives, the authors tell us that " Totemism, if such a term is applicable here, is an institution altogether apart. The totems are inherited taboos of a certain kind which affect all the kin, causing them to abstain from eating certain articles of food. The children inherit from the father, in a few cases from the mother as well ; but generally the mother's totem is disregarded by her children, and never, at the present day at least, descends to her grandchildren. Since most, if not all, of the inhabitants of a hamlet are connected by kinship, and have in consequence inherited the same totems, one may speak of a hamlet as having a certain totem or totems of its own. Other natives, however, living in the same hamlet, but either not related at all to the rest or related only by marriage, have their own peculiar totems, so that in one and the same hamlet there may co-exist two or even more totemic groups. Thus in Mataita (a village or district of Goodenough) some of the inhabitants of Ululu recognise a species of grasshopper (*vagita*) as their totem, the rest the dog (*koko*). It is seldom possible in such cases to discover which group was earliest on the spot, for history amongst these people is short-lived, and an event of twenty years back is almost outside the range of memory.

" The origin of the totems is, of course, far beyond their ken, shrouded in the mists of the past. Their ancestors in the youth of the world came up out of the ground at Gauyaba, in the centre of the island. It was they who imposed the taboos, for a reason known to themselves alone. One man conjectured that their spirits passed at death into their totems, and hence the totem has received the name of ' grandparent ' (*kubuku*) ; but others emphatically denied this doctrine. The word *talagi* for totem is as common as *kubuku* ; so too is *tabu*, whether it be an introduced word or not. But whatever be the mystic bond which unites the native with his totem, there are, or were, very material penalties for any infringement of it. Eyes and cheeks will swell, the hair will drop out, ulcerous sores will cover the body of the man who dares to kill or eat it. Death will follow quickly unless for three days, morning, noon, and night, he washes in the sea, and three times during the hours of darkness inside his hut. Kinsmen dare not go near him, but friends whose totems are different must take care of him ; thus only is there any hope of his recovery. Even if, wandering in the woods, a man should set his foot on his dead totem, his foot will be covered with ulcers ; or should it be cooked and eaten in his village by another native, he will die, and the native who cooked it must pay the blood-price to his relatives. Some, when they see their totem lying dead in the track, make a wide detour to avoid it, others flee, and pay a friend of another totem to go and bury it. There is no connexion between totemism and the rules regulating marriage : on this point the natives were emphatic. Persons whose totems are the same can marry, and have done so in two cases with which we are familiar. It is not common, because marriage cannot occur within the kin, and neighbours who have the same totem are usually connected in some way by kinship.

" The totem may be a bird, a fish, an animal, or a plant.

Some Wailaka [1] people gave even a rock as their totem, and some Waibulaus [1] the Pleiades and Venus (or possibly Sirius) ; but these should be considered doubtful. It is probable that they are taboos of another kind, in the case of Pleiades and Venus possibly a taboo on the names. The prohibitions attached to the totem seem invariably to refer to the eating of it, or, in the case of the plants, to their use for flavourings with food. All the plant totems, as far as we know, can be, and are, so used by other natives with different totems, and all the birds and fish and animals. This is all the more strange because at Kiriwina, in the Trobriands, the totems are said to be quite different. There, marriage within the totem is forbidden, although stray cases were known in the old days, regarded much as we should regard a brother and sister marriage ; the father's totems may not be eaten there, although the mother's, which alone the man inherits, may be eaten freely. The so-called link totems are unknown on Goodenough. The totem of a family may be a bird, a fish, a plant, or an animal, one or all of these, or several of any one ; in fact any combination of them at all with no apparent system. Bird totems slightly preponderate." [2]

In Dobu, an island of the D'Entrecasteaux Archipelago lying off the south-eastern extremity of New Guinea, the rules regulating totemism seem to be somewhat different, for on this subject Mr. R. F. Fortune tells us : " Each village has a set of linked totems, a bird ancestor, a fish, and a tree. Every person may make free with his or her own totemic objects, provided spouse or father is not also of the same totem. No person may eat the bird, eat the fish, or use the tree for firewood of the spouse's village ; no person may eat bird or fish or use the tree for firewood of the father's village. Deference is paid to the linked totems of a spouse even where they are also own totems, and deference is paid to the linked totems of the father, even where they are also own totems. . . ." [3]

[1] Parts of Goodenough Island.
[2] D. Jenness and A. Ballantyne, *The Northern D'Entrecasteaux* (Oxford, 1920), pp. 66 *sqq.*
[3] R. F. Fortune, *Sorcerers of Dobu* (London, 1932), p. 36.

CHAPTER X

TOTEMISM IN THE TROBRIAND ISLANDS

THE Trobriand Islands are a group of islands lying a little way to the north of the D'Entrecasteaux Archipelago. The natives, who are Melanesians, have a system of totemism which has been described as follows by Professor B. Malinowski, our principal authority on the islanders.

" Right across the political and local divisions cut the totemic clans, each having a series of linked totems, with a bird as principal one. The members of these four clans are scattered over the whole tribe of Boyowa,[1] and in each village community, members of all four are to be found, and even in every house there are at least two classes represented, since a husband must be of a different clan from his wife and children. There is a certain amount of solidarity within the clan, based on the very vague feeling of communal affinity to the totem birds and animals, but much more on the many social duties, such as the performance of certain ceremonies, especially the mortuary ones, which band the members of a clan together. But real solidarity obtains only between members of a sub-clan. A sub-clan is a local division of a clan, whose members claim common ancestry, and hence real identity of bodily substance, and also are attached to the locality where their ancestors emerged. It is to these sub-clans that the idea of a definite rank attaches. One of the totemic clans, the Malasi, includes the most aristocratic sub-clan, the Tabalu, as well as the lowest one, the local division of the Malasi in Bwoytalu. A chief of the Tabalu feels very insulted if it is ever hinted that he is akin to one of the

[1] Boyowa is the largest island of the Trobriand group.

stingaree-eaters of the unclean village, although they are Malasi like himself. The principle of rank attached to totemic divisions is to be met only in Trobriand sociology ; it is entirely foreign to all the other Papuo-Melanesian tribes." [1]

[1] B. Malinowski, *Argonauts of the Western Pacific* (London, 1922), pp. 70 *sq.* An earlier, and somewhat more detailed account, of totemism in the Trobriands is given by Dr. C. G. Seligmann in his book, *The Melanesians of British New Guinea* (Cambridge, 1910), pp. 677 *sqq.* His account has already been reported by me in *Totemism and Exogamy*, iv. 280 *sq.*, and need not be repeated here. The names of the four totemic and exogamous clans mentioned by Professor Malinowski in the passage quoted in the text are Malasi, Lukuba, Lukosisiga, and Lokulobuta.

CHAPTER XI

THE large islands of New Britain and New Ireland, lying to the north of the eastern extremity of New Guinea, are the most northern members of the Melanesian chain. Their totemic system has been briefly but clearly described by Dr. George Brown, an experienced missionary who had the good fortune to know the natives intimately at a time when they were still little affected and corrupted by contact with European civilisation. His description runs thus :—

" In describing the family life of the New Britain people, it must be remembered that all the people in New Britain, Duke of York,[1] New Ireland, are members of two exogamous classes named respectively, at Duke of York, Pikalaba and Maramara. These classes live together in the same village. The totem of the Maramara class is an insect called *ko gila le*, which means the leaf of the horse-chestnut. The insect is so called because it mimics the leaf of that tree, and when resting on it it is very difficult to distinguish between the leaf and the insect. The totem of the Pikalaba class is the *kam* (*mantis religiosus*). Each class calls its respective class *takun miat*, which means ' our relatives,' but I do not think they believe they were descended from them. It appears to me to be a term expressing the close and intimate connection between the members of each class and the totem to which they respectively belong. Neither class will injure

---

[1] The Duke of York is a small island lying off the eastern extremity of New Britain, and intermediate between it and New Ireland. Dr. Brown was particularly well acquainted with it. I had the advantage of knowing and esteeming him personally.— J. G. F.

its totem, and any injury inflicted by one class on the totem of the other would certainly be considered as an insult and would occasion a serious quarrel. All lands, fruit trees, fishing-grounds in the lagoon belong definitely to the respective classes. A Maramara cannot set his fish-trap on Pikalaba fishing-stones, and *vice versa*. Such an act would certainly cause a fight.

" Intermarriage in either class is absolutely forbidden. Any such marriage would be considered incestuous, and would bring speedy punishment ; in fact the whole of the people would be horrified at such an event, and the parties would almost certainly be killed. They also called incestuous (*kuou*) any one who killed or ate any portion of a person of the same class as himself, *e.g.* a Maramara who killed or ate a Maramara. The children all belong to the mother's class. These respective classes are well known, but there are no outward signs or marks to distinguish them. I think that in theory, but in theory only, every Maramara woman is every Pikalaba man's wife, and *vice versa*, but there is no trace, so far as I know, of anything like communal marriage ; on the contrary, it appears to me that the regulations prohibiting the intercourse, or even mentioning the names of relatives, show that this was very repugnant to public sentiment and feeling.

" The children of two brothers would belong to a different totem from their own and in theory a man might marry his niece, but this was never done, so far as I know. A man, however, could not possibly marry his sister's daughter, because she would be of the same totem as himself."[1]

The social and totemic system of the natives of New Ireland has been investigated and described by Dr. Hortense Powdermaker, who spent ten and a half months, from March 1929 to February 1930, at Lesu, a village on the east coast of the island. Her account of the system runs as follows :—

" Cutting across the local groupings are the lines of kinship. The society is divided into two exogamous moieties, *Telenga*, the fish-hawk, and *Kongkong*, the eagle. The members of each moiety regard themselves as related to each other in a classificatory manner. Each moiety is

[1] G. Brown, *Melanesians and Polynesians* (London, 1910), pp. 27 *sqq.*

divided into a number of clans, an extended family group, all the members of which are related in the female line. The Hawk and Eagle moieties appear to extend over all of New Ireland and the Tabar Islands too, and the rule of exogamy functions wherever the moieties are found. The subdivision into clans, however, seems to vary in different linguistic units. Because of the rule of matrilocal residence, members of a clan may reside in different villages, usually in near-by ones of the same linguistic unit. If, for example, a Lesu man marries a woman from Ambwa, he will usually go to live there, leaving his clan relatives at Lesu. But he will return to Lesu for all rites and events in which the latter are concerned, and will be buried there. The female members of the clan, because of the same rule of matrilocal residence, are more likely to reside in the same village and hamlet. Also, as marriages within the same village are quite common, a man will frequently not have to change his residence upon marriage.

" Although Eagle and Hawk are the names of the two moieties, there is, as far as I could learn, no theory of descent from either animal. The native explanation of the origin of the moiety and clan structure, as well as of the whole social organization and of the culture itself, is contained in a myth about their ancestral heroine, Tsenabonpil. The narrative relates in detail how the people of Lesu went to one of the Tabar islands near by because they were afraid of a pig named Luana, who ate people. The old woman, Tsenabonpil, was left behind because she had a swollen leg (probably elephantiasis) and it was feared that she would sink the canoe. After people left, she had intercourse with a *kiwiwi* bird, and she gave birth to twin boys, Daror and Damuramurari. When the boys grew up Tsenabonpil told them that they must kill the cannibalistic pig, Luana. After many adventures they succeeded in capturing and killing him. Then the old woman sent some of the hair of the pig, attached to a coconut leaf, to Tabar, to indicate to the Lesu people that the pig had been killed. They returned in their canoes to Tabar (Lesu ?), and now Tsenabonpil gave them their totemic structure and all knowledge. She cut marks on a tree to designate the two moieties, and then made further markings as she called out the names of all the clans. At the same time she gave them knowledge of magic, of medicine, of all their crafts, and of everything else they now know. After this she and her two sons disappeared. . . .

" Each clan is associated with a small piece of ground, occasionally with a part of a reef, or a passage of water, and sometimes all three. This clan or *tsenalis* ground is owned communally by the clan members, and on it is supposed to dwell a totemic pig or snake (sometimes both), or, in the case of water, a shark. The adjective *tsenalis* is also used to describe the animal, which is friendly to people of its class, but hostile to those of others. The animal is supposed to have lived on this ground for ever, and it is believed that it will continue to do so." [1]

" Besides the clan animal each piece of clan land is inhabited by the *gas*, a double of each living member of the clan. It is difficult to get a very exact idea of the *gas*, other than that each man, woman, and child possesses one, that it dies when its human counterpart dies, that it may take different forms (in one tale it appears as a dwarf), that it lives in a *lima* tree, and that it is rarely seen by its human counterpart. However, occasionally the folk-tales recount a meeting between a human being and a *gas*. . . ." [2]

" The clan and moiety are much more than mere totemic divisions of the society, for they are also very active functioning units. Since the moieties are exogamous, they set the structure for sex life. Members of the Hawk moiety must pick their mates from the Eagle moiety and *vice versa*. Transgressing this rule, either in or out of marriage, is the worst crime of Lesu society. Between the moieties there is a set of reciprocal duties, including an exchange of food at pregnancy, birth, circumcision, first menstruation, marriage and death rites. As the members of a moiety are scattered through households, hamlets, and villages, they generally function as a unit only at these rites. The clan, on the other hand, functions frequently as an economic unit, the members assisting each other in all their important undertakings." [3]

---

[1] H. Powdermaker, *Life in Lesu* (London, 1933), pp. 33 *sqq.*

[2] H. Powdermaker, *op. cit.* p. 39.

[3] H. Powdermaker, *op. cit.* pp. 40 *sq.*

BOOK III

TOTEMISM IN NEW GUINEA

CHAPTER I

TOTEMISM IN BRITISH NEW GUINEA (PAPUA)

THE native population of British New Guinea is racially divided into two sections, an eastern and a western. The eastern section are Melanesians, who are believed to have immigrated into New Guinea from the islands of Melanesia. The western section are Papuans, who may be supposed to be the aborigines. They are relatively tall, dark-skinned, frizzly-haired, while the Melanesians are smaller and lighter in colour. The line of cleavage between the two races occurs about Cape Possession on the eastern side of the Gulf of Papua.[1] In representatives of both races the institution of totemism has been recorded. For the Melanesians the evidence has been given by Dr. C. G. Seligman in his book *The Melanesians of British New Guinea*. That valuable work reached me too late to allow me to incorporate its results in the body of *Totemism and Exogamy*; but in an appendix to that book I gave a summary account of the evidence adduced by Dr. Seligman of totemism among the Melanesians.[2] Here I will notice only such evidence of totemism in British New Guinea, whether among the Melanesians or the Papuans, as has come to light since the publication of Dr. Seligman's work and my own.

Thus among the eastern or Melanesian people totemism has been found and described by Mr. Henry Newton, a missionary attached to the Anglican Mission at Samarai, which is the extreme south-eastern point of New Guinea.

---

[1] C. G. Seligmann, *The Mela-nesians of British New Guinea* (Cambridge, 1910), p. 1.

[2] *Totemism and Exogamy*, iv. 276 *sqq.*

His knowledge of the natives seems to extend at least to Wedan on the east coast of New Guinea and to Boianai on the south coast.[1] His account of totemism among these people runs as follows :—

" One cannot have much to do with the natives of New Guinea without being struck with the important part played by totemism in their lives and thoughts, and the influence it has upon their dealings with one another. . . . Totemism represents the principles which regulate the social life of the people. It regulates marriage, it decides the section of the community to which the offspring belongs, it enters into the ceremonies connected with death, it creates a sort of freemasonry or family relationship which influences the behaviour of people to others far removed from them in place of abode, in dialect, in customs. All who have the same totem are looked upon as being related one to another, and wherever they go they can claim hospitality and protection from all whose totem is the same. People go to a district they have never been to before, there they find fathers and mothers, grandfathers and grandmothers, and they puzzle you as they talk about them, till you remember they are totem relationships, not family ones.

" The people can give no definite tradition as to how they came to be connected with the bird or fish or animal they revere as their totem. Sometimes men have said, ' Our bird came from such-and-such a direction '—the direction from which the particular sept is supposed originally to have come —' and settled here '—presumably leading the early settlers— ' and allotted to us this part of the village and portioned out to us our garden land, and we hold it now by that title of possession.' All of one sept, those who claim a particular totem, claim to have sprung from a common origin, to have sucked originally from a common breast ; those of another sept, to have had another and different origin. . . . Each sept has two or more branches, claiming the same chief totem—though there may be subsidiary totems which are different—all the branches claim a common origin, but the differentiation has come about in the course of time, and the different branches within the one sept have duties and

[1] Henry Newton, *In Far New Guinea* (London, 1914), p. 163.

responsibilities to one another which they only can fulfil, and which cannot be fulfilled by members of a distinct sept.. A sept that is weak in numbers may be absorbed into another sept.

" Totemism is wider than some other things in New Guinea. Thus though the Boianai people and those farther west know nothing of the Walaga,[1] and take no part in it, while the shore people from Wedan eastwards do, yet totemism brings the people of Boianai and those farther west into close relationship with the people of Wedan and those farther east.

" The commonest totem is a bird, so much so that the usual way of asking a man what is his totem is to ask him what is his bird. Another way is to ask him what is his ' bariawa,' a word expressing what is out of the ordinary run of human experience. . . . There are other totems nearly always subsidiary to a bird, as fish and snakes, and also more rarely stones and trees.

" A man may not kill his totem, much less eat it, and for any one to kill it in his presence is to confer a deadly insult. A missionary when he first came was asked what his totem was, and unthinkingly, or not knowing what it involved, said it was a Torres Straits pigeon, and he caused great indignation later on by shooting the pigeons for the pot. . . .

" Men and women of the same totem do not intermarry ; to do so would be to commit incest. A young man will come to the missionary and ask advice as to whom he should marry, as there is no one of a suitable age in the village whom he can take to wife, and you suggest a name. ' She is my sister,' he will answer in astonishment, and you, bewildered because you thought you knew all his relations, ask, ' How is she your sister ? '—to be told, ' Our origin is the same,' and you understand it is a totem relationship, as close for marriage as a blood relationship.[2]

---

[1] The Walaga is a festival and dance that is celebrated only every six or seven years. A new village is constructed for the celebration. A mango sapling is cut down and brought into the new village, where it is set up on a platform, and the people dance and sing round it. See H. Newton, *op. cit.* pp. 148 *sqq.* His description of the ceremony reminds us of the Maypole and the May-dance in Europe.

[2] By totem relationship the writer clearly means what is now regularly called classificatory relationship. All totemic peoples, without any exception, appear to possess a classificatory system of relationship.—J. G. F.

" Usually the child is of the same sept as the mother, and takes her totem ; the system is matriarchal, but this is by no means universally so, and it seems that quite frequently a youth elects to go either to his father or his mother's sept, ' to eat with these or those.' Hence it is that the uncle on the mother's side is a nearer relative to the child than its own father, so far as relationship implies control over the child's actions and its future. . . . So for the marriage of minors who are orphans, our custom is to obtain the consent that is required by the law from the uncle on the mother's side as being the guardian according to native custom. . . .

" When a person dies, it is someone connected with his sept or a branch of his sept who digs the grave, the people of his own sept provide the death feast, and a branch of his sept eat it, and the dead are buried with their feet in the direction from which the ancestors originally came when led by the totem.

" All the members of a sept help each other in such work as digging up the garden ground, in the building of houses, and any other work which calls for help. Each sept may also have its own club-house, and they build their own houses together in one section of the village.

" Totemism decides for a man to whom he will go when travelling, on whom he will quarter himself in a strange village. He may quite rightly, as a matter of course and without any sense of shame, go and live with people of the same totem as himself, and if he is of any importance in the sept his hosts will kill a pig for him and his, and when he goes home load him up with presents of cooked food for his journey. The visitor does not feel that he is imposing, for are they not his own people, and will he not show the same hospitality to them when they visit his village. . . .

" It is said that should a castaway drift to a strange place the people who know nothing of him at all would take him in and befriend him if he gave them to understand his totem was that of a sept living in the place, and that sept would provide him with garden land, keeping him till his food was grown and he could keep himself. On the other hand, should his totem be unknown he would most probably be killed." [1]

Orokaiva is the name now given to a group of tribes who inhabit the greater part of the Northern Division of Papua from Oro Bay north-westwards to the borders of the Mandated Territory. All the tribes included in this area speak dialects of a common language : the best known of them are the Binandele, who live in the north of the division, on the Mambare river.

All these tribes are divided into clans, each of which has what Mr, Williams calls an emblem. The emblem is usually, though not invariably, a plant or tree. The name of the emblem varies from tribe to tribe. The Aiga tribe, with which Mr. Williams is most familiar, call it *heratu*, and this name he adopts in speaking of the Orokaiva generally ; but *kenatu* is the form of the name in the Binandele and Tain-Daware languages, and in Wasida a different word, *hae*, is used. The Orokaiva are mostly forest people, which may partly explain their preference for a plant emblem. But besides the plant emblem there are certain bird associates and simple emblematic devices.

For example, in the Wasida tribe Mr. Williams came across three bird associates, *Kombu*, a certain black bird whose name, *Kombu*, is meant to reproduce its cry ; *Hiviki*, the hawk, and *Hororo*, a small ground forager. These were all subsidiary emblems, and the clans to which they belonged had *heratu* or emblems of the ordinary botanic kind. Further, the birds in these cases were not, as far as Mr. Williams could ascertain, used for the regular purpose of the *heratu*, namely, as a badge or token of identity. However, among the Binandele the *Diriu* or common blue pigeon is the emblem of a clan, the Diriu clan, and among the Tain-Daware the *Bangai* or eagle-hawk is the emblem of the Bangai-unji clan ; and Mr. Williams was told that the feathers of both these birds were used as identity marks.

A man uses both the paternal and maternal *heratu*. The *heratu* proper is the former, and the contrary instances which do occur are exceptional. The *heratu* of the father is passed on by inheritance, whereas that of the mother is

[1] Henry Newton, *op. cit.* pp. 160 *sqq.*

not normally handed down beyond the generation of her off-spring.[1]

On the whole, then, there are some grounds for regarding these *heratu* or plant emblems of the Orokaiva as a form of totemism, and this possibility is considered by Mr. Williams himself, who in conclusion sums up the case for totemism as follows :—

" Throughout this chapter I have avoided the word ' totem,' using in preference the non-committal, if awkward phrase ' plant emblem.' I may now review the evidence which might have justified the use of the former term.

" (1) The *heratu* is normally connected with a definite social group, viz. the clan (though sometimes with the individual and his immediate family).

" (2) The clan is usually exogamous in practice, though by no means strictly so.

" (3) The clan commonly, in the typical case always, takes its name from the *heratu* or, more strictly, is synonymous with the *heratu*.

" (4) The clan uses its *heratu* first and foremost as a badge.

" (5) The *heratu* is called an ancestor (though the Orokaiva does not really believe that his ancestor can be plant or tree).

" Thus far it would seem the *heratu* has conformed very nearly to the tenets of totemism. It remains to be considered whether the clan possesses any magico-religious sentiment for its *heratu* such as typically unites the group and its totem.

" The evidence is here somewhat conflicting. Generally speaking, the plant emblem is treated with no semblance of respect or reverence. In clearing the bush, a man will fell his *heratu* tree without a thought ; if it bear edible fruit like *topu*, the wild fig, he will eat it ; if it be, as in one case it is, *ambe* or sago, he will not forswear one of his principal means of subsistence. There is a large clan, the *Umondaha*, one of whose *heratu* is nothing more or less than ' Water.'

" In one or two instances, however, informants have claimed that they will not cut down their own tree ; though such are distinctly exceptional. No case has come to light

[1] F. E. Williams, *Orokaiva Society* (Oxford, 1930), pp. 112 *sqq.*

of a useful *heratu* which its owner will not use.   With the
rare bird *heratu* the case is almost the same.   A Diriu man,
ex-constable, averred that he had shot many *diriu* (blue
pigeon) for his master, and would be only too glad to shoot
and eat another if I would lend him a gun. . . . A man whose
subsidiary *heratu* is the bird *Kombu* says that while he
would not hesitate to kill it (if he could get near it), he would
still refrain from eating it.   It is apparently for reasons of
sentiment alone that he would not eat it, for he declares there
would be no evil effects upon him if he did (as I believe he
might) yield to the temptation.

    " On the other hand, however, a man of the Bangai-unji,
or ' children of the eagle-hawk,' who use one of its speckled
feathers for their mark, avers that he would neither kill
nor eat the bird ; and, further, volunteers that if a *bangai*
fledgling, being caught and kept in the village, were to die, it
would not be eaten or thrown away, but buried.   Lastly,
there is one isolated note which may have some significance.
The bird *Hororo* belongs especially to a certain man, Erupa.
Should its cry be heard near the village, the people would say,
' Erupa will be successful in the hunt to-day.'

    " In passing, I may mention a point of some interest.
Among the Orokaiva there are certain strict rules of etiquette
between relatives by marriage (particularly between the man
and his parents-in-law), exemplified by a very strict name-
avoidance.   Now, although a man will cut down his own
heratu tree without mercy, he will hesitate to do the same
with a tree that happens to bear the name of his *atovo* or
imboti, *i.e.* his father-in-law or his mother-in-law, and may
request one of his companions in the clearing to fell this
particular tree for him.   Similarly he will not eat any food,
animal or vegetable which happens to be synonymous with
either of his parents-in-law.   Now this rule is based on
sentiment ; there are, as far as my knowledge goes, no
magico-religious sanctions to it ; and where a similar tabu is
observed with regard to the *heratu* we may probably assume
that this is no more than a sentimental avoidance. . . .

    " The conclusion of the present chapter may be sum-
marised very briefly.   The clan's *heratu* originates from the
individual *heratu* of its leader or ancestor ; and the individual

heratu is some plant which serves as a token of identity because it bears the name of its owner." [1]

In the western or Papuan area of British New Guinea, or Papua, as it is now called, the Kiwai-speaking Papuans inhabit the large island of Kiwai, and certain other islands in the estuary of the Fly River, a couple of villages on the left (north-eastern) bank of the river, the right bank of the estuary, and the sea coast towards the west as far as Mabudavane. Their social and totemic systems have been carefully examined and described by the Finnish ethnologist, Professor G. Landtman, who spent two years among them, from April 1910 till April 1912.[2]

The totems of the Kiwai islanders, as enumerated by Professor Landtman, are thirty-three in number and include the following : wild pig, cassowary, crocodile, small crab, grasshopper, a mythical animal called *ateraro*, the coconut palm (*oi*), the coconut, the sago palm, the nipa palm, the banana, a wild fruit-tree (*mipari*), two kinds of croton (*mobea* and *oso*), seven species of wild trees (of which Professor Landtman gives the native names), the north-west wind (*Surama*), and a plaited mat (*sawa*).

Professor Landtman found that the term *nurumara* (totem) was somewhat ambiguously used by the natives, some of whom wanted to include in the list of totems various other things, although their opinion was strongly resisted by the rest.

Every person in the island of Kiwai has one totem only. Professor Landtman heard indeed of one man who had two totems, the croton and the grasshopper ; but it appears that his true totem was only the croton, to which he had added the grasshopper totem, because he had been, for some time, the guardian of a house belonging to the grasshopper clan.

Totems chosen from the vegetable kingdom predominate in Kiwai island and may be regarded as characteristic of the natives. Not only are they far more numerous than the rest, but the people with any other kind of totem are very few. All the animal totems are also found at Mawak, a village on

[1] F. E. Williams, *op. cit.* pp. 126 *sqq.*
    G. Landtman, *The Kiwai*   *Papuans of British New Guinea* (London, 1927).

the coast of the mainland to the west of Kiwai island, except the wild pig, which is a very rare totem on Kiwai island, but it is also a totem at Masingle, another village on the coast. The commonest animal totems, in a relative sense, on Kiwai island, are the crab and the cassowary. It is curious that though cassowary is a totem in Kiwai, the bird itself is not found on the island, which seems to show that as a totem it must have been introduced from elsewhere. On the whole, the non-vegetable totems are mostly represented in the villages of Sumai and Iasa on the south-west coast, which are in frequent communication with the villages in the Mawata region.

The *oi* and *neiabo* clans both have the same totem (the coconut palm), but the clans are regarded as distinct. The *oi* clan is one of the most widespread in the island, and the palm is probably indigenous, while the *neiabo* clan, which is represented only by a very few people, properly belongs, it is said, to the Dibiri people in the east.

The clans of the nipa palm and crab are connected with each other, just as are the palm and the crab, for the crab lives under the roots of the palm. In Kiwai island, Professor Landtman met with one instance only of a name being used for a totemic group other than that of their totem, a practice which is so common at Mawata.[1]

One of the principal dissimilarities between the Kiwai islanders and the Mawata group of people on the coast to the west, in most respects so alike, is presented by their varying totemic system.[2]

At Mawata each person has one chief totem and several, in most cases an almost indefinite number, of subsidiary totems. For example, one of the leading men, Gamea, a very good informant, declared to Professor Landtman that his principal totem was the dog and that he had three secondary totems, an eel-like creek fish, a creeper with red flowers, and a fresh-water tortoise. All these he inherited from his father. But it turned out that Gamea had a number of other totems, though he did not consider them as important as his totems proper. A number of secondary totems are in fact common to different totemic divisions. Even the chief totem

---

[1] G. Landtman, *op. cit.* pp. 185 *sqq.*

[2] On totemism at Mawata, com-pare *Totemism and Exogamy*, ii. 25 *sqq.*

of one group may be treated as a totem by the members of another group as well.

For this reason the Mawata totems do not furnish any definite means of dividing the people into clans. There exist, however, five very distinct clans, each one known by a name of its own, which is not that of any totem. The five clans with their principal totems are as follows : *Hawidaimere*, chief totem *umu* (dog) ; *Marowadai*, chief totem *divare* (cassowary) ; *Doriomo*, chief totem *hibara* (crocodile) ; *Gaidai*, chief totem *gera* (sea-serpent) ; and *Gurahi*, chief totem *apiteri* (moth). In speaking of the clans, a person will commonly give the name of the clan, not the name of its totem, though the name of the totem is sometimes added by way of explanation. A man will generally mention his first few subsidiary totems in a certain order, but generally he does not even remember all the rest at the same time.

It is claimed that all persons belonging to one and the same clan possess its subsidiary totems as well as its principal one. This rule, however, can hardly be followed very strictly, in view of the uncertain character and even number of the subsidiary totems ; moreover a man will sometimes adopt his mother's chief totem also.

The clans, as enumerated above, are very important divisions of the people ; among other things, they regulate marriage, all of them being strictly exogamous. A marriage, on the other hand, is not prohibited between a man and a woman who have any secondary totems in common.[1]

The Masingle tribe is situated a little way inland from Mawata. Their totemic system has several features in common with that of the Mawata. All the totems of the Masingle, except possibly one, are animals : dog, pig, wallaby, bat, cassowary, gaura pigeon, black cockatoo, white cockatoo, hawk, two species of the bush-fowl, pelican, six other species of bird, a fish, crocodile, and five species of snake. Some people said that the bull-roarer was also a totem.

Every person has one chief totem and a number of subsidiary totems. Those of one of the old leaders named Webamu were the following : pig (head totem), wallaby,

[1] G. Landtman, *op. cit.* pp. 187 *sqq.*

gaura pigeon, a kind of wild fowl, and five other species of bird. He belonged to the *obentobe* clan. The whole population is divided into similar clans, all the members of each having the same chief and subsidiary totems. In several cases different clans have the same chief totem but different subsidiary totems. The clans form together two large groups, named after the two leading clans, the *mlobe* (chief totem pig) and the *dariame* (chief totem cassowary). The two groups are exogamous, but any man of one group can marry any woman of the other.[1]

The totemic system of the Kiwais is primarily of social, not religious, significance. Everything that affects the ceremonial life is kept extremely secret, whereas the people speak of their totems quite openly in the hearing of anybody. The totems are never made the objects of any rites whatever, although, on the whole, observances of some kind or another entirely fill the people's life.

In spite of the people's seeming willingness to impart everything they know about their totems, it proves very difficult to determine the true nature of these. A person's totem is an object to which he is bound by intangible ties sanctioned by tradition, but although the moral character of this obligation is recognised by everyone, no explanation can be given by the people themselves as to what their relations to the totems really are. Implicitly following the rules which have come down to them from their fathers, they never seem to question the purpose or meaning of these. It is possible, however, that the people have an instinctive notion regarding the importance of the totemic system, as a safeguard against certain dangers to the community (particularly marriage between close relatives, which is guarded against by the rule of exogamy), and that in this way the indications of nature itself have taken the form of a social routine.

The rules incumbent on a person as regards his totem are mostly of a prohibitory character ; the principal one is not to harm or kill it (in case of a tree not to fell it) and not to eat any part of it. Indeed, not to eat an otherwise edible animal or plant and to have it for a totem are by the natives considered almost synonymous. Professor Landtman often

[1] G. Landtman, *op. cit.* pp. 189 *sq.*

observed that when men of the cassowary clan were out hunting they would not kill a cassowary, and that they also abstained from eating it if it had been killed by somebody else. If, however, the hunter's dogs had caught and damaged a cassowary, he would kill it and let somebody else have it. The punishment for either killing or eating the totem is usually said to be illness. Some people explain that they do not want to kill or eat their totem animal because they have been taught to feel sorry for that thing ; and one man added as a reason that he and the totem were all of the same blood. In former times not even a man of the crocodile clan would kill his totem, but nowadays he is said not to spare the beast any more than he expects to be spared by it. A crocodile-man, however, never takes part in the eating of his totem. Dugong, although it is a subsidiary totem of the *doriomo* clan of Mawata, is nevertheless eaten by the members of that clan, probably because the rules are not considered so stringent in the case of subsidiary totems, and because the dugong is perhaps the most important article of animal food.

Utility seems further to be the reason why, among the vegetable totems, coconuts are eaten by members of the coconut clan. Professor Landtman's informants wanted to regard this instance as the only real exception to the general rule against a person eating his own totem, and in fact in that country coconuts are almost indispensable both as food and drink. However, the members of the *tamane* (wild yam) clan also eat their totems. If a man of the bamboo clan needs a bow, he does not cut down his totem to make one, but obtains the bow ready made from a friend.

All totems rank as equal in social estimation, and everybody cares for his or her totem, without expecting any actual benefit from it. Occasionally a certain affinity is thought to exist between a clan and their totem animal ; thus the men of the dog clan of Mawata were accused of going much after the women, and very dissolute in their habits, so that they would have connection even with a sister.

The first institution of the totems is occasionally attributed to Marunogere or some other mythical hero, but only as a vague idea. The numerous myths and folk-tales of the people do not contain any actual information as to the origin of the totems.

The totems are strictly hereditary in the male line. A married woman retains her own totem ; for instance, a *novai* girl, even after her marriage, refrains from eating the *novai* fruit, although she cooks it for her husband and children, boys and girls, who eat it. A Mawata girl who marries a cassowary-man may eat cassowary, although her husband and children do not. Generally, however, a wife seems to respect, to a certain extent, her husband's totem as well as her own. At her husband's death she returns to her own clan, her children remaining in their father's.

Certain conventional marks representing the totem at festivals and on other great occasions are often painted on the bodies of the totemites, or, in the case of plant totems, leaves of these are attached to the dress. Houses and temporary huts also are often decorated to show off the totem of the people to whom they belong. One purpose of this custom is said to be to inform people from other villages where their friends of the " blood " live and also to enable the women to entertain their clansmen with food. On returning home from war the men often put on their clan marks. Some of the Mawata clans at least have a particular war-cry, referring to their respective totem animals, and this cry the men will utter in the act of killing an enemy.

In former times it seems to have been the rule that every sufficiently large totem clan in a village occupied a communal house of its own, which bore the same name as the clan. It appears to have been the pride of every powerful clan to possess a separate long-house. The *darimo* alone, which accommodated all the men, was named independently of totems. Even at the present time, in villages with long-houses, all the members of a certain clan will almost invariably be found living in the same house, and not infrequently occupying it alone. The modern comparatively small houses—for instance at Mawata—accommodate two to four families, and these without exception have the same totem.[1]

We possess another account of Kiwai totemism written by Mr. W. N. Beaver who, as Resident Magistrate in the

[1] G. Landtman, *op. cit.* pp. 191 *sqq.*

Western Division of Papua or British New Guinea for twenty-seven years, had ample means of acquainting himself with the facts which he describes. It confirms, and on some points supplements, the account given by Professor Landtman. It runs as follows : " There are thirteen totem clans among the people of Kiwai, and plant totems are the predominating feature, as distinct from those of Mawata or Parama or Wabada.[1] In fact, only four, namely, the Crab, the Cassowary, the Catfish, and the Crocodile, are birds or fish.

" As usual, the totem descends through the father. The late Mr. Hely, R.M., stated that a woman must take the totem of her husband, and that this is the reason why a man must always give a female relative of his own in exchange for his own wife, in order that the relative strength of the clans may be maintained.[2] People of the same totem must not intermarry, but this rule is breaking down, especially among the younger generation. Not very long ago at Ipisia two young people came to me with a complaint that their parents objected to their marriage. There seemed to be no reason why they should not marry, and I did not discover for some time that the old people's opposition was due to their being of the same totem. In cases of this kind I think it is generally unwise to give any direct decision, the matter being much better left to the good sense of the people themselves. There is no objection to persons of the same name marrying. The late Mr. Chalmers stated that a man may marry a stepdaughter and even his own daughter. I have a recollection of an instance of this latter at Sumai, but I am at a loss to see how it fits in with the rule that all the children take the totem of the father. I was and still am under the impression that this was a very exceptional case, one of incest both from our and from a native point of view. Totemism is found among the people of the Mamba and Kumusi, although in no advanced stage as regards exogamy, or perhaps one might say in a degenerate stage, and I believe incest of this

---

[1] As to Mawata, see above, p. 337. The Parama occupy Bampton Island, and the Wabada occupy Wabada Island, both in the estuary of the Fly River.

[2] See *Totemism and Exogamy*, ii. 35 *sqq.*

kind is not unknown.   I have a personal knowledge of at least one case of recent date where a father married his daughter and had two children by her, both of which he killed.   Brothers and sisters of course may not marry among the Kiwais, nor may cousins, although it is well known that among certain native races, notably the Fijians, a first cousin marriage, but only between the children of a brother and a sister, is the best marriage.

" Totems may not be either killed or eaten, and I think in the main this prohibition is pretty strictly observed, even if some of the rising generation do not object to eating a totem animal killed by somebody else.   Plant totems having so strong a position in Kiwai, the application of this rule is extended much further.   For instance, if a tree happens to be a clan totem, the members of that clan cannot eat its fruit or use it in any way.   Thus the Soko (nipa palm) clan may not roof their houses with nipa leaf, but must use sago leaf instead.   The Duboro (pandanus) clan must make their sleeping mats from banana leaf and similarly the Gagari (bamboo) and Buduru (fig tree) clans may not use their special totems.

" This totem clan organisation is in reality almost a brotherhood in which members of a totem are bound by strong social ties, and are entitled to look for assistance and hospitality from each other on all occasions..   If this assistance is withheld, the offender may be liable to a certain amount of social ostracism.   The punishment for a break of totem rule, such as killing a totem, recoils on the person's own head, or even the whole clan may suffer for the fault of one member.

" I suppose the one feature that appeals most strongly to almost every traveller in the West is the long clan house, chiefly, I think, owing to its great size.   The long-house is a form of communal dwelling in which a whole clan or, in cases where there is only one house in a village, a whole series of clans lives under one roof.   In such case as Oromo-sapua, on Kiwai or Kowabu on the mainland and numerous other instances where there is but one house, each clan has its own special section in it.   On Kiwai, where, as a rule, the villages are large, each totem clan builds and occupies its own house, and there are or used to be objections to members

of other totems eating or sleeping in it.   Where, in addition
to the long-house, a Darimu or a number of them (man-
house) is found, it is occupied by the unmarried men and
very often by those who are married, especially on ceremonial
occasions and when a married man should refrain from living
with his wife.   It might be mentioned that there is no difference in appearance or construction between the Darimu and
the ordinary long-house.   The Darimu may be used by a
single totem clan, but it is more common to find it in possession of a group or associated group of them." [1]

Further Mr. Beaver has recorded a system of totemism
among the Girara, a tribe of the mainland, who inhabit a
territory between the Fly and the Bamu Rivers.   On this
subject he writes as follows : " I am not prepared to offer
any theories as to the racial history of the Girara-speaking
villages, but one thing is certain and that is that their language is a Papuan one.   The following story of their origin
was told me at Barimo by the people themselves.   At a spot
not far from Gaima (this was pointed out to me, when we
came back there) a very long time ago a man married a dog.
The offspring of this match consisted of three sons, the two
elder of whom were the ancestors of Daumori and Pagona
(villages on the Fly) and settled in these places.   The youngest
son quarrelled with his brothers and went inland.   He saw
that the country was good and decided to settle there, and it
was he who became the ancestor of the Girara-speaking
villages. . . . As far as the Girara are concerned, however, I
have not found that the Dog forms any of their totems.   I
was told that these were first allotted by a person named
Ibare and are five in number—the Pig (Itira), the Pigeon
(Boboa—I think this is the Goura pigeon), the Crocodile
(Dupa), the Cassowary (Goragora) and the Snake (Amura).
This seems to me to be a small number for such a large
number of people, and very probably I have not been told
the full list, or it is quite possible that these five form principal
groups.   The totems descend through the father, and the
customs do not differ materially from those of the other
Western tribes.   A man must not marry in his totem nor
is he allowed to kill or eat his totem.   People of the same

[1] W. N. Beaver, *Unexplored New Guinea* (London, 1920), pp. 180 *sqq.*

cognisance, though belonging to different villages, are always treated as friends and brothers. There appears to be some objection to a man allowing his totem animal to be killed in his presence. As we were travelling through a belt of scrub, a large cassowary stalked across the track. The native sergeant at once threw forward his carbine (he was a Parama Sting-Ray man) ; but one of the guides sprang in and knocked up the weapon, crying that the cassowary was his ' father.' " [1]

Further, a system of totemism has been discovered and described by Mr. F. E. Williams, Government Anthropologist to the Territory of Papua, among the Keraki and kindred tribes, Gambadi and Semariji, who inhabit the Morehead district near the western boundary of British New Guinea or Papua. Between 1926 and 1932 Mr. Williams spent altogether ten months in the district, the natural features of which he paints in colours which are not alluring. He says : " The country itself is one of strange extremes and few attractions. Its climate is by turns very pleasant and superlatively unpleasant. Its scenery often has a mild, almost dainty attractiveness in detail, but represents on the whole the extreme of monotony. It supports only a poor and scattered population, and from the European's point of view its economic prospects would seem to be practically nil. In fine, regarding at least that portion which is known as the Morehead District, one feels inclined to applaud the opinion of one of the earlier magistrates : ' There is nothing to induce settlement nor would I ever advise any one to go there.' " [2]

The Morehead district is defined by Mr. Williams as lying south of the low divide and between the Bensbach River on the west and the latitude of the Mai Kussa on the east. The Morehead River runs through the centre of it. Of the tribes inhabiting the district Mr. Williams devoted his attention chiefly to the Keraki.

With regard to the totemic system of the tribes who inhabit the region, Mr. Williams tells us that " a great number of natural species in the Morehead district are thought to have special relations with the various groups of

[1] W. N. Beaver, *op. cit.* pp. 201 *sq.*
[2] F. E. Williams, *Papuans of the Trans-Fly* (Oxford, 1936), p. 1.

its human inhabitants, and without being able to define these relations in any set manner, I propose to refer to the species in question as totems.   Their incidence, or their appropriation to the various social groups, reveals some confusion, and is at many points inconsistent with the division of the population into the Bangu and Sangara moieties.   Furthermore, their social functions are of relatively small consequence. Many of them appear indeed to play a very insignificant part in the lives and thought of the present-day native, and it is no exaggeration to say that those of minor importance are frequently forgotten altogether.   Any individual informant finds it difficult to enumerate his totems off-hand ; and the ethnographer's attempts at verification by appeal to independent witnesses may disclose not only a lack of knowledge on the native's part, but serious inconsistencies in different versions. . . . It is only, in fact, from a group of informants who can jog one another's memories, and thrash out disputed points together, that one can expect anything like a complete or reliable list.   Altogether, in view, firstly, of the inconsistencies between the totemic system and the present-day moiety organization, and secondly, of the social unimportance of the totems and the all-too-common uncertainty or ignorance regarding them, we are, I think, at liberty to infer an advanced degree of disorganisation and decadence.

" The main outlines of the totemic system are common to the whole Morehead district, *i.e.* to the Keraki, Gambadi, and Semarji peoples ; but what information I have been able to gather relates mainly to the Keraki.   Here the totem is most generally referred to as *yuvi*—' untouchable ' or ' forbidden.'   It cannot be claimed that this word is synonymous with ' totem,' for it is obviously of wider range ;   but having been driven to the conclusion that no special term for ' totem ' existed in the native language, I nevertheless found that the question, ' What are your *yuvi* ? ' would always elicit the same sort of answer, viz. a list of natural species which the particular group recognised as its own and yet regarded as in some manner forbidden.   These *yuvi* species are also referred to as *kaki*, ' ancestors,' though there seems to be a total absence of any idea, either in mythology or in present-day thought, that the creatures or plants in question are really ancestors of the groups which acknowledge them. A third term, *tuarar*, is distinguished in use from *kaki*, and although the distinction is not maintained with anything like exactitude it becomes evident that the two words stand for two separate categories, *i.e.* the species known as *kaki* are not *tuarar*, and *vice versa*. We may go on to consider the first sort of totems, viz, those which the native calls his *yuvi* or, rather less often, his *kaki*. . . .

" Throughout the whole district these totems may be classified under the following heads :—

> 1. Birds (*a*) Hawks
>   (*b*) Miscellaneous
> 2. Aquatic creatures
> 3. Lizards and snakes
> 4. Trees and plants " [1]

" The principal totems throughout are the hawks. Now, the Morehead district, with its numerous wide swamps, has a rich avifauna, and the predatory birds are correspondingly numerous. I have often watched the hawk perched on the bough of a dead tree and surveying the flat expanses with a sort of malignant quiet, and I have often admired him in his splendid flight ; but my feelings of interest or admiration were not obviously shared by those who held him as a totem. The native has a good eye for birds, and is always ready to point one out to the less observant European ; but he does so in the hope that the bird will be brought down by the European's gun, and I have been asked to shoot a whitefish-hawk by its Sangara totemites, to whom the exultation that would follow a successful shot meant more than any consideration they might have for the bird. It is hardly necessary to say that under ordinary conditions the hawks are almost entirely beyond the power of the native's arrow. It is glibly said that the Bangu men will not eat the hawk *wana*, and that Sangara men will not eat *inifiak*. They are rules that can be kept without difficulty, for it is hard to imagine when a native would get a chance of eating either. The hawks are, in fact, not to be considered as possessing any practical value. The only relation that they bear to economic needs is an indirect

---

[1] F. E. Williams, *op. cit.* pp. 85 *sq.*

one : in some connections they are said to typify the successful hunter, who can see everything and strike infallibly.

" Among the class of miscellaneous birds some are more easily approachable and worth the killing, such as the scrub hen (*udaga*) and the black cockatoo (*toguia*), the latter being not only a good eating bird but supplying in his crest and beak a fine ornament. But, on the whole, the birds, although so numerous in many parts of the district, are again of little economic value to its inhabitants. As food they are hardly worth considering, while their feathers—the most effective material for self-decoration which the Papuan native possesses —are not greatly in evidence in the Morehead district for the sole reason, of course, that they are so seldom caught or killed.

" The aquatic creatures are all edible, though the primitive forms of fishing practised in the streams and lagoons by the Keraki bush-men and their neighbours are somewhat ineffectual, and do not constitute an important phase of the food-quest. Of still smaller value are the lizards and snakes mentioned as totems.

" Among the botanic totems there is one of real importance, viz. the *karose* or ti-tree, the bark of which provides the indispensable material for thatching, and is adapted to many minor purposes. A number of other useful trees are found in the list ; four of them for instance bear edible fruits ; one has leaves useful for cigarette making ; and one is a wild edible tuber. But for some others I have not been able to discover any value at all. In fine, we may safely reassert as a generalization that with certain exceptions the natural species which are held as totems in the Morehead district possess relatively small economic value and exercise but little material influence upon the lives of its inhabitants.

" Their influence on social regulations and on the magico-religious life is in many cases hardly more significant. Here, however, we encounter considerable variation : while many of the totems remain quite insignificant, some few are found to have important religious and mythical associations, and yet others are the centres of magical rites. (It should be remarked in passing that some of the creatures which play leading parts in Morehead mythology are never referred to as *yuvi*, *kaki*, or *tuarar*, so that mythical associations do not in themselves suffice to turn a natural species into a totem.)

" Generally speaking we find that the totemic species is allocated to some social group. . . . Again, it is commonly referred to as *yuvi* or forbidden, and the members of the group refuse to eat it. Lastly, it may be spoken of as *kaki*, or ancestor. In view of these considerations, it seems permissible to use the expression ' totem.' The child always takes the totems of its father.

" We may first briefly consider the hawks, which alone find a wide and more or less consistent distribution as totems for the two moieties. The two principal species which are commonly acknowledged by Bangu and Sangara respectively are *wana* and *inifiak*. The former is the large brown kite with white breast, which hunts for snakes and bandicoots ; the latter is a smaller white-headed hawk.

" We have already observed that these birds are nominally forbidden as food, though the prohibition can never cause any serious prohibition to the totemites. The results of a hypothetical breach were pictured for me in imagination : the man who killed or ate his hawk would shut his eyes and stagger, and then (the thought of the bird's talons being in my informant's mind) would scratch himself with clawed fingers. The sanction is thus clearly envisaged as automatic, and the notion of punishment is effected by a sort of metaphorical association, as when the crocodile totemite for instance conjures up the picture of a roughened, horny skin as the automatic penalty for eating crocodile.

" These more dire results of eating the totem are restricted to the totemites, but it is interesting to note that the prohibition may be extended in a milder degree to both moieties. At Tonda, for instance, I recorded an allegedly historical incident in which a Bangu man named Bitu offended the Sangara people of his village by killing and eating their totem, the hawk *inifiak*. By way of requital, the story says, a Sangara man named Tabaru thereupon killed the Bangu hawk *wana* and called on his fellows to eat it. In this somewhat improbable story we see an example of the mutual regard for one another's totems which, appearing to be somewhat unusual in the case of the hawks, is frequently met with in the case of other totemic species.

"Without ever having been able to test sincerity by actual observation I have been assured that a Sangara man would grieve over the death of an *inifiak*. If he chanced upon the bird lying dead he would wrap it carefully in bark and place it in the branches of a tree. . . .

"When the hunter brought down a wallaby he might exclaim, *wana* ! or *inifiak* ! according as he was Bangu or Sangara ; and when the raider had killed his man and was about to behead him he would, I am told, utter shrill cries of triumph in the same spirit : if Bangu he would call ' *Sikakakaka . . .* ! ' in imitation of the *wana* or *sikaka* ; if Sangara, ' *Gangangangan . . .* ! ' in imitation of the *inifiak* or *ganagan*.

"The more obvious purpose here, and the only one which suggests itself to the native, is that of advertising the killer's success : his fellow totemites, rushing to the scene, would join in his cry and feel the pleasure of reflected glory. But there is, perhaps, a more deep-seated motive. While the native apparently does not in the moment of triumph directly ascribe his success to *inifiak*, there is evident, in some connections at any rate, a feeling that the hawk can really exercise an influence in the hunter's favour. I shall record presently what I know of the ritual of the hawk-stone shrine at Kuramangu, and it will appear that it is at least in part a hunting rite. How far the influence of *inifiak* is felt to extend is indeed uncertain. I have no doubt as to the authenticity of the procedure, since I have been privileged to see the highly secret hawk-stone, *inifiak*, and a mock performance of the ceremony on the actual site. But it seems plain that this is no more than a local ritual, being one of the kind associated with the *tuarar*, which we shall have to consider separately. It may be that the totem *inifiak* is regarded throughout the Morehead district as having some influence on hunting, but its special cult belongs to the Keraki Proper, and its only shrine, as far as I could discover, is at Kuramangu. I know of no parallel ritual nor of any shrine for the Bangu hawk, *wana*.

"When we come to consider more generally the rather

lengthy list of remaining totems we find the same sort of rules observed with greater or less degree of strictness. They are said to be *yuvi*, and those of an edible nature are not to be eaten by the people to whom they belong, because, as it has been explained, this would mean that they are eating their *budar*, ' friends ' or ' kinsmen.' Bangu men of the Kaunje tribe, for instance, who call the crocodile their *kaki* or ancestor, will not eat it (and for the exception to prove the rule they ascribe the recent death of one of their number to a breach of this law). But they have no hesitation in killing this hated creature when they get the chance to do so, and then they are content to absent themselves while the Sangara people cook and eat it.

" In some cases, while the particular totem is predominantly either Bangu or Sangara, it is found that both sections in a given district refuse to eat it. From among many examples I may cite those of the *tumbabw'r* (eel) and *udaga* (scrub hen) among the Keraki Proper. Both are associated with the Bangu moiety, but the former in particular and the latter in a somewhat lesser degree are regarded as sacred by Sangara as well as Bangu ; and, although they are highly valued as food, no man or woman of the Keraki Proper would eat them. When they are caught and killed they are eaten by those among the wives who happen to have come from distant parts and are thus exempt from the prohibition.

" As for help or favour derived from the totem, I have discovered hardly any evidence for such a conception. And furthermore it must be said that there is little trace of any real reverence or special regard. Indeed it would appear that, in the absence of such beliefs and sentiments, the majority of totems are virtually no more than symbols or badges, and half forgotten at that, of the groups that own them.

" There are, however, some few cases, such as those of the above-mentioned eel and scrub hen, where the totem is really sacred and may be made the object of some ritual. . . . We may note here that a certain creek called Tarekor, which leads into the Wassi Kussa, is regarded as one of the sacred places of this creature, the eel. Until recently there was to be seen here the half-submerged trunk of the *chevem* tree which had been the dwelling-place of *tumbabw'r* at Boigu, and which, together with the eel itself, had been borne up the Wassi Kussa in the original flood. Nowadays after fishing in the Tarekor creek it is customary to lower one fish, attached to a length of cane, into the water and leave it there. But my informants did not say that this was an offering to *tumbabw'r*, as one might rather have hoped. All that they could say was that it was an old custom. . . . Perhaps, however, we shall be justified in seeing in this the remnant of a rite of placating the totem." [1]

With regard to the marriage system of the people, Mr. Williams tells us that the favourite marriage is with the classificatory cross-cousin (mother's brother's daughter or father's sister's daughter). Of the forty-six marriages examined in this respect, 44 per cent were of this nature. There were solitary cases of marriage with classificatory junior sister and classificatory daughter. In the remaining cases, amounting to 32 per cent, the husband was unable to say in what relation his bride had stood to him. Marriage with the true cross-cousin is, according to informants, in no way condemned, though it occurs rarely. [2]

In that part of Northern New Guinea which formerly belonged to Germany, Mr. Gregory Bateson found a social system which he regards as totemism in the Iatmul people on the Sepik River. Among these people a perfect village is divided longitudinally by the big dancing ground on which the ceremonial houses stand. On one side of this are the houses of one patrilineal moiety, with those of the other moiety opposite. On the upper river the two moieties are called " mother people " and " sun people." These names refer to important totemic emblems, the vulva and the sun respectively. In Palimbei the mother *versus* sun division is the basis of organisation of initiation ceremonies. The men of the sun moiety scarify and initiate the boys of the mother moiety and *vice versa*. In Mindimbit, Tambunum, and neighbouring villages, where the totemic moieties are less important, there is a distinct patrilineal division which is concerned with initiation. These two moieties do not coincide with the totemic divisions, and have no totemic

[1] F. E. Williams, *op. cit.* pp. 85 *sqq.*   [2] F. E. Williams, *op. cit.* p. 128.

significance. In Mindimbit neither of the systems of dual division controls marriage in a simple way. There is a definite preference for clan exogamy.[1]

To return to local organisation, the moieties (sun and mother) are further subdivided into a large number of totemic groups, membership of which (as also of the moieties) is determined by patrilineal descent. Where circumstances permit, this subdivision is brought out in the arrangement of houses. So that we have the village divided longitudinally into two moieties, and each of these divided transversely into patches of ground apportioned to each totemic group. Marriage is patrilocal as a rule, the wife going to live in the husband's totemic group.

The smallest local group is the household—those relatives who live together in one house—a man, his wives, and their children, and it is usual to find two or three of these groups living together in one big house. Most generally we find two own—or close classificatory—brothers living together— each with his wives and children ; one family at each end of the house, but with no partition between them.

Among the Iatmul two men may be connected according to no less than six different methods of reckoning which frequently conflict.

(*a*) Kinship by genealogy. By his genealogy at birth a man is provided with a series of relatives and also potential wives. According to this system of reckoning a man's possible wives are the women of his father's mother's clan.

(*b*) Kinship by marriage. The exchange of sisters in marriage is common.

(*c*) Kinship by *Tambinien*, an ambiguous term. *Tambinien* are partners, and their children ought to marry, with brother-sister exchange. The mother's brother is in a very real sense a male mother.

(*d*) The Iatmul have a very marked sentimental feeling, not only for their mother, but also for the mother's brother, and indeed for the whole of the mother's clan, including its totems.

(*e*) Reckoning by clans and moieties.

[1] Gregory Bateson, " Social Struc- ture of the Iatmul People of the Sepik River," in *Oceania*, vol. ii. No. 3 (March 1932), pp. 256 *sqq.*

A man is called by the same totemic name as his father's father (real or classificatory), and a woman by the name of her father's father's sister.[1]

A child is obliged to inhale the smoke of totemic ginger in order that he may learn the difficult lists of totemic names.

A celebration is held after a successful raid when young men have killed for the first time, and in this celebration the mother's brother plays a curious part, in connection with his sister's son, who has killed an enemy for the first time. The killers are bathed in the river. After bathing, the young man's mother's brother is naked and tied down on a sort of stretcher. The father of the young man puts into his hand an adze. Meanwhile a number of men raise the stretcher, swinging it violently and singing songs, in which they call out the names of the mother's brother's clan. After this the young man is placed on the belly of his recumbent mother's brother, cuts his bonds with the adze, and presents the adze to him. His uncle then sits up on the stretcher and raises himself, using the adze as support.

Another incident of the same celebration is as follows: The mother's brother of the young man will kill a fowl and prepare the feathers as a headdress. This is given to the father's sisters dressed and ornamented as men. Then the mother's brother's wives dressed as men lie down on the ground. The father's sisters go stepping across them carrying the feathers. The mother's brother's wives snatch the feathers and run off with them. The ceremony ends with a dance of the women at night, wearing masculine ornaments.[2]

In the tribe polygamy is allowed, and a man may have as many as ten wives.

Certain plants, animals, etc., belong to various clans, and are identified with the *ngwail* or ancestor of the clan to which they belong. Thus the system appears to be closely allied to totemism, each clan having dozens or even hundreds of *ngwail* (totemic ancestors). For example, the Mwai-lambu *ngavva* clan belonging to the mother moiety includes among its totems shamanic spirits, pigs, houses, ceremonial houses, ancestral heroes, canoes, land north of Sepik River, masked figures, fire, water, ginger, turmeric, many plants,

---

[1] G. Bateson, *op. cit.* pp. 267 *sqq.*   [2] G. Bateson, *op. cit.* pp. 276 *sqq.*

animals and birds, pots, brooms, bamboo hoe, and so forth.[1]

There is a difference between the totems of the moieties. Thus the clans of the Sun moiety tend to have suns and stars and clouds for their ancestors and to place their ancestral pigs, canoes, and so on, in the sky. The clans of the mother moiety, on the other hand, connect their ancestors with the earth. Some clans say that they have totems connected with the bush, while others are specially connected with the river. The most important are common to all clans : shamanic spirits, fire, water, dwelling-houses, ceremonial houses, crocodiles, ginger, masks, eagles, and many other important categories.

Collectively the objects and ancestors of the clan are spoken of as *nyai' ngwail* (the fathers and fathers' fathers). This combination fits clearly with the division of the clans into lines, whereby all ancestors are either fathers or father's fathers.

A man takes his father's names and applies them to his own sons. Similarly he takes his father's sister's names and applies them to his daughters . . . As a man grows older and his son's sons appear, his totemic clan names are one by one taken away from him and given to his grandsons, while he is still alive. Finally, he is only left with the names given to him by his mother's brother. With these names he is said to go to the land of the dead.[2]

The Mwailambu clan keeps somewhere in one of its houses, somewhere behind its pots, or hung up high in the roof, a plaited basket, carefully sewn up, in which are the precious relics of its totemic ancestors. The Kwosamba clan possessed a similar small hoard. The relics are produced on special occasions for a ceremony called *pwivu*, the eating of the relics.

The *pwivu* basket of the Mwailambu contained three human bones and a variety of other articles. Another clan *pwivu* was said to be the tooth of a totemic pig.

At a *pwivu* for a little girl who had caught a fish, scrapings from the three bones and the club, and so on, were mixed

[1] G. Bateson, "Social Structure of the Iatmul People of Sepik River," Part iii., *Oceania*, vol. ii. No. 4 (June 1932), p. 401.

[2] G. Bateson, *op. cit.* pp. 409 *sq.*

with the milk and flesh of two coconuts, and spells were pronounced over the mixture, which was eaten by the young people of the village, who came up and ate it direct, dipping their heads down into the bowl. After two adults had tasted, a crowd of children of the village ate. Any children, especially unmarried girls, were encouraged to eat of it, regardless of clan.

After eating, small scars were cut in the forearm of the children, and they had to observe certain food taboos. For five days they were forbidden water and washing. They drank coconut milk. After this initial period certain taboos continued, and they might not eat fish, especially big fish. These taboos lasted till the next planting of turmeric. In another case the mixture contained small fish, which had to be swallowed whole, in imitation of the egret, but Mr. Bateson did not know whether the egret was a specially important totem of this clan.[1]

Generally speaking it may be said that all Iatmul ceremonial involves the chanting of names, and the exhibition of representations of totems.

Many representations of totems are not used in any ritual but are merely standing visible as carvings. In most cases the totemic representation is the centre of ritual performances, at least when it is set up.

Certain totemic representations are specially exhibited by the sister's children of the totem's clan. For example, masks are worn by the sister's children, flutes are blown by the sister's children, and certain objects are exhibited by the sister's children during mortuary ceremonies for the dead of the mother's clan whose totem they represent.[2]

There is no serious scruple against killing and eating the totem. The only plant with which a man may decorate himself is that of his mother's totem. Though the structure of the institutions is patrilineal, a man's first duty is towards his mother's totem.

In discussing the question whether the social system of the Iatmul is totemism or not, Mr. Bateson tells us that the system lacks some of the marks which are usually associated with totems. First, it is not clear that any of the Iatmul

---

[1] G. Bateson, *op. cit.* p. 429.   [2] G. Bateson, *op. cit.* p. 430.

ngwail are species. Certainly the most important are individual spirits, while the less important are, in many cases, primarily individuals whose names are loosely extended to apply to any other individuals of the same species. Further, there is no taboo on eating the *ngwail*: there are no ceremonies to increase or multiply the *ngwail*: there is no belief in the rebirth of totemic ancestors, nor in the reappearance of ancestors in totemic form in dreams.[1] On the whole, then, we may say that if the system described by Mr. Bateson is to be called totemism, it is an irregular or anomalous form of the institution.

[1] G. Bateson, *op. cit.* pp. 444 *sqq.*

CHAPTER II

DUTCH NEW GUINEA comprises, roughly speaking, the western half of the great island. The south-eastern corner of the territory, bounded by the sea on the south, and by Papua or British New Guinea on the east, is occupied by the Marind, or Marind-Anim tribe, possessing a complex totemic system which has been examined and described by a Swiss ethnologist, Dr. P. Wirz.[1] Brief summaries of his description of the system have been published by Dr. A. C. Haddon and Professor Landtman.[2]

The whole tribe of the Marind are divided into two principal groups, *Geb-ze* and the *Sami-rek*. These two groups are quite independent and unconnected, though the members of each group claim to be closely related to each other. While the *Geb-ze* group forms a complete unity in itself, the *Sami-rek* is divided into a number of exogamous sub-groups, or sub-groups which may be called totemic societies. These totemic societies are further subdivided into what may be called totemic unions. The *Geb-ze* are similarly divided into a number of totemic unions. Thus they distinguish, for example, the coconut union, the banana union, and so on. The connection of these totemic unions with the totemic societies of which they are subdivisions is of different kinds : but it is founded upon some mythical or legendary relationship or on totemic friendship or totemic relationship. Thus, for example, all coastal animals and coastal plants are related

---

[1] Dr. P. Wirz, *Die Marind-anim von Holländisch - Sud - Neu - Guinea* (Hamburg. 1922).

[2] G. Landtman, *op. cit.* pp. xv, 190 *sq.*

to each other and belong to the coast totemic union. To these totemic unions belong the personified forces, the ancestors (*Dema*) and originators of these objects, and further the clans, which stand in close relation to these ancestors and their totemic descendants.

The totemic union is also a complete unit of the social structure, with strict exogamy and patriarchal descent. A totemic union sometimes includes several clans, which may be connected with each other only in some mythical or totemic way, that is, may have the same totemic relations and the same principal totem, which regularly gives its name to the whole totemic union.

The clans finally are divided into single families, which take their name either from a male ancestor, or from a settlement which has once been inhabited by their mythical ancestor.

The present structure of the Marind tribe has been brought about by migrations and blendings, which have been spread over a long period. The settlement in any case originally consisted in original groups or families, and we must suppose that the original settlements consisted of clans only. The clan organisation forms the foundation of the tribal structure. The clans are named after early ancestors and immigrants, the *Dema*, or, if the settlement was completed by a single group, after a canoe in which the *Dema* ancestors have immigrated, or finally after a place which was originally settled or has been for a long time inhabited.

Besides the wanderings of the ancestors (*Dema*), in the course of time many extraordinary incidents or experiences have furnished materials for myths, such as, for example, the discovery of certain plants, hunting adventures, feasts, and the like, which form the foundation of the clan myths and the totemic relationships. As the myths relate, the ancestors and early immigrants are regarded as extraordinary beings and the originators of certain objects, and have qualified as *Dema*. The descendants of *Dema*, that is the clan itself, have thus entered into a specially close connection with the corresponding totemic object.

The wife of Wokabu (a *Dema*), so a myth tells us, produced or gave birth to the sago, or rather the sago *Dema* (it is thought of as a piece of sago endowed with special power). Hence all the descendants of Wokabu are related to the sago, and belong to the sago totemic union (*Boan*). The sago itself is called *Amai*, which means ancestors, as also is Wokabu. Other objects, which in some way or other are mythically connected with sago or with Wokabu, are also spoken of as *Amai*. These stand with other words in close mythical and totemic connection with the clan : to these belong, for example, all parts of the sago palm, all the products of the sago palm, the implements for preparing sago, and animals which feed principally upon the sago or live close to the sago palms.

It is quite possible that such myths as that of the origin of sago and the connection of the sago with Wokabu are founded upon a true tradition, namely that Wokabu as one of the first immigrants came into possession of many sago trees· and planted them out, for sago is nowhere extensively found on the coastal region of British New Guinea, and there the chief source. of food is not sago but yams and taro. This was probably also the case with the early Marind, when they still inhabited the eastern coastal region.

The totemic outlook of the Marind thus arises directly from the myths of the *Dema* (ancestors), and from the belief in their supernatural powers and abilities, as a consequence of which they could transform themselves into and produce different objects of Nature and are regarded as the originators of the whole universe. They also begat human offspring, which by successive generations shed their extraordinary powers and became ordinary human beings. Men, animals, plants and other objects, which go back to the same ancestor (*Dema*), are thus blood relations to one another. The Marind say in such cases that these beings are their *Amai* (forefathers, or early ancestors).

The totemic relationship thus flows directly from the belief in the *Dema* ancestors. The object into which the *Dema* (ancestral being) can transform himself, or which he has produced, generally becomes the clan symbol or the chief totem, after which the whole clan is named. A group named after a chief totem is called by the Marind a *Boan*. This includes one or more clans : with all the mythical totemic objects of the *Boan* the clan stands in close connection. For example, the *Mahu-ze* clan belongs to the dog *Boan*, for Mahu, according to the myth, was the originator of the dog. On the other hand, all dogs belong to the *Mahu-ze* clan, since they originate from Mahu, and everything which is connected with the dog, and all objects which are mentioned in the myth of Mahu, belong also to the *Mahu-ze* clan.[1]

There exist certain food taboos. These do not include all totem animals, but according to the Marind are concerned mainly with birds, but even in these cases they are not very strict. For example, they would never apply these restrictions to a cassowary or a species of pigeon or a large duck ; but with an expression of regret to their ancestors would devour them without scruple.

The Marind thus stands, by means of his *Dema* (forefathers) and the myths, in a certain totemic relation with all existing things. This is so extensive that an enumeration of all totemically connected objects is quite impossible. It may even include certain activities such as sleeping and marrying as totemic activities of certain clans or clan unions, as when for example a clan has the tradition of its *Dema* (ancestor) that he slept a great deal or led a loose life. Certain characteristics may also be regarded as distinctive totemic marks, such as bald-headedness or ringworm, if the myth relates that these marks originated with the *Dema* or that they go back to the time of the *Dema*.

Generally the clan members stand in close relation with everything that is mentioned in the myths of their forefathers. Thus the idea of totemism can only be applied with certain reservations to the Marind. It is not always possible to speak of totemic relationship. Often a clan connection depends only upon certain events, wanderings, and adventures of the ancestors (*Dema*).[2]

As we have seen, the *Geb-ze*, one of the two principal divisions of the Marind, includes several totemic unions. Among these are the coconut and the banana *Boan*. The coconut *Boan* includes the clan of the coconut with the undivided blossoms, and the clan of the ordinary coconut. The banana totemic union (*Boan*) includes among others the clan

---

[1] P. Wirz, *op. cit.* Bd. I. Part ii. pp. 28 *sqq.*
[2] P. Wirz, *op. cit.* I. ii. pp. 33 *sqq.*

of the pearl mussel. A third totemic union is that of the fan-palm, which stands in a close mythical connection with the coconut *Boan*. The first coconut is said to have sprung miraculously from the grave of a man who had been murdered by magic. It bore fruit the same day, or according to another version, a whole grove of palm trees sprang from the grave the same day. Coconuts had been unknown before, and the people now flocked to gather and enjoy the newly discovered fruit.[1]

The *Sami-rek*, the second great group of the Marind, is subdivided, as we have seen, into four sub-groups. The first of these sub-groups includes the cassowary or fire, kangaroo, and stork totemic unions (*Boan*). To these *Boan* belong a number of clans which possess special mythical and totemic connections. Such are the smoke clan, the special fire clan, the special cassowary clan, the rattan clan, which all belong to the cassowary or fire *Boan* in a wider sense. The stork *Boan*, which in its entirety is also called the bird society, includes two clans, that of the giant stork (*Xenorhynchus asiaticus*) and a sub-species of the same. The second sub-group of the *Sami-rek* includes the areca, crocodile, the sea, fish, and birds of prey. The third sub-group of the *Sami-rek* is that of the sago, with the dominating sago *Boan*, which is divided into the clans of the dog and the shad. The fourth sub-group of the *Sami-rek* is named after a special mythical object, the rainbow. To it belongs only one *Boan*, that of pigs.[2]

Among the Marind the marriage regulations are such that husband and wife must always belong to different totemic societies.[3] The system of relationship is classificatory: all male contemporaries in the same totemic union are called brothers, all brothers of the father are called fathers, and all sisters of the mother are called mothers, and even the sisters-in-law of the mother are addressed as mothers.[4]

---

[1] P. Wirz, *op. cit.* I. ii. pp. 69 *sq.*
[2] P. Wirz, *op. cit.* I. ii. pp. 37 *sq.*
[3] P. Wirz, *op. cit.* I. i. p. 68.
[4] P. Wirz, *op. cit.* I. i. p. 75.

BOOK IV

TOTEMISM IN INDIA

§ I. *Totemism of the Birhors*

ELSEWHERE I have shown that the institutions of totemism and exogamy are found to linger among some of the backward indigenous tribes of India, who in their fastnesses of the forest or the mountain have been able to retain their primitive culture, little affected by contact with invading races.[1] Here I will adduce some fresh evidence of such survivals.

Thus the Birhors, a primitive Dravidian tribe of Chota Nagpur, are divided into a number of totemic and exogamous clans called *gotras*, mostly named after some animal, plant, fruit, flower, or other material object. Of their totemism Mr. Sarat Chandra Roy tells us that " the Birhors appear to have preserved or developed a few interesting features in their totemism which I have not yet met with among any other totemic tribe in Chota Nagpur, and which, as far as I know, have not been recorded of any other tribe in India.

" It is interesting to note that the few families that compose a Birhor *tanda* or food-group do not all belong to the same clan or kinship-group. Chance, or, more often, marital connections, would appear to have originally brought together in a *tanda* families belonging to different clans. And through long association in the food-quest, families of different clans composing any particular *tanda* appear to have attained a comparatively greater cohesion than different families of one and the same clan belonging to different *tandas*. But

[1] *Totemism and Exogamy*, ii. 218-327.

even this cohesion is seldom so strong as to prevent any family from leaving its old *tanda* and joining a new one when it feels inclined to so so." [1]

The totem clans among the Birhors, so far as Mr. Sarat Chandra Roy could ascertain them, are :—

1. Andi (wild cat).
2. Bonga Sauri (a kind of wild grass).
3. Bhat (name of a Hindu caste).
4. Bhont or Bhuntil (a kite).
5. Bhuiya (name of a tribe).
6. Chauli Hembrom (*chauli* = rice ; *Hembrom* = betel palm).
7. Ganda Garua (a large species of vulture).
8. Geroa (a small bird).
9. Gidhi (vulture).
10. Goar (milkman caste).
11. Guleria or Galaoria (pellet-bow).
12. Gundri (a kind of bird).
13. Hembrom (betel palm).
14. Here Hembrom (*here* = rice husk).
15. Induar (eel).
16. Jegseria Latha (*latha* = a cake made of *mohua* flowers).
17. Kauch or Horo (tortoise).
18. Kawan Hembrom.
19. Keonduar (a kind of fruit).
20. Khangar (name of a sub-tribe of the Mundas).
21. Kharea (name of a tribe).
22. Khudi Hembrom (*khudi* = broken grains of rice).
23. Ludumba = a kind of flower.
24. Lundi jal (= *Lakur chata*).
25. Lupung (*myrobalan* tree).
26. Maghaia Hembrom (*Maghaia* = belonging to Magha or Bihar).
27. Mahali (name of a tribe).
28. Modi (name of caste or section of a tribe).
29. Murum (nilgai or *Portax pictu*, a wild deer).
30. Nag (cobra) or Nagpuria (belonging to Chota Nagpur).
31. Sada (*white*).
32. Samduar (*sadom* = horse).
33. Saunria (a kind of wild grass).
34. Sham-jhakoa (a composition used in whetting weapons).
35. Singpuria (*singhara* fruit or *Trapa bispmosa*).
36. Suia (a kind of bird).
37. Toriar (belonging to Pargana Tori in the Palamau district).

" A few of these names, such as Nagpuria and Toriar, are derived from names of localities, whereas a few others,

[1] S. C. Roy, *The Birhors* (Ranchi, 1925), pp. 89 *sqq.*

such as Bhat, Goar, Bhuiya, Khangar, and Mahali, would appear to be derived from names of other tribes, with some of whom at any rate there are reasons to believe there have been miscegenation in the past."

A Birhor's totem is hereditary, not acquired.

There are no sex or associated totems.

The members of a clan do not wear any badge or distinguishing emblem or peculiar dress, nor make up their hair in any distinctive fashion nor get representations of their totem cut or tattoed on their persons or carved or painted on their houses or on any personal belongings. But during sacrifices to the Spirits, known variously as *Ora-bongas* (' home gods '), *Buru-bongas*, (hill gods) or ' Khunt bhuts ' (clan spirits), some emblem of the family totem is placed by the side of the sacrifice, and this emblem is always carried about with it wherever the family migrates.[1]

" The few legends that the Birhors tell about the origin of some of their clans do not point to any belief in the descent of men from their totems. All that they indicate is that the totem plant or animal had had some accidental connection with the birth of the reputed ancestor of the clan. Thus, the ancestor of the Gidhi (vulture) clan, it is said, was born under a wide-spreading tree, and, as soon as he was born, the egg of a vulture which had its nest on the overhanging branches of the tree dropped down on the babe's head from the nest. Hence the baby and his descendants came to form the Gidhi (vulture) clan. Similarly the ancestor of the Geroa (small bird) clan is said to have been born under the wings of a Geroa bird, and the ancestor of the Lupung clan under the shade of a *lupung* tree.

" But although the Birhors of our days do not believe in the actual descent of a clan from its totem, they appear to find some resemblance in the temperament or physical appearance of the members of a clan to that of their totem animal or plant. Thus, it is said, people of the Gidhi (vulture) clan have usually little hair on the crown of the head, and members of the Lupung clan are generally short but plump like the *lupung* fruit. . . .

" As with other totemic peoples, a Birhor must abstain

[1] S. C. Roy, *The Birhors* (Ranchi, 1925), pp. 89 *sqq.*

from killing, destroying, maiming, hunting, injuring, eating, or otherwise using the animal, plant, or other object that forms his clan totem, or anything made out of or obtained from it ; and, if possible, he will also prevent others from doing so in his presence. Some of the clans carry the principle to curious extremes. Thus, the men of the *Murum* clan cover their eyes when they chance to come across a *murum* stag. . . .

" It is worthy of note, however, that all totem taboos have to be strictly observed only by married men, for it is not until he is married that a Birhor is considered to become a full member of his clan. Eating, killing, or destroying one's clan totem is regarded by the Birhor as equivalent to killing a human member of his own clan, and the reason usually assigned by the Birhor for abstaining from or preventing others from killing or destroying his totem is that if the totem animal, plant, or other object diminishes, the clan too will suffer a corresponding decrease in numbers. Although it is believed that a particular clan will multiply in proportion as the totem species or class multiplies, no Birhor clan resorts to any magical process, like the Australian *intichiuma* ceremonies, for the multiplication of its totem species or class. Individuals of the tribe not belonging to a certain totem do not hold those who do responsible for the ensuring of a supply of the totemic animal or plant for their benefit, nor are the former required to obtain the permission of the latter to eat their totemic animal or plant. Marriage between persons of the same clan is considered incestuous.

" Descent is reckoned in the male line, and a man has the same totem as his father. The mother's, or rather the mother's father's totem, is not respected ; for, in fact, a female is not supposed to have any clan ; she is not a recognised member either of her father's or of her husband's clan, and has not, therefore, to observe the taboos relating to their totems. She must not, however, kill the totem animal or destroy the totem plant of her husband's clan, as that would, in the Birhor's estimation, be equivalent to killing the husband himself. When a Birhor unwarily happens to eat, kill, or destroy his totem animal or plant, his clan-fellows impose on him, according to his means, a fine of either five four-anna bits or five two-anna bits, or five annas. He is also required to provide a feast, if not to all the members, at least to one member of each clan in his settlement or encampment. The spirits of the dead are not supposed to enter their totem animals, nor are the spirits of a dead totem supposed to enter the wombs of the wives of men of that totem. A meeting of the totem animal is not considered, save among the Murums, to affect one's luck ; nor does a Birhor make obeisance to his totem animal when he meets it. But should he ever happen to come across the carcase of his totem beast or bird, he must anoint its forehead with oil and vermilion, although he has not actually to mourn for the dead animal or bury it.

" There is another practice connected with Birhor totemism which, even if it may not have an essentially religious or magico-religious significance, is at any rate intimately associated with Birhor religion. Every Birhor clan has a tradition of its ancient settlement having been located in some hill or other within Chota Nagpur. And once a year at every Birhor encampment or settlement the men of each clan assemble on some open space outside their group of leaf-huts to offer sacrifices to the presiding spirit of their ancestral hill. This spirit is called *Ora-bonga* by the migratory Birhors and *Buru-bonga*, or mountain god, by the comparatively settled Birhors. At these sacrifices, in which members of other clans may not take part, the eldest member present of the clan officiates as sacrificer. A mystic diagram with four compartments is drawn on the ground with rice-flour, and in one of these compartments the sacrificer sits down with his face turned in the direction of the ancestral hill of his clan and with some emblem of his totem species placed in another compartment of the diagram. Thus, men of the Ludumba clan place a *ludumba* flower before the sacrificer ; those of the Murum (stag) clan place a bit of a horn or skin of the *murum* ; those of the Kendua clan place a twig of the Keond tree ; those of the Geroa clan place a wing of the *Geroa* bird. . . .

" In the case of bird or beast totems, the skin, horn, claw, or wing used as an emblem to represent the clan is obtained by members of the clan, not by killing or destroying the bird or beast with their own hands, but through men of some other clan to whom they are not taboo. So intimate and vital is the connection between the clan and its totem, that the totem emblem thus used is regarded as representing the clan as a whole. And the invocation at such a ceremony begins thus : ' Behold such-and-such a clan has come to offer sacrifices to thee, O spirit of such-and such hill." [1]

Although the men of every Birhor clan annually offer sacrifices to the presiding spirit of their ancestral hill, so great is their fear of the spirit that no member of a Birhor clan will, on any account, enter or even go within a distance of a mile or two of the hill or jungle reputed to be its former home, unless some family of the clan is still residing there and regularly propitiating the local spirits. Even when, in the course of their wanderings, a group of migratory Birhors happen to come near such hill or jungle, they must turn aside and take a different route. The reason now assigned for such avoidance is that the spirits of such a hill or jungle who have not had any sacrifices offered to them since the men had left the place might cause them harm for such neglect. . . .

" The situation of these traditional homes of a few of the clans is believed to have endowed them with specific magical powers. Thus, the Here Hembrom and Khudi Hembrom clans are said to have powers over the weather. It is said that when high wind is approaching, if a man of either of these clans pours a jug of water on the *thhan* (spirit-seat) or in front of the tribal encampment and bids the storm turn aside, the storm will immediately take a different direction, and even though it may blow hard on the country all around, the hill or jungle in which these clans may be encamping will remain quite calm and undisturbed. The reason why the men of these clans are said to be *maliks* or masters of the storm, is explained by saying that their *Buru-bongas* (mountain gods) or *Ora-bongas* (home gods) are situate in the north, which is the home of storms. Members of the *Jegseria Latha* clan, whose ancestral home and ' home god ' (*Ora-bonga*) are farther north than those of the Here Hembrom and Khudi Hembrom clans, are credited with the power of controlling monsoon rains and high winds in the same way. . . . It is said that monsoon winds and rains will always

[1] S. C. Roy, *op. cit.* pp. 102 *sqq.*

abate their force when they approach a settlement of this clan. Of the *Kawan* clan—one of the wildest of Birhor clans —it is said that tigers, on certain occasions, serve them as friends and servants. When a Kawan woman is about to be confined, her husband makes for her a separate shed with leaves and branches, in which she is left alone. As soon as a baby is born to her, a tiger, it is said, invariably enters the shed, cleanses the limbs of the baby by licking them, and opens a back door to the shed for the woman to go out and come in during her days of ceremonial taboo." [1]

" Although all the Birhor clans agree in excluding females (with the exception of little girls who have not yet attained puberty) from their spirit-huts (*bonga-oras*) and in excluding married daughters and other women not belonging to the family from their spirit-seats (*thhans*), and in pro- hibiting women from eating the heads of animals caught in the chase or sacrificed to the spirits, different clans observe different rules about the ceremonial pollution attaching to females during menstruation or in child-birth. Thus, among the Maghaia Hembrom clan, as soon as a woman menstruates a small new door is opened in the wall of the hut for her use during the next eight days, and she is not allowed to use the main door of the hut or to touch any food or other thing in the house or do any work, whereas in most other clans, although she is not allowed to touch anything in the house, a new door is not opened for her. In addition to these restrictions, a menstruous woman of the Kawan clan must go out of, and enter, the hut through the newly-opened door- way in a sitting posture—that is to say, on her buttocks and not on her legs."

In the presence of so many points of difference in custom between the different clans, it is no wonder that a Birhor should identify " clan " with *jat* or caste, and that there is as yet hardly any real tribal sentiment or any cohesion between the members of the different clans. But, inasmuch as members of two or three clans generally form one food-group, camping together in the same *tanda* or settlement or wandering about and hunting in the same jungle, there has sprung up a well recognised connection of some particular clan with certain

[1] S. C. Roy, *op. cit.* pp. 106 *sqq.*

other clan or clans. Thus, for instance, the *Geroa* and *Murum* clans are generally found associated together, and the *Saunria* clan is usually found associated with the *Ludumba* clan. Although the Birhors assert that these associations of particular clans have existed from the beginning of time, there are reasons for supposing that such association originated from sons-in-law or other near relations by marriage joining the groups of their fathers-in-law or other relations on the wife's side.

There is thus hardly any social integration between the different clans forming the tribe. Even the different families of the same clan living at a distance from one another do not recognise the idea of collective responsibility as illustrated, for instance, by the law of the blood-feud, but only, and that dimly, the existence of an ultimate relationship. It is only in the families composing one settlement or encampment, although generally belonging to more than one clan, that we meet with a certain amount of social solidarity. Even the birth-pollution and death-pollution of any family in the local settlement is shared by all the other families of the settlement to whatever clan they may belong. Although their ancestral spirits and home spirits are different, they join in sacrifices to the same local spirits and the same spirits of the hunt.

Although a few clans, as we have seen, are supposed to have a magical control over certain departments of Nature, such power is now said to belong to them not directly on account of their totem, but on account of the situation of their traditional homes. There is no specialisation between the different clans, which are all considered as equal in rank.

" Such are the main features of Birhor totemism so far as I have hitherto been able to ascertain them. As with most other Dravidian tribes in Chota Nagpur, the Birhor totemic clan is exogamous and·the system of relationship is classificatory. The respect which a man owes to his totem prevents him from killing or eating it. But the respect for the totem does not appear to have developed into an actual worship of the totem animal or plant. The Birhor has not come to regard his totem as a god, but looks upon it more in the light of a fellow-clansman. Although the Birhor identifies himself and his fellow-clansmen with his totem, he does not, like certain Central Australian Blacks, occasionally kill and eat his totem for a more complete physical identification with it. Nor does a Birhor clan breed or tame its totemic animal.

" One peculiar feature of Birhor totemism that I have noticed is the belief in the magical power of certain clans over wind and rain. But the tribe is not at the present day, at any rate, organised, like the Arunta, as a co-operative supply association, composed of groups of magicians, each group charged with the management of particular departments of Nature.

" The totemism of the Birhors would appear, however, to have not been without its influence on the growth of their religion. The most noteworthy feature in Birhor totemism appears to me to be the belief in the vital connection between the human clan, their totem, and the hill which is reputed to have been their original home, or rather the spirit of such hill." [1]

§ 2. *Totemism of the Oraons*

Another Dravidian tribe of Chota Nagpur who possess a system of totemism are the Oraons. Their system has already been described in my earlier work,[2] but some fresh light has been thrown on it by the eminent Indian ethnographer, Mr. Sarat Chandra Roy, who has made a special study of the tribe, and has reported the results of his enquiries in two valuable monographs.[3] I will quote what he says on the subject of Oraon totemism for comparison with my former account.

" The present social organisation of the Oraons is the archaic organisation of the ancient Oraon hunting communities adapted to the needs of the more complex agricultural village-communities of later days.

" Totemism, which was the basis of the social and political organisation of the Oraons in what may be roughly called the hunting and pastoral stages of Oraon culture, still forms the fundamental feature of their social organisation in so far as kinship, marriage, and relations of the sexes are

---

[1] S. C. Roy, *op. cit.* pp. 119 *sqq.*
[2] *Totemism and Exogamy*, ii. 284 *sqq.*
[3] S. C. Roy, *The Oraons of Chota Nagpur* (Ranchi, 1915) and *Oraon Religion and Customs* (Ranchi, 1928).

concerned. For purposes of exogamy the whole tribe is to this day divided into a number of clans or *gotras*. Individual totems, sex totems, or associated totems are unknown. The fauna and flora of their past and present habitats naturally supply the bulk of the totem names. With the acquisition of a knowledge of agriculture and the use of metals, a few new totem names have been since added. The existing Oraon totems so far as known to us may be classified as follows :—

(i) Beast Totems

1. Addo (ox).
2. Alla (dog).
3. Bando (wild cat).
4. Barwa (wild dog).
5. Chidra (squirrel).
6. Chiglo (jackal).
7. Ergo (rat).
8. Gari (common monkey).
9. Halman (baboon).
10. Khoea (wild dog).
11. Kiss or Suar (pig).
12. Lakra (tiger).
13. Osga (field rat).
14. Runda (fox).
15. Tig (a species of monkey).
16. Tirki (young mice).

(ii) Bird Totems

1. Bakula (paddy-bird).
2. Dhechua (a small black bird with a long tail).
3. Garwa (stork).
4. Gede (duck).
5. Gidhi (vulture).
6. Girlihi (a species of bird).
7. Khakha (raven).
8. Kerketa (hedge-sparrow).
9. Kokro (cock).
10. Orgora (hawk).
11. Tirkuar (the Tithio charai bird).
12. Toppo or Lang toppo (a species of long-tailed bird).

(iii) Fish and other Aquatic Totems

1. Aind (a subdivision of the eel).
2. Beah (a large fish with thorns on the back).
3. Ekka (tortoise).
4. Godo (crocodile).
5. Ken (a species of fish).
6. Khalkho ,, ,,
7. Kinduar (a species of fish).
8. Kosuar ,, ,,
9. Kosuwa ,, ,,
10. Linda (a subdivision of the eel).
11. Lita (a species of fish).
12. Minj ,, ,,
13. Sal ,, ,,
14. Tirn (a species of fish).

(iv) Reptile Totems

1. Khetta or Nag (Cobra).

(v) Vegetable Totems

1. Bakhla (a species of grass).
2. Bara or Bar (*Ficus indica*).
3. Basa (a kind of tree).
4. Gondrari ,, ,,
5. Kanda (sweet potato).
6. Kaithi (a curry vegetable).
7. Kendi (a kind of tree).
8. Keond (a kind of fruit).

9. Kheksa (a curry vegetable).
10. Khes (paddy).
11. Kinda (date palm).
12. Kujur (a kind of fruit).
13. Kundri (a curry vegetable).

14. Madgi (the mohua tree).
15. Munjniar (a kind of creeper).
16. Pusra (a kind of *kusum* tree).
17. Putri (a kind of tree).
18. Rori (a kind of tree).

19. Augal toppo (a kind of bush).

(vi) MINERAL TOTEMS

1. Panna (iron).   2. Bekh (salt).

(vii) PLACE TOTEMS

1. Bandh (an embanked reservoir of water).

2. Jubbi (a marsh or surface-spring).

(viii) SPLIT TOTEMS

1. Amri (rice-soup).   2. Kispotta (pig's entrails).

" (In the list given in Sir Herbert Risley's *Tribes and Castes of Bengal* a few of the totem names are given twice over, once in Oraon and again in their Hindi forms. Thus Lakra and Bagh are given as two different names, and similar mistakes are made with regard to ' Dhan ' and ' Khes,' etc.)

" The Oraons retain very few traditions as to the origin of particular totem names. Such traditions as they have do not reveal any belief in the descent of men from their totems. All that they indicate is that the totemic animal or plant is believed to have helped or protected the human ancestor of the clan, or been of some peculiar service to him. Thus, it is said, that while an Oraon had fallen asleep under a Kujur plant, a flexible twig of the plant entwined round his body and protected him from molestation. Accordingly the man took the Kujur plant for his totem, and his descendants now form the men of the Kujur clan.

" Some legends, on the other hand, refer the origin of a few clan names to some help or protection extended by a man to some animal or plant. Thus, it is said, that while a certain Oraon of olden times was about to catch a tortoise, the latter exclaimed : ' I am your *jat* (caste-fellow).' And so the man desisted from catching it, and his descendants came to form the Tortoise clan. The origin of the Kispotta (pig's entrails) clan is stated to be as follows. An Oraon killed a pig and ate its flesh, but threw away its entrails. The life of the pig remained in the entrails, so that the slain pig was soon afterwards found moving about in actual bodily form. Thenceforth pig's entrails became taboo to the slayer of the pig and his descendants, and they came to constitute the Kispotta clan. More matter-of-fact is the account given as to the origin of the Khalkho Fish clan. An Oraon was fishing in a stream. A Khalkho fish which was caught in his net managed to escape. Thenceforward, the Khalkho fish became taboo to the man and his descendants, who came to be called men of the Khalkho clan.

" Although the members of an Oraon clan do not believe in their actual descent from their totem animal or plant, they regard themselves as descendants of a common ancestor, and, as such, blood-relatives between whom marriage or sexual intercourse is not permissible. Although an Oraon will strongly protest that such a union is an incest (a ' brother-sister union ' as he calls it) which can never be permitted, the genealogical method of inquiry will occasionally reveal an instance here and there of such endogamous union. But in each of the few instances of this sort of union that you may come across, you are sure to find on inquiry that some pre-marital intrigue leading to inconvenient consequences resulted in a permanent union which was ultimately sanctioned by the village and the Parha [1] to which the man belonged, only on the latter having paid a fine and provided a feast to the ' Parha brethren.' After the offending pair are thus formally re-admitted into the tribe, and their union thus legalized, their sons are considered as good as legal heirs born of lawful wedlock. But of every case of such union, if the parties are no longer in the land of the living, you will be told that such a union could not endure, and that, ' as was but inevitable,' one of the pairs died within a few years of the union. . . . As totemism is now a dying institution amongst the Oraons except in its relation to marriage, you will find many Oraons of the present generation ignorant of the *gotras* of such near relatives as their mother's father and the husband of either their mother's sister or father's sister. Although an Oraon may not marry into his own totem, he may marry into the totem of his mother.

[1] Federation of villages.

" As a general rule, an Oraon must abstain from eating or otherwise using, domesticating, killing, destroying, maiming, hurting, or injuring the animal or plant or other object that forms his totem ; nor must he use anything made of it or obtained from it, and, when practicable, he will prevent others from doing so in his presence.   In the case of tree-totems, the men of the clan will neither go under the shade of the tree nor cut or burn its wood nor use its produce in any shape.   When, however, the totem is an animal or plant or other thing which forms an indispensable article of diet or household use, considerations of necessity or expediency appear to have introduced a modification of the taboo against using it.   Thus, instead of abstaining altogether from the use of paddy, Oraons of the *Khes* or paddy clan abstain only from eating the thin scum that forms on the surface of rice-soup when it stands unagitated in a cool place.   Similarly, instead of avoiding the use of salt altogether, Oraons of the Salt clan have only to abstain from taking raw salt unmixed with any food or drink, but may take food or drink to which salt has been added in cooking or in which even raw salt has been mixed beforehand.   In the same way, men of the Iron clan have only to abstain from touching iron with their lips or tongue, but may use iron in any other way they like ; and men of the Pig clan may eat all parts of the pig except only the head.   Men of the Bara clan may not eat the *bar* fruit by splitting it up in two, but are allowed to eat it whole.

" From similar considerations, some of the class of totems that Dr. Frazer [1] calls ' split-totems ' may have arisen.   Such are the *Kis-potta* (pig's entrails) and the *amri* (rice-soup) clans.   Some may have arisen, as Dr. Frazer suggests, by ' the segmentation of a single original clan, which had a whole animal for its totem, into a number of clans, each of which took the name either of a part or of a sub-species of it.' [2]

" If in the cases of certain clans the totem-taboo has been thus modified to suit the convenience of men of the totem— in a few cases, on the other hand, the taboo has been extended by the law of similarity to other objects that have a

[1] *Totemism and Exogamy*, i. 10.   [2] *Totemism and Exogamy*, i. 58.

real or fancied resemblance to the totem or may happen to
bear the same or a similar name to the totem's.   Thus men
of the Tiger (*Lakra*) clan, besides the various taboos they
have to observe in connection with the tiger and the wolf,
have also to abstain from eating the flesh of the squirrel, inasmuch as the squirrel's skin is striped like the tiger's.   Men
of the Kerketa (hedge-sparrow) clan, in addition to the usual
taboos with regard to the ' Kerketa,' observe a similar taboo
with regard to the Dhichua or King-crow which has also a
long tail like the Kerketa.   In some localities, again, an
Oraon of the Tiger (Lakra or Bagh) clan may not marry
in the month of Magh (December or January) inasmuch as
the word ' Magh ' rhymes with ' Bagh '—the Hindi name for
a tiger.   Similarly, men of the Monkey (Gari) clan besides
observing the taboo against killing, hunting, domesticating,
or eating the flesh of a monkey, have also to abstain from
sitting under the shade of a tree bearing the same name
(Gari) or cutting or burning its wood. . . .

" In a few cases a double totem appears to have arisen
from the anxiety felt by a particular totem to change a totem
name, now considered opprobrious, into a more respectable
name.   Thus in a few villages, we have found members of
the *Kis-potta* (pig's entrails) clan, when asked as to their
gotra or clan give their gotra-name as *kasai* (a kind of tree) ;
and, on enquiry, we found that while observing the customary
taboos with regard to pigs, they observe in addition further
taboos with regard to the ' Kasai ' tree, under which they do
not sit, whose branches they do not burn, and whose fruit
they do not eat.   Fusion of clans may be a possible explanation for such a transformation of the totem name." [1]

" Whether in its origin the institution of totemism had
any relation to religion or not, certain practices still survive
here and there among the Oraons to indicate that at a certain
period in the history of the tribe religion was intimately
associated with Oraon totemism.   So far as the actual
animals, plants, or other objects that form the totems of the
different Oraon clans are concerned, they no longer appear
to be objects of any definite religious observances unless the
taboos attached to the clan totems may have owed their

[1] S. C. Roy, *The Oraons of Chota Nagpur*, pp. 324 *sqq.*

origin to an appreciation and are of a certain *mana* or sacredness inherent in them.

" The totem-emblems of a few Oraon clans, however, still appear to receive divine honours and even sacrifices and offerings. Thus in the village of Amboa (within the Police Circle of Lohardaga) where the *Bhuinars* or descendants of the original Oraon founders of the village belong to the *ekka* or tortoise clan, one wooden image of a pig with two wooden images of the tortoise (said to be the offspring of the pig) are kept in the village priests' house and on the day preceding a *jatra* or dancing-tryst held periodically in the neighbourhood, the wooden images are ceremonially bathed in water, painted in appropriate colours and anointed with vermilion and offered a libation of rice-beer and the sacrifice of a chicken. Similar rites are observed with respect to two wooden images of tigers at village Jamgain (in the Police Circle of Lohardaga) where the Oraon *Bhuinars* belong to the Lakra or tiger clan and the wooden images of a fish (together with similar images of crocodiles) in the village Kanjia (Police Circle, Mandar) of which the Oraon *Bhuinars* belong to the Khalkho fish clan. And the images of their clan-totems are carried as fetishes to the *jatra* ground on the shoulders of young men. On their way to the *jatra* ground, these totem-symbols receive offerings of bits of various articles of merchandise from people carrying such merchandise for sale to the market or *jatra* fair. And in whichever Oraon village on their way the party happen to make a temporary halt, the images are placed on the village dancing-ground (*akhra*) and the Oraons of the village offer a libation of rice-beer and in some cases a chicken which is not, however, killed but is fastened to the wooden plank on which the images are carried. Such a chicken is released on the return of the party from the *jatra* ground, and may be taken away by anyone who likes. In some villages, before the party start for the *jatra* ground, a chicken is ceremonially fed on *arua* rice and set apart with a vow to offer it in sacrifice to the wooden or brass emblem of the village when the party return home with success in any fight that may ensue at the *jatra*.

" It has to be noted that in the majority of cases the

wooden or metal images nowadays carried to the *jatras* do not represent the totems of the present Bhuinhars or other Oraon residents of the village at all ; in most cases they appear to be emblems arbitrarily adopted in comparatively recent times according to whim or fancy or chance. In some of these cases, perhaps, they may represent the totems of the first Oraon settlers who have since been displaced by later immigrants ; but of this I have no positive evidence. In all cases, however, these and similar emblems connected with Oraon villages or *Parhas* (federations of villages) are believed to be connected with the ' luck ' (*ban-gi*) of the village or *parha* concerned, and receive divine honours and offerings." [1]

[1] S. C. Roy, *Oraon Religion and Customs.*

CHAPTER II

§ 1. *Totemism of the Bhaina*

THE Bhaina are a primitive tribe peculiar to the Central Provinces and found principally in the Bilaspur District and adjoining area, that is, in the wild tract of forest country between the Satpura Range and the south of the Chota. Nagpur Plateau.[1] The region has been called the Highlands of Central India, and in it a number of primitive tribes have been able to bid defiance to their enemies of the lowlands.

The Bhaina tribe is divided into a number of totem clans or septs, named after animals or plants. Such are Nag the cobra, Bagh the tiger, Chitwa the leopard, Gidha the vulture, Besra the hawk, Bendra the monkey, Kok or Lodha the wild dog, Bataria the quail, Durgachhia the black ant, and so on. Members of a clan will not injure the animal after which it is named, and if they see a corpse of their totem animal or hear of its death, they throw away an earthen cooking-pot and bathe and shave themselves as for one of the family. Members of the Baghchhal or tiger clan will, however, join in a beat for tiger though they are reluctant to do so. At weddings the Bhainas have a ceremony known as the *gotra* worship. The bride's father makes an image in clay of the bird or animal of the groom's clan and places it beside the marriage-post. The bridegroom worships the image, lighting a sacrificial fire before it, and offers to it the vermilion which he afterwards smears upon the forehead of

---

[1] R. V. Russell, *Tribes and Castes of the Central Provinces of India* (London, 1916), ii. 223.

the bride. At the bridegroom's house a similar image is made of the bride's totem, and on returning there after the wedding she worships this. Women are often tattooed with representations of their totem animal, and men swear by it as their most sacred oath. A similar respect is paid to the inanimate objects after which certain clans are named. Thus members of the Gawad or cowdung clan will not burn cowdung cakes for fuel ; and those of the Mircha clan do not use chillies. One clan is named after the sun, and when an eclipse of the sun occurs these perform the same formal rites of mourning as the others do on the death of their totem animal. Some of the groups have two divisions, male and female, which practically rank as separate clans. Instances of these are the Nagbans Andura and the Nagbans Mai or male and female cobra clans ; the Karsayal Singhara and Karsayal Mundi or stag and doe deer clans ; and the Baghchhal Andura and Baghchhal Mai or tiger and tigress clans. These may simply be instances of subdivisions arising, owing to the boundaries of the sept having become too large for convenience. In the Census of 1911 the number of the tribe was returned as seventeen thousand.[1]

§ 2. *Totemism of the Bhils*

The Bhils are another primitive tribe of mountaineers in the Central Provinces who retain a system of totemism, some account of which has been given in my earlier work.[2] At the present time the Bhils of the Central Provinces have only two subdivisions based on religion, the Muhammadan Bhils, who were forcibly converted to Islam during the time of Aurangzeb, and the remainder, who, though they retain many animistic beliefs and superstitions, have practically become Hindoos. The Muhammadan Bhils only number about three thousand out of twenty-eight thousand. Both classes are divided into septs or clans, generally named after plants or animals to which they still show reverence. Thus the Jamania clan, named after the *jaman* tree, will not cut or burn any part of this tree, and at their weddings the

[1] R. V. Russell, *op. cit.* ii. 228.
[2] *Totemism and Exogamy*, ii. 218 *sq.* ; iv. 292 *sq.*

dresses of the bride and bridegroom are taken and rubbed against the tree before being worn. Similarly, the Rohini clan worship the *rohan* tree, the Avalia clan the *aoula* tree, the Meheda clan the *bahera* tree, and so on. The Mori clan worship the peacock. They go into the jungle and look for the tracks of a peacock, and spreading a piece of red cloth before the footprint, lay their offerings of grain upon it. Members of this clan may not be tattooed, because they think that the splashes of colour on the peacock's feathers are tattoo-marks. Their women must veil themselves if they see a peacock, and they think that if any member of the clan irreverently treads on a peacock's footprints he will fall ill. The Ghodmarya (horse-killer) clan may not tame a horse nor ride it. The Masrya clan will not kill or eat fish. The Sanyan or cat clan have a tradition that one of their ancestors was once chasing a cat, which ran for protection under a cover that had been put over the stone figure of their goddess. The goddess turned the cat into stone and sat on it, and since then members of the clan will not touch a cat except to save it from harm, and they will not eat anything which has been touched by a cat. The Ghattaya clan worship the grinding mill at their weddings and also on festival days. The Solia clan, whose name is apparently derived from the sun, are split up into four subclans : the Ada Solia, who hold their weddings at sunrise ; the Japa Solia, who hold them at sunset ; the Taria Solia, who hold them when stars have become visible after sunset ; and the Tar Solia, who believe that their name is connected with cotton thread and wrap several skeins of raw thread round the bride and bridegroom at the wedding ceremony. The Moharia clan worship the local goddess at the village of Moharia in Indore State, who is known as the Moharia Mata ; at their weddings they apply turmeric and oil to the fingers of the goddess before rubbing them on the bride and bridegroom. The Maoli clan worship a goddess of that name in Barwano town. Her shrine is considered to be in the shape of a kind of grain-basket known as *kilia*, and members of the clan may never make or use baskets of this shape, nor may they be tattooed with representations of it.

A man may not marry in his own clan nor in the families of his mother's and grandmother's. The union of first cousins is thus prohibited, nor may girls be exchanged in marriage between two families. A man may not marry his wife's sister during his wife's lifetime. The Muhammadan Bhils permit a man to marry his maternal uncle's daughter, his first cousin, and though he may not marry his wife's sister he may keep her as a concubine.[1]

§ 3. Totemism of the Gonds

The Gonds are the principal tribe of the Dravidian family, and perhaps the most important of the non-Aryan or forest tribes in India. They belong properly to the Central Provinces, though some of them are found in Chota Nagpur and other parts of Bengal. They have a system of totemism, of which some account has been given.[2] A later and fuller account of it is given by Mr. R. V. Russell in his valuable work on the *Tribes and Castes of the Central Provinces of India*. He tells us that many of the Gond clans are named after animals and plants. Among the commonest clans in all districts are Markam, the mango tree ; Tekam, the teak tree ; Netam, the dog ; Irpachi, the *mahua* tree ; Tumrachi, the *tendu* tree ; Warkara, the wild cat, and so on. Generally the members of a clan do not kill or injure their totem animals; but the rule is not always observed, and in certain cases they have now some other object of veneration, possibly because they have forgotten the meaning of the clan name, or the object after which it is named has ceased to be sacred. Thus the Markam clan, though named after the mango, now venerate the tortoise, and this is also the case with the Netam clan in Bastar, though the clan is named after the dog. In Bastar a man revering the tortoise, though he will not catch the animal himself, will get one of his friends to catch it, and one who reveres the goat, if he wishes to kill a goat for a feast, will kill it not at his own house but at a friend's house. The meaning of the important clan names Marabi, Dhurwa, and Uika has not been ascertained, and the members of the clans do not know it. In Mandla the Marabi clan are divided into the Eti Marabi and Padi Marabi, named after

[1] R. V. Russell, *op. cit.* ii. 285 *sqq.*
[2] *Totemism and Exogamy*, ii. 222 *sqq.*

the goat and pig   The Eti or goat Marabi will not touch a goat nor sacrifice one to Bura Deo.   They say that once their ancestors stole a goat and were caught by the owner, when they put a basket over it and prayed Bura Deo to change it into a pig, which he obligingly did.   Therefore they sacrifice only pigs to Bura Deo, but apparently the Padi (pig) Marabi also both sacrifice and eat pigs.   The Dhurwa clan are divided into the Tumrachi and Nabalia Dhurwa, named after the tendu tree and the dwarf date-palm.   The Nabalia Dhurwas will not cut a dwarf date-palm nor eat its fruit. They worship Bura Deo in this tree instead of in the *saj* tree, making an iron doll to represent him and covering it with palm-leaves.

In Betul the Gonds explain the totemistic names of their clans by saying that some incident connected with the animal, tree or other object occurred to the ancestor or priest of the clan while they were worshipping at the Deo-khulla or god's place or threshing-floor.   The reason why these stories have been devised may be that the totem animals or plants have ceased to be revered on their own merits as ancestors or kinsmen of the clan, and it was therefore felt necessary to explain the clan name or sanctity attaching to the totem by associating it with the gods.   If this were correct the process would be analogous to that by which an animal or plant is first held sacred of itself, and, when this feeling begins to decay with some recognition of its true nature, it is associated with an anthropomorphic god in order to preserve its sanctity.   The following are some examples recorded by Mr. Ganga Prasad Khatri.   Some of the examples are not associated with the gods.

Gajjami, subclan of the Dhurwa clan.   From *gaj*, an arrow.   Their clan ancestor killed a tiger with an arrow.

Kusadya Dhurwa (Kosa, tasar silk cocoon).   The clan ancestor found a silk cocoon on the tree in which he worshipped his gods.

Kohkapath.   Kohka is the fruit of the *bhilawa* or marking-nut tree, and *path*, a kid.   The first ancestor worshipped his gods in a *bhilawa* tree and offered a kid to them.   Members of this clan do not eat the fruit or flowers of the *bhilawa* tree.

Jaglya.   One who keeps awake, or the awakener.   The

clan ancestor stayed awake the whole night in the Deo-khulla, or god's threshing-floor.

Guddam. Gudda is a place where a hen lays her eggs. The clan ancestor's hen laid eggs in the Deo-khulla.

Admachi (the *dhaura* tree). The clan ancestor worshipped his gods under a *dhaura* tree. Members of the clan do not cut this tree nor burn its wood.

Watka (a stone). Members of this clan worship five stones for their gods. Some say that the clan ancestors were young boys who forgot where the Deo-khulla was and therefore set up five stones and offered a chicken to them. As they did not offer the usual sacrifice of a goat, members of this clan abstain from eating goats.

Tumrecha Uika (the *tendu* tree). It is said that the original ancestor of this clan was walking in the forest with his pregnant wife. She saw some *tendu* fruit and longed for it and he gave it to her to eat. Perhaps the original idea may have been that she conceived through swallowing a *tendu* fruit. Members of this clan eat the fruit of the *tendu* tree, but do not cut the tree nor make any use of its leaves or branches.

Tumdan Uika. *Tumdan* is a kind of pumpkin or gourd. They say that this plant grows in their Deo-khulla. The members drink water out of this gourd in the house, but do not carry it out of the house.

Gadhamar Uika (Donkey slayer). Some say that the gods of the clan came to the Deo-khulla riding on donkeys, and others that the first ancestor killed a donkey in the Deo-khulla.[1]

A man may not marry in his own clan, nor in one which worships the same number of gods, in localities where the classification of clans according to the number of gods worshipped obtains. Intermarriage between clans which are *bhaiband* or brothers to each other is also prohibited. The marriage of first cousins is considered especially suitable. Formerly, perhaps, the match between a brother's daughter and sister's son was most common; this is held to be a survival of the matriarchate, when a man's sister's son was his heir. But the reason has now been generally forgotten,

[1] R. V. Russell, *op. cit.* iii. 67 *sqq.*

and the union of a brother's son and sister's daughter has also become customary, while, as girls are scarce and have to be paid for, it is the boy's father who puts forward his claim. Thus in Mandla and Bastar a man thinks he has a right to his sister's daughter for his son on the ground that his family has given a girl to her husband's family, and therefore they should give one back. The children of two sisters may not, it is said, be married, and a man may not marry his wife's elder sister, any aunt or niece, or his mother-in-law or her sister. But marriage is not prohibited between grandparents and grandchildren. If an old man marries a young wife and dies, his grandson will marry her if he is of proper age. In Bastar a man may marry his daughter's daughter or maternal grandfather's or grandmother's sister. He might not marry his son's daughter or paternal grandfather's sister, because they belong to the same clan as himself.[1]

§ 4. *Totemism of the Kharia*

The Kharia are a primitive Dravidian tribe found in the Central Provinces. A branch of the tribe inhabits Chota Nagpur. Both branches possess a system of totemism. The totemism of the Chota Nagpur Kharias has been described by me elsewhere.[2] In the Central Provinces the tribe is divided into totems and exogamous clans, which pay reverence to their totems. Thus members of the Kulu (tortoise), Kiro (tiger), Nag (cobra), Kankul (leopard), and Kuto (crocodile) clans abstain from killing their totem animal, fold their hands in obeisance when they meet it, and taking up some dust from the animal's track place it on their heads as a mark of veneration. Certain clans cannot wholly abstain from the consumption of their clan totem, so they make a compromise. Thus members of the Baa, or rice clan, cannot help eating rice, but they will not eat the scum which gathers over the rice as it is being boiled. Those of the Bilum or salt clan may not take up a little salt on one finger and suck it, but must always use two or more fingers for conveying salt to the mouth, presumably as a mark of respect. Members of the Suren or stone clan will not make

---

[1] R. V. Russell, *op. cit.* iii. 71 *sqq.*   [2] *Totemism and Exogamy*, ii. 295.

ovens with stones, but only with clods of earth. The tribe do not now think that they are actually descended from their totems, but tell stories accounting for the connection. Thus the Katang Kondai or bamboo clan say that a girl in the family of their ancestors went to cut bamboos and never came back. Her parents went out to search for her and heard a voice calling out from the bamboos, but could not find their daughter. Then they understood that the bamboo was of their own family and might not' be cut by them. The supposition is apparently that the girl was transformed into a bamboo.

Marriage between members of the same clan is forbidden, but the rule is not always observed. A brother's daughter may marry a sister's son, but not *vice versa*.[1]

§ 5. *Totemism of the Kols*

The Kols or Hos are a great tribe of Chota Nagpur which has given its name to the Kolarian family of tribes and languages. A branch of the tribe inhabits a district bordering on Chota Nagpur, in Bengal. Its system of totemism has been described in my earlier work.[2]

In the Central Provinces the Mandla Kols have a number of totemic clans. The Bargaiyan are really named after a village Bargaon, but they connect their name with the *bar* or banyan tree, and revere it. At their weddings a branch of this tree is laid on the roof of the marriage-shed, and the wedding-cakes are cooked in a fire made of the wood of the banyan tree and served to all the relations of the clan on its leaves. At other times they will not pluck a leaf or a branch from a banyan tree or even go beneath its shade. The Kathotia clan is named after *Kathota*, a bowl, but they revere the tiger. Bagheshwar Deo, the tiger-god, resides on a little platform in their verandas. They may not join in a tiger-beat nor sit up for a tiger over a kill. If they did sit up they think that the tiger would not come and would be deprived of his food, and all the members of their family would fall ill. If a tiger takes one of their cattle, they believe that there has been some neglect in their worship of him.

[1] R. V. Russell, *op. cit.* iii. 447 *sq.*　　[2] *Totemism and Exogamy*, ii. 294 *sq.*

They say that if one of them meets a tiger in the forest he will fold his hands and say, " Maharaj, let me pass," and the tiger will then go out of his way. If a tiger is killed within the limits of his village a Kathotia Kol will throw away his earthen pots as in mourning for a relative, have his head shaved, and feed a few men of his clan. The Katharia clan take their name from *kathri*, a mattress. A member of this clan may never have a mattress in his house nor wear clothes sewn in cross-pieces as mattresses are sewn. The word *kathri* (mattress) may never be mentioned before him, as he thinks some great misfortune would thereby happen to his family, but this belief is falling into abeyance. The name of the Mudia or Mudrundia clan is said to mean shaven head, but they apparently revere the white *kumrha* or gourd, perhaps because it has some resemblance to a shaven head. They give a white gourd to a woman on the third day after she has borne a child, and her family then do not eat this vegetable for three years. At the expiration of the period the head of the family offers a chicken to Dulha Deo, frying it with the feathers left on the head, and eating the head and feet himself. Women may not join in this sacrifice. The Kumraya clan revere the brown *kumhra* or gourd. They grow this vegetable on the thatch of their house-roof, and from the time of planting till the fruits have been plucked they do not touch it. The Bhuwar clan are named after *bhu or bhumi*, the earth. They must always sleep on the earth and not on cots. Other clans are Nathunia, a nose-ring ; Karpatia, a kind of grass ; and Binjhwar, so named from the tribe of that name.

Marriage within the clan is prohibited, but violations of this rule are not infrequent. Outside the clan a man may marry any woman except the sisters of his mother or step-mother. Where, as in some districts, the clans have been forgotten, marriage is forbidden between those relatives to whom the sacramental cakes are distributed at a wedding.[1]

§ 6. *Totemism of the Majhwar*

The Majhwar are a small mixed tribe who have appar-

[1] R. V. Russell, *op. cit.* iii. 510 *sq.*

ently originated from the Gonds, Mundas, and Kawars. They have no subdivisions, but a number of totemic clans. Those of the Bhainsa or buffalo clan are split into the Lotan and Singhan subclans, *lotan* meaning a place where buffaloes wallow and *singh* a horn. The Lotan Bhainsa say that their ancestor was born in a place where a buffalo had wallowed, and the Singhan Bhainsa that their ancestor was born while his mother was holding the horn of a buffalo. These clans consider the buffalo sacred and will not yoke it to a plough or cart, though they drink its milk. They think that if one of them killed a buffalo their clan would become extinct. The Baghani Majhwars, named after the *bagh* or tiger, think that a tiger will not attack any member of their clan unless he has committed an offence entailing temporary excommunication from caste. Unless this offence has been expiated his relationship with the tiger as head of his clan is in abeyance, and the tiger will eat him as he would any other stranger. If a tiger meets a member of the clan who is free from sin, he will run away. When the Baghani clan hear that any Majhwar has killed a tiger they purify their houses by washing them with cowdung and water. Members of the Khoba or peg clan will not make a peg or drive one into the ground. Those of the Dumar or fig-tree clan say that their first ancestor was born under this tree. They consider the tree to be sacred and never eat its fruit, and worship it once a year. Members of the clan named after the *shiroti* tree worship the tree every Sunday.

Marriage within the clan is prohibited and for three generations between persons related through females.[1]

§ 7. *Totemism of the Nahals*

The Nahals are a forest tribe who are probably a mixture of Bhils and Korkus. They have totemic exogamous clans. Those of the Kasa clan worship a tortoise and also a plate of bell-metal, which is their family god. They never eat off a bell-metal plate except on one day in the month of Magh (January), when they worship it. The members of the Nagbel clan worship the betel-vine or " snake-creeper," and refrain

[1] R. V. Russell, *op. cit.* iv. 151 *sq.*

from chewing betel leaves, and they also worship the Nag or cobra and do not kill it, thus having a sort of double totem. The Bhawaria clan, named after the *bhaunr* or black bee, do not eat honey, and if they see a person taking the honeycomb from a nest they will run away. The Khadia clan worship the spirits of their ancestors enshrined in a heap of stones (*khad*), or according to another account they worship a snake which sits on a heap of pebbles. The Surja clan worship Surya or the sun by offering him a fowl in the month of Pus (December–January), and some members of the clan keep a fast every Sunday. The Saoner clan worship the *san* or flax plant.

Marriage is prohibited between members of the same clan, but there are no other restrictions and first cousins may marry.[1]

§ 8. *Totemism of the Parja*

The Parja are a small tribe, originally an offshoot of the Gonds, who reside in the centre and east of the Bastar State. They have exogamous totemic clans, as Bagh a tiger, Kachhim a tortoise, Bokda a goat, Netam a dog, Gohi a big lizard, Pandki a dove, and so on. If a man kills accidentally the animal after which his clan is named the earthen cooking-pots of his household are thrown away, the clothes are washed, and the house is purified with water in which the bark of the mango tree has been steeped. This is done in sign of mourning, as it is thought that such an act will bring misfortune. If a man of the snake clan kills a snake accidentally he places a piece of new yarn on his head, praying for forgiveness, and deposits the body on an ant-hill, where snakes are supposed to live. If a man of the goat clan eats goat's flesh it is thought he will become blind at once. A Parja will not touch the dead body of his totem animal, and if he sees anyone killing or teasing it when alive he will go away out of sight. It is said that a man of the Kachhim (tortoise) clan once found a tortoise while he was on a journey, and, leaving it undisturbed, passed on. When the tortoise died it was reborn in the man's belly and troubled him greatly, and since then every Parja is liable to be afflicted in the same

[1] R. V. Russell, *op. cit.* iv. 259 *sq.*

way in the side of the abdomen, the disease which is produced being in fact enlarged spleen. The tortoise told the man that as he had left it lying by the road, and had not devoted it to any useful purpose, he was afflicted in this way. Hence, when a man of the Kachhim clan finds a tortoise nowadays, he gives it to somebody else who can cut it up. The story is interesting as a legend of the origin of spleen ; but has apparently been invented as an excuse for killing the sacred animal.

Marriage is prohibited in theory between members of the same clan. But as the number of clans is rather small, the rule is not adhered to, and members of the same clan are permitted to marry so long as they do not come from the same village ; the original rule of exogamy being perhaps thus exemplified.[1]

§ 9. *Totemism of the Rautia*

The Rautia are a cultivating caste of the Chota Nagpur plateau, but they are also found in the Central Provinces. The tribe has totemic clans, and retain some veneration for their totems. Those of the Bagh or tiger clan throw away their earthen pots on hearing of the death of a tiger. Those of the sand or bull clan will not castrate bullocks themselves, and must have this operation performed on their plough-bullocks by others. Those of the Kansi clan formerly, according to their own account, would not root up the *kans* grass growing in their fields, but now they no longer object to do so Other clans are Tithi, a bird, Bira, a hawk, Barwan, a wild dog, and so on.

Marriage is forbidden within the clan, but is permitted between the children of a brother and a sister or of two sisters.[2]

§ 10. *Totemism of the Bhuinars*

Around Pathalgaon in Udaipur State the Bhuinar are divided into a number of exogamous clans (*gotras*), which are definitely totemic. Among the totems are Dumen (the dumen tree), Murhi (a vegetable), Sali (a tree), Nag (the cobra), Sukra (spear grass), Maji, Chitki, Raki and Ali. In

[1] R. V. Russell, *op. cit.* iv. 373 *sq.*   [2] R. V. Russell, *op. cit.* iv. 481 *sq.*

Jashpur State, the clans seem to be different. The following totems are there found : Ahind (eel), Harhuria (a species of snake), Kirketta (a species of bird), Goha (gecko), Beng (frog), Thithio, Tope, Saras (various kinds of birds), and Chorant (spear grass). Veneration of the totem is observed in various ways ; for instance people of the Chorant clan take a ceremonial bath if there is a forest fire. It may be noticed that in Jashpur the totem names are the same for many neighbouring tribes.[1]

§ 11. *Totemism of the Pandos*

The Pando tribe is found in several villages of Udaipur State and probably elsewhere. The Pandos acknowledge relationship with no other castes or tribes, but there are two sub-tribes known as Utarha and Surgujiha. They have exogamous clans *(gotras)*, and give the following names of them :—Jau, Takey, Naupan, Jissey, Karwayhan, Kanhariya, and Jannoo. Additional names of clans found in various villages are Baren (fig tree), Ithi (an insect), Kirketta (a bird), Gohity (a gecko, a species of lizard), and one or two others. Many of these clans are evidently totemic in their origin, but the history of the names of some of them is unknown. People of the *baren* clan will not eat figs, those of the *gohity* clan will not eat the gecko, those of the *kirketta* will not eat the kirketta bird, and so on. Information regarding the clans is given to the tribes by their Baigas or Goonias, that is, their priests.[2]

[1] *Census of India*, 1931, vol. i. Part iii., ed. by J. H. Hutton (Delhi, 1935), p. 90. [2] *Census of India*, 1931, vol. i. Part iii. p. 86.

CHAPTER III

TOTEMISM IN THE BOMBAY PRESIDENCY

MANY survivals of totemism in the Bombay Presidency have been discovered and recorded by Mr. R. E. Enthoven in his standard work on *The Folklore of Bombay*.[1] On this subject he writes : " The most interesting feature of the primitive religion in the Presidency is to be found in the widespread survival of totemism. Neither the Vedas nor subsequent orthodox Hindu writings contain any mention of the worship of trees, animals, and other objects in connection with a belief that they are in the position of ancestors, and that all who worship the same object should refrain from inter-marrying. It may be assumed that the survival in full vigour of the worship of totems in the south of the Presidency, as well as the unmistakeable traces of a former totemistic organisation found throughout the Deccan and Konkan, are indications of a culture that is not Aryan in origin. Recent research has brought to light a number of totem divisions among the Marathas and the occupational castes of the Deccan allied to the Marathas by common descent. In full vigour, the totemism of Bombay means the worship of a tree, animal, etc., on important occasions such as marriage, the first occupation of a new house, or the setting-up of a thresh-ing-floor at the commencement of harvest. The totem must not be injured by its adherents, they must not use its products, *e.g.* the fruit or wood of a totem tree, or the ivory from the tusk of an elephant totem. The ban on intermarriage between those worshipping the same totem is complete in the Kanarese districts, where the system is still in full vigour.

[1] Oxford, 1924.

Over eighty totems have been identified. The totem is there known as a *bali*. In the Deccan and Konkan the totem organization that formerly prevailed has been overlaid by a system of family stocks, but the totem object, known as a *devak*, is still worshipped. In many instances it still acts as a barrier against intermarriage, though this is by no means invariably the case. Campbell, who drew attention to the existence of these totems among Marathas of the Deccan, in his Kolhapur volume of the *Bombay Gazetteer*, described them as 'marriage guardians.' Subsequent research has discovered over 80 *devaks* in the Deccan and Konkan, and leaves little doubt that they possess, or once possessed, all the essential attributes of a real totem.

" It has already been remarked that totemism is not, so far as we are aware, a social organization known to the Aryans when they entered India. On the other hand, Risley and Russell, writing of the tribes and castes of Bengal and the Central Provinces, show that the primitive tribes in those areas possess numerous totems that are not only similar to those discovered in Bombay, but in some instances are identical with them. We have, therefore, in the totem trees and animals the undoubted remains of an early form of primitive religion, unknown to the Aryan invaders. Investigations of the subject in Bombay have so far only touched the surface. Further study offers the promise of interesting developments." [1]

" Among the more primitive elements of the population in India generally, the worship of trees, animals, weapons, and implements of industry on the occasion of marriage, and in such fashion as tends to justify the inference that the object worshipped is regarded as an ancestor, is common and widespread. In the Bombay Presidency these objects are known as *devaks* in the Deccan and as *balis* in the Karnatak, and are a common feature of many tribes and castes in the Deccan, Konkan, and Karnatak. The significant points of this *devak* worship are :—

" (1) Those who own the same *devak* may not intermarry.

" (2) The *devak* must in no circumstances be injured by those who acknowledge it. It and its products, *i.e.* the fruit

[1] R. E. Enthoven, *op. cit.* pp. 18 *sqq.*

if it is a tree, or the parts of it if it is an animal, *e.g.* the tusks of an elephant if the elephant is the *devak*, must be treated with respect, not used for food or ornament, or injured in any way.

" The preparation of a complete list of the *devaks* and *balis* of the Bombay Presidency would necessitate a special inquiry. A large number, however, will be found in the pages of *Tribes and Castes of Bombay*,[1] under the article on Marathas. It will be sufficient to give a few examples here.

TREES AND PLANTS

1. Mango.
2. Babul (*Acacia arabica*).
3. Bel (*Aegle Marmelos*).
4. Bor (*Zizyphus Jujuba*).
5. Chinch (*Tamarind*).
6. Kadamb (*Anthocephalus Cadamba*).
7. Rui (*Calotropis gigantea*).
8. Shami (*Prosopis spicigera*).
9. Nim (*Melia Azadirachta*).
10. Banyan tree and others of the fig class.

ANIMALS AND BIRDS

1. Horse.
2. Mouse deer.
3. Pig.
4. Eagle.
5. Tortoise.
6. Crow pheasant.
7. Buffalo.
8. Peacock.
9. Cobra.
10. Goat.
11. Elephant.
12. Elk (*sambhar*).
13. Monkey.
14. Porcupine.
15. Wolf.
16. *Chital* (*Axis maculata*).

IMPLEMENTS OF INDUSTRY

1. Spinning-whorl (*chat*).
2. Axe.
3. Potter's patter.
4. Oil-mill.
5. Blowpipe ⎱ of the goldsmith.
6. Pincers ⎰
7. Knife.
8. Sword.

" The following are instances illustrative of the abstention, on the part of those who worship such *devaks*, from using or injuring the same, as well as their products, in any way :

" Those of the elephant *devak* will not injure an elephant

---

[1] R. E. Enthoven, *The Tribes and Castes of Bombay*, 3 vols. (Bombay, 1922).

or wear ornaments of ivory made from its tusks. Those of the elk *devak* will not injure the elk. Members of the tiger group are very averse to injuring a tiger, as for instance the Bhils, amongst whom the Vaghs or tiger section worship the tiger and grieve when they hear of a tiger being killed. They are said to prostrate themselves when they encounter a tiger. Among the Kunbis, the Shelar or goat section will not eat the flesh of a goat, and those of the More or peacock section abstain from eating the flesh of a peacock. Among Bhandaris, the Padwals, or snake-gourd section, will not eat the snake-gourd. Those who respect the Banyan tree as a *devak* will not use the leaves of this tree for any purpose. Certain families among Kunbis, of the Banyan section, will not even take food from leaf-plates fashioned from Banyan leaves. Maratha traders of the Jack-fruit tree section will not eat the Jack-fruit. Similar instances can be multiplied indefinitely.

" It has been noted that the special occasion for the worship of the *devak* is marriage. It is, however, a common custom to worship it also—

(1) on the occasion of occupying a new house for the first time ;

(2) at the time of preparing the threshing-floor in the field when the harvest has been gathered ;

(3) on the occasion of performing the thread-girding ceremony.

" If the houses of the bride and bridegroom are in the same village or town, the installing, or setting-up for worship, of the *devak* takes place on the marriage day. Otherwise it takes place two or three days previously. In installing the *devak* the first step is to worship the household gods. The company then repair to Maruti's temple, the bride carrying a platter containing the *devak* or an image of it and an offering of food. Here the *devak* is formally worshipped, and then brought back to the bride's house, where it is either affixed to the marriage booth or placed with the household gods until after the completion of the marriage ceremony. Sometimes, after visiting Maruti's temple with the *devak*, the bridal party repair to the village potter's house, where the *devak* is again worshipped. This is an indication of the primitive nature of the rite.

" Another method of *devak* worship is as follows : A small quantity of rice is put into a winnowing fan and with it six small sticks of the *devak*, each covered with Mango leaves and cotton thread. These are worshipped as deities. Near the winnowing-fan is kept an earthen or copper vessel filled with rice, turmeric, red powder, betel-nuts, sweet-balls made of wheat flour, *ghi*, and sugar ; and on the top of the vessel is a small sprig of the *devak* and a coconut covered with cotton thread. This vessel is also worshipped as a deity, and offerings of sweet eatables are made to it. The winnowing-fan is taken to the temple of Maruti. After the worship of this vessel, the regular ceremony of holy-day blessing is performed. Twenty-seven mothers, or village and local deities, represented by betel nuts, are consecrated in a new winnowing-fan or a bamboo basket. Seven mothers are made of Mango leaves, six of which contain *Durva* (*Cynodon Dactylon*) grass, and the seventh *Darbha* (*Eragrostis cynosuroides*) grass. Each of them is bound with a raw cotton thread separately. They are worshipped along with a copper vessel as mentioned above. The copper vessel is filled with rice, betel-nuts, turmeric, etc., a sprig of Mango leaves is placed on the vessel and a coconut is put over it. The vessel is also bound with a cotton thread. Sandal paste, rice, flowers, and *Durva* (*Cynodon Dactylon*) grass are required for its worship. An oil-lamp is waved round the *devak*, the parents and the boy or the girl whose thread or marriage ceremony is to be performed. An unwidowed woman (*suvasini*) is called and requested to wave this lamp, and the silver coin which is put into the lamp by the parents is taken by her. The father takes the winnowing-fan and the mother takes the copper vessel, and they are carried from the marriage booth to the *devak* consecrated in the house. A lighted lamp is kept continually burning near this *devak* till the completion of the ceremony. After completion of the thread or marriage ceremony the *devak* is again worshipped, and the ceremony comes to an end. The deity in the *devak* is requested to depart on the second or the fourth day from the date of its consecration. No mourning is observed during the period the *devak* remains installed in the house.

" In the Deccan, on the day before the marriage, the

twig of the *devak* is brought home and worshipped. It is then carried, first to Maruti's temple and then to a potter's. After worship at both places, it is brought to be tied to a post of the *Mandap*." [1]

The worship thus paid to *devaks* or *balis* seems to prove that they are not common totems, but that, if, as appears probable, they once were so, they are now in process of developing into a sort of minor domestic divinities. It is not surprising to find old totems thus passing into new gods. We have seen indications of a similar promotion of totems in Tikopia. Gods are subject to evolution like animals and men.

[1] R. E. Enthoven, *op. cit.* pp. 208 *sqq.*

CHAPTER IV

TOTEMISM IN MYSORE

OF totemism in Mysore I have given an account in *Totemism and Exogamy*.[1] That account was based on the preliminary issue of H. V. Nanjundayya's *The Ethnographic Survey of Mysore* (Bangalore, 1907). It has since been repeated by Mr. L. K. Ananthakrishna Iyer, in the first volume of his work, *The Mysore Tribes and Castes* (Mysore, 1935), pp. 246 *sqq.*, where it will be more accessible to students than in the preliminary reports from which I drew it. I need not repeat it here.

[1] *Totemism and Exogamy*, ii. 269 *sqq.*

CHAPTER V

TRACES OF TOTEMISM IN THE PUNJAB

THE Punjab has long been the gateway through which the tide of invasion has, age after age, flowed into India from the west. We need not therefore expect to find in it at the present day any of those primitive Dravidian tribes which, elsewhere in India, behind the safe barriers of their mountains and forests, have retained their primitive systems of totemism to the present time. However, some traces of totemism survive in the taboos observed by various sections (*got*) of the Chuhra, the despised and out-caste sweepers and scavengers, who occupy the lowest rung on the social ladder. On this subject I will quote the evidence of Mr. H. A. Rose in his *Glossary of the Tribes and Castes of the Punjab and North-West Frontier Province* (Lahore, 1911), vol. ii. pp. 188 *sq.* :—

" The Gil will not eat *bataun*, the egg-plant (*bhata bart*) : the Lute do not eat hare or rabbit : the Kanare abstain from cloves : the Sahotre refuse to look on a tiger ; at marriages, however, they make the images of a tiger which the women worship : the Bhatti will not sit on a bench of boards or bricks : no Chuhra will eat *seh*, or hedgehog.

" The Sarwan Chuhras do not dye cloth with *kasumba*, saffron, and will only use thatch for their roofs. In Dera Ghazi Khan the different sections reverence different animals, *i.e.* the Sahota respect the lion, the Athwal or Uthwal the camel, and one section the porcupine, while bricks are said to be reverenced by the Gil, men bowing and women veiling their faces before them. Thus the Sindhu *muhin* or *got* respects indigo ; the Kandiara respects the horned rat ;

while the Khokhar *got* is said to avoid eating *bharta*, *i.e.* anything roasted on a fire. The Khokhar *got* is also said to abstain from the flesh of dead animals as well as from eating the heart, which all other Chuhras will eat.

" The flesh of the hare is also avoided by Chuhras generally—a tabu explained by the following legend :—Once a Chuhra by chance killed a calf, and hid it under a basket, but its owner tracked it to the Chuhra's house. The Chuhra declared that the basket contained a hare, and when it was opened it was found that the calf had turned into a hare, so from that time all the Chuhras have given up eating hare. Some, however, do not abide by this rule. In Kangra it is said that once a hare sought Balmik's protection, and thus the tabu arose. In Montgomery the avoidance of hare's flesh is ascribed to the influence of the Makhdum Jahanian of Sher Shah, those who are not his followers disregarding the prohibition. In Dera Ghazi Khan the current legend is that once Bala Shah, the ancestor of the Chuhras, and Mullah Nur, the Mirasi, were in God's *dargah* or court. The latter asked Bala Shah not to sweep, whereupon a quarrel arose and Bala Shah struck the bard with his broom, knocking out his right eye. Mullah Nur appealed to God and produced a hare as his witness—so now the sweepers do not eat hare's flesh. In Gurgaon, however, the prohibition is said to be confined to the Sus Gohar *got*, or, according to another account, to the Balgher *got*. In Maler Kotla it is confined to the Sahota *got*. About Leiah, women are said to eat the hare, but not men."

BOOK V

TOTEMISM IN AFRICA

§ 1. *Totemism of the Basuto (Sotho) and Nguni (Angoni)*

THE latest account of totemism among the Basuto or Sotho, as the name appears to be given more correctly, is contained in the following passage, which I extract from *The Bantu-Speaking Tribes of South Africa*.[1] " Most offshoots of the Nguni group, such as the Southern Transvaal Ndebele, the Swazi, the Rhodesian Ndebele, and the Ngoni of Nyasaland and Tanganyika, have preserved the same fundamental social system. But there are one or two new principles which must be noted. Among the Southern Transvaal Ndebele, each *isibongo*, or clan, has a special species of animal linked with it, known as its *zila* or taboo, which may not be named or eaten or used by the members of that clan. This feature has undoubtedly been copied from the surrounding Sotho tribes."[2]

" In all the Sotho tribes we find a wider grouping which cuts across the limits of the tribes. The members of such a wider group (for which there is no special native term) all regard themselves as intimately bound up, in some mystical way, with some species of animal or natural object, known as their *seano* (object of reverence), *sereto* (honour), *seila* (taboo), or *seboko* (praise-name). The name of this animal or object is used as a ceremonial or laudatory form of address, just as is the *isibongo* of the Nguni tribes. There are special myths telling how each group originally obtained the *seano*, and all the members of a group have to observe various taboos and other usages in connection with the animal or object.

[1] Ed. by I. Shapera (London, 1937).   [2] *Op. cit.* p. 86.

Formerly,. if it was an animal, no one of that group might eat its flesh, use its skin, or even touch it, lest some serious misfortune befall him.   Still less would he dare kill it, unless it was harmful and did manifest damage, and in that case he had to be ceremonially purified afterwards.   There is no bar to marriage of people having the same *seano*, but in cases of mixed marriage the children take the *seano* of their father. There also does not appear to be any social solidarity among the members of such a group.   Frequently they may be scattered over many different tribes, as in the case of those whose *seano* is the crocodile (*kwena*) ;   they are found all over the Sotho area.   On the other hand, a single tribe can also include members of many different *seano* groups.   In a single Ngwato ward, the following *seano* are to be found :— *kwena* (crocodile) ;   *moyo* (heart) ;   *tlou* (elephant) ;   *phuti* (duiker) ;   *nare* (buffalo) ;   *kxabo* (ape) ;   *tau* or *sebata* (lion) ; *kubu* (hippopotamus) ;   *kolobe* (boar).   Sometimes a group, or part of a group, would for some historical or political motive discard its existing *seano* and adopt a new one, with a corresponding change in the taboos which it had to observe."[1]

§ 2. *Totemism of the Bushmen of the Kalahari Desert, the Hottentots, and the Bechuanas*

Totemism was discovered among the Bushmen of the Kalahari Desert by Mr. S. S. Dornan, who found it also among the Hottentots of the Orange and Vaal Rivers, and among the Bechuanas, among the last of whom it had been well known before.   I will extract Mr. Dornan's notices of the institution in his own words.   Speaking of the Bushmen, he says :   " Totemism existed amongst them to a slight degree, but was not nearly so elaborate as amongst the Bantu or the Australians.   A man of the Eland clan would not marry a woman of his own clan as a rule, neither would he kill nor eat the animal if he could help it." [2]

" Most of the clans (of the Bushmen) are still further subdivided, sometimes on a totemistic basis, as the Hiech-ware Masarwas of the Sansokwe River are the Koha Kee or

[1] *Op. cit.* pp. 91 *sq.*
[2] S. S. Dornan, *Pigmies and*   *Bushmen of the Kalahari* (London, 1925), p. 55.

zebra clan, those of the Tuli river are the Du Kee or eland
clan, and so on, while the Madenassena are the Pidi Kee or
goat clan, and the Khabo are the Khabo Kee or monkey
clan." [1]

" Marriage (among the Bushmen) takes place within the
clan, that is, a man can take another woman of the same
clan, but she must not have the same totem as himself, or
bear the same surname, for all members of the same totem
bore that as a surname. In the same clan there might be
several different totem families. Totemism is not well developed amongst the wild Bushmen. It is only in its initial
stages, and so far as I know, or have learned, was never very
rigidly carried out. According to the Bushmen themselves
some tribes had none of it at all." [2]

" Among the Kalahari Bushmen totemism is not highly
developed. . . . The Bushmen are too much children of the
wild to have an advanced system of totemism. Some call
themselves the Zebra clan, as those of the Sansokwe river,
others the Eland clan, or the Duiker clan, while the Madenassena Bushmen call themselves the Goat clan. These latter
are partially tame Bushmen. While as a rule they avoid
killing and eating the totem animal, or reject certain portions
of it when eating, as the Duiker clan may eat all of that
animal except the heart ; still, if pressed by extreme hunger
they will not scruple to dispense with even this restriction.
I have heard of a clan, whose totem was the wild buffalo,
who did not scruple to eat any portion of an ox, although they
looked upon oxen as tame buffaloes. Thus taboo is by no
means strict with the Kalahari Bushmen." [3]

Again, speaking of the Hottentots, Mr. Dornan says :
" When a man wanted to marry he had to go outside his
own clan ; he was obliged to give presents to the relatives
of the bride, just as the Bantu do. Some of the clans along
the Orange and Vaal rivers were named after various animals,
as the Springboks, Scorpions, Wild Cats, Zebras and Hippos.
Thus a member of the Scorpion clan could not marry a
Scorpion, but marry a Wild Cat or a Zebra. Though this
custom does not absolutely prove totemism, I think, as in the

[1] S. S. Dornan, *op. cit.* p. 68.   [3] S. S. Dornan, *op. cit.* p. 161.
[2] S. S. Dornan, *op. cit.* p. 128.

case of the Bushmen, it was the beginning of a system of totemism, which had not developed very far." [1]

Once more, writing of the Bechuanas, Mr. Dornan observes : " The *seboko* (pina), or tribal emblem of the Bahlaping is the fish, of the Baphuti the duiker, of the Bakuena the crocodile, of the Batlokwa the wild cat, of the Baphiri the hyena, and so on. All these little clans are Bechuanas, but each has its own *seboko*, tribal emblem or totem." [2] " A young man could not marry a girl with the totem of his own clan, that is, Wild Cat could not marry Wild Cat, but Wild Cat might marry Porcupine, or Wild Vine, and so on." [3]

§ 3. *Totemism of the Bavenda*

The Bavenda are a Bantu tribe who occupy approximately a third of the inhabited territory of the Zoutpansberg district in the Northern Transvaal. They have a system of totemism ; but it is in a decadent condition. Of this subject Mr. Stayt, who has published an excellent monograph on the tribe, gives us the following account, in which he speaks throughout of the totem-clan as a sib.

" In addition to being a member of a patriarchal family and of a strong matrilineal group, every Muvenda [4] belongs also to a sib, *mutupo*. These sibs were at one time exogamous and of a totemic character ; they are now broken down and have been replaced by the extended family. As the members of a sib increased in numbers small families began to break away from the original stem and to start independent groups in different localities. These new groups often retained the original name of their sib, while gradually ignoring its peculiar character. As the connexion with the original stem grew more remote, the rule of exogamy also lapsed. Many old men still express horror at the thought of a marriage between a man and woman of the same sib, considering such a union to be incestuous, all siblings to them being brothers and sisters. Among the younger people, however, provided the interested parties live some distance

---

[1] S. S. Dornan, *op. cit.* p. 216.
[2] S. S. Dornan, *op. cit.* p. 244.
[3] S. S. Dornan, *op. cit.* pp. 277 *sq.*
[4] Muvenda is the singular of Bavenda.

apart and cannot trace genealogical relationship, these unions frequently occur.

" Members of a sib are called by the name of some animal, plant, or object, between which and themselves they conceive there is an intimate relationship, and which is always regarded by them with considerable respect. It is difficult to collect accurate information concerning the various sibs and sub-sibs and their totems. The people seem reluctant and almost afraid to mention their sib names, and there are few men who have any knowledge of more than five or six. The difficulty is increased still further by the fact that there are different methods of answering a question about the sib. When possible the name of the totemic animal or object is avoided and the praise-name of the group substituted, or the name of one of the original ancestors, or the name of the elder sister of the headman of the sib, or that of the locality with which the sib is chiefly associated. A man, in taking an oath, always uses the name of his *mutupo*. Many sibs are commonly called by the name of the totem animal with the prefix *vha* ; *e.g.* Vha Dau are the people of the lion. Others have the word *ila* interpolated between the prefix and the name of the totem ; *e.g. Vha-ila-mbudzi* are the people forbidden the goat. A man has no objection to eating animals which are taken to another sib, but he usually respects his wives' totems and avoids eating them in their presence, or conforms with the required ritual behaviour. A man whose totem is the pigeon will frighten away any pigeon on his premises to avoid its being killed, but if he catches one in a trap accidentally he is not unduly worried, but gives it to a friend belonging to a different sib to eat. Every sib has one or more honorific phrases, *tshikodo*, associated with it. The *tshikodo* is addressed to a chief when entering a village or when he has performed a noteworthy action ; it is often used by a visitor in greeting him as a sign of respect and politeness. A father may reply to the greeting of his child, using the sib *tshikodo*. A woman may use the words in thanking a man for a service that he has rendered her. . . .

" The following sibs are found in Vendaland to-day :—

" (1) *Vha Dau* (people of the lion) have their sacred

mountain at Maungani. The totem animals of this sib are lions, leopards and all felines.

" (2) *Vha Kwebo* (people of the dove) have traditional homes on the mountains at Tshiendeulu and Luonde. The totem animals of the *Vha Kwebo* are the dove and the pig.

" (3) *Ndou* (elephant) (the sib who tabu the elephant) have traditional sacred homes at Tshiruluuluni, Fundudzi, Thengwe, Ha Manenzhe, and Kokwani. The members of the sib who come from Kokwani are also forbidden to eat the small figs from the root of the fig-tree.

" (4) *Ma Khwinde*, or *Vha-ila-mbudzi* (the people who tabu the goat) have their ancestral home at Dzata. The Ma Khwinde totem animal is the goat, which may not be eaten unless it is eaten with a special ritual. The skin on the goat's tail must be peeled back and the tail cut off at the root ; all blood must be washed off and the animal left standing for a short time before it is killed by having its throat cut. All the important chiefs belong to this, the largest and most honoured of all Venda sibs. Chief Mphaphuli, whose ancestors were not Ma Khwinde (I was unable to discover to what sib they originally belonged), now claims to be a Ma Khwinde, distinguishing his section of the sib by calling it *Gutame*, the name of one of his father's sisters.

" There are many other alternative names and praise-names applied to branches. The great praise-name *Singo* (elephant's trunk) is used in addressing an important chief. . . .

" (5) *Vha Laudzi*, with their sacred mountains at Vhu-lorwa, Tshingani, and Lwamondo, have no actual totem animal or object ; they are forbidden to work in their gardens on the day after they first see the new moon. Those from Lwamondo are of Ba Sutho stock, from Palabora. Another section of this sib has its mountains at Masia and Tsianda ; they have adopted the goat as their totem and practise all the Ma Khwinde tabus and are probably of Ba Thonga stock.

" (6) *Vha Dau* (2) (People of the Lion). There are several unrelated sections of this sib, all having for their totem animals the lion and all felines. . . .

" (7) *Vhatwamamba*, with its important branch sib the *Vha Leya*, have their ancestral home at Tshivhula in the

Blaanberg ; they were originally of Sutho stock.   It is tabu for members of this sib to eat anything that has touched the cooking-stones by the fire.   If they are to eat a sheep, it must be stabbed in the back, and while it is dying one of its forelegs must be skinned.   They are also forbidden to eat snails.   The Bavenda used to carry salt in snail-shells, so that it was tabu for members of this sib to eat anything which had been cooked with salt.

" (8) *Vha Nyai*, now a Venda sib, were originally a group of people living north of the Limpopo.   There are two sections of this sib ; one section may not eat sheep unless the shoulder has been cut off before the animal is dead ; the other section may not eat porridge that has been touched by the handle-end of the porridge-stick.

" (9) *Vha Khomolo* are a small sib, with their ancestral mountain in Southern Rhodesia. Their totem animal is the buffalo, and they may not eat the heart of the buffalo or the hoof of cattle.

" (10) *Mbedzi*.   This is a large sib, probably one of the earliest arrivals in the Zoutpansberg from Southern Rhodesia. This group occupies the extreme east of Vendaland and has given its sib name to that part of the country.   The Mbedzi totem animal is the crocodile, and all river animals are also tabu to them.   There is a tradition among the old Ma Khwinde people forbidding their men to marry women of the Mbedzi sib, as such unions are supposed to result in the formation of disfiguring growths on the faces of the husbands. I could obtain no history of this tabu, which is gradually being allowed to lapse.

" (11) *Vhafu-a-madi* (Dead of the water).   This was at one time a praise-name of the Vha-Kwebo sib, but is now the name of a separate sib, which has completely severed its connexion with the Vha Kwebo.   It is tabu for a member of this sib to eat from the porridge-stick, which must always be put into a pot of water as soon as porridge is ready.

" (12) *Vha Dzivhani* (At the pool).   This sib, like a section of the Vha Dau, is supposed to have been one of the Ba Ngoni sibs.   It is tabu for its members to drink the water of the Mutali river where it runs into Lake Funduzi.

" (13) *Vha Pfumbe*.   Most of the Bavenda who are now

living in Southern Rhodesia are called Vha Pfumbe ; many of them are descended from members of Mphephu's following who remained in Southern Rhodesia when Mphephu returned to Zoutpansberg after his exile. They are now considered as a separate Venda sib.

" There are among the Bavenda some families among whom there is a definite connexion between the original ancestor and the totem. Nemaungani, of the Vha Dau sib, whose totem animals are lions and all felines, believes that his first ancestor was transformed into a leopard and still accompanies him wherever he goes, stalking beside him invisible, but always alert and ready to kill his enemies ; he is often called Nemaungani vha Nngwe (of the leopard) on this account. Chief Lwamondo, whose village is situated nearly at the top of Lwamondo Kop, belongs to the Vha Laudzi sib, who venerate the new moon. All Vha Laudzi living on the kop have also a very intimate connexion with the baboon, and are to-day generally called the Vha-ila-Pfene (*pfene*, baboon). Junod [1] describes what he considers to be the proper Venda theory on this point in the following way :—

" ' It is believed that these baboons are the Badzimu (ancestral spirits) themselves. Each Mu Laudzi, when he dies, becomes a baboon and goes to the sacred hill of Lomondo to dwell there. There is a specially big baboon amongst them. It never utters a cry. It is very old. It is the chief of the flock, and the principal ancestor god. Only when a great misfortune threatens the tribe one will hear it coming out of the forest and shouting loudly. Should a member of the clan die away from Lomondo, it is the old baboon which will go, accompanied by others, to fetch the new Mudzimo (ancestral spirit), who has been transformed into a baboon, and it will bring the new god to the sacred hill. At the time of the first fruit ceremony, the consecrated beer will not only be poured on the back of the ox-grandfather, but part of it will be brought to the forest of the gods and poured on a rock for the baboon god. And when the party which went into the forest returns to the village, one will hear a loud cry. It is the old baboon, who once more has abandoned its

[1] H. A. Junod, " Some Features of   *South African Journal of Science*, xvii.
the Religion of the Bavenda," *The*   (1921) pp. 218 *sq*.

obstinate mutism to express thankfulness for the offering. Then all the women assembled in the villages at the foot of the hill will burst into cries of joy, those same peculiar yells with which they greeted Raluvimbi when he visited the country.'

" Junod considers that this connexion between the totem animal and the ancestor god is a very unusual conception. In most history origins of the sib the totem object gives birth to a human being from which all the members of the sib are descended. Here there is a belief of the transmigration of souls into the totem animal. Junod does not record the interesting origin of this metamorphic conception, which led to the very natural identification of the baboon with the Vha Laudzi ancestors. According to Chief Lwamondo and several other informants, it happened that during the Swazi invasions towards the end of the last century, the presence of the Swazi impi, stealthily climbing the kop with the intention of attacking the village unawares, was betrayed by the sudden loud barking of a baboon. This timely warning led to the discovery of the enemy impi and to its utter defeat in an encounter which would otherwise have ended disastrously. Surely the ancestors must have been responsible for the opportune bark of the baboon, warning them of the terrible danger at the critical moment ! The baboon must then be a reincarnation of their first ancestor, and probably all other baboons on the kop are similarly inhabited by ancestor spirits ! The veneration described by Junod readily followed ; the conception of metamorphosis is vague, and apparently only applies to baboons actually living on the kop. Chief Lwamondo tells of a European hunter who wished to disprove the sacred character of these baboons ; he fired twelve shots at a monster baboon, but of course failed to make a hit ! This anecdote, by which a portion of the Vha Laudzi sib have become the *Vha-ila-Pfene*, is a good example of the manner in which a sib-name, through some accidental circumstance, may be changed and an entirely new totem adopted. Possibly many of the overlapping and obscure totems have been the result of similar accidents ; in time the history origin of the sib-name and totem is forgotten." [1]

[1] H. A. Stayt, *The Bavenda* (London, 1931), pp. 186 *sqq.*

Among the Bavenda cross-cousin marriage with the mother's brother's daughter is practised whenever possible, and is an essential feature in the society. The only other marriage that is permitted within the family group is with the wife's brother's daughter, under special conditions. Otherwise a man may marry anybody, from anywhere, provided that person is not connected by blood with either the father's or mother's family group. Except in the above cases the rule of exogamy is strictly adhered to, and applies to the remotest blood relatives and even to many people in the family group with whom there is no blood relationship at all.[1]

§ 4. *Totemism of the Pedi*

" If we cross the plain of the Sabi and reach the Drakensberg, we find that all the Pedi tribes dwelling together with the Thongas in the Leydenburg and Zoutpansberg district possess laudatory names which they also call *seboko*, the same word as *shibongo* ; but most of these names are names of animals, and are called by the technical term *muthupu*, totem ; the animal is the emblem or totem of the group. The Pedi clans are totemic. This means that, not only do they glorify themselves by comparing themselves with an animal and taking its name, but they think that there is a mysterious vital connection between it and their social group. I cannot give here all the facts I collected amongst them on the subject. . . . Let me merely mention the following details. The Khahas of the Shiluvane valley have the small grey antelope, called duyker, as totem. They salute each other in these words : ' Goni ! Phudi ! ' *Goni* is probably the name of an old ancestor, the same as Nkuna for the Ba-Nkuna ; but *phudi* means duyker. They consider it taboo to make a *nteke* of its skin for their children. Some of them do not eat the flesh of that antelope, fearing that their children would become idiotic, or be covered with boils. They will not sit near a man of another clan who is handling a duyker. The Mashilas (Sekukuni's people), who have the porcupine as totem, say : ' It is taboo even to tread on its dung ; the soles of the feet would become sore.' Many clans are afraid to

[1] H. A. Stayt, *op. cit.* p. 175.

kill the animal which is their totem ; this is not a law enforced by the chiefs ; the totem itself punishes them if they
transgress it.   However, nowhere did I find the idea that they
are descended from the totem.   They say : ' The old people
noticed that the flesh of such and such an animal made the
people of their clan ill ; so they proclaimed it taboo.'   Among
the Vendas, or at anyrate amongst certain Venda clans (Ba-
Laudzi, Ba-Ngwe, Ba-Shidzibe) the totem is connected with
the ancestor-gods.   At his death each member is transformed
into the animal venerated by his clan and joins his congeners
in the sacred wood where they live.

" Nothing of this kind is met with amongst the Thongas.
The Thonga clans are *atotemic*.   Many men bear the names
of animals, but this is merely a means of glorifying themselves ; there is no taboo with regard to the flesh, skin, or
dung of that animal.   I have come to this conclusion after a
careful investigation." [1]

[1] H. A. Junod, *The Life of a South African Tribe*, Second Edition (London,
1927), i. 367 *sqq.*

CHAPTER II

TOTEMISM IN RHODESIA

§ 1. *Totemism of the Mashona*

THE Mashona, a group of Bantu tribes of Southern Rhodesia, have a system of totemism, of which the chief features are the following :—

1. The *mutupo* or totem is a cognomen used in the Roman sense, and
2. serves as such as a ceremonial and laudatory form of address.
3. It acts (with modifications) as a bar of consanguinity to ensure exogamy in the sense of agnatic relationship ; the *mutupo*, in these tribes, descending from father to son.
4. It is a social bond between members of the same clan.
5. A taboo, or partial taboo, is attached to the animal, part of carcass, plant, or even " element " whose name is used or implied.
6. There are magical sanctions enforcing such taboo, for example, the loss of teeth by the eater of an animal tabooed.

" When we say that the *mutupo* is a cognomen, and serves as a ceremonial and laudatory form of address, we must add modifications. To begin with, the *mutupo* is frequently not the commonly used name of the totem animal or object which is tabooed. For example, those of the zebra totem do not swear by *mbizi* (zebra), but by *tembo* (the striped one). . . .

" A woman will not call her husband by his *mutupo*

name in public, nor, indeed, elsewhere than in the privacy of her own hut.   Likewise .it is in such circumstances only that he uses her totem name. . . .   Generally she is called ' amai wa ningi ' ' mother of So-and-so,' even as she says : ' Father of Mugaro ' to her husband, if Mugaro be the name of their son.   But note how a man is not ashamed to use the totem name to his wife's younger sister, *before he marries her*. Nor does he hesitate to ask a strange woman her totem name, so that he may thank her correctly by using it when she has brought him water.   The woman should respond by using the man's *chidawo*,[1] not his *mutupo* : the use of the *mutupo* itself would be an indication of undue familiarity.

" As regards the other attributes tabulated, let us take examples of actual *mitupo* (totems), and get a view of the natives' own ideas, regarding ' totemism.'

" *Dziwa*, the pool, is a well-known *mutupo*.   The pool in the river is big, and contains many creatures—*nzwidz*, the otter, *howe*, the fish, *mvuwu*, the hippopotamus, *ngwena* or *garwe*, the crocodile, and *shanga* or *chipu*, the river reed. So that, when a man is heard to be addressed as Dziwa, another of the *mutupo* may say, ' What of the pool are you forbidden ? '   And so he will get an indication of the close- ness of their relationship.   So with those of the *chibgwa mutupo*.   They may be cats which roar, that is lions, lynxes, or even jichidza, the big owl which hoots like a lion.

" People of these unreal divisions intermarry in these times of freedom, and ease their minds of any scruples they may have by ' cutting the kin ' (*ku cheka wukama*).   This is done by sacrificing the ox.   The chief of the tribe should carry out this rite, and he gets his portion of the meat for his good offices.   But the strict old conservatives do not approve. ' *Zwi cha ira zwomene*,' they say, and wait expectant for a dire result of the marriage.

" . . . Before European influences were felt, Mashona of the same *mutupo* (totem) but of differing *zwidawo* (sub- divisions), intermarried.   The *chidawo*, then, was of im- portance in its uses, as well as of significance as an index to the origin and essence of totemism.   It was quite possible that two unrelated agnatic groups might have the same

---

[1] The *chidawo* is the general name for a subdivision of the totem clan.

mutupo or totem, but hardly the same *chidawo*. Therefore the natives considered that those of the differing *zwidawo* might marry."[1]

Fourteen years earlier Mr. Bullock had suggested that the subdivisions (*chidaiwo*) of the totem clans were introduced for the purpose of allowing marriage between distant members of the same agnatic group or totem clan. He still thinks that there is an element of truth in the suggestion, but that it is not the whole truth.[2]

For a full account of Mr. Bullock's views on the subject I must refer the reader to his own work. Mr. Bullock gives the native names of a hundred and forty-six Mashona totems, but without their English equivalents.[3]

§ 2. *Totemism of the Ila-speaking Peoples of Northern Rhodesia*

The Ila-speaking peoples of Northern Rhodesia inhabit the country lying to the north of the Batoka plateau, above the middle Zambesi. They are divided into at least ninety-three totemic clans. The clans are strictly exogamous. For example, no leopard man may marry a leopard woman. Members of different clans living in the same village may marry ; but members of the same clan though they live even a hundred miles apart, may have neither regular nor irregular intercourse. Wilful breaches of the law have occasionally occurred, but they are regarded by the people with the utmost abhorrence. Cases have happened when the breach has been committed in ignorance, and the relationship of the couple has not been discovered till after marriage. In such cases no punishment is meted out to the offenders ; the marriage is simply dissolved, or the pair are left to suffer what is regarded as the inevitable fate of those who break a taboo. The general rule is that children, both male and female, take the clan of their mother, not of their father, though in a very few instances men on being questioned as to their clan have mentioned the clan of their father.

The exogamous clan is called a *mukoa*. The members of

[1] C. Bullock, *The Mashona* (Johannesburg, 1927), pp. 78 *sq.*

[2] C. Bullock, *op. cit.* p. 77.
[3] C. Bullock, *op. cit.* pp. 81 *sqq.*

the clan call themselves by the name of some animal or plant or natural object between which and themselves they conceive to be a certain relationship, and which they accordingly regard with considerable respect. Messrs. Smith and Dale, to whom we owe a very valuable account of these Ila-speaking people, have compiled a list of ninety-three of their clans, with the names of their totems. Among these names we may note : zebra, vulture, ground hornbill, elephant, wart-hog, hare, river-monster, barbel-fish, cattle, ring-dove, hyena, kite, goat, baboon, scavenger beetle, lion, wild dog, crab, hartebeest, crocodile, wasp, small bird (*intite*), monkey, termite ant, genet, buffalo, jackal, squirrel, crow, hippo-potamus, scorpion, hornet, eland, snake, palm, palm-leaves, *mayovu* (a tree which is said not to shake in the wind), palm-bush, baobab tree, *masale* (a kind of grass), *mankonte* (a kind of edible root), wild orange, honey, grain, rain, river, iron, wind.

Messrs. Smith and Dale never heard of any ceremonies performed for the increase of a totem, such as the Australian aborigines so often observe. " The Totemism of the Ba-ila," they say, " exists as a feature of their social organization, not as part of their religion : the only semi-religious feature in it is in the reverence in which the totem is held. In the case of the animal totems this is shown in their not being killed or eaten by the clan. If you ask a man whether he eats his totem, he will protest vigorously against the idea. . . . Katumpa, of the dog clan, when asked if he ate dogs, said, ' Shall I eat a man ? ' Yet this is not now a universal feeling. In this respect the totemism of to-day is a degeneration. Old men will refrain from killing or eating where young men will have no scruples. One young man said when we asked whether he would eat his kinsman the lion, ' Yes, even if it had just devoured my father. I would take him out of its stomach and eat the lion.' Generally speaking, we may say that where the totem animal is edible the younger men will eat it, and will only refrain when the animal is in itself un-palatable. Thus the Bakubi clan, whose totem is the vulture, the Bachiwena (Crocodiles), the Banaumpe (Wild-dogs) do not, and are hardly likely to break the ancestral custom ; while on the other hand the Bono, whose totem is cattle,

.the Basantis (Oribis), Banakonzes (Hartebeestes), etc., are strongly tempted to eat, and as a matter of fact the younger generation do eat, the totem.   In former days the Bono refrained not only from eating beef but also from drinking milk.   In respect to totems other than animals and birds we can hardly understand in what ways reverence was shown them.   The Banamaila could hardly have refrained from eating grain, or the Batunga from drinking water." [1]

Messrs. Smith and Dale attempted to test some current theories of the origin of totemism by questioning the Ila-speaking people about their totems, and though the results of their enquiries were negative, they are not the less instructive, if only as a warning against premature generalisations. I will therefore quote their own account of their enquiry. They say : " Why do a number of people associate themselves with and call themselves by the name of a particular class of animals, plants, or things ?   The clans are connected in some way with certain localities, and it might be thought that the totem is an animal or plant living or growing especially in those places.   But none of the totems is sufficiently localised to support such a conjecture.   Duikers and lions and pigeons and baobab trees, and what not, are found in every district ; so we must certainly rule out that suggestion.   We must also reject the theory by which Dr. Theal tried to account for the remnants of totemism among the tribes of South Africa.   The Ba-ila do certainly believe in transmigration ; but there seems to be little or no connection between their totemism and their conceptions of metempsychosis. . . .

" The Banachibizi do not pass after death into zebras, nor the Banasulwe into hares.   The number of the animals into which the Ba-ila do pass, or believe they pass, is strictly limited in number ; and people of any clan can pass into them —into lions, for example.   We cannot indeed find in the facts before us any reason to support any of the current theories as to the origin of Totemism.   Nor is that to be wondered at. The Ba-ila are far from ranking among the most primitive people of the world ; they are far advanced beyond the

[1] Rev E. W. Smith and Captain   *of Northern Rhodesia* (London, 1920), A. M. Dale, *The Ila-Speaking Peoples*   i. 287 *sqq.*, and 310 *sqq.*

Australian aborigines, for example, who know nothing of working in metals or agriculture. Sir James Frazer may find justification in their ignorance of elementary physiological facts for his ' conceptional ' theory, but, whatever it may have been in the past, any such theory would now only provoke the Ba-ila to ridicule. Like the Australians, the Ba-ila believe implicitly in reincarnation, but not without the ordinary processes of nature. With Sir James Frazer's theory in mind we put the question to one of the oldest men in the country, whether he had ever heard, or whether his fathers had ever told him, of a child being born in that manner. Without any hesitation, and with the air of one who closes a subject with a word, he asked, ' Did you ever know of a cow calving without a bull ? ' A pastoral people are not likely to remain in ignorance of such matters.

" We cannot hope, in fact, to offer any suggestion as to the origin of Totemism. We have put questions in various forms, direct and indirect, to many people, and have specially questioned the old men as to what they learnt from their fathers, but no rational answer can be obtained. Nor can we offer our readers any legends like those recorded by Messrs. Spencer and Gillen, and other writers. The totem is regarded as a relation, but how or why it is so they can offer no explanation." [1]

The Ba-ila, that is, the Ila-speaking peoples, have the classificatory system of relationship. With regard to the marriage of cousins, which is a crucial point in the social institutions of so many totemic and exogamous peoples, Messrs. Smith and Dale observe : " If I am a male, I address my male cross-cousin as *mulongwangu* (' my friend '), and my female cross-cousin as *mwinangu* (' my wife ') ; if I am a female I address him as *mulumi angu* (' my husband '), and her as *mukazhima* (' my fellow-wife '), that being the proper term used by one wife of a polygamist to another. This form of address found here and elsewhere is one of the most curious things in the system. Why should the children of a man and his sister address each other respectively as man and wife ? It is because, according to clan rules, they might marry. Intercourse between the children of two

[1] E. W. Smith and A. M. Dale, *op. cit.* i. 289 *sq.*

sisters are regarded as incestuous because they have the same totem, but these are of different clans. . . . But as a matter of fact, latter-day custom does not allow such marriages; while I may marry the daughter of my father's sister, I may not marry the daughter of my mother's brother. . . . Of the four possible cousin marriages, therefore, the Ba-ila nowadays only allow one." [1]

§ 3. *Totemism of the Ba-Kaonde*

The Ba-Kaonde is a Bantu tribe which, with its neighbours, inhabits the Kasempa District of Northern Rhodesia. An account of the social and totemic system of the tribe has been given us by Mr. F. H. Melland, who was Magistrate for the Kasempa District from 1911 to 1922.[2] He tells us that " the Kaonde tribe, as at present constituted, appears to be of mixed origin; but there can be small doubt that the main stocks forming it are all parts of the Luba family and represent some stages of the great migration that swept over all this part of Africa, starting some three to five centuries ago, and coming from somewhere in the north-west." [3]

With regard to the totemic system of the tribe, Mr. Melland informs us that " it is generally accepted that totemism is connected with exogamy (marrying outside the family), and on these grounds the *mukoka* must be called a totem. The whole essence of the *mikoka* is exogamous. Except for this one feature, however, it cannot be said that totemism is of much importance to the Ba-Kaonde (and other similar tribes) nor of much interest ethnographically.

" It is said that Mulonga and Mwinambuzhi ('Adam' and 'Eve') had very many children, who chose names for themselves, and chose those of familiar objects around them Thus one called him (her-) self *chulu* (ant-hill), another *mbowa* (mushroom), another *mulonga* (water), a fourth *kasaka* (kaffir corn), and so on. (Parenthetically it may be noted that many words used as the eponyms of the totems are, in all tribes, often archaic, and form—frequently—

---

[1] E. W. Smith and A. M. Dale, *Africa* (London, 1923).
op. cit. i. 318 *sq.*
[2] F. H. Melland, *In Witch-Bound*
[3] F. H. Melland, *op. cit.* p. 28.

connecting links between tribes. For instance, *kasaka* (as above) is not used nowadays in Chikaonde[1] for kaffir corn, *mebele* being the word. But *masaka* is the Chiwemba for the same grain. The Wawemba call the duiker *mpombo*, but as an eponym they use the word *kashya*, which is the modern name in Chikaonde for the same antelope ; *mulonga* is used in Chiwemba for a stream (or running water), but is only used now in Chikaonde as a totem—with the same meaning, and so on.

" These children of Mulonga and Mwinambuzhi in their turn had children, and the name of the children of the first couple remained as the family (or totem name) : the descendants of Kasaka, for instance, being known as Benasaka. Thus it became a rule that one of the Benasaka could not marry another of the Benasaka, nor one of the Benachulu another of the same totem. There are no beliefs, practices nor taboos connected with the eponym, for in the first case it was but a chance-chosen name, and had no direct reference to its origin. Thus a member of the Benambuzhi will not hesitate to eat goat flesh : one of the Ben-angi fears the leopard as does one of another totem, and will kill it readily if he gets the chance. No one worships, prays to, or offers sacrifices to the eponym of his totem.

" Long ago, among the Ba-Kaonde, a man would forgive certain sins if committed by one of his totem—especially adultery and larceny of crops (never in the case of assault). This does not hold good nowadays.

" Hospitality is still shown to a stranger of one's totem : a hut to sleep in, food (even a fowl) and so on. If one does not do this it brings shame (*mbumvu*). A common way of finding one's totem mate is as follows :—

> *Stranger in Village :* ' Here is some (money or goods), please sell me some food, for I am hungry.'
> *Villagers* produce some food.
> *Stranger :* ' That is poor measure for my money. It may be, perhaps, that it is one of your own totem whom you are cheating.'
> *A Villager :* ' What is your totem ? '
> *Stranger :* ' So-and-so.'
> *2nd Villager (sitting at some distance) :* ' What's that ? What did you say your totem was ? '

[1] The language of the Kaonde.

Stranger : ' So-and-so.'

2nd Villager : ' Whence come you, and where were you born ? '

Stranger : ' I am of the —— tribe, and was born in the village of So-and-so, under the great chief X.'

2nd Villager : ' And you are of the —— ? ' (name totem).

Stranger : ' Yes, indeed.'

2nd Villager : ' Then come and be my guest, for you are my relation.'

" To kill a fellow totem-man is no more and no less a crime than to kill any other.

" In war a man would not spare his totem mate, even if he knew his totem.

" Curiously enough this totemism which, though so unimportant, is so widely spread amongst this and the adjoining Bantu tribes is not found among the neighbouring Alunda. The Ba-Kaonde say of this lack of totemism, ' A Kalunda can marry his niece,' implying (rightly or wrongly) much less strict rules as to exogamy among their western neighbours." [1]

§ 4. *Totemism of the Awemba*

The Awemba or Wemba is a Bantu tribe which inhabits, with other Bantu tribes, the great plateau of Northern Rhodesia, in the north-eastern part of the territory. The social and totemic systems of the tribes inhabiting the plateau have been investigated and described by Messrs. C. Gouldsbury and H. Sheane, who tell us that one of them had for many years questioned the older men as to their ideas on the origin of totemism, but without receiving any satisfactory answers. Some of the natives said that the creator Leza had at the beginning, before the dispersal (*chipanduko*) created the totems ; but the usual reply was : " We have the same name as the animals, and that is all." The institution and ordinances of the totem clans are accepted as something consecrated by immemorial usage, as to which it is vain and foolish, perhaps even impious, to enquire.[2]

" Wemba totems fall under the broad headings of animate, such as animals, reptiles, fish, birds, and insects, and

[1] F. H. Melland, *op. cit.* pp. 248 *sqq.*

[2] C. Gouldsbury and H. Sheane, *The Great Plateau of Northern Rhodesia* (London, 1911), p. 93.

inanimate, such as minerals and artificial objects. Plants and vegetable products, and nature phenomena, also supply totem names. The following list is given to show their variety :—

Animals.—Crocodile (*bena-ng'andu*, modern form *ng'wena*), elephant (*benansofu*), lions (*bena-nkalamo*), leopard (*bena-ng'o*, modern form *mbwiri*), dog (*bena-mbwa*), goat (*bena-mbushi*), pig (*bena-nguruwe*), fish (*bena-isibi*, and of certain species as *bena-mpende*), bees (*bena-nshimu*), birds (*bena-nguni*), mouse (*bena-mpuku*), tortoise (*bena-nkamba*), frog (*bena-fyula*), otter (*bena-mbowo*), duiker (*bena-nsengo*), ant (*bena-milongo*).

Minerals.—Slag-iron (*bena-mbulo*).

Artificial Objects.—Cooking-pot (*bena-'nongo*), drinking-bowl (*bena-nsupa*), but totems of such artificial objects are rare.

Nature Phenomena.—Rain (*bena-mfula*).

Plants. etc.—Porridge (*bena-bwali*), millet (*bena-male*) ; to this phratry belong men who are chosen to be priests at Mwaruli ; castor-oil (*bena-mono*), mushroom (*bena-boa*), plum (*bena-masuku*), banana (*bena-nkonde*), tree (*bena-miti-nsengo*), grass (*bena-chani*).

" Some of these names are old and ancient ones given to the animal which are nowadays not employed (compare the Wiwa totem name for lion and Muwaya for guinea fowl as different from the usual words used to denote them).

" It is interesting to note that many of these clan names are common to many of the Plateau tribes, such as the Awemba and the Amambwe, who until quite recently were at war with each other, and it seems as if these phratries were constituted before the separation of the various tribes. In the olden times, possession of the same totem as some phratries of alien tribes carried with it valuable privileges. If a stranger captured in war could prove that he was of the same totem as any of his captors, he would not be put to death. Even nowadays a travelling native will prefer to stay at the house of a man of the same totem, as he has the right to be suitably entertained by him. In some cases certain clans have become very numerous and powerful ; so on Lake Bangweolo we find the totem names of Bena-ng'ona and Bena-ng'oma used in a general fashion to designate the two main branches of the tribe, and almost what we might term tribal totems. The same word *bena*—' the masters, or owners of '—is used not only to prefix totems, but also to prefix the name of the locality, so the Bena-Luwumbu or Bena-ng'umbo are territorial terms adopted by the Bisa dwellers in that region, and not totemistic. Among the Awiwa there is no special reluctance to give their totem names except that of the chief, which is often noticed when questioning Awemba and Walungu. Among the Awiwa the totem descended on the father's side, but among the Awemba the maternal totem was the greater of the two.

" Following the law of exogamy, no sexual intercourse is allowed among members of the same totem, for which crime the olden time punishment was death by burning. But whether this practice originated from natural horror of incest or from definite rules of exogamy or of totemism is hard to say. . . .

" When a member of the family dies, when burying him they turn his *face* to the quarter from which the original founder of the clan is supposed to have come ; this place is called Chipanduko (the place of the dispersal of the clans). The *head* itself, however, will be always turned facing the east. Among the Awemba, certain totems are considered higher than others ; for instance, a man who is Mwenamfula (rain totem) is considered to be of good lineage and respected accordingly.

" Unfortunately, every year these survivals of totemism are becoming fainter, especially amongst the Awemba. There is a tradition among the Awiwa that their ancestors would not eat or kill these animals, and that men of the Simwanza and Siwale (bird totems) would formerly release these birds if found in snares, and would not eat them. But nowadays the totem animal is in no way respected, and is killed and eaten like any other animal, without any feeling of remorse or any special ceremonies of the nature of a sacrament. Among the older men there is still a lingering feeling that there is some mystic and indefinable affinity between them and the totem. When a lion is heard at night roaring outside a village they exclaim *Lavwe mukanda*, at its fierceness, and use the same expression when they see a member of the lion totem in a passion." [1]

---

[1] C. Gouldsbury and H. Sheane, *op. cit.* pp. 93 *sqq.*

CHAPTER III

TOTEMISM IN EAST AFRICA

§ 1. *Totemism of the Elgeyo Tribe*

ON the eastern edge of the fertile Uasin Gishu plateau, in the highlands of Kenya colony, lies the long narrow strip of country—four hundred and three square miles in area—reserved for the Elgeyo tribe. The tribe keeps cattle and practises agriculture. In the rainy season they grow *wimbi* and maize for food, and in the dry season, when the irrigation system is used, they plant *mtama* to provide beer and food.

" Each location, that is, each of the sixteen chief sections of people in the district, contains several hamlets, each of which is a totemic group. The totemic condition dates back to the time when the country, now known as the Elgeyo reserve, was reinhabited after the great desolation which drove out the ' Kurut.' Each of the groups has associated with it the totem adopted in those early days. Animals (elephant, leopard, frog, etc.), birds (hawk, etc.), the moon, and thunder are among the things then chosen.

" Each group may intermarry with such other groups only as tradition has decreed. One of the first enquiries a father makes as to a suitor's credentials is respecting his totem. No marriage between parties of the same group, or of groups between which union is forbidden, is sanctioned, as it is firmly believed that the offspring of such a marriage would be defective. A man or woman of a Buffalo group may take a mate from an Elephant, Leopard, Baboon, or Rhinoceros group. An Elgeyo of the Kaptorgog section of Rokocho location, which is of the Rhinoceros totem, may marry one of the Moon group in Changach. The Thunder group found in Kaptoyo of Rokocho may wed the Leopards from Kobil section of Changach, or the Moons of Nandet in Marichor. The Hawk group at Kapsogom in Sego may intermarry with the Buffalo group living in Singori in Rokocho. Each group has several other groups from which to select mates. Though every totem is not represented in every location, a native has a wide choice of areas in which he may seek for a wife. The only case where a person may marry one of his own totem is among the Buffaloes—and even here there is the restriction that he must choose the Buffalo he wants from another location, not from his own community. The rule is relaxed in this totem because its members are more numerous than those of other groups. Full brothers must marry into different groups. For example, if the eldest brother, a Leopard, has married a woman of the Buffaloes, the next brother will avoid that totem, and marry, perhaps, a Thunder woman.

" The object associated with each totemic group does not appear to be regarded with special reverence. All the natives delight in killing big game. Black ants, totems of one group, take the same risks as any others. In no case is homage of any kind paid to the totem." [1]

§ 2. *Totemism of the Embu Tribes*

The Embu are a group of primitive tribes inhabiting the vast southern slopes of Mount Kenya. Isolated in their forests and gorges, they have remained in a backward state down to the present time.[2]

" The social organization of all the Embu tribes includes loose and vague grouping into families or clans. This arrangement, however, is not very conspicuous, and appears to have little actual effect except in the matter of marriage, union within the clan being regarded as incestuous. The clan is hereditary, the wife taking the husband's clan, as do the children. The members are supposed to be specially

---

[1] J. A. Massam, *The Cliff Dwellers of Kenya* (London, 1927), pp. 151 *sqq.* Mr. Massam is, or was, a District Commissioner in Kenya.

[2] G. St. J. Orde Browne, *The Vanishing Tribes of Kenya* (London, 1925), p. 24. The author, Major Orde Browne, was Assistant Commissioner at various Government posts in the area in question.

friendly and hospitable to each other. There appears to be a trace of what may be described as totemism : various animals and insects being regarded as the special signs of certain clans. This, however, does not appear to be of great importance, and it is quite common to find a man who knows his clan, but does not know of any special totem appropriate to it. In Ndia certain clans appear to have different hereditary characteristics. The Akiuru (totem, the frog) are regarded as being able to pronounce curses of special potency, though these can be guarded against by recourse to a doctor. The Ithaga are the smiths, and appear to practise their art as an hereditary profession : they are also the masters of particularly potent curses, and in addition have influence over the rain, being able to detect its approach and to prevent it if they wish.

" Certain other clans have special habits or restrictions ; for instance, the Agachiku (totem, the ostrich) will not eat the breast of goats." [1]

§ 3.   *Totemism of the Lango*

The Lango are a Nilotic tribe of Uganda, whose country lies in the upper valley of the Nile, touching Lake Kioga on the south. In the south the country is flat and intersected by innumerable marshy rivers whose sluggish current is almost blocked by the thick vegetation, while in the north the valleys are more marked and the banks of the rivers more definite, and there is less vegetation on the streams. Hence the water flows more readily, and being unretarded in its course dries up in the hot season. Elsewhere nearly all the rivers contain some water at all times of the year, with the result that the greatest population is to be found along the watercourses.[2]

The Lango are divided into many exogamous clans, which either are, or seem formerly to have been, totemic. The system has been described as follows by Mr. J. H. Driberg in his excellent account of the tribe, among whom

---

[1] G. St. J. Orde Browne, *op. cit.*   *Nilotic Tribe of Uganda* (London,
pp. 39 *sq.*   1923), pp. 42 *sq.*
[2] J. H. Driberg, *The Lango, a*

he lived for some years in an official capacity as a member of the Uganda Civil Service.

." Lango clans are numerous. . . . They have no very coherent notions on the origin of a clan system, being content with the thought that their remote ancestors founded the clans, and that the wisdom of their ancestors is justified in their children. The basis of the system consists of numerous tabus or prohibitions, which vary according to the clans, and it is probable that they were in origin totemic, though the totemism appears to have broken down many generations ago, and at the present time the word is hardly applicable in its accepted significance.

" With rare exceptions, there does not appear to be any intimate connection between the clan and the thing tabued. In many cases, indeed, there are several tabus attached to the one clan, which tends to dispose of any suggestion of the idea of co-birth with the tabu. On one point, however, there is no doubt, namely that all prohibitions are rigidly observed.

" The exceptions which indicate a totemic origin (so strongly, indeed, that such an origin must be ultimately premised for all the clans) are the clans *Jo Ayom*, *Jo Akwaich* and *Jo Akarawok me Jo Amor*, which alone are named after the object tabued. The *Jo Ayom* mourn as for a man if a patas monkey (*ayom*) is killed, just as the *Jo Akwaich* mourn on the death of a leopard (*kwaich*), as they are said to be *danogi* (their man, *i.e.* a member of their clan). Tradition has it that in the old days the *Akwaich* clan used to place their babies without risk in the mouth of a leopard, and for ever afterwards no leopard would harm them. The *Jo Akarawok me Jo Amor* (the *Amor* subdivision of the *Akarawok* clan) will not kill a duiker (*amor*), and, if they accidentally kill one, they bury it and cover its grave with leaves.

" The clans are exogamous, marriage not being permitted into either the paternal or maternal clans, and a woman enters the clan of her husband and conforms with its rules, the old prohibitions of her family's clan being allowed to lapse. Moreover, on divorce a woman observes the tabus of her late husband's clan, and does not revert to her own, and this rule holds good even if she contracts a second marriage into another clan.   While observing her new husband's tabus (though they are not binding, and it is rather a matter of courtesy), she still remains constant to those of her first husband.   Children follow the father's clan even should they accompany their mother on divorce.   Illegitimate children enter the clan of their mother's family or her husband's family according as she is unmarried or married, but a lover who begets a child by an unmarried girl, by marrying her secures the child for his clan." [1]

The rule prohibiting the marriage of relations is very strict.   No one may marry a girl however remotely connected by blood on either the father's or the mother's side, that is, all marriage is forbidden within the father's or the mother's clan ;   and even certain distant step-relationships, in which there is no blood-tie whatever, are a bar to marriage.[2]

§ 4.   *Totemism of the Nilotic Tribes on the Upper Nile*

Totemism of the Shilluk

Totemism is also found in a more or less pronounced form among a series of Nilotic tribes whose country lies along the course of the Upper Nile.   They have all been investigated by Dr. and Mrs. Seligman.   It will be best to quote the evidence of these experienced observers in their own words, taking the tribes in geographical order, from the Shilluk in the north to the Bongo in the south.   Speaking of the Shilluk, they say :   " There are numerous observances connected with animals, including some which might be called taboos, but we did not ourselves discover any evidence of totemism, though clan exogamy prevails.   On the other hand both Westermann and Hofmayr consider that totemism exists. Westermann gives the following example :—

" ' The ostrich and the crow and the crow and Deng were split out of the gourd, all three are three-twin brothers.   Deng went into a certain village, the ostrich went into the bush, and the crow flew up.   We were born by Deng.   Akwoe (the son of Deng) came in the time of Duwat . . . he came into the Shilluk country to the people of the king (that is to

[1] J. H. Driberg, *op. cit.* pp. 189 *sqq.*   [2] J. H. Driberg, *op. cit.* p. 156.

Fashoda). And when we became many some went to Feni-kang Odurojo, but some remained at Fenidwai. Thus we separated from each other. . . . That is the beginning of (the village of) Adelfalo—the ostrich and crow are of our family. They are not eaten by us on account of the *dwalo* sickness.' [1]

" Westermann states that the common ancestor to whom members of a clan trace descent is in most cases a man, but that some of the clans claim descent from an animal.[2] Hofmayr states that the number of totems among the Shilluk is small, and gives the following examples : ostrich, hippopotamus, Veranus lizard, giraffe, *gu* (a fish), a gourd, *ayiado* (a bean), *cwa* (tamarind), and *tuko* (hearth-stone). This seems to imply a wide distribution of particular clans. He also cites *curro* (a fish), the crocodile, the crested crane, and the knee-joint as totems of Tonga in the extreme south.[3]

" As to the origin of these totems, if totems they be, we were informed that the prohibition to eat the fish *curro* was directly due to Nyakang,[4] who told his people to bring him all the fish they caught in the river. Although they brought him many fish, they kept back one, and Nyakang, who knew this, as in dreams men are aware of things happening at a distance, told his people, *i.e.* the Shilluk, that this fish must always be unlawful food to them. Concerning the crocodile, we were informed that all might eat it except those possessed by Nyakang or his mother, who if they ate it would die. . . .

" Considering the data just cited we are struck by the fact that Westermann's example is almost in the typical Dinka form of totemism (twin birth of totem animal and human progenitor of clan), while the example given by Hofmayr is from Tonga at the extreme south of the Shilluk country, where, as we discovered, mixed marriages resulting in a mingling of Dinka and Shilluk cults were by no means uncommon. We are then inclined to consider that Shilluk totemism—as far as it exists—is due to Dinka influence. In

[1] C. G. and B. Z. Seligman, *Pagan Tribes of the Nilotic Sudan* (London, 1932), pp. 41 *sq.*, referring to Westermann, *The Shilluk People* (Philadelphia, 1912), pp. 178 *sq.*

[2] Westermann, *op. cit.* p. 127.

[3] Seligman, citing W. Hofmayr, *Die Schilluk. Geschichte, Religion, und Leben eines Niloten Stammes* (Wien, 1925), p. 236.

[4] The mythical or semi-historical founder of the Shilluk dynasty.

any case, while exogamy is generally observed, the association of particular groups of men and animals seems to make
no great emotional appeal to the Shilluk—to be but little
loaded with effect—compared with the similar feelings among
the Dinka." [1]

Totemism of the Dinka.—With regard to totemism
among the Dinka, the neighbours of the Shilluk upon the
south, Dr. and Mrs. Seligman tell us : " Dinka totems are
usually animal, sometimes plant, more rarely a natural
object or process, and occasionally it seems that certain
spiritual agencies are regarded in very much the same way.
Confining ourselves to the more usual beliefs, the clans
speak of certain animals as their ' ancestors,' *kwar* being
the word used by the Than tribes ; usually the *kwar* has
nothing to do with a man's personal name (one man, whose
name signified hyaena, had a crocodile as his *kwar*) but, in
the words of one of our Than informants, ' the *kwar* is the
animal which is the spirit (*jok*) of the clan (*gol*).' Further,
ruai, the word ordinarily meaning ' related,' is used when
speaking of the bond between a man and his *kwar*, *i.e.*
they are *ruai*, ' relatives.' No man injures his *kwar* animal,
but all respect it in various ways. Sometimes the *kwar*
is a plant, as in some Agar and Cic clans, who treat the totem
plant with much the same reverence as is commonly shown
to the totem animal.

" Most of the Dinka clans whose *kwar* is an animal
derive their origin from a man born as one of twins, his
fellow-twin being an animal of the species that is the totem
of the clan. Sometimes the association is not quite so close,
in which case the totem animal usually lays certain commands
upon one of the members of the clan, offering in return
certain privileges. Commands and privileges alike show the
close relationship existing between the animal and the man
who is traditionally looked upon as the ancestor of the clan.
Although children take their father's totem they respect
their mother's totem animal or plant, and an animal may be
avoided for several generations for this reason. Thus, a
man whose paternal grandmother had the poisonous snake
anong as totem said that if he saw anyone kill a snake of

[1] Seligman, *op. cit.* pp. 41 *sqq.*

this species he would bury it, because it was the totem of his father's mother ; the same man refrained from eating the flesh of hippopotamus because it was the totem of his mother's mother. Further, it is customary for both sexes to avoid eating their spouse's totem animal, though this rule seems to be kept more strictly by women than by men, presumably on account of the ancestral spirits of the children. The clans are usually designated by the name of their traditional human ancestor ; comparatively few are spoken of by the name of their animal, though there is a Niel (snake) clan, and even a Niel tribe among the Danjol Dinka in the neighbourhood of Khod Adar.

" A Ngong Nyang man gave the following account of his conduct towards snakes of the *aro* species, his mother's totem animal. If he saw one of these snakes in the forest he would sprinkle dust on its back, for otherwise the snake might upbraid him for lack of friendliness. If the snake were angry and tried to bite him, dust sprinkled on its back would propitiate it, but if he could not appease it and it bit him he and the animal would both die. This man's children show the same reverence for the snake as their father. If the snake bit a man of an entirely unrelated stock the man would die, but not the snake, for the snake and the folk of foreign clans are not related *ruai*.

" The following are specific examples of beliefs concerning the origin of various clans of the Ngong Nyang tribe and of the relationship existing between their members and their totems.

" Gol e Mariak has as totem the snake, *niel*. Long ago one of these snakes came into the hut of one Mariak, and there gave birth to its young. The snake spoke to Mariak, telling him not to hurt it or its children : ' If you see a man hurt one of my children tie the mourning-band of palm-leaf round your head.'

" Gol Akon Chang Jurkwait is so called from the name of the son born to one Nyanajok Alerjok as one of twins, his fellow-twin being an elephant. The boy was brought up in the village in the usual way, but the elephant was turned loose in the jungle.

" Gol e Luel has the crocodile for totem. Long ago Luel

found the eggs of a crocodile ; he put them in his canoe, and when he reached home buried them under the floor of his hut. One night, as the eggs were hatching, the old crocodile came and scratched them up and then led the young to the river. Before leaving the hut the crocodile said to Luel : ' Do not hurt us, and we will not hurt you. Wear mourning on your head and stomach if any of you see another man kill one.' A man of this clan will not hesitate to swim in the river, even at night, for the crocodiles will not hurt him.

" Gol e Yukwal e Lukab e Lerkwe has the hippopotamus as totem.

" Gol e Yicol has the lion as totem, the founder of this clan being the twin brother of a lion. While men of other clans have to barricade themselves in their houses, Col of this clan can—as he affirms—sleep in the open ; when a lion kills game it calls to Col at night, who goes out next morning and finds the meat, and when Col kills a hippopotamus he in turn leaves some of the meat in the forest for the lions. If Col were not of the party no one would touch a lion's kill, for to do this would offend the lion, who would then attack them, but if Col were with them no one would hesitate to take the meat. If a lion suffered from a splinter of bone or portion of gristle becoming wedged between its teeth it might roar round the hut in which Col lay, until he came out and removed the source of its discomfort."[1]

Totemism of the Nuer.—The Nuer inhabit the swamp region on either side of the White Nile south of its junction with the Bahr el Ghazal. Concerning the totemism of the Nuer tribe Dr. and Mrs. Seligman inform us that " it is nearly quarter of a century since we discovered totemism of the twin pattern, identical with that of the Dinka, among the Nuer, later confirmed by Mr. Jackson and Professor Evans-Pritchard, who has written that ' certain lineages of pure Nuer . . . ancestry are associated with groups of animals or objects, and this association is sometimes based on the idea of a twin birth of the ancestor of the lineage and a particular animal or object.' Like ourselves he heard of clans with lion and crocodile as their totems, in each case

[1] Seligman, *op. cit.* pp. 142 *sqq.*

the animal being twin with the founder of the clan, but he states that though all the descendants of Kir, who form the nucleus of the Jekan tribes, respect gourds because their ancestor was enclosed in a gourd, it is possible that they were originally Dinka, since they are not recognised as being of the same origin as the bulk of the Nuer clans. This applies equally to the Gaawar, the descendants of War, who respect the *nyuot* tree and the fish *nyiwar* because when their ancestor came down from heaven he held a branch of the tree in his hand and was accompanied by the fish. Now all this, though it would equally apply to the Dinka—and we may add that totem animals have spirit names just as among the Dinka—does not seem to us necessarily to imply Dinka origin, for we consider that the similarity is best explained by the origin of the two peoples from a common stem or stock.

" The Leng sub-clan stand in the same relation to the lion as do the Dinka of the Gol e Yicol clan of the Ngong Nyang tribe. Not only do they share their ' kill,' but much the same rules of justice are applied to lions as to man. A man of this clan killed a lion ; afterwards a lion took some twenty head from his herd. It was decided not to hunt the beast, since the latter was within its rights, but twenty cattle were exacted from the man who had killed the lion, a sacrifice was made, and the affair ended. An instance is cited of a man who killed a lion in defence of his cattle. ' He had no sense at all,' said Professor Evans-Pritchard's informant. ' When he came home he bent his fingers like claws and behaved as though he wanted to eat people.' A sheep was quickly sacrificed to the lions, and all was well.

" Other instances conform less to totemic type, just as among the Dinka. Thus the Bul respect the *kac* tree, because their miracle-working ancestor used to sit under it, and the same tree is, we believe, respected by the Jidiet clan because their ancestors were killed with clubs made of its wood.

" Men of the Juak clan reverence the river (they originated near the river Gwol and their honorific clan name is Gat Gwol). When a man of this clan wants to cross the river he will pull a bead off his necklace or other ornament and throw it into the water, saying : ' Grandfather, take this, let me cross without harm.' A married woman of this clan will not cross a stream naked, but with her *yet* (petticoat) or *yoah* (fringed garment) on.   Should she forget and step into the water naked she will go back, pull off a strip of her *yoah*, and throw it into the river, saying : ' Grandfather, take this, I did not purposely offend you.' " [1]

Totemism of the Bari.—The territory of the Bari-speaking tribes lies to the south of the Dinka country, embracing both banks of the river. " The Bari are divided into a number of exogamous clans, called *dunget* (pl. *dungesi*) with male descent ; there are certain prohibitions, for the most part connected with animals or food, which each clan should observe.   There are no clan marks for men or women, but the ears of sheep and goats are cut or notched conventionally to indicate the clan of their owner.   The food avoidances of the Bari are far from simple, and although it is unlikely that all are clan prohibitions, some certainly are. . . .

" The Dung clan refuse to eat hartebeeste and giraffe ; no reason is given, and it is said that the younger generation pay little attention to this prohibition.

" The Kamyak clan refuse to hunt or kill elephant, whom they call brothers, nor will elephants damage Kamyak cultivation.   The lion is also called a brother and may not be killed ; if a lion takes a Kamyak cow that lion is almost certain to die shortly for not observing the clan prohibition.

" The Rito clan refuse to eat elephant and fig, lest they be afflicted with disease.

" The Lokuamiro clan do not kill the lion, and call it brother ; no lion will touch a clansman or his property." [2]

Totemism of the Lotuko.—The Lotuko-speaking tribes occupy an area on the east bank of the Nile east of the Bari and north of the Acholi.

" The clans of the Tarangole group with their totem animals are as follows :—

Igago, with its sub-clans Kidongi, Marabat, Lejong, Katang, and possibly some others (all having arisen as divisions within Igago) having the crocodile as totem.
Lowudo, *namalong*, a monkey.
Lomini, the elephant.
Lomia, *manga*, the winged white ant.
Idjogok, *amunu*, a snake. . . .

[1] Seligman, *op. cit*. pp. 212 *sq*.   [2] Seligman, *op. cit*. pp. 244 *sq*.

" Descent is patrilineal, and the clans are exogamous; thus Igago, Lowudo, Lomia, and Lomini clans may all intermarry, but Kidongi, Marabat, Lejong, and Katang, are regarded as divisions that have split from Igago and so do not intermarry with each other or with Igago.

" There is no objection to marrying into the mother's clan, so long as the relationship is not too close. Several such marriages are recorded in our genealogies. We are not prepared to define the expression ' too close ' precisely. It is, however, certain that a man may not marry the daughter of his mother's sister."

Sympathy is supposed to exist between men and their clan animals, into which they are transformed at death. " As regards the change, the usual idea is that the animal which was the dead man is at first small, *e.g.* in the case of the Igago clan, whose members become crocodiles, tends to linger near the dwellings of the living. Later, it increases in size, and takes to the water, but often not before the *ibwoni* (medicine man) has treated it. So when a Lomini man dies, a herd will come and take with them the new elephant, while a troup of monkeys will fetch away the new monkey that was a Lowudo." [1]

Totemism of the Bongo.—The Bongo are a group of tribes inhabiting a territory on the Bahr el Ghazal or Blue Nile. " Each tribe (*kohu*) is divided into a number of patrilineal exogamous totemic clans, moreover a man may not marry a woman of his mother's clan. In some tribes certain clans appear to be more closely connected than others and will not intermarry, but two clans having the same totem are not necessarily debarred from marriage. The Bongo deny that they pass at death into their clan animal, and the main feature of their totemism appears to be a taboo on eating the clan animal." [2]

[1] Seligman, *op. cit.* pp. 310 *sq.*   [2] Seligman, *op. cit.* p. 466.

CHAPTER IV

TOTEMISM IN UGANDA

THE Protectorate of Uganda may on account of its geographical position be called the Heart of Central Africa. It is inhabited by many different tribes, most of them of the Bantu stock, who are divided into totemic and exogamous clans. The totemism of some of the principal of these tribes has already been described by me in *Totemism and Exogamy*.[1] My principal authority was my friend, the late Canon John Roscoe, who furnished me with a good deal of unpublished information, much of which he later published in his book, *The Northern Bantu* (Cambridge, 1915). Afterwards, in the years 1919 and 1920, through the generosity of the late Sir Peter Mackie, my friend was able to return to Uganda, and to visit and describe a number of tribes which he had not dealt with before. In what follows I shall endeavour to report the discoveries which he made in this his last expedition to the country which he knew so well, and in which he had spent the best years of his life.

Totemism of the Basabei.—On the north and northeastern slopes of Mount Elgon there is to be found a semipastoral tribe, divided into two sections, the Basabei and the Bambei.

" The Basabei said that at first their tribe was composed of three clans :—

1. *Gibisisi*, who avoided dogs (*embwa*).
2. *Goboro*, who avoided a kind of mushroom (*butiko*).
3. *Kyemwehe*, who avoided all kinds of vegetables.

" The founders of these clans were said to have come into

---

[1] *Totemism and Exogamy*, ii. 451 *sqq.*

the country with a cow and a calf and a bride named Yoboro.

" The tribe has now two main divisions, Basabei and Bambei, and the clans are numerous, though the tribe is numerically small, not amounting to more than several hundreds. Each clan has its own totem, which was, however, known only to a few of the principal members, who could not be induced to divulge it. The clans were all exogamous, and, with the exception ˜f a few dwellers near rivers, none of them would eat fish.'· [1]

Totemism of the Bakama.—" On one of the plateaux of Mount Elgon people were found who were called the Bakama, and who were regarded as a clan of the Sabei tribe. On investigation these were found to be one of the agricultural or artisan clans of Kitara,[2] who came to Mount Elgon from Buruli about the time Kamrasi reigned in Kitara, and who took the name .Bakama because of their allegiance to the Mukama of Kitara. Their totems were *nkima*, the black-faced monkey, and *kisanki*, the grass used for thatching houses ; and, as they understood smelting and general iron-work, they were important additions to the Sabei tribe, whose customs they to a large extent adopted." [3]

Totemism of the Bakonjo.—The Bakonjo were a small tribe inhabiting the eastern slopes of Mount Ruwenzori, a lofty mountain in the south-western part of Uganda, situated between Lake Albert on the north and ·Lake Edward on the south. The tribe seemed to be native to that region and numbered only a few hundreds.

" They were a totemic tribe, divided into a number of clans which followed the usual custom of clan exogamy. There is little doubt that each clan had a secondary as well as a primary totem, but during the short visit of the expedition to that region, it was not possible to discover it. The names of the clans with their primary totems were—

Baswaga,	totem *njoju*,	elephant.
Ahera,	,, *ngabi*,	antelope.
Abaswi,	,, *ekisuba*,	heron.
Abakira,	,, *mpunu*,	pig.

[1] J. Roscoe, *The Bagesu and other Tribes of the Uganda Protectorate* (Cambridge, 1924), p. 52.

[2] Kitara is the country of the large Bakitara or Banyoro tribe in the west of Uganda.

[3] J. Roscoe, *op. cit.* p. 83.

Abahambo,   ,,   *nseri*, crocodile.
Abasukari,   ,,   *mbogo*, buffalo." [1]

Totemism of the Bambwa.—The Bambwa were a mountain tribe living on the western slopes of the Ruwenzori range.
They were a turbulent people and were never completely
subdued, though in the past they were regarded as free-men
under the king of Kitara.

" Neighbouring tribes declared that the Bambwa were
cannibals ; and though the people themselves denied this,
the evidence pointed to the truth of the assertion. In fact
when I visited the western slopes of the mountain some
twenty-two years ago, I found them actually using human
flesh. . . .

" The tribe was divided into a number of totemic clans
which in most cases seemed to use the name of their totem
as the name of their clan :—

1. *Engo*, leopard.	11. *Njaza*, antelope.
2. *Nkende*, a kind of cat.	12. *Njojo*, elephant.
3. *Ngeye*.	13. *Nsumba*, cat.
4. *Nko*, a cat.	14. *Musu*, rat.
5. *Nsugu*.	15. *Omwaga*.
6. *Ntale*, lion.	16. *Mbuku*.
7. *Mpuru*, pig.	17. *Kapude*.
8. *Nsenge*.	18. *Kabebe*.
9. *Mbogo*, hippopotamus.	19. *Kakereme*.
10. *Mpara*, red buck.	20. *Kigasi*, monkey.

" Clan exogamy was practised, no man being permitted
to marry a woman whose totem was the same as his own." [2]

Totemism of the Bakunta.—The Bakunta are a small tribe
found on the shores of Lake Edward.

" The names of their clans with their totems were :—

1. Mamba,	totem	*mamba* (lung-fish).
2. Mamba Basonga,	,,	*mamba* (lung-fish) and *butiko* (fungus).
3. Bagahyi,	,,	*tseri* (frog).
4. Bakulungu,	,,	*ngobe* (monkey).
5. Nsenene Basonga,	,,	*nsenene* (grasshopper).
6. Abaitiri,	,,	*nte* (cow that had been with the bull).
7. Bayangwe,	,,	*nkuni* (antelope).
8. Abaluwha,	,,	*njovu* (elephant)." [3]

[1] J. Roscoe, *op. cit.* p. 137.   [2] J. Roscoe, *op. cit.* pp. 147 *sq.*
[3] J. Roscoe, *op. cit.* pp. 159 *sq.*

Totemism of the Bakyiga.—The Bakyiga occupy the southern part of the Ruwenzo͡ range of mountains, bordering on Lake Edward.

" I managed to obtain the names of some forty-eight clans, but only in a few cases could I find out their totems, though there was every reason to believe that each clan had one."

Among the clans were—

1. Basige (totem, *ente ngobe,* a cow with short straight horns. If such a cow was born in a man's own kraal, his people might drink its milk and eat its flesh, but if it was born anywhere else they had to avoid it).

2. Abageyho (totem, *epu,* meaning uncertain, possibly a kind of antelope).[1] Of the remaining forty-six clans Canon Roscoe gives the native names but without the English equivalents, which he could not ascertain.

Totemism of the Bahima or Banyankole.—The Bahima or Banyankole are a pastoral tribe inhabiting the district of Ankole, situated in the extreme south of Uganda, and to the west of Lake Victoria Nyanza. They have a system of totemism which has been already described on Canon Roscoe's authority in *Totemism and Exogamy.*[2] But on his last expedition to their country Canon Roscoe discovered some further details concerning it, which I will here subjoin in his own words.

" The marriage customs of the pastoral people of Ankole differed from those of many of the surrounding tribes in that they were not entirely exogamous. They had no rule to prevent members of different subsections of the same great clan from intermarrying. A man might marry a woman whose primary totem was the same as his own, provided that her second, or even a third totem differed. Thus the royal clan, *Abahinda,* had as totem *nkima,* a monkey with a black face *(colobus ?)* and millet *(bulo)* uncooked and unhusked. They might not marry into divisions of the clan which retained only these two totems, but they might marry into such divisions as the *Abasonga* which had a third totem, *kozi,* a black cow. The members of the three great clans of the tribe, the *Abahinda, Abasambo* and *Abagahe,* might intermarry without further enquiry, but within the clans marriage

[1] J. Roscoe, *op. cit.* p. 164.   [2] Vol. ii. pp. 532 *sqq.*

between members of the subdivisions was forbidden unless
they differed in at least one totem." [1]

Totemism of the Bakitara or Banyoro.—The Bakitara
or Banyoro are one of the largest tribes of Uganda. Their
country lies in the western part of the Protectorate. Of their
totemic system I have given some account in *Totemism and
Exogamy*,[2] in great measure from private information furnished me by my friend Canon John Roscoe. Since then
Canon Roscoe revisited the tribe for the last time during his
expedition of 1919–1920. He spent a considerable time
investigating the social structure and religious institutions of
the people with the personal aid of the king, who furnished
him with much valuable information. At the risk of repeating some details that have been given in my earlier work,
I will here subjoin Canon Roscoe's latest and fullest exposition of the totemic system of the Bakitara.

" The people of Kitara belong to two distinct races, but
by intermarriage an intermediate group was formed and the
lines of demarcation between the three groups have become
more and more vague and are rapidly disappearing. This
was the result of a policy, adopted, it is said, by a king who
ruled not many generations ago, by which certain restrictions
on intermarriage were removed, and some of the more pro-
gressive men of the agricultural class or serfs were raised to
the rank of free-men and permitted to marry women of the
pastoral clans.

" The two classes of which the nation was originally composed were (*a*) the *Bahuma*, or pastoral cow-men, who in-
vaded the country and conquered (*c*) the *Bahera*, agricultural
people and artisans, who were regarded as serfs. The third
group, which came into being later, was composed of (*b*) the
Banyoro, or free-men, the wealthy and important members
of class (*c*), who had been raised from serfdom and might
marry women from (*a*), the pastoral people, (*c*) the serfs, or
(*b*) their own class, so long as they did not marry women of
their own totemic clans. . . .

" The Bakitara are a totemic nation, divided into clans
numbering over one hundred. They can give no account

[1] J. Roscoe, *The Banyankole* (Cambridge, 1923), p. 119.
[2] Vol. ii. pp. 513 *sqq.*

of the origin of their totems, though one or two men say that their fathers warned them to avoid some particular kind of food which became taboo and their totem. The greatest use of the totemic system seems to be for defining consanguinity in connection with marriage regulations. This is by no means the only benefit of such a scheme of differentiation, for the system serves innumerable social and economic uses in daily life.

" With the existence of the three classes, we get three distinct groups of totems, one belonging to class (*a*), the pastoral people, one to class (*b*), showing the mixture or union of classes (*a*) and (*c*), and one to class (*c*), the agricultural people. Some of the clans, doubtless those of the pure pastoral people (*a*), have totems which relate to cattle alone ; the totems of others are connected with both cows and vege-tables and are evidently those of men who have sprung from mixed marriages ; while the agricultural class naturally have totems connected with the field. Some of the pastoral clans have totems which pertain to cows at certain times, after which time, when the conditions change, the animal is no longer a totem. For example, when a cow has drunk salt water she is a totem to a certain clan during that day, and her milk may not be drunk by any member of that clan ; but the next day the cow is no longer a totem and her milk may be drunk ; again, for five days after a cow has mated, she is a totem to certain clans who may not drink milk from her nor eat the meat should she be killed, but after the five days that cow ceases to be a totem. Other clans have a part of a cow as their totem ; some must avoid the tongue, others may not touch the heart, while others again refrain from eating the intestines. In each of these instances only this part of the animal is taboo ; they may eat freely from any other part and they may drink the milk.

" The royal family have as their principal totem the bush-buck (*ngabi*), which is somewhat difficult to understand, for we should have expected a cow. It is possible that the present dynasty, which is said to have come over the Nile from Bukedi, was originally not of pure pastoral stock, or, at any rate, had not been so strict in adhering to pastoral customs. It is also rather peculiar that there are many other clans, not royal, which have the bush-buck as their totem. Possibly these were in existence in the country before the arrival of the present royal family. There are also many branches of the royal clan, but it is difficult to discover any reason for their splitting off.

" Though most if not all clans have a second totem, few of them pay much attention to it ; it is seldom named, and, so far as I can discover, is only mentioned when it is necessary to distinguish between persons having the same primary totem. Owing to the slight importance of the secondary totem, which, in many cases, is not generally known, it has been impossible to secure as much information concerning the clans as is desirable.

TOTEMS OF GROUP (A), THE PASTORAL PEOPLE

Name of Clan	Totems
1. Babito (royal clan)	Ngabi, bush-buck. Maleghyo, rain water from the roof of a house.
2. Bachaki	Ngabi, bush-buck. Maleghyo, rain water from a house (subsection of Babito).
3. Abangamwoyo	Same totems, also a subsection of Babito.
4. Abachwa	,, ,,
5. Abagweri	,,
6. Abagumba	,,
7. Ababambora	,,
8. Abandikasa	,,
9. Abahangwe	,,
10. Abategwa	,,
11. Abachwera	,,
12. Abanyakwa	Ngabi, bush-buck. Ngobe, cow with short straight horns.
13. Abalebyeki	Ngabi, bush-buck.
14. Abanyuagi	,, ,,
15. Ababoro	,, ,,
16. Abakwonga	,, ,,
17. Abadwalo	,, ,,
18. Abajagara	,, ,,
19. Abagomba	,, ,,
20. Abamori	Koroko, hippopotamus. Ngabi, bush-buck.
21. Abagorongwa	,, ,,
22. Abaziraija	,, ,,
23. Abapasisa	,, ,,
24. Abagaya	,, ,,

TOTEMS OF GROUP (A), THE PASTORAL PEOPLE—*continued*

Name of Clan	Totems
25. Abatabi . . .	Koroko, hippopotamus. Ngabi, bush-buck.
26. Abahemba . .	,, ,,
27. Abatwairwe . .	,, ,,
28. Abapina . . .	,, ,,
29. Abasita . . .	Ente emira, cow which has drunk salt water. Maleghyo, rain water from the roof of a house.
30. Abasita . . .	Busito, cow after mating. Muka, dew on the grass.
31. Ababyasi . .	Busito, cow after mating.
32. Abacwezi . .	Ente emira, cow which has drunk salt water. Busito, cow after mating.
33. Abahemba . .	Busito, cow after mating.
34. Abaisanza . .	Etimba, cow marked red and black. Butweke, woman who enters a kraal, solicits the owner's son, and bears a child to him. She must never enter a kraal of the clan again, nor may any member of the clan hold converse with her.
35. Abakurungo . .	Etimba, cow marked red and black. Butweke, woman who enters a kraal, solicits the owner's son, and bears a child to him.
36. Abagabu . .	Nkira, tailless cow. Ezobe, cow of a particular colour.
37. Abasaiga . .	Nkira, tailless cow.
38. Abasengya . .	Ngobe, cow with straight horns. Lulimi, tongue of animals.
39. Abasingo . .	Mulara, black cow with white stripes down face and back. Busito, cow after mating.
40. Abangoro . .	Mulara, a black cow with white stripes. These split from Abasingo because their companions had killed a man and they feared the consequences.
41. Abami . . .	Mpulu, spotted cow.
42. Abayanja . .	Kitara, white cow.
43. Abazima . . .	Mgobo, black cow.
44. Abasonda . .	Cow marked like a zebra.
45. Abatembe . .	Ngabi, bush-buck.
46. Ababyasi . .	Ekuluzi, cow with calf for the second time.
47. Abakwakwa . .	Ngobe, cow with short straight horns.
48. Abatwa . . .	Milch cow. Nsugu, grass which has been put into the mouth.

TOTEMS OF GROUP (B), THE FREE-MEN

Name of Clan	Totems
1. Abanyonza . .	Etima, red and black cow. Ngobe, cow with short straight horns.
2. Abalanzi . . .	Etima and Ngobe.
3. Abalisa . . .	Etima, red and black cow. Maleghyo, rain water from the roofs of houses.
4. Abasumbi . .	Etimba, red and black cow. Ngobe, cow with short straight horns.
5. Abagahe . . .	Etimba, red and black cow.
6. Abafunjo . .	Munyere, cow of some particular colour. Ngobe, cow with short straight horns.
7. Ababworo . .	Cow marked red and white. Maleghyo, rain water from the houses.
8. Abalebeki . .	Same totems.
9. Abagimu . . .	,, ,,
10. Abairuntu . .	Mulara, black cow with white stripes. Mjojo, the elephant.
11. Abanyama . .	Mutima, heart of animals.
12. Abaitira . .	Eseleke, cow of a particular colour. Isereke, woman who is a stranger and is nursing a female child.
13. Abarega . . .	Maleghyo, rain water from houses.
14. Abarigira . .	The same.
15. Abangali or Abagabo .	Nkira, tail-less cow.
16. Abakwonga . .	Ngabi, bush-buck.
17. Abayangwe . .	Nkondo, grey monkey. Nkobe, large monkey.
18. Abagweju . .	A house burned down. The place is avoided and no vessel from such a place used.
19. Abatongo . .	Amara, the stomach of animals.
20. Abasengya . .	Ngabi, bush-buck. Maleghyo, rain water from houses.
21. Abakimbiri . .	Isereke, woman nursing a female child.
22. Abysima . .	Ngabi, bush-buck.
23. Abaraha . .	Akanyamasole, wagtail.
24. Abalageya . .	Nlegeya, bird.

TOTEMS OF GROUP (C), THE SERFS

Name of Clan	Totems
1. Abafumambogo	Abazaza nedongo, twins. Nsenene, grasshopper. Mbogo, black cow.
2. Abayaga . . .	Kanyamukonge, bird. A fly. Millet.
3. Abahinda . .	Nkonde, monkey.
4. Abasambo . .	Obutweke, girl who has gone wrong. Kaibo-hasa, empty basket.
5. Aberi . . .	Enyangi, bird.
6. Abasuli . .	Mbuzi, goat.
7. Abalaha . .	Akatengetenge (?).
8. Abasonga . .	Nesenene, grasshopper.
9. Abahango . .	„ „
10. Abakami . .	Akamyu, hare.
11. Abasogo . .	Akaibo batera omutwe, basket put on the head.
12. Abagombi . .	Biweju, sugar-cane.
13. Abachubo . .	Echu, kind of fish.
14. Ababopi . .	Ekigangoro, centipede.
15. Abazazi . .	Echu, kind of fish. Mamba, lung fish.
16. Abango . .	Akabaimbira, skin of leopards. These came from Abasingo, and separated because of a quarrel over a skin.
17. Abaregeya . .	Njobi, monkey. Musokisoki, bird.
18. Abaisanza . .	Epo, kind of antelope.
19. Ababiiro . .	Ndaha, guinea fowl.
20. Abanana . .	„ „
21. Abaduka . .	The old skin of a drum.
22. Abahenga . .	Kagondo, small black water bird.
23. Abaho . .	Kalozi, fungus growing on trees.
24. Abanyampaka .	Kagondo, small black water bird.
25. Abanyonza . .	Nyonza, bird. Kaibo hasa, empty basket.
26. Abagimu . .	Mpulu, spotted cow. Maleghyo, rain water from houses.
27. Abahembo . .	Kaibo-hasa, empty basket.
28. Abasengya . .	Lugara, a wooden spoon.
29. Abagere . .	Njaza, an antelope.
30. Ababoro . .	Mutima, heart of animals. Kaibo-hasa, empty basket.
31. Abasanza . .	Maleghyo, rain water from houses.
32. Abakimbiri . .	Bumpa, potters' clay. Grain left in the field all night at harvest.
33. Abasihiri . .	Yam." [1]

[1] J. Roscoe, *The Bakitara or Banyoro* (Cambridge, 1923), pp. 12 *sqq.*

" Among both the pastoral and agricultural tribes of Kitara, with the exception of the royal family, clan exogamy was enforced, and it was a criminal offence for a couple who belonged to the same clan to form an alliance. The guilty pair would be condemned by all the members of their clan, with the complete assent of their respective parents.

" Blood relationship was also carefully considered, for a man might not marry into the clan of his parents or of his grandparents, though he might marry into the clan from which any of his grandparents had come. The totem was the chief guide as to relationships." [1]

Totemism of the Baganda.—The Baganda, the principal tribe of Uganda, to which they have given their name, have a complete system of totemic and exogamous clans. I give an account of the system in *Totemism and Exogamy*,[2] mainly from private information furnished to me by my friend Canon John Roscoe. That account has since been substantially repeated by him in his book *The Baganda*,[3] to which I would refer the reader for a comparison with my statement of the facts.

[1] J. Roscoe, *op. cit.* p. 264.
[2] Vol. ii. pp. 463-513.
[3] Rev. J. Roscoe, *The Baganda,*

an Account of their Native Customs and Beliefs (London, 1911), pp. 133-185.

CHAPTER V

TOTEMISM IN KIZIBA

KIZIBA is a district in Tanganyika, situated on the west shore of Lake Victoria Nyanza, to the south of Ruanda. The natives of the district belong to two distinct stocks, the Bairu, the aboriginal inhabitants, and the Bahima, who are immigrants from the north. But the Bahima form only a small percentage of the population.

The royal family bears the name of Bahinda. There are besides twenty-seven clans. All members belonging to a clan have the same totem (*muziro*), which is regularly some edible animal. But the totem may also be some other tabooed object. If anyone injures his totem animal or eats the food forbidden to his clan, he suffers from an irruption of the skin on the arms and hands.

Not only does a human being stand in a peculiar relation to his or her totem, but the totem itself stands in a like peculiar relation to other objects. For example on the wood of a certain totem tree (*muziro nyama*) no flesh may be cooked, or again with a stick of another kind of tree (*nkoni etarer'omunyanya*) a man may not strike his sister, and similarly cattle may not be struck with the wood of another totem tree (*nkoni etater'ente*).

The natives can tell in each case why a certain clan may not eat the flesh of a particular species of animal. Generally the reason assigned is that an animal or animals of that species have rendered some service to the ancestors of the clan.

Members of the same clan (*ruganda*) may not intermarry. The children, both male and female, belong to the clan of their father.

The royal family stand in a special totemic relationship to snakes. The *nkoronkima* snake is the totem of the males, and the *mpiri* snake is the totem of the female members of the house. When a male member of a royal family dies his ghost or spirit passes out from his head through the wall of the hut, and enters into the body of his totem snake (*nkoronkima*). So also when a princess dies her ghost or spirit enters into the body of her totem snake (*mpiri*).[1]

[1] H. Rehse, *Kiziba Land und Leute* (Stuttgart, 1910), pp. 84 *sqq.*

CHAPTER VI

TOTEMISM OF THE BARUNDI

URUNDI is a district of Tanganyika that lies south of Ruanda, between Lake Victoria Nyanza on the north-east, and Lake Tanganyika on the south-west. The population is composed of three elements : firstly, the Bahutu, an agricultural Bantu people ; secondly, the Batussi, a pastoral Hamitic people ; and thirdly the Batwa, a hunter and forest pigmy people. The Batwa are the oldest element in the population. The Bahutu came from the east, destroying the forests in their advance. The Batussi have adopted the Bantu language.[1]

The totemic clan is the basis of the social organisation of Urundi, as in Ruanda, Karagwe, Kiziba, Ankole, and elsewhere. Many of the clan names of the Barundi are found in Ruanda, Chyoro (Kitara), and Ankole. Many of the clannames are common to the Batussi and Bahutu ; some are common to the Batwa.

The chief features of the totemic system common to all the clans are : the patriarchal character of its structure ; the exogamy of the clans ; the totemic nature of the clans and the associated taboos and restrictions, especially food taboos, imposed upon their members. The communism of the clan is another of its characteristics.

Descent of the clan is in the paternal line, and every child belongs from birth to the clan of its father. Strict exogamy is the rule. Marriages between members of the same clan are forbidden, and a clan member may take a wife only from another clan. Moreover it seems that the members of a clan are not free to marry members of any other clans, but

[1] H. Meyer, *Die Barundi* (Leipzig, 1916), pp. 6 *sq.*

that they are restricted in their choice to a certain number of clans. The royal clan (the Baganwa) are not strictly exogamous. In Urundi, as in Ruanda, the king may or must marry his own sister or daughter.

Several clans have the same totem : probably these formed originally a single clan, which was broken up and dispersed.

The totem is an object of respect, if only in the negative sense that everything connected with it must be strictly avoided by the members of the clan. In the great majority of cases the totems are animals or parts of animals : much less often they are artificial objects like baskets or cushions ; still less frequently they are plants or parts of plants. They have also split totems, for example the liver, heart, or entrails of an animal. They believe that the soul of a dead clansman passes into his totem animal.

The totem is the object of shy avoidance : to injure or kill the totem animal is an offence that can be expiated only with difficulty. It is forbidden to eat its flesh or blood or to drink its milk. Out of these taboos has been developed the present strong belief that the flesh, blood, and milk of a totem animal are unclean and will harm the clan member who partakes of them. This pollution can only be expiated by elaborate ceremonies. A breach of the totem taboo, especially of the food restriction often results in the sickness of the transgressor or even in his death. Respect for the totem leads members of a clan to avoid all contact with the members of other clans who eat the totemic animal. The totemic restrictions on food are not binding upon children, though they are so upon women. In the inner organisation and life of the clan the strong feeling of solidarity of its members finds expression in a far-reaching communal system. The clan community is ruled by an elected elder or headman, and the land is the common property of the clan.

The feudal organisation of the country under the king tends to break up and destroy the social and economic organisation of the totemic clans, which, however, long retain their clan names, their totems, and their old customs. One element of the ancient social organisation of the totemic clans is retained under the new political order, namely, the custom of blood revenge, which is still the strongest safe-guard of the individual, though public and private security has increased under the strong rule of the feudal lords. Under the rule of the kings the blood revenge of the clan is exercised in secret, no longer openly as in former times.[1]

[1] H. Meyer, *op. cit.* pp. 98 *sqq.*

CHAPTER VII

TOTEMISM IN NORTHERN NIGERIA

Totemism of the Bachama and Mbula.—Totemism is widely diffused among the tribes of Northern Nigeria, and it is found in the form both of clan totems and individual or personal totems. On this subject Mr. C. K. Meek tells us : " A feature of the social and religious life of the Bachama (as also of the Mbula, Kanakuru and Longuda tribes) is the presence of totemic beliefs. These occur in two forms, viz. (*a*) a sense of relationship between an extended family or kindred and a species of animal, and (*b*) a sense of relationship between an individual and an animal. As regards the former the totem is transmitted in the male line, the family group being formed on patriarchal principles : but in the latter case the totem is transmitted by females, so that there is (or may be) a totem kin as distinct from the family group. But not all kindreds, nor yet all individuals, have totems. Indeed, the possession of a totem appears to be exceptional, and there are reasons for believing that such totemism as exists was introduced from the Mbula tribe, a people who speak a language which is definitely Bantoid.

" The Mbamo kindred respect the bush-cat, and . . . carry out harvest rites at the bush-cat shrine, just as though the bush-cat were some deity. If a Mbamo loses his way in the bush he will call on the bush-cat to show him his way home, in the same way as members of other tribes will call on the sun or the Supreme Being. The Mbamo regard themselves as the ' children ' of the bush-cat, and believe that all that they have in life—their food, their health and children—

are the gifts of the bush-cat. If they fall sick, or if anything goes wrong, they resort to the bush-cat shrine at Bolen ; and one whose son has been sick for a considerable period will hand him over permanently to the priest of the Bolen cult. So much do they respect the flesh of the bush-cat that it is taboo to eat the flesh of any animal bearing similar stripes. No Mbamo, therefore, will touch the flesh of a leopard or hyena. If any non-Mbamo had killed a bush-cat and subsequently touched the person of a Mbamo the body of the latter would immediately be covered with sores, and he would have speedily to find a ' medicine.' There is, however, no personal association with individual bush-cats, though an enemy of the Mbamo may charge one of their number with having, as a bush-cat, stolen one of his chickens during the night. On the other hand the bush-cat takes a personal interest in the welfare of all members of the Mbamo clan. If anyone thieves from a Mbamo the bush-cat will cry outside the thief's house, and the members of the household will know that one of their number had committed an offence against one of the Mbamo group. The thief, stricken with fear, will, it is said, betake himself forthwith to the person from whom he stole, confess his offence and solicit his protection. The Mbamo concerned will take him to the shrine at Bolen and say to the priest of the cult : ' This man stole from me : I bring him to the bush-cat, for the bush-cat went to him.' The priest will question the thief who will straightway confess his guilt and offer to the priest a white cloth in recompense. This the priest binds on to the roof of the shrine. He then takes some cotton and passes it round the offender's head, and there the matter ends. . . . It is of interest to note that stolen goods subsequently restored become the property of the priest and are not returned to the complainant. The bark of the Bauhinia Reticulata tree is sacred to the bush-cat, and strips are deposited beside the symbol of the cult. These strips are issued as charms by the priest to members of the clan ; bracelets for men and necklaces for women. The priest is attended by a boy who, every evening, is required to light a fire in the hut of the priest. Some of the embers are carried to the shrine, as the bush-cat is believed to be fond of warmth.

" There are one or two other kindreds which have totem animals. Thus the Ndaka of Yimburu associate themselves with water-tortoises. But the water-tortoise does not appear to be a totem for the whole Ndaka clan, as there is a group of Ndaka in the Bata district which has no totem. It may be said generally that the majority of the Bachama kindreds or clans are non-totemic.

" Turning now to the individual relationship of a man or woman to some animal, derived from his or her mother, this appears to be fairly common. The general conception is that the man and his animal counterpart are each the double or *alter ego* of the other. The fortunes of the two are so closely bound together that nothing can happen to the one without a corresponding reaction on the other. The sickness or death of one connotes the sickness or death of the other. The man can influence and direct the movements of his animal counterpart, and the latter can visit at night his human counterpart and warn him of possible dangers. If a man who is associated with a hippopotamus knows that his fellow-townsmen are going to hunt hippopotami he can warn his hippopotamus *alter ego*, together with other hippopotami who are its relatives, to leave the herd that day. If a hippopotamus upsets a canoe his human counterpart is fully aware of the fact, however far away he may be. If the man is himself in a canoe, and his hippopotamus *alter ego*, or even hippopotami who are counterparts of members of his totem-kin, come to attack his canoe he merely orders them to be gone, and off they go. Totemic conceptions of this character occur among the Bura, Kilba, Kanakuru and Yungur tribes. Among the last, for example, there is a kindred at Waltandi which has a special association with roan antelopes. None of the kindred, therefore, may shoot a roan antelope. Any member of another kindred who wishes to shoot a roan antelope will first present himself before one of the roan kindred with a gift of a pot of beer and two hoes, soliciting the assistance of the kindred. The person approached will then indicate to the petitioner where the roans are accustomed to graze, but he will warn the hunter that he must avoid shooting the leader of the herd, as the leader of the herd is his own second self. From this it appears that although all of the roan kindred have animal counterparts not all roans have human counterparts." [1]

From the preceding account it appears that among the Mbamo the bush-cat receives a form of worship, and has therefore made some progress towards becoming a god.

Totemism of the Bata-speaking Peoples.—"Totemic ideas do not play any significant part in the life of the Malabu.[2] It was stated that the royal clan respect the crocodile, on the ground that once upon a time a Baza maiden was, on the day of her marriage, seized by a crocodile. The Gogen also respect the crocodile. The Magdari, Tara and Jekin have a special association with leopards, and this would suggest that all these three kindreds belonged, as their tradition indicates, to a common stock. The association is ascribed to the circumstance that an ancestress of the group bore twins, one of which was a leopard and the other a boy. The two lived in close association, the leopard visiting the boy at night and bringing him a share of his quarry, and the boy feeding the leopard when the leopard had failed to kill game. And just as the original leopard and man were brothers so their offspring also became brothers, each assisting the other, and being identified, so that any (human) of the three kindred could turn himself into a leopard if he so desired. In later times the association became lost because the ' medicine ' necessary for its maintenance was destroyed in a fire." [3]

We have seen that similarly among the Dinka the origin of a totem clan is often ascribed to the twin birth of a human being and the animal totem.[4]

Totemism of the Bura and Pabir Tribes.—Among these people, " the clan does not coincide with the local group, for in most village areas you find groups of several clans living together, and where this is the case the authority, civil and religious, is usually vested in the senior member of the senior clan. The clan as a whole is, however, localised (in contradistinction to the phratry which is scattered). Descent is patrilineal, but the sense of kinship is not confined to the clan

---

[1] C. K. Meek, *Tribal Studies in Northern Nigeria* (London, 1931), i. 10 *sqq.*

[2] The Malabu are a group of the Bata-speaking people.

[3] C. K. Meek, *op. cit.* i. 97.

[4] See above, p. 433.

(in which the descent from a common ancestor may be fictitious or at anyrate cannot be demonstrated), but extends to relatives on the mother's side whose relationship can easily be traced. Among the Bura all cousin marriage is forbidden, but among the Pabir cross-cousin marriage is practised in the Woviri or royal family group.

" The sense of association with a totem is vague. In some instances the clan disclaimed any such associations, but it is possible that in such cases a closer enquiry than I was able to give would have revealed the totem. Thus the Gamsana clan of the Mbeiya phratry, while stating that one of the African mahoganies (*Afzelia africana*) might not be burnt by any Gamsana (if it were their children would be injured by fire), could give no account of this taboo. Usually all the three main characteristics of totemism could be traced, viz. the association of an animal or tree species with the exogamous group (clan), the belief in the sense of relationship between the members of the clan and the animal or tree, and the respect shown by the members of the clan to the animal or tree.

" In at least two instances the name of the totem was identical with that of the social group. The Bwola phratry respects the *Ficus platyphylla* and the name for this tree in the Bura language is Bwola. The Minta clan of the Pabir respects the *Afzelia africana* tree and the Pabir name for this tree is Minta. The members of a clan refer to the totem animal species as their brethren, but they do not usually claim descent from the totem (as is the case with some of the Zaria tribes). The relationship is rather one of alliance. The following are instances of how the relationship is said to have arisen. The Lasama totem is the *Mamba*. Once upon a time a Lasama was captured in war and was put in the stocks to await sacrifice. In the early morning a *Mamba* crawled up to him and so frightened him that he gave a lurch, which freed his legs and he escaped. All *Mambas* were therefore proclaimed to be friends of the Lasama and no Lasama may kill or injure a *Mamba*. *Mambas* will not, it is said, injure a Lasama, and any Lasama coming across the dead body of a Mamba must bury it.

" The Mbeiya of Sakwa state that their totem is the *tsala kokwa* snake. The founder of the clan was troubled because he was getting old and had no children. In his sleep he dreamed that someone bade him go and dig in the ground, and when he found the tail of a living thing he was to cut it off, sew it up in leather, and give it to his wife ; so he dug and came across a tail and gave it to his wife and she bore a child and eventually had a large family. The man wondered at the marvel, and went again to the hole and dug deeper and found the body of the snake. And so he forbade any of his children to kill any of that species of snake, and if they came across its dead body they were to bury it.

" The totem of the Gauja clan is the *Varanus niloticus* Any member of the clan eating it would be covered with sores, and his body would waste away. The dead body of a *Varanus* must be buried respectfully, ' its secret must not be discovered.' An injured *Varanus* in the possession of any member of another clan must be ransomed." [1]

Totemism of the Mumuye and neighbouring Tribes.—" It appeared that formerly each kindred had its sacred or taboo animal. Thus the We-Passe avoided eating the flesh of bush-pigs, the We Gaure of rock coney, the We Kenna of jackal, and the We-Guda of bush-cat. Anyone breaking the taboo would be assailed by leprosy. Little importance is attached to these taboos nowadays, and there is no prohibition against marrying a person whose taboo animal is the same as his own. For the rule of exogamy is only carried out as far as second cousins, so that a We-Passe man may marry a We-Passe woman provided she is not a first or second cousin." [2]

Totemism of the Katab.—" Some of the Katab clans have certain animal or plant taboos, but these do not appear to be closely associated with the system of clan exogamy or to play a prominent part in maintaining the sense of relationship between the members of the clan. . .

" The Agbat clan respects the crocodile (*tsang*). It is their friend and brother (*nauyuk*) and on it they swear oaths. An Agbat, it is said, can play unharmed with a crocodile in the water. If he sees its dead body, he hastily retreats, or buries it. He will not even touch a piece of crocodile skin. If he kills a crocodile by accident he must hurry off to the forest for some

[1] C. K. Meek, *op. cit.* i. 148 *sqq.*　　　　[2] C. K. Meek, *op. cit.* i. 498.

special medicine ; if he kills it by design the entire clan will,
it is believed, perish.   The reason assigned for this association
is that once in ancient times the *Katab* were flying from their
enemies and came to an unfordable river.   Crocodiles formed
a bridge for the Agbat, but swam away when the other
Katab clans tried to cross by the same means.   An Agbat
can frighten a crocodile by merely calling out the name of
some other clan than his own.   There does not appear to be
any belief nowadays that an Agbat, on dying, turns into a
crocodile, but it was stated that when an old Agbat man dies
his friends sing : ' The water is all astir—the crocodile is
entering.'   An Agbat woman does not cease to respect the
crocodile on her marriage, and it was said that the son of
an Agbat woman, though he takes his exogamic unit from
his father, shows respect to his mother's totem as well as to
his father's.   The Agbat also, apparently, respect the leopard.
If an Agbat kills a leopard he is required by custom to perform
certain rites designed to protect him from the ghost of the
dead animal.   He sends a friend or relative to a neighbouring
tribe (Kagoro) for medicine, some of which he drinks and
some of which he smears on his body.   He will not eat
leopard's flesh or wear a leopard's skin.   The reason now
assigned for this respect is that once in bygone days an
Agbat ate leopard's flesh and his body became covered with
boils.   The Agbat do not call themselves ' Leopards,' but
they state that in battle they were always put in the van, and
as they rushed forward they shouted ' We are leopards ; we
cannot run away.'

" The Shokwa clan respect the *tatong*, one of the lizard
family.   The association of the *tatong* with the Shokwa clan
was begun, it is said, in the following way.   Shokwa, the
founder of the clan, was sitting alone in his house lighting a
fire.   A *tatong*, hearing the noise, came and spoke to Shokwa,
asking who he was and where were his relatives.   Shokwa
replied that he had no relatives, and the *tatong* then assured
him that God would increase his family.   This prophecy
came true, and Shokwa ordered all his children to respect
the *tatong* for all time.   And so no man of Shokwa may
injure a *tatong*, and if he finds one he takes it to the priestly
head of the Kuzat family who houses it in a granary, feeds it

with beniseed and finally releases it with blessings. For
the Shokwa regard the *tatong* as a relative, and if they find
the body of a dead *tatong* will cover it with earth reverently,
holding a funeral feast as they would for one of their old
men.   Should a Shokwa man kill a *tatong* accidentally rain
would fall, even in the middle of the dry season.   The most
binding oath a Shokwa can make is by the *tatong*.   The
respect shown by the Shokwa is shared by all the Katab
clans, and any member of another clan living near Shokwa
who accidentally killed a *tatong* would take its body to
Shokwa for burial.   The Shokwa people do not, however,
call themselves by the name of their emblem animal.   On
the contrary, the *tatong's* name is taboo." [1]

Totemism of the Kurama of Zaria Province.—" The
following is a list of some of the Kurama clans :—

" (1) The Asare, with exogamous subdivisions scattered
throughout the tribe.   The clan emblem is the crocodile,
which is regarded as a relative for the following reason.
One of the Har Asare tried to commit suicide by drowning
himself.   A crocodile appeared in the river, and said to him :
' You are related to us and are therefore one of us.'   And so
he was transformed into a crocodile.   Later, as a crocodile,
he was lying on the bank when one of his late fellow-villagers
appeared and drew an arrow on him.   The crocodile said to
him : ' Stay, for I am your brother and dwelt with you in
the village on the hill.'   In this way all the Har Asare were
made aware that crocodiles were their relatives.   The informant was unable to say whether the crocodiles contained
the souls of living or dead Har Asare, but stated that if
accidentally they killed a baby crocodile during a fishing
drive then one of their children would die simultaneously in
the village.   An Asare can play fearlessly with a crocodile.
If he inconveniences a crocodile during his fishing he will
be assailed with sickness.   If he catches a young crocodile
in his net he must abandon the net and any fish he may have
netted.   If he sees the corpse of a crocodile he must dig a
grave for it and bury it reverently, pushing the corpse into
the grave with sticks, for he may not touch it with his hands.
The use of crocodile's skin for any purpose is taboo, and an

[1] C. K. Meek, *op. cit.* ii. 6 *sqq.*

Asare will even avoid eating food cut up by a knife the sheath of which had been made of crocodile's skin. An Asare woman who is enceinte and eats crocodile's flesh will promptly abort. The Asare do not call themselves by the name of their emblem animal.

" (2) The Kamau are a small exogamous group entirely localised at Garu. Their emblem is the *bahawa*, an animal which they say resembles a red buffalo but is much smaller, and is not found in the country now inhabited by the Kurama, an indication that some at least of the Kurama came from distant parts. . . .

" (3) The Lisha are found (*a*) at the villages of Jura, Galma, and Oroko, and (*b*) at Muda kare. Each section is exogamous, but any man of (*a*) may marry any woman of (*b*) and *vice versa*. Moreover, sections (*a*) and (*b*) have distinct emblems, that of the former being the *bahawa*, that of the latter being the red frog (*okave*). Each section has its own hereditary social chief, who is the arbiter of quarrels between members of his own subdivision. These facts would seem to indicate that each section originally belonged to a different clan. . . . The reason assigned for the association with the *bahawa* was as follows : some women of the Lisha (*section* (*a*)) were out farming one day, and had left their babies under the trees. Hunters came along and scattered a herd of *bahawa* among the babies. But when the mothers returned not a single child had been injured, and so the *bahawa* were known to be their relatives. Oaths are sworn on the *bahawa*, and it was said that formerly when the Lisha lived in the country of *bahawa*, it was customary to cover the dead body of a *bahawa* with leaves.

" (4) The Areru are localized at Garu and Dama Kasua. They are exogamous and appear to respect the cock (*bug-wara*). It was stated that if the husband of an Areru woman had had a cock cooked in the compound he had subsequently to purify the place where it had been cooked by sweeping it with the leaves of the locust-bean and shea trees. The place would be taboo to his wife for two days. The husband, moreover, might not sleep with his wife on the evening of the day on which he had eaten the cock's flesh. . . ."[1]

[1] C. K. Meek, *op. cit.* ii. 166 *sqq.*

Totemism of the Kare-Kare of Bornu Province.—" The (Kare-Kare) tribe consists socially of a number of exogamous divisions, each division being composed of one or more kindred which are believed to be related. . . .

" Each of the social divisions appears to associate itself to some extent with some species of animal, but such evidence as I was able to obtain in the very short time spent among the Kare-Kare showed that totemism, or what used to be described as totemism, is now breaking down. The Dagare division, for instance, does not appear to have any emblem at all other than the sacred spear. The Masgabai stated that they respected the *Shamwa* stork. But the Arku and Jellam divisions (and also the villagers of Kurfa and Dalmari) made a similar statement, and it appeared, indeed, that the *Shamwa* was to some extent respected by most of the Kare-Kare. If the *Shamwa* was ever a ' totem,' then the totemic grouping was much larger than the exogamous grouping of to-day. Similarly the leopard was stated to be taboo to at least four of the social divisions, viz. Langawa, Deguri, Aisa, and Sikau (between whom there is no prohibition of intermarriage). Incidentally, the Aisa and Langawa divisions of the Kare-Kare gave the same reason for respecting the leopard as was given by the Masgabai division of the Ngizim tribe, viz. that when the wife of one of the ancestors of the division found herself without any means of carrying her newly-born babe a kindly leopard brought to her house a dead gazelle, from the skin of which she was able to manufacture a satchel. . . .

" Descent is reckoned patrilineally, but intermarriage with close relatives on the mother's side, *e.g.* first, second, or third cousins, is against the tribal custom. The junior, but not the senior, levirate is practised, and sons inherit, and may marry, the widows of their fathers' and other paternal uncles." [1]

Totemism of the Ngizim of Bornu Province.—" The social organization (of the Ngizim) resembles that of the Kare-Kare, *i.e.* the tribe consists of a number of divisions fairly well localized, each of which is exogamous and each of which is associated (though frequently in a vague way

[1] C. K. Meek, *op. cit.* ii. pp. 220 *sqq.*

only) with some species of animal.   Thus, in the vicinity of
Potiskum (Southern Ngizim) we find the following social
divisions :—

(*a*) Mugunum	associated with the		hyena.
(*b*) Patiskum	,,	,,	hyena.
(*c*) Masgabai	,,	,,	leopard.
(*d*) Daja	,,	,,	snakes.
(*e*) Yenuwak	,,	,,	crane.
(*f*) Zumi	,,	,,	centipede.
(*g*) Jellam	,,	,,	hyena.
(*h*) Guzhagum	,,	,,	stork.
(*i*) Audassa	,,	,,	leopard.
(*j*) Makinmu	,,	,,	frog.
(*k*) Dagazurwa	,,	,,	stork.

" Each of these divisions is exogamous, that is to say (*e.g.*),
no Daja man may marry a Daja woman.   But any Daja
man may marry any woman of any other division.   There
is an exception, however, to this rule ; for a Mugunum man
may not marry a Patiskum woman, on the ground of some
supposed relationship between these two divisions.   Both
have the hyena emblem, and it is probable, therefore, that
Mugunum and Patiskum are merely localized groups of some
former larger social division, which possibly also included
Jellam ; for it was stated that intermarriage between the
Patiskum and Jellam stocks was not permitted, both divisions
having the hyena emblem, *i.e.* considering themselves related
to or allied with the hyena. . . .

" The Zumi social division respect the centipede, the
Ngizim word for which is *zumi*.   Thus we have here an
instance of a social division calling itself by the name of its
emblem. . . . The reason assigned for the association of the
Zumi division with the centipede is that a centipede once
stung one of the ancestors of the Zumi.   Thereafter the name
of Centipedes was adopted for the group, and in consequence,
no Zumi has ever since been stung by a centipede.   It was
said that in former days any Zumi could play unharmed with
a centipede, but that nowadays they do not attempt to do so.

" Those who respect the hyena (viz. the Mugunum,
Patiskum, and Jellam divisions) bury the dead body of a
hyena if they come across it in the bush.   They would not
think of killing a hyena themselves, and might take action

2 H

against any local resident of another division who had killed a hyena. They would refuse to share a meal with him and would even thrash him ; for they would consider that the blood of the hyena was on their head and that in consequence they might be attacked by leprosy. Hyenas in turn, they say, respect their human relatives, and refrain from visiting their compounds to steal.

" The Masgabai respect the leopard for the same reason as was given in the notes on the Kare-Kare, viz. that a leopard had provided the wife of an ancestor with a gazelle in order that she might make a satchel in which to carry her new-born babe. The Audassa, who also respect the leopard, stated that in former times any Audassa woman who was about to bear a child was favoured in this way.

" The Daja appear to respect all snakes rather than any particular species, but further enquiries might show this to be incorrect.

" The sense of association with the emblem animal is not always very potent, and in some cases the informants had to think twice before they could say what their emblem animal was. It was stated that husbands respected the emblems of wives ; but on two occasions the husbands had first to refer to their wives before they were able to give the names of their wives' emblems. On the other hand, the sense of kinship between members of the same social division is so strong that the idea of intermarriage is totally repugnant.

" Descent is among all the Bornu tribes patrilineal. It was stated that children of women of the same clan would not be allowed to intermarry until at least four generations had passed." [1]

Totemism of the Kanakuru of Adamawa Province.— " The Kanakuru system of social organization is the counter-part of that of the Longuda. For whereas among the latter there is a matrilineal organization for purposes of inheritance, residence and authority in the family, and a patrilineal organization for certain religious purposes, the reverse is found among the Kanakuru, who for the normal ordering of social life follow the patriarchal rule, while in religious matters, in particular those relating to totemism, they follow the

[1] C. K. Meek, *op. cit.* ii. 248 *sqq.*

opposite principle, the totem being handed down in the female line.

"The patrilineal grouping is known as the *mumu*, the matrilineal as the *kinikinik*. . . . The *mumu* is an exogamous unit, that is to say, for example, that no male of the Kamo Reau may marry a female of the Kamo Reau. It is also prohibited for a man to marry any close relative of his mother's. But he may marry a distant relative of his mother's and may thus marry a woman who has the same totem as himself. . . .

"Property which belongs to the *mumu* as a whole passes from the head of the *mumu* to his successor, who may be a brother (by the same father), or a cousin, or possibly a grown-up son. Personal property is also transmitted patrilineally within the family group, which may coincide with the *mumu* or may be smaller than the *mumu*, owing to the *mumu* having more than one branch. . . .

"Turning now to the matrilineal organization which centres primarily round the totem, heritable through the mother, the matrilineal group is presided over by one known as the Naya, who is regarded as the custodian of the souls of the members of the group and whose animal counterpart is leader of the herd of animals which are the counterparts of the human members of the Naya's group. The totemic grouping is not obviously exogamous, for it was stated that a man whose mother belongs, for example, to a crocodile totem-kin may marry a woman who also belongs to the crocodile kin, provided the partners to the marriage are not close blood-relatives, *i.e.* they are not first or second cousins. But I was unable to obtain an instance of a marriage of this character. . . . It cannot, therefore, be definitely said that there is no connection between totemism and exogamy among the Kanakuru. Nevertheless the native point of view appeared to be that there was no objection to two persons of the same totem marrying, as only one of the two, viz. the woman, is capable of transmitting the totem.

"Among most non-Muslim tribes of the Northern Provinces, certain animals are taboo to certain kindreds; and the reason usually assigned is that those animals are reputed to have assisted the forefathers of the kindred in enabling them to escape from their enemies. In some cases no other reason is given for the respect accorded to the animals than that they are sacred to the religious cults. The respect shown is due to a tradition and not to a living faith. But among the Kanakuru, Mbula, and Bachama, and also, I believe, among the Kilba and Bura, the sense of a mystic relationship with some species of animal is a living religious belief. Between the animal and the man the closest bonds exist, and each participates in the nature and qualities of the other, and what happens to the one happens also to the other. If the one falls sick the other falls sick. If the one dies the other dies. Their destinies are so interwoven that it behoves the one to protect the other ; and the animal, therefore, acts as the guardian of the man, and the man in his turn sees that other men do not injure the animal. The animal may visit him at night and give him counsel, and he in turn may give orders to the animal. So closely are they identified that the one may transform himself into the other. That such conceptions had at one time a wider distribution than they have to-day in Nigeria is evidenced by the common belief, even among professing Muslims, that certain men or certain families are able to convert themselves into a certain species of animal. And in the language of the Hausa, all of whom are professors of Islam, there is even a special word, viz. *rikidda*, which means ' to turn into an animal.'

" When a child is born an animal of the species which is the totem of the mother is also born, the two together being, as it were, twin souls. As soon as the child is weaned, the mother takes it to the Naya ; and with gifts of a goat and hoe, beseeches the Naya, as head of the family group and leader of the animal herd, to care well for her child. This the Naya undertakes to do. If the child falls ill at any future time the mother repairs at once to the Naya who enters the sacred hut where the totem souls assemble and deposits a calabash of grain, saying, ' Here is one of our children who is ill. If it is you who have caused the illness, then may his face, as a result of this offering, be changed (for the better) by the morning.' This prayer is addressed by the Naya to his own *alter ego*, the leader of the herd, who may have caused the child's illness by injuring the child's animal counterpart or allowing it to be injured.   If the offering has been accepted there will be signs in the morning that the grain had been disturbed.   Similarly if a grown-up person is ill he will go to the Naya in order to discover if the illness proceeds from his totemic group.   (Among some groups it appears that if the corn, sprinkled with sand, remains undisturbed it is a sign that the disease was caused by the totem, whereas if marks are seen on the grain such as might have been made by a rat, then it is concluded that the totem is not responsible for the disease.)   Every two or three years the totemic group assembles to pay honour to the Naya and thank him for having cared for their souls during the preceding period. The Naya makes offerings of beer and pieces of the flesh of a goat to the totemic souls, and all present partake of a ceremonial meal of beer and food.

" The Naya is treated with the utmost respect ;   for as custodian of the totem he can injure any of the group by causing injury to his animal counterpart.   Thus if the totem is the crocodile he can, by driving a particular crocodile into some place from which there is no egress, cause a particular man to die slowly of some wasting disease.   An unscrupulous Naya may, therefore, carry on a regular system of blackmail among the members of the totemic group of which he is the head.   A Naya cannot be deposed from his office ;   but it is said that a man of more powerful soul-substance than himself may rob him of his herd or flock, taking the animal-souls away at night to some distant secret place.   This belief provides an excuse for a Naya who might otherwise be charged with causing excessive sickness within the group. He may refuse to treat sick people on the ground that another had robbed him of his authority.   When he becomes old he may voluntarily hand over the care of the totem to a brother (by the same mother), or to a sister's son.   In practice these totemic beliefs are mainly used for the treatment of disease. . . ." [1]

Totemism of the Jukun.—The Jukun-speaking peoples of Nigeria occupy that part of the Benue basin which is bounded by Abinsi to the west and Kona to the east, Pindiga to the north, and Donga to the south.   They

[1] C. K. Meek, *op. cit.* ii. 316 *sqq.*

appear to have had formerly a system of totemism, but it has largely broken down at the present day. On this subject Mr. Meek tells us that : " Before proceeding to examine the constitution of the family and household a few remarks may be made about the totemic ideas of the Jukun. Just as there is no clan organization, so there is no totemic organization in any of the Jukun groups. If there ever was a totemic organization it was bound to have broken down in the disorganization consequent on the clash between patrilineal and matrilineal ideas, and we might expect at the present time to find a plurality of totems or emblems in each family group and great diversity of opinion as to the mode by which the emblems are transmitted. This is what is actually found, and though most Jukun continue to respect a large number of animals or plants they do so in a half-hearted manner. Many of the young people are quite ignorant of the family taboos, and others do not hesitate to break the taboos when they feel inclined.

" One of the Jukun kindred to which the python and a number of other animals are sacred stated that he had no longer any respect for the animals he had been brought up to regard as taboo. For he had once been confronted with a python and had killed it, and being hungry had eaten it.

" No evil results followed ; and so he has not hesitated to break the other taboos when opportunity occurred. . . . I have even known cases of men breaking the taboo against eating the flesh of a crocodile, the most sacred of all Jukun animals. Before proceeding to eat it they will safeguard themselves by making some fictitious statement such as ' This is cow's (or goat's) flesh.' "[1]

[1] C. K. Meek, *A Sudanese Kingdom* (London, 1931), pp. 74 *sq.*

CHAPTER VIII

TOTEMISM IN CENTRAL NIGERIA

The Kwotto, a tribe of Central Nigeria, have a regular system of totemic and exogamous clans. The system has been described as follows by Captain J. R. Wilson-Haffenden, who spent some time among the tribe as an Administrative Officer of the Nigerian Service.

" The Kwotto tribe is divided into a number of totem clans, all the members of each of which regard themselves as descended from a common ancestor. This sentiment of common relationship is so strong that marriage within the clan—*i.e.* of any clansman with any of his fellow-clanswomen —is forbidden as incestuous.

" Totem descent is reckoned through males ; therefore children belong to the clan of their father, and a person's mother always belongs to a different clan than himself or herself.

" But each individual, by virtue of the nature of his birth, is regarded as possessing not only what I propose to call a ' pattern ' or ' paternal ' soul (*ekiti*), but also a ' matter ' or ' maternal ' soul (*kofi*). The former is derived from the father (or, more strictly, from one of the father's paternal ancestors). It is associated with the totem, and regarded as normally resident in the head. The latter is derived from the mother, and is associated with the ' matter ' of the body in general, and the blood in particular. . .

" The totems of the Kwotto clans are all named after different animals, mostly wild ones. For example, there are lion, leopard, crocodile, python, and monitor clans. One clan only, that of the goat, is named after a domestic animal.

" Each individual animal belonging to each totem species is regarded as connected with each member of the clan named after it by a mystic relationship, and the souls of prominent members of each clan are believed after death to be born again in the shape of the clan totem. Any sudden appearance of a totem animal at night, during either a man's waking or dreaming hours, is often interpreted as a warning of the imminent death of a fellow-clansman.

" Members of a clan are addressed by their fellow-members, and by members of other clans, by the name of their totem animal. . . .

" No member of a totem clan may kill his totem animal, but a member of one clan may kill the totem of another, even if it be the clan of his wife or mother. This is subject to the proviso that, after killing any of the more powerful totem animals, the slayer would have to propitiate the chief of the clan to which the totem belonged, in order to escape the spiritual danger to which he would otherwise become liable. . . .

" If the members of a clan desire the death of one of their totem animals for any reason—*e.g.* of a leopard having caused havoc in a town or of a goat required to be killed for sacrifice—they request the members of another clan to kill it for them. At the same time they offer propitiatory sacrifices to the spirit of the totem, pointing out that they are not killing it of malice, but only from necessity, and, further, that they are not killing it with their own hands. But clansmen will not readily be persuaded of the necessity of killing their totem. For example, if a leopard causes harm to the members of the leopard clan, many propitiatory sacrifices would first be offered to the totem ancestor before they would become convinced of the necessity for killing it. Their first impulse would be to regard the trouble as due to their lack of attention to their ancestor, who, in consequence, had adopted an aggressive attitude towards them

" All clans prohibit the eating of their totem, but a man may eat the totem of another clan, even that of his wife or mother. He would not offend the feelings of the clans-people in question, however, by eating their totems in their presence.

" A number of legends explaining the origin of these totemic beliefs are current among the Kwottos. They are varied, and it is doubtful whether one can look with assurance to any one of them for an authoritative solution of the problem which they purport to solve. But their general drift would certainly seem to throw some light on the possible ultimate cause to which the beliefs may be referred.

" A legend explaining the origin of the lion totem is to the effect that, seven days after the death of the first chief of the lion clan, persons visiting his grave saw a lion standing on the top of it. This unusual and unexpected sight was taken by the witnesses as proving that the chief had actually turned into a lion on death . .

" A parallel story is told to explain the origin of the leopard as a totem and the belief that chiefs and important persons change into leopards when they die.

" A crocodile myth runs as follows. Many years ago, when the Kwottos were at war with neighbouring tribes, the inhabitants of a certain village were in danger of being attacked and overwhelmed by superior forces of the enemy. The latter were advancing along the path leading to the forest, in the heart of which the village was situated. The invaders, when they had nearly reached the village, found the only available path blocked by a crocodile lying across it. This cast such fear into them that they retired. Villagers who had observed their miraculous deliverance through the agency of the crocodile reported it to the village chief. He then decreed that henceforward the crocodile species were to be regarded as their friends, and were not to be killed. Eventually, through the friendship thus established between the crocodile and villagers, a mystical relationship grew up between them. In time they became so closely associated with each other that the human chiefs and elders acquired the power of changing at death into these saurians.

" An alternative version has it that the crocodile clan originated as follows. At Toto, which is the headquarters of the clan, there is a river named Kunama, which contains many crocodiles. The founder of the clan, one Ohitoto, the first Village Head of Toto, was definitely seen by witnesses regarded as reliable to change from human form to that of a crocodile on the banks of this river seven days after death. It is noteworthy how the mystical number ' seven ' recurs in these legends.

" An etiological myth, parallel in its essentials to the first-mentioned story of the crocodile, is told to account for the ability of members of the python clan to change into pythons and for the various taboos in connection with this totem animal—that is to say, the acceptance of the belief in the kinship tie between the clansmen and the python is explained as based on the circumstance that the ancestors of the human group were saved from a perilous situation by the ancestors of the animal group. The latter were then in gratitude con-secrated, as it were, as blood-brothers by the humans. Later, the mystical relationship subsisting between them gave each the power of changing into the other.

" The legend narrated to account for the adoption of a goat as a totem is as follows. One day a slave felt hungry, and ate a portion of his master's yams. On the return of the owner he endeavoured to avoid the punishment which his irate master was about to inflict on him by making out that a goat close by, and not he himself, had eaten them. At this juncture the goat obligingly came up and ate the remains of the yams which the slave had left, thus proving to the satis-faction of the master that the slave was innocent. This kindness on the part of the goat caused the slave to set up the goat as his totem in gratitude for services rendered. Although this totem, which is the only one consisting of a domestic animal, was thus originally adopted by a slave—presumably a member of another tribe captured in war—the majority of the goat clan at the present day, it is pointed out, are regarded as being as pure Kwottos as the members of other clans." [1]

Among the Shulabwe (and presumably the Kwottos) " the most favoured type of marriage is that of patrilineal cross-cousins (*i.e.* of a man or woman with his or her father's sister's child). Next in favour comes marriage between patrilineal ortho-cousins (*i.e.* of a man or woman with his or her father's brother's child). That form of cross-cousin

[1] J. R. Wilson-Haffenden, *The Red Men of Nigeria* (London, 1930), pp. 150 *sqq.*

marriage by which a man marries the daughter of his mother's brother, although not forbidden, is definitely looked on with disfavour. For it tends to destroy the solidarity of the patrilineal group, which marriage with the daughter of the father's sister or father's brother tends, on the other hand, to cement."[1]

1 J. R. Wilson-Haffenden, *op. cit.* p. 107.

CHAPTER IX

TOTEMISM IN SOUTHERN NIGERIA

On the subject of totemism in Southern Nigeria Mr. P. A. Talbot, who in his official capacity as Resident has lived long in the country and knows the people well, tells us that " there are traces of totemism in nearly all tribes, though in some more than others, and it is possible that long ago a real totemic system obtained, and that most men were divided into totemic clans or classes, but the people have now outgrown the beliefs, mainly infantile, connected with such ideas of plants and animals."[1] However, true totemism appears to linger in a few isolated cases.

Thus among the Ekiti, a sub-tribe of the Yoruba people and neighbours of the Edo, families have to observe a totemic taboo (*Orile*) towards certain animals. For example, those of the Effan Orile cannot eat buffalo, while those of the Agbourin (harnessed antelope), Edun (monkey), and Ekkun (leopard) Orile are not allowed to touch the flesh of the animals after which the family or clan is named.[2]

" More traces of totemism are to be found perhaps among the Edo, especially the Bini branch, than any other Southern Nigerian tribe. Each family has several tabus connected with it, generally consisting of animals or vegetables, of which they must on no account partake ; the prohibition descends from the father to the children. Even here, however, it seems doubtful whether true totemism is much concerned."[3] Of Bini totemism I have given some account in

[1] P. A. Talbot, *The Peoples of Southern Nigeria* (London, 1926), ii. 252.

[2] P. A. Talbot, *op. cit.* ii. 256.

[3] P. A. Talbot, *op. cit.* ii. 257.

Totemism and Exogamy based on manuscript materials kindly furnished by Mr. N. W. Thomas, Government Anthropologist for Southern Nigeria,[1] who in a later work gives the evidence for totemism among the Edo more briefly, as follows :

" Over the whole area occupied by the Edo-speaking people, the ordinary rule of prohibited degrees is that a man may not marry a woman who belongs either to his father's or his mother's family. Precisely how far the limits of the family extend is difficult to ascertain. It seems to be clear that no marriage will be permitted where any family relationship is recognised, but it seems to be equally clear that, after a certain point, a family breaks up. In certain communities the test of membership of a family is whether they sacrifice to the ancestors in the same place. In the kingdom of Edo, so far as the father's family is concerned, the test is a simpler one. The majority of families have a totem, known as Awa or Awaigbe, that is, family prohibition or totem. The totem may be an animal, a plant, an object of domestic use, or a certain action or form of words. The plant or animal may not be eaten nor used, and the form of words or objects is likewise forbidden to be used. Only during the burial ceremonies are these prohibitions relaxed. These prohibitions descend from father to child, and in no case is a man married to a woman who has the same prohibitions as himself." [2]

---

[1] *Totemism and Exogamy*, ii. pp. 587 *sqq.*

[2] N. W. Thomas, *Anthropological Report on the Edo-Speaking Peoples of Nigeria*, Part i. (London, 1910). p. 61.

CHAPTER X

TOTEMISM IN ASHANTI AND THE NORTHERN TERRITORIES OF THE GOLD COAST

§ 1. *Totemism in Ashanti*

THE natives of Ashanti are divided into a number of totemic and exogamous clans, each of which is called a *ntoro*. The totems of the clans recorded by Captain R. S. Rattray of the Gold Coast Political Service are as follows :—

Clan	Day set aside for Observance	Totems or Taboos	Remarks
1. Bosommuru	Tuesday.	1. Python. 2. Ox, cow. 3. Species of monkey called *kwakuo*. 4. Dog. 5. Wild dog. 6. Species of bird called *asokwa*. All these could not be killed or eaten. Besides these palm wine or Indian corn would not be drunk or eaten on a Tuesday.	The Bosommuru is a river in Akyem. This is held to be the most important of all the *ntoro* divisions, partly no doubt owing to its having been the *ntoro* of no less than eight Ashanti Kings; and partly because the Ashanti think it was the first *ntoro* ever given to man.
2. Bosompra	Wednesday.	1. Leopard. 2. White fowl. 3. Species of yam called *afasie*. 4. Bush buck. 5. *Kwakuo* (species of monkey).	

478

Clan	Day set aside for Observance	Totems or Taboos	Remarks
		6. *Tamiriwa* (large edible snail).	A river rising in Ashanti and flowing into the sea near Shama.
		7. Tortoise.	
		8. *Aboka, i.e.* any animal found dead.	
3. Bosomtwe	Sunday.	1. A species of monkey called *kwakuo*.	A large lake in Central Ashanti.
		2. The Bush buck (*nwansane*).	
		3. *Tamiriwa* (a species of edible snail).	
4. Bosommaram	Saturday.	1. Palm wine (but may drink European spirits).	
		2. Cow.	
5. Abankwadie	Sunday.	1. Ox or cow.	Derivation doubtful.
		2. *Tamiriwa* (snail).	
		3. Tortoise.	
6. Agyinadie	Wednesday.	1. Crocodile.	Derivation doubtful
		2. *Afasie* (a species of yam).	
7. Akankadie	Tuesday.	1. *Abuburo* (dove).	
		2. Dog.	
		3. Wild dog.	
8. Agyimadie	Sunday.	1. Bush buck.	
		2. *Okankane* (serval).	
		3. *Tamiriwa* (snail).	
		4. Tortoise.	
		5. Palm wine (on Sunday only).	

" The above list comprises all the *ntoro* that have so far come under my notice, but very possibly does not exhaust the total number of these divisions, nor must my information be regarded as final."

The following myth—a translation of an account in the vernacular—gives the origin of the first *ntoro* ever bestowed upon man, the Bosommuru *ntoro* :

" Very long ago one man and one woman came down from the sky and one man and one woman came up from the earth.

" From the Sky God (Onyame) also came a python (*onini*),

and it made its home in the river now called Bosommuru.

" At first these men and women did not bear children, they had no desire, and conception and birth were not known at that time.

" One day the python asked them if they had no offspring, and on being told they had not, he said he would cause the women to conceive. He bade the couples stand face to face, then he plunged into the river, and rising up, sprayed water upon their bellies with the words *kus kus*, and then ordered them to return home and lie together.

" The women conceived and brought forth the first children in the world, who took Bosommuru as their *ntoro*, each male passing on this *ntoro* to his children.

" If a Bosommuru *ntoro* man or woman sees a dead python (they would never kill one) they sprinkle white clay upon it and bury it. (A Bosompra man treats a leopard in the same manner).

" *Agyinadie ntoro.* This *ntoro* is supposed to have been given to man in a somewhat similar manner, by the crocodile.

" *Bosomtwe ntoro.* This *ntoro* is supposed to have been given to man by Twe, the anthropomorphic spirit god of the lake.

" *Akankadie ntoro.* 'Nyame (the Sky God) very long ago sent down a dove to the earth to a certain man and woman there with his blessing and a promise of children. The Ashanti say that persons of this *ntoro* are to be distinguished by their peaceful natures even to this day.

" Myths and traditions in connection with the remaining *ntoro* have not yet been traced.

" An examination of the above myths and of the tables of the *ntoro* divisions shows that one aspect at least of the *ntoro* is totemistic. We have a mythical spirit ancestor who was a python, a crocodile, an anthropomorphic water god, etc., with whom its descendants claim *ntoro* relationship, and this relationship is expressed in certain funeral customs.

" Now evidence of participation in a funeral custom is held by the courts to be evidence of joint responsibility for a clansman's debt as proving kinship. The sprinkling of white clay and the burying of python or leopard therefore have a considerable significance.

" With regard to other animals, plants, etc., which might be regarded as associated totems or sub-totems, their position is less clear.   The Ashanti say they do not respect them in any particular way.   They do not eat them, it is true, because they say that if they did they would be ill.   These taboos, they state, were established long, long ago because these particular things were found to disagree with their ancestors ; new taboos are not now created in this sense."[1]

The Ashanti have the classificatory system of relationship, with the many prohibitions which it entails on marriage with persons of near or distant relationship, as we should esteem them.   On the other hand, marriage is allowed with the father's sister's daughter, indeed it is not only allowed, but privileged or enjoined, and with the mother's brother's daughter marriage is also enjoined.[2]   In short, marriage is enjoined with cross-cousins of the first degree.

§ 2. *Totemism in the Northern Territories of the Gold Coast*

Many of the tribes inhabiting this area are divided into totemic and exogamous clans.   The system was recognised and recorded for the first time, so far as I am aware, by Mr. A. W. Cardinall.   I will give his general account of the system, only premising that in it he seems to include both clan totems and individual or personal totems.

" The subject of animals leads one to the question of totems.   In its usually accepted meaning the term is not quite accurate if applied to the customs of these people. Everyone has some animal which is a species of *alter ego*—not to be slain or eaten, an animal which is recognized as one's friend, one's brother.   Most noteworthy of these animals is the crocodile, which is called by the Paga people their soul.   The life of a man or woman is identical with that of his crocodile *alter ego*.   When he is born the crocodile is born ; they are ill at the same time ; they die at the same time.   It is said that when a man is at the point of death one can hear at night the groaning of his crocodile.   These crocodiles congregate chiefly in one large pool and are very numerous.

---

[1] R. S. Rattray, *Ashanti* (Oxford, 1923), pp. 45 *sqq.*
[2] R. S. Rattray, *op. cit.* pp. 37 *sq.*

Women and children walk among them without fear to get the water, and the crocodiles are at liberty to get any goat or sheep rash enough to go within reach of their maws.

" Other totems are the python, iguana, squirrel, civet, mole-cricket, monkey, green-snake, mouse, partridge, and dog. Some trees are also totems, notably the *kapok*. It would seem that women have no such totems. They are generally forbidden to eat fowls, dogs, or monkeys. . . .

" A man usually has two totems. One he inherits from his father and the other he obtains at the ceremony of *seem*, a kind of baptism. . . Occasionally an animal is taken as a totem at the instigation of a sorcerer, who may detect in it the malign influence which has caused the misfortunes that prompted the consultation. For instance, at Pagabru a man slew two leopards. This was an event of no small order. Shortly after, several people in his compound died. The sorcerer was visited, and as a result the man learned that the leopard was a totem or, rather, taboo for him. He therefore modelled two clay leopards outside the gate of his compound and sacrificed to them. Be it noted, again, how the man himself associating the two events—the slaying of the leopards and the death of his relatives—on consulting the sorcerer obtained a reply quite in accordance with his own natural conclusions. In the opposite way, a man whose friends attribute their good fortune to the kindness of their totems will be persuaded to adopt those particular animals. To do so one merely sacrifices a goat or fowl and begs for their protection. . . .

" The origin of these totems is usually traced to some event in the past in which the animal chosen has aided the family. A small boy who joined my household—a Nankanni —had as his main totem the python. It appears that his father was out in the bush with some friends, when they angered a python, which slew them but left him. This was an evident sign of partiality for him on the part of the snake, who thus became the boy's father's totem.

" The chief of Navarro's totem is a crocodile. The family received this in the following manner. Long ago the Kamboin-zono, coming from the south, had chased the Nankanni in a northern direction. One of the invaders was left at Zekko with his wife, because of an injury to his leg. No remedy could heal him. One day, when he was near to dying, a squirrel jumped down from a branch of a tree on to the wound. The Kamboin-zono in his agony cried out, but the pain was relieved almost immediately. He felt sure that he could recover, and sent his wife to go and bring him some water. She took her pot and went in search of it. Finding none, and meeting a crocodile, she ran back to him and told him what she had seen. He told her to go back quickly and follow the crocodile, for it would show her where a water-hole would be found. She went back and, following the crocodile, found a large pond. She filled her water-pot and returned to her husband, who, recovering, built his compound at the place and begat many children. After many generations these fought together, and some were driven from Zekko. These men came and settled in Navarro, retaining the memory of the friendly aid of the crocodile.

" At Mayoro I learned how one day a blacksmith went to the bush to kill bush-cows ; meeting one, he shot an arrow and wounded it. The bush-cow charged. The blacksmith ran. Seeing an ant-eater's earth he crept in, just escaping the bush-cow. It remained there waiting for him to come out. But, being seriously wounded, it died, and fell on top of the hole. The blacksmith could not push the corpse away and remained imprisoned. A mole-cricket was there also, and began to bore an exit. Through this small orifice a ray of light came to the unfortunate hunter, who enlarged it with his knife and succeeded in extricating himself. Thus the mole-cricket became the totem of the blacksmiths." [1]

Totemism of the Nankanse.—A fuller and more precise account of totemism in this region has been given by Captain R. S. Rattray in his monograph on the tribes of the Northern Territory. Thus he tells us that the Nankanse, the largest of this group of tribes, are divided into some twenty-six totemic clans (*bute*, plural *bura*), each of which is patrilineal and exogamous.

" The history of any of these tribes," he says, " is always a composite record ; it is the history of every clan of which

[1] A. W. Cardinall, *The Northern Territories of the Gold Coast* (London, N.D.), pp. 39 *sqq.*

the tribe is composed. The history of a clan is the history of the first head of that clan. . . . To write the history of the origin of the Nankanse would therefore entail the study of the migrations and vicissitudes of each of the twenty-six or more clans which now constitute this tribal division. It would clearly be impossible to do so, and would serve little purpose. One example must therefore suffice.

" *History of Winkono, the Head Settlement of the We'ba Clan* (*We'ba*, lit. bush-dog, *i.e.* the leopard). ' Before the Dagomba came, and before the Europeans came, the *Ten'dana*, Anvenyo, was head *Ten'dana* of all the *weba kyiseba* (lit. those who taboo the leopard). The clan is divided into three (main) *yi-zuto* (lit. chief or head compounds), each tracing descent from one of three 'half-brothers' by the same father but by different mothers. This common father was called Abonposogo (lit. Rotten Thing). He was the ' father ' of the leopard clan, and the first of that clan. It came about thus : He had become blind, when a leopard came and licked his eyes, which then opened. He thereupon took an oath that neither he nor any of his children would ever eat or kill a leopard again. After regaining his sight he married and begat Atonaba. Atonaba, when still an infant, was saved from being burned to death by a hen which gave the alarm when the hut in which the infant was asleep caught fire. Abonposogo then took another oath, that no first-born of his should ever eat a fowl. Atonaba begat Avila (alias Akungue ?). Avila begat Anude. The clan became known as *we'ba la noa kyiseba* (they who taboo leopard and fowl). When an old man of the clan falls ill, we see a leopard among the compounds, and, on death, he ' rises up ' a leopard.

" *Violation of the Totem.*—On the death of a clansman, a fowl is killed, and one leg placed on the mat beside the corpse, and this is later buried with it, the following words being spoken : ' Receive this, your fowl, to-day, because you are departing.'

" Women of the clan do not turn into leopards, nor do young children who die before they have begun to keep the taboos, nor children who die before their mother has given birth to another child, because no proper funeral custom is held for such and they are not full and proper members of the clan.

" If a clansman sees a dead leopard he will touch it with his finger and then touch his own head, and will dig a hole and bury it. If someone kills a leopard, and you have power over him, you will take it from him and bury it, and afterwards bathe. No second funeral custom is made because the leopard is my ancestor who has already died and for whom a second funeral has already been held. . . . A full-grown man who dies will turn into a leopard, but not a person who has not had a proper funeral custom. We (leopards) do not eat people unless they owe us a debt. When this happens we (the living) consult a soothsayer and find out the reason why a leopard has killed some one, and make satisfaction. Clansmen cannot become leopards while alive, but when a man is about to die a leopard will come to the compound. When a clansman meets a leopard, he will salute it by slapping his thigh or clapping his hands. If a leopard begins to kill the live-stock, it is liable to be killed, but later an offering will be made at the sacred grove (*tingane*) and a report made— that ' your (*i.e.* the ancestor's) child was a thief and was punished.' "

Of the remaining clans, which to-day form what may be called the Nankanse Tribe, the following are a fairly representative list :—

Clan	Totem	Clan	Totem
1. Wobogo	Elephant.	14. Wafo or Wa'gyifo	Python.
2. Ebega	Crocodile.	15. Woo	Water-lizard.
3. Mena	Water-tortoise.	16. Sebega	Hartebeest.
4. We'ba la noa	Leopard and fowl.	17. Punyono	Big Crocodile.
5. Dulugu	Giant hornbill.	18. Tunena	A kind of fish.
6. Gwegene	Lion.	19. Yowa zifu	Yowa fish.
7. Bugum-nwabiliga	Crown-bird.	20. Yiu	Iguana.
8. Tenanbona	Lit. earth-donkey (ant-eater ?).	21. Nwana	Monkey.
9. Ene	Hippopotamus.	22. Kyia	Janet.
10. Sase	Hyena.	23. Wurega	Canary.
11. Ko	Roan.	24. Sakuri	Porcupine.
12. Gonafo	Bush-cow.	25. Bu	Goat.
13. Tugfo	Eagle.	26. Pesego	Sheep.[1]

[1] R. S. Rattray, *The Tribes of the Ashanti Hinterland* (Oxford, 1932), i. 232 *sqq.*

Totemism of the Builsa.—The Builsa are a large tribe, ranking as the second largest tribal group inhabiting the Northern Territories. They are situated west of the Nankanse.

The Builsa have the same totemic organisation which was found in the tribe already investigated. " It is not easy at the present day—largely owing to the effects of civil wars and slave-traders—to allocate particular clans to particular towns. These are tending to become cosmopolitan. I will not therefore attempt to do so, but merely note the names of such clans as are met with. These are :—

Pa or *Paau* (a cricket).	*Gwobeag* (lit. Bush-dog ?).
Nau (crocodile).	*Puig* (hyena).
Way-kpwem (python).	*Gbwegen* (lion).
Wanu (monkey).	*Kirr* (a kind of squirrel).
Feok (Colobus monkey).	*Tunin* (a kind of fish).
Warek (leopard).	*Yogeu* (a wild cat ?). . . .

" The same reasons as are given elsewhere to account for the respect accorded to certain animals, etc., are here repeated. The clan totems assisted the clansmen's ancestors in some way or other. Sergeant-Major Solla, who belongs to the *Feok* clan, states, ' Our ancestor was nursed by a monkey, when he had been lost in the bush. When we die, or even before we die, our *kyik* (soul) becomes a monkey.' " [1]

Totemism of the Dagaba.—The Dagaba number, according to the last Census Report (1921), 36,500 souls. The word *bure* (pl. *bura*) is used to designate their totemic, exogamous, patrilineal divisions. The Dagaba totem clans recorded include the following :—

Kpwire (Small mouse).	*Zibu* or *Zigi* (Python).
Nwana (Monkey).	*Wabo* (Snake).
Loara (Leopard).	*Eba* (Crocodile).
Sieni (Porcupine).	*Bona* (Lizard).
Kunkuni (Tortoise).	*Gangane* (Grasshopper).

The clan totem is known as *kyirun* (pl. *kyire*) which means simply, " the avoidance," " the taboo."

" The following is the account given to me of how the *kunkuni* (tortoise) came to be the *kyirun* of that clan.

" ' A wife of our ancestor went to the water and left her infant in a basket. When she returned, she found that a

---

[1] R. S. Rattray, *op. cit.* ii. 399 *sq.*

tortoise had entered the basket. She picked it up and threw it away. It hit a stone and died, and soon after the infant also died. The Elders said the tortoise was our kyirun. When a clansman sees a dead tortoise he sews it in a cloth ; if he did not do so, he could not be given a proper funeral when he died. Any one who killed a tortoise in the olden days would have been killed. When a man dies, a tortoise dies ; when a child is born, a tortoise is born. I have white mottled legs, my tortoise has the same ; I am getting blind, so is my tortoise. When a man dies, he goes to *Dapane* (land of dead) ; his tortoise also goes there.'

"Some of the totems given above are undoubtedly associated totems and sub-totems. A clansman of the *Kpwire* group stated that while the *Kpwire* (mouse) was his ' avoidance,' being that of the first ancestor from which his clan traced descent, his particular kindred group, however, also tabooed *Wabo* (snake), because its less remote ancestor had once been lost and was dying of thirst, when a snake showed him where to find water. This ancestor in consequence adopted the snake as his own private (avoidance), but in the following generation it became that of his descendants who inherited the medicine or roots connected with it. There are many instances of this splitting up or forming of these subsidiary avoidances which in time tend to submerge or supersede the older more remote ancestral *taboo* and give birth in this manner to new clans. This curious and interesting fact accounts in many cases for the existence of more than one *totem* or avoidance by a single person and a single kindred group. The whole system of totemism in these parts seems to have originated in this manner." [1]

Totemism of the Lobi.—The Lobi inhabit the extreme north-western area of the Northern Territories, spreading south along a narrow strip bounded on the west by the Black Volta. They are perhaps the most primitive of any of the tribes in the Northern Territories.

Lobi clans are divided into patrilineal totemic groups, known elsewhere as *bute* (with its variants), and known among the Lobi as *dogoro*. The *dogoro* are possibly the orthodox totemic clans, but for the purposes of recognition

[1] R. S. Rattray, *op. cit.* ii. 404 *sq.*

and description, the totem occupied quite a secondary place, clans being known, not by their particular avoidances, but by names which are, or are associated with, the clansmen's common remote ancestors. The following is a table showing the *dogoro* with their accompanying avoidances, where known:—

Dogoro	Totem or Avoidance (Kyiru)
1. Kusele	*Zun* or *jun* (a snake). *Pie-puo-sab* (eating food out of a basket, a sub-totem ?).
2. Boyele	*Kaukoo* (water in which *dawa-dawa* has been put).
3. Somale	*So-kyera-puo-sab* (eating food at cross-roads). *Kyie* (a kind of squirrel).
4. Metoor	(*a*) *Kyie* (a squirrel); (*b*) *Nwanzie* (red pigeon); (*c*) *Onzie* (red mouse).
5. Zage	*Nabars* (a blackbird).
6. Nabele	*Chapila* (paddy bird).
7. Kpele	*Pie-puo-sab* (see above, No. 1).
8. Bekone	*Nyusabla* (black cat).
9. Bimbile	To have no taboo of any kind is the curious taboo of this group.
10. Kowere	(*a*) *Chapila* (paddy bird); (*b*) *Zun* (the snake); (*c*) *Duolo* (mud fish).
11. Gane	*Nyuoba* (leopard).
12. Gbane	?
13. Banyine	*Sen* (porcupine).
14. Yipale	(*a*) *Kyie* (squirrel); (*b*) *Senale* (small mouse).
15. Sanyile	(*a*) *Nwam* (monkey); (*b*) *Duolo* (mud fish); (*c*) *Nwanzie* (red pigeon).
16. Nauyole	?
17. Nayile	?
18. Sanbale	*Senale* (small mouse).
19. Pureyile	*Zun* (snake).
20. Bowale	(*a*) *Kyie* (squirrel); (*b*) *Wun* (snake).
21. Zenzule	*Wulpill* (roan).
22. Basiele	*Zompo* (hedgehog).
23. Bakyele	?
24. Donale	?
25. Nwanbule	*Zun* (snake).
26. Kazile	*Vur do puo sab* (eating after porridge stick left in pot).
27. Birepole	(*a*) *Senale* (small mouse); (*b*) *Kyie* (squirrel).
28. Yerse	?
29. Butule	*Wulpill* (roan).
30. Nakyele	(*a*) *Kyie* (squirrel); (*b*) *Bazuo* (also a kind of squirrel.[1]

[1] R. S. Rattray, *op. cit.* ii. 425 *sqq.*

Totemism of the Isala.—The Isala were returned in the 1921 Census as numbering 21,698 persons.

" There are two ways of enquiring of an Isal to what clan he belongs ; one may ask, ' What do you swear by ? ' (*Ben nwehe?*) or ' What do you avoid ? ' (*Ben vea?*). The nouns formed from these verbs appeared to be used for what we would call the clan totem, *i.e. nwean* and *viero* or *vero*— the thing you swear by, the thing you avoid. The latter word is the one most commonly used, and when coupled with the name of the totem, gives us the clan name ; thus *Ganga-vera* (s. *Gangavera*), those of the crow clan, lit. crow-avoiding persons ; *Nyevera*, those who avoid crocodile ; *Sanvera*, those who avoid porcupine, etc. etc."

A clansman may not marry a clanswoman ; the son acquires the clan of his father. The following is a list of Isala clans :—

Clan Totem	English
1. *Gangan*	Crow.
2. *Gama*	Crown-bird.
3. *Hene*	A small red pot.
4. *Pwei*	Leopard.
5. *Sam*	Porcupine.
6. *Gangachoho*	A kind of wood used for ceilings of huts.
7. *Piesu*	Sheep.
8. *We'ten*	Skin of *weme*, a small antelope.
9. *Heli* or *Hel*	Jerboa ?
10. *Non-bu ar nwam*	Grindstone hole and monkey.
11. *Kantile*	A small mouse.
12. *Ban* or *Bala*	Iguana.
13. *Nantebe*	Slipper.
14. *Changbei*	Frog.
15. *Nyeva*	Crocodile.
16. *Kwai*	Dung-beetle.
17. *Gunguro*	Hyena.
18. *Dol*	Python.
19. *Pie-ten*	Goat skin (a sub-totem of the *Hene* clan).[1]

Among the Isala marriage within the clan is forbidden : each clan is exogamous. Besides being excluded from marrying any woman of his own clan, a man may not marry any woman of his mother's clan, even when the woman lives in

[1] R. S. Rattray, *op. cit.* ii. 466 *sqq.*

a town other than that from which his mother came. Marriage with a father's sister's daughter and with mother's brother's daughter is prohibited. A man may not marry the daughter of his wife's sister " because his wife calls that woman her daughter." He may marry—indeed it is considered a natural union—his wife's brother's daughter. The Isala permit a man to marry two sisters, but if both conceive about the same time, the younger is sent to another compound for her confinement. A brother and sister may not marry a sister and brother, " it would cause quarrelling." A man may not marry a woman, and also marry her daughter (by another man). If a father gives his daughter to a man in marriage, he may not later take a wife from the section from which his son-in-law comes. A violation of some of the above prohibitions would, it is supposed, result in death.[1]

[1] R. S. Rattray, *op. cit.* ii. 503 *sq.*

ON the Ivory Coast, which adjoins the Gold Coast on the west, a system of totemism has been found in two of the tribes.

Totemism of the Koulangos.—The Koulangos offer sacrifices to animals, especially to serpents and above all to pythons. As to lions, leopards, hyenas, and elephants, some people will not kill them, because their family is descended from a lion, a panther, a hyena, or an elephant. In this case it is believed that the animals cannot injure their human descendants. Other people may not touch these animals because they can transform themselves into these creatures.[1] For the Koulangos have a belief corresponding to the European belief in were-wolves. They think that certain persons can change at will, some into leopards, some into hyenas, and others into other animals. They do not thus transform themselves in order to attack other men, nor to play tricks upon hunters. They only do it for a defensive purpose, for example to protect their plantations by night. In order to accomplish the transformation, they bathe in water into which they have put a certain drug.

Certain families change thus into a certain animal. Those who can transform themselves into certain animals cannot and ought not to eat of the flesh of the animals into which they turn. Thus persons who change into leopards may not eat the flesh of the leopard, and persons who change into lions may not eat the flesh of the lion.[2]

The Koulangos are reported to practise neither exogamy

---

[1] L. Tauxier, *Le Noir de Bondoukou* (Paris, 1921), p. 175.
[2] L. Tauxier, *op. cit.* pp. 197 *sq.*

nor endogamy. A man is free to take a wife from his own household, and still more from his own village. But they also marry a wife from outside their house, their family, or even of their village. However, a brother may not marry his sister. Children of two brothers or of two sisters may not marry, but children of a brother and sister may marry.[1] In other words, cross-cousins may marry, but ortho- or parallel cousins may not.

Totemism of the Dyoulas.—The Dyoulas have *diamous* or clan names such as Ouatara, Bane, Derebou, and so forth, which are the names of the *n'tanas* or sacred animals which they may not touch.

The Ouatara have for their *n'tana* (totem) the leopard. They say that the ancestor of the Ouatara was a leopard. When an Ouatara sees a leopard in the forest he holds out to the animal both his hands, with the fingers stretched out fan-wise, and the thumbs hidden in the palms of his hands. If he is a true Ouatara the leopard will not touch him. Naturally the Ouatara have no right to hunt or kill, or even touch the animal from which they are descended.

Members of another clan, the Kamarate, have also the leopard for their totem (*n'tana*).

When a leopard is heard to cry, it is because someone is about to die in their quarter.

The old men used to say that formerly their souls after death entered the bodies of leopards. But since their conversion to Mohammedanism they no longer believe in this transmigration of their souls. They say, too, that formerly their forefathers could change themselves into leopards, but nowadays they are no longer able to do so.

Members of the Bane clan have for their totems (*n'tana*) the serpent and the palm-rat. Their ancestors changed themselves into serpents. Accordingly, in those days they respected serpents, but they have now lost this power of transformation.

Members of this clan still respect the palm-rat, because formerly when they went to war they took with them a drug as a charm to protect them against the bullets of the foe. But the person who gave them the drug had told them that if they touched a palm-rat, or ate of one, the drug would have

[1] L. Tauxier, *op. cit.* p. 160.

no power to ward off the bullets and they would certainly be killed. At the present day some of them eat the palm-rat because under French rule there is no longer war and consequently no need to guard themselves against the shots of an enemy. But some who are more warmly attached to old customs still adhere to the practice of not eating palm-rats.

Members of the Derebou clan have for their totems the leopard and the hare. They spare the leopard because their grandfathers believed that the leopard was their ancestor. But now that they are Muslims they believe it no longer. Formerly they tied up goats in their quarter for the leopards to eat.

As to hares, they may not eat them, for they believe that if they did so they would become blind. One of their ancestors, who had made a powerful drug, attached it to a hare which had a white spot on its front, and set it free in the forest. They declare that since then they may not touch hares lest the drug should lose its potency.[1]

---

[1] L. Tauxier, *op. cit.* pp. 271 *sqq.*

CHAPTER XII

TOTEMISM IN LIBERIA

THE Kpelle, a negro tribe whose country lies along both banks of the Paul River, have certain sacred animals and plants which may, though perhaps in a qualified sense, be described as totemic.

No person may eat his *sala* or totem animal : it is taboo to him. A man who has the leopard for his totem may not, further, eat the flesh of any animal which a leopard has killed and left behind, for the spittle of the leopard has fallen upon it. On the other hand, the fruit of a totem tree may be enjoyed by its owner and his kinsfolk ; but it must first be struck with a stick or cut with a knife.

Sacrifices are regularly offered by the totemite to his totem every month. The offerings consist of cooked fowl and rice, or if the man cannot afford that, then kola nuts will suffice. It appears that when a man has a son born to him he offers a sacrifice to his totem animal, which is also the totem animal of his new-born son.

The totem with its attendant taboos is inherited from father to son and from mother to daughter.

What Professor Westermann calls the totem plant is always individual : a certain plant belongs to a certain man, and is planted for him. Not so with animals : whoever has the leopard for his totem respects all leopards ; but Professor Westermann does not know whether or not the man regards any one individual of the species as specially associated with himself.

The names of the totem animals, so far as Professor Westermann could ascertain them, were as follows : Leopard,

Elephant, several kinds of Antelope, Wild Pig, Chimpanzee, Porcupine, Tortoise, Crocodile, Water Snake, Dog ; of the totem plants, Banana Tree, Kola Tree, Oil Palm, Raffia Palm, and Manioc Plant ; among natural phenomena, the Wind.[1]

But Professor Westermann tells us that what he calls the totemic animals and plants form no bar to the marriage of individuals who possess them.[2] Thus the totems, if they can be called such, of the Kpelle lack one of the most important characteristics of true totemism.

[1] D. Westermann, *Die Kpelle* (Gottingen and Leipzig, 1921), pp. 216 *sqq.*

[2] D. Westermann, *op.* cit. p. 62.

CHAPTER XIII

TOTEMISM IN SIERRA LEONE

TOTEMISM appears to be, or to have formerly been, widespread among the tribes of Sierra Leone. The following account of it is given by Mr. N. W. Thomas, Government Anthropologist:

" A number of facts came to light which suggest that totemism, somewhat overlaid perhaps by other prohibitions, exists among most of the Sierra Leone tribes. It is true that the name of the clan is not derived from the forbidden animal, so far as can be seen, nor are the clans invariably exogamous ; but the exogamous rule clearly existed in the past, and in the main the prohibitions are of the totemic type ; the only attempt to account for the prohibitions asserted that they were acquired by ' experience.' The main indication of totemism is the (rare) assertion that animal and man are of the same family.

" In general the totems, if such they are, appear to be of small importance in the life of the people, if we except the Kuruma and Bokoro clans. The existence of the clans is, however, at once proclaimed in the Timne country by the custom of appending the clan name to that of the individual ; it is, in fact, on the way to becoming a surname.

" *Timne.*—In a certain number of cases the exogamous rule held good ; but it is clearly in process of being abrogated, as there were cases in my genealogies in which members of the Kamara clan intermarried ; and it was more than once expressly stated that by means of sacrifice the ' nearness ' could be overcome, especially if no other woman were available. The suitor sacrificed a sheep and bread in the presence of all the people ; in some places all ate ; in others, some asked a blessing and handed their meat to others. Some say that the suitor should not eat. In other cases, no sacrifice was needed ; but it is probable that the wife would come from another village.

" The respect for the totem is usually shown by abstention from killing and eating it, or using the tree for firewood ; in some cases touching, especially the dead animal, is or was forbidden ; Kagbo clan may give *ranink* (their totem fish) to one who is not a Kagbo, but must wash hands after touching it ; eating the fish, on the other hand, brings on the head of the offender a penalty that cannot be avoided. Bangura clan avoids leopard but may touch a leopard skin without precautions. In some cases it is not forbidden to kill the totem and sell it to others. If Kamara eats a forbidden animal, they tie a yam leaf in a big leaf to rot and rub on the spots, which then disappear.

" A Kamara man who sees a living python will die ; and he will not touch a dead one, though he will tell a man who can eat it where it is to be found. He will not, however, allow one to be killed in his presence, and will offer money to secure the release of a young python kept in captivity. Probably all these customs are more or less in abeyance, for I kept a python in captivity for some months and received no offer from any Kamara man.

" In the ordinary way the descent of the totem is patrilineal ; but one or two informants respected their mothers' totems, though the prohibition would not be passed on to their children. A wife must respect her husband's totem when she is pregnant or suckling a child ; she may not cook his forbidden animal in his pots.

" In many cases the penalty for breach of a prohibition seems to be related to the forbidden animal ; thus spots on the skin and the leopard, red marks and a red bird, cracked feet and the crocodile (skin), and so on. In no case did I hear of any remedy for a breach of the tabu." [1]

With regard to marriage rules in Sierra Leone Mr. N. W. Thomas informs us that " cross-cousin marriages and other

[1] N. W. Thomas, *Anthropological Report on Sierra Leone*, Part i., *Law and Custom of the Timne and other Tribes* (London, 1916), pp. 132 *sqq.*

BOOK VI

TOTEMISM IN NORTH AMERICA

CHAPTER I

TOTEMISM OF THE WINNEBAGO INDIANS

THE Winnebago are an Indian tribe in the State of Wisconsin. They were discovered by the Frenchman Nicollet in 1634, when they were settled on Green Bay in Lake Michigan. To the west they were in intimate contact with a kindred tribe, the Iowa, who in turn were neighbours of the Oto and Missouri. These four tribes, the Winnebago, Iowa, Oto, and Missouri, all belonging to the Siouan stock, speak dialects naturally intelligible to one another, and show many cultural similarities. On the other hand, the Winnebago show many cultural similarities with their Central Algonquian neighbours, particularly in all that pertains to material culture and art, and this double influence, that from their Siouan neighbours and that from their Algonquian neighbours, must be borne in mind in any attempt to understand the Winnebago culture.[1]

The Winnebago social organisation is based on two phratries or moieties, known respectively as the Upper or Air and the Lower or Earth divisions. The Upper division contains four clans, Thunderbird, War People, Eagle, and Pigeon (extinct), and the Lower division eight clans, the Bear, Wolf, Water-spirit, Deer, Elk, Buffalo, Fish, and Snake. The moieties were exogamous. A member of the Upper moiety must marry a member of the Lower moiety and vice versa. While there is no law forbidding marriage between the clans of the two moieties, there is some evidence showing a tendency of certain clans to intermarry. The Thunderbird and Bear

[1] F. W. Hodge (editor), *Handbook of American Indians*, ii. (Washington, 1910) p. 958.

clans are regarded as the leading clans of their respective moieties. Both have definite functions. The lodge of the former is the peace lodge, over which the chief of the tribe presides, and in which disputes between Indians are adjudicated. No person might be killed in the lodge, and an offender or prisoner who escaped to it was protected so long as he was within its precincts. The lodge of the Bear clan was the war or disciplinary lodge : prisoners were killed, and offenders punished in its precincts. Besides these functions, the Bear clan possessed the right of " soldier killing " and was in charge of both ends of the camping circle during the hunt. Each clan has a large number of individual customs, relating to birth, the naming feast, death, and the funeral wake. In this connection the most notable rule is that a member of one clan cannot be buried by the members of another clan of the same moiety.[1]

Some twenty years ago the tribe was examined afresh for the Bureau of American Ethnology by Mr. Paul Radin. The results of his careful examination of the social and totemic organisation of the tribe are best given in his own words, as follows :

" The Winnebago are divided into two divisions, the one known as the *wangeregi herera*, ' those who are above,' and the other as the *manegi herera*, ' those who are on earth.' Descent was reckoned in the paternal line. But these appellations refer to the animals after whom the clans are named, the name *wangeregi* covering the birds, the term *manegi* land and water animals. So firmly has the idea of division of animal forms become associated with the two divisions that were a new clan introduced now among the Winnebago its position would depend exclusively upon the nature of the animal associated with it. As similar reasons dictate clan groupings among some of the Central Algonquian tribes, a few words concerning this type of association will not be amiss. The grouping of the fauna into a distinct number of categories is extremely common in North America. Among the Winnebago, a number of other Siouan, and Central Algonquian tribes, there was a fivefold classification ; earth animals, sky animals, empyrean animals, aquatic animals, and sub-

[1] F. W. Hodge, *op. cit.* ii. 959 *sq.*

aquatic animals. Among the Winnebago, the thunderbird belongs to the empyrean ; the eagle, hawk, and pigeon to the sky ; the bear and wolf to the earth ; the fish to the water ; and the water-spirit below the water. This religio-mythological conception has unquestionably received a certain amount of sympathetic elaboration at the hands of shamans, and particularly at the hands of the leaders of such ceremonies as the Winter Feast, the Clan Feast, and the Clan Wake, as well as at the hands of those who had in their keeping the clan origin myths.

" The characteristics of the thunderbird, eagle, bear, and water-spirit as clan animals, and as animals connected with a division of fauna, are also related to the general conception of these animals *per se*. The eagle and hawk are birds of prey ; the thunderbird is generally a deity granting long life, and associated with peace, although his connection with war is also common. Similarly the bear is supposed to have a ' soldier ' nature, and the water-spirit is intimately associated with rites pertaining to crossing streams, calming the sea, and ownership of water property. This correlation unquestionably indicates an influence of the religio-mythological conception of the animal upon the social group with which it is associated. How far this can go is abundantly attested by the names and behavior of the *wangeregi* and *manegi* divisions.

" On the other hand, we may legitimately ask what influence the two divisions had in molding the attributes of these animals, or upon the behavior of the groups with which their name was associated. The functions of a warrior may have determined, as they certainly have accentuated, the ' warrior ' characteristics of the eagle and hawk, nor is there any easily intelligible reason why the thunderbird should be associated with peace. From our knowledge of the social organization of other Siouan tribes, the political functions of the clan seem to be the characteristic feature of the organization, and this being the case, the possibility of associations of warlike and peaceful attributes with animals may as much be ascribed to the influence of the social unit as vice versa. With regard to such functions as the exogamy of the two divisions or that of the clans, or of the reciprocal burial

relationship of the *wangeregi* and *manegi* divisions, we, of
course, know that the characteristics of the animal in question
have nothing to do with the matter. We must then realize
that we are dealing with reciprocal influences—with the re-
ligio-mythical conception of animals on the one hand, and of
political functions of social units on the other. In some cases,
such as the specific associations with the water-spirit, it is
probable that the religio-mythological conception of the
animal is dominant. The association of the thunderbird with
fire has likewise not been due to any activity of the social
unit; and thus examples might be multiplied. In this connection, the fact that animals with whom a multitude of
associations have already been established are subsequently
associated with social units is fundamental. From this point
of view, the animal names of social organization are intrusive
features, and we will consequently expect to find historical
adjustments. This, we think, is what has taken place here.
The animal name with its religio-mythological conceptions
was a remarkably strong unit, and as a result reciprocal
influences took place. Although the religio-mythological
influence must thus have been marked, it appears to have
changed none of the marital and other functions of the two
divisions nor the political functions of the clans. What it did
change, and change fundamentally, was the interpretation of
the social organization.

" The only function that the *wangeregi* and *manegi*
divisions seem to have had was the regulation of marriage.
A *wangeregi* man had to marry a *manegi* woman, and vice
versa. The only other function was, according to some informants, reciprocal burial. Here the religio-mythological
interpretations seem in part to have determined this relation,
for a *mangeri* man buried a *wangeregi* man because, as a
' land division,' it pertained to him to place a corpse in the
earth. This, however, seems to be a doubtful function, for
earth burial seems in olden times to have been characteristic
only of the *manegi* division, the *wangeregi* clans employing
scaffold burial. In addition, the burial relation was one of
the many reciprocal duties of the ' friend-clan,' and if it was
ever postulated of the *wangeregi* and *manegi*, this was likely
due to the fact that the ' friendship ' relation seems also to

have existed between two clans belonging to the two different divisions. According to one myth, however, the four clans of the *wangeregi* paired off as ' friends ' with four clans of the *manegi*. This would then be practically equivalent to saying that the *manegi* buried the *wangeregi*.

" Thus far we have spoken only of the socio-political functions. The two divisions, however, play a part in a number of social and ceremonial connections : first, in the organization of the village ; second, in the arrangement of the clans while on the warpath ; third, as the basis of organization at the ' chief ' feast ; and lastly, as the basis of organization of the ceremonial lacrosse game.

" According to the majority of the older people, when the old social organization was still intact, each village was divided into two halves by an imaginary line running due north-west and south-east, the *wangeregi* clans dwelling in one half, with the chief's lodge in the south, and the *manegi* clans dwelling in the other half, with the bear or soldier clan in the north. Although this arrangement has now become almost legendary, it was corroborated by many of the older people. To what extent every village was organized on this basis it is impossible to state. When this question was directly put to individuals, the answer was always in the affirmative. Quite a number of old individuals, however, denied vigorously that such had ever been the organization of the village, and claimed instead that the lodges of the Chief and the Soldier (Bear) clan were in the center of the village.

" In looking over the clan affiliations of the informants we noticed, however, that the first arrangement was always given by members of the bird clans, and second arrangement by members of the Bear clan and generally also by others on the *manegi* side. This fact, of course, makes the decision as to the relationship of these two types of village organization quite difficult. There can be no question as to the existence of a twofold division of the tribe as far as marital relations were concerned, nor as to the segregation of specific clans in different villages. When on the warpath the twofold division manifested itself in the arrangement of fireplaces, so that the question to be resolved here is whether we can credit the statements that this twofold division expressed itself in the arrangement of the village, and, if it did, whether this was characteristic of the whole tribe or only of parts of the tribe. That this was true for part of the tribe can be accepted. Whether it was true for the whole tribe, however, can not be definitely answered until we know more of the Dhegiha and Tciwere. . . .

" The twofold organization is reflected in the arrangement of the fireplaces when on the warpath, each division having two fireplaces, whose location is determined by the direction in which the party is going. When going west, for instance, the two fireplaces for the *wangeregi* are on the south, and the two for the *manegi* on the north side. However, when on the tribal move or hunting, no indication of the division exists.

" As the basis of ceremonial organization, we find the twofold division present only once—at the chief feast (*hunk woha*), but as this feast is to all intents and purposes a feast given by the bird clans in general, there is really nothing surprising about its use. The name *hunk woha* would seem to indicate that we are dealing simply with a feast of the Thunderbird clan, and this indeed may have been the case historically. *Hunk* to-day, however, is frequently used to indicate the *wangeregi* division.

" As the basis of organization in a game, the twofold division finds expression in ceremonial lacrosse. There the *wangeregi* are pitted against the *manegi*. A well-known myth is associated with this arrangement, according to which the animal ancestors of the *wangeregi* and *manegi* decided their respective rank by playing a game in which they were organized on this basis. The *wangeregi* won and for that reason the chiefs of the division have been selected from this division. A division into two halves when playing ceremonial lacrosse is characteristic not only of the Winnebago but of the Omaha, Menominee, Sauk, Fox, and other tribes. Among the former two, these sides are identical with two aforementioned political divisions of the tribe, but among the latter two where no such division exists, the tribe seems to divide itself into two halves merely on this occasion." [1]

[1] Paul Radin, " The Winnebago Tribe," in *Thirty-seventh Annual Report of the Bureau of American Ethnology* (Washington, 1923), pp. 185 *sqq*.

Among the Winnebagos " generally a man took but one wife, although he was permitted to marry more than one if he wished. In polygamous marriages the second wife was usually a niece or a sister of the first wife. According to a very reliable informant it was the wife herself who often induced her husband to marry her own niece " [1]

[1] Paul Radin, *op. cit.* p. 138.

CHAPTER II

THE remains of Indian tribes that belonged to the Creek Confederacy in the State of Oklahoma were investigated by Mr. John R. Swanton for the Bureau of American Ethnology in the years 1911 and 1912. With reference to the totemic system of these tribes, he tells us : " Regarding the origin of clanship itself, which is practically bound up with several of the larger clans, such as the Wind, Bear, Panther, Raccoon, Alligator, and Deer, there are several stories, some simple, some more complex, but all we have left is evidently only a fragment of the original mass of lore on the subject. While I was told, as a matter of common report, by certain very good informants that the people of each clan were descended from the totem animal, such a suggestion is almost always lacking in the myths dealing with the subject, as, for instance, the Wolf-Bear myth. According to Legus Perryman, each clan, or, rather, each exogamous division, was descended from an eponymous female ancestor called Bird-woman, Panther-woman, etc. The female ancestor of the Bear clan was not, however, named from the common black bear, but from one called the Howling or Whooping Bear. Some people now identify it either with the grizzly bear or the polar bear. . . .

" A Coweta Indian stated that in the beginning human beings and animals were coming across the ocean in a gar-skin boat. On the way the human beings named themselves after the different animals. One said, ' I belong to the Panther family,' another ' I belong to the Bird family,' and so on. They kept on this way until they were about to land, when all of the animals were used up. One man remained, however, and they said to him, ' To what clan will you belong ? ' He answered, ' To the clan of that which you hear making a noise above my head.' He referred to the wind humming overhead, and therefore his family came to be called the Wind clan. According to another informant the people formerly came to a body of water, and they jumped into it one after the other. As they did so one said ' I'll be a Bird,' another, ' I'll be a Bear ' ; and so on. In accordance with still another legend, people came out from a cavern in the earth, and as they emerged a man standing at the entrance bestowed their various clan designations. In fact, they seem to have been in animal forms or to have been accompanied by animals, for it is related that when the Beaver appeared he plunged into a near-by pond, and on a tree by the bank the Bird was sitting. Then the Bear came out so fast that he slid on into the water where was the Beaver." [1]

" Clanship had an important influence on the relations between men, extending into the smallest matters of everyday life, and much of Creek etiquette was based upon it. Thus a Creek could tell by the attitude of any two members of his tribe towards each other—whether they joked with one another and so on—in what manner they were related. Persons having parents of the same clan used to joke with each other. This ' joking relationship ' thus included the entire clan of the mother ; it also included those whose fathers belonged to one's own father's clan, and according to Jackson Lewis it included one's own father's father and those women who had married into the father's clan. It was etiquette to talk disparagingly of one's own clan, even in the presence of other members of it, what was said being understood in a contrary sense. On the other hand, one must always back up his father's clan and those belonging to it and must speak well of it and of them.

" A similar etiquette extended to objects connected with the clan, particularly the animal from which it was named. I was told that if a person killed a totem animal the people

<hr />

[1] J. R. Swanton, " Social Organization and Social Usages of the Indians of the Creek Confederacy," in *Forty-second Annual Report of the Bureau of American Ethnology* (Washington, 1928), pp. 110 *sq.*

belonging to the clan from which it derived its name would compel him to make them a payment. A man of the Bird clan would say to one who had been shooting birds, ' You have killed my parents ; you will have to pay me for it,' and the other would give him something. . . .

" Although the infliction of fines is here spoken of as modern, my own information is to the effect that these observances have, in recent years, been viewed as subjects for jest rather than matters worthy of serious consideration, and it appears that animal names were matters of jest as far back as Adair's time. The custom must certainly have been little more than formal in some cases ; otherwise the Deer and Bear clans would have been obliged to abstain from meat almost entirely and the rest of the nation would have been under constant tribute to them. The late Chief Grayson informed me that upon one occasion he killed a fawn and made a cap out of its skin for one of his sons. Afterwards he met a man of the Deer clan who took him to task for this but was finally mollified by the assurance that it was so used, not out of disrespect, but because it was held in honour. A man was also supposed to see that proper respect was paid to the totem animal of his father's clan. An instance was related to me in which a man was called to account for having killed a wolf, by another man whose father belonged to the Wolf clan. It was from this clan association that the Creeks applied terms of relationship to animals. According to one informant the Bird people call the buzzards, and all other kinds of birds in fact, ' my father,' and he added that this form of address was usual with other clans. It is, however, more likely that the term given by way of illustration was applied by persons whose fathers were from the Bird clan. If they themselves had been Birds, they would probably have said ' my uncle.' " [1]

" The Indians of the Creek Confederacy had numerous totemic clans divided into two moieties which settled certain social functions but did not determine marriage. The·towns of which these clans were composed were again divided into two moieties which were opposed in the ball games and tended to keep apart from each other." [2]

[1] J. R. Swanton, *op. cit.* pp. 168 *sq.*   [2] J. R. Swanton, *op. cit.* p. 695.

CHAPTER III

TOTEMISM OF THE CHITIMACHAS

SPEAKING of the tribes of the Lower Mississippi, Mr. John R. Swanton tells us that " the Chitimacha resembled the Natchez and some other tribes of the Lower Mississippi in having a distinct class of nobility, with different terms of etiquette for each. This is affirmed by the living Indians and fully confirmed by the following statement : ' There are distinctions of rank recognized among them ; the chiefs and their descendants are noble, and the balance of the people are of the class of commons. An old man of this latter class, however great may be his age, will use to the young noble, however young he may be, respectful expressions which are only employed towards the nobility, while the latter has the right of speaking to the former only in popular terms.'

" This strongly recalls the Natchez system and adds importance to a tradition that the Chitimacha had come from the neighbourhood of the Natchez tribe.

" Instead of marrying among the common people, however, it is affirmed that the Chitimacha nobles were constrained to take partners in their own class, which is tantamount to the admission that a true caste system existed. If a noble married among the common people, the writer was informed, he would have to stay with them, and for that reason many refused to marry at all when no women of their own caste were to be had, and thus hastened the extinction of the tribe.

" Totemic clans also existed, but only the wolf, bear, dog, and ' lion ' (*'haimasi'ks*) are remembered. The wolf clan is said to be entirely extinct, and the lion clan is represented by

only one woman.   It is probable that there was a snake clan
also.   When angry, people would say to each other, ' You are a
bear,' ' You are a wolf,' etc.   A person belonged to the same
clan as his mother, relationship on her side being considered
closer.   Benjamin Paul states that his father's mother, who
explained the totemic system to him and who belonged to the
wolf clan, used to talk to the wolves when she was out in the
woods, and thought that she could induce them to go away.
Benjamin Paul's father was also a wolf, of course, while he
and his mother were of the dog clan.   The former chiefs,
Champagne and Soulier Rouge, were bears." [1]

[1] J. R. Swanton, *Indian Tribes of the Lower Mississippi Valley and Adjacent Coast of the Gulf of Mexico* (Bureau of American Ethnology, Bulletin 43, Washington, 1911), pp. 348 *sq.*

INDEX

513

THE END